Zope 3

DEVELOPER'S HANDBOOK

Zope 3

DEVELOPER'S HANDBOOK

Stephan Richter

DEVELOPER'S
LIBRARY

Sams Publishing, 800 East 96th Street, Indianapolis, Indiana 46240 USA

Zope 3 Developer's Handbook

International Standard Book Number: 0-672-32617-5

Library of Congress Catalog Card Number: 2003109347

Printed in the United States of America

First Printing: February 2005

08   07   06   05   4   3   2   1

Trademarks

Warning and Disclaimer

Bulk Sales

Sams Publishing offers excellent discounts on this book when ordered in quantity for bulk purchases or special sales. For more information, please contact

U.S. Corporate and Government Sales
1-800-382-3419
corpsales@pearsontechgroup.com

For sales outside of the U.S., please contact

International Sales
international@pearsoned.com

Acquisitions Editor
Shelley Johnston

Development Editor
Damon Jordan

Managing Editor
Charlotte Clapp

Project Editor
Dan Knott

Copy Editor
Kitty Jarrett

Indexer
Ken Johnson

Proofreader
Andy Beaster

Technical Editors
Eckart Hertzler
Robert Barksdale
Paul Everitt
Jim Fulton
Patrick Reilly
Kai Wu

Publishing Coordinator
Vanessa Evans

Book Designer
Gary Adair

❖

To my family, especially my wife, parents, brother, and grandparents.

❖

Contents At a Glance

Table of Contents

V   Other Components

25   Building and Storing Annotations   235

26   New Principal-Source Plug-ins   247

27   Principal Annotations   257

About the Author

Stephan Richter is a doctoral student in physics at Tufts University in Somerville, Massachusetts. He has been part of the Zope community since the summer of 1999. He has been involved in many community activities, such as documentation and organizing the first EuroZope conference. Stephan has also consulted with many Zope solution providers, developed many add-on products, and published two community-written books on Zope. Since attending the first public Zope 3 sprint early in 2002, Stephan has been actively involved in developing Zope 3, and he has taken command of several sub-projects, such as internationalization and documentation.

Acknowledgments

Many thanks to the following community members for their feedback and invaluable help:

- **Lex Berezhny**, who proofread many chapters and sent in corrections. He also provided general feedback about the book as a whole.

- **Brad Bollenbach**, who gave useful feedback and corrections on several chapters, especially Chapter 18, "Internationalizing a Package."

- **Marcus Ertl**, who provided feedback on the early version of the chapters in Parts III and IV and corrected bugs.

- **Paul Everitt**, who proofread some chapters and pointed out unclear paragraphs and fixed grammer and spelling mistakes while the book was in development.

- **Ethan Fremen**, who pointed out several typos and technical inaccuracies that were due to rearranged APIs.

- **Egon Frerich**, who pointed out a few typos and a resulting technical bug.

- **Marius Gedminas**, who provided technical insight and sample code for Chapter 4, "Setting Up Virtual Hosting."

- **Florent Guillaume**, who found an inaccuracy that was due to a change in the framework.

- **Eckart Hertzler**, who updated and reviewed many of the chapters in Parts III and IV before the book was sent to the publisher for editing.

- **Michael Howitz**, who pointed out a procedural mistake due to a late change in the API.

- **Sutharsan Kathirgamu**, who commented on early versions of Parts III and IV and made suggestions.

- **Max M**, who pointed out a mistake with a URL in the text.

- **Ken Manheimer**, who provided a different point of view on metadata for Chapter 11, "Metadata and the Dublin Core."

- **Lalo Martin**, who corrected some typos in the early stages of the book.

- **Peter Mayne**, who pointed out some technical and many grammar/spelling mistakes during the final stages of the book.

- **Gintautas Miliauskas**, who fixed numerous typos and corrected some mistakes.

- **Gustavo Niemeyer**, who pointed out several technical mistakes during the final stages of the book.

- **Garrett Smith**, who provided the original version of Chapter 3, "Installing New Zope Packages."

- **Christian Theune**, who pointed out a missing import in a code snippet.

- **Philipp von Weitershausen**, who pointed out a couple technically unclean coding practices.

We Want to Hear from You!

As the reader of this book, *you* are our most important critic and commentator. We value your opinion and want to know what we're doing right, what we could do better, what areas you'd like to see us publish in, and any other words of wisdom you're willing to pass our way.

You can email or write me directly to let me know what you did or didn't like about this book—as well as what we can do to make our books stronger.

Please note that I cannot help you with technical problems related to the topic of this book, and that due to the high volume of mail I receive, I might not be able to reply to every message.

When you write, please be sure to include this book's title and author as well as your name and phone or email address. I will carefully review your comments and share them with the author and editors who worked on the book.

Email: opensource@samspublishing.com
Mail: Mark Taber
           Associate Publisher
           Sams Publishing
           800 East 96th Street
           Indianapolis, IN 46240 USA

Reader Services

For more information about this book or another Sams Publishing title, visit our website, at `www.samspublishing.com`. Type the ISBN (excluding hyphens) or the title of a book in the Search field to find the page you're looking for.

Introduction

W<small>HAT IS</small> Z<small>OPE</small>? A<small>LTHOUGH THIS SOUNDS LIKE</small> a simple question that could be answered in a line or two, it is inadequate to say that it is an open-source application server or that it is a content management system. Both of these descriptions are true, but they really put a limit on Zope that simply does not exist. So, before we look at a more complete definition of Zope, let's discuss some of the solutions Zope has been used for.

As mentioned previously, many people use Zope as a content management system (CMS). CMSs are usually Web-based (browser-managed) systems. Basically, a user can manage the content of a page through a set of web forms, workflows, and editing tools. However, people have also used Zope for an entirely different CMS genre. Some companies, such as struktur AG, have successfully used Zope to interface with the XML database Tamino (from software AG).

Zope is also commonly used as a Web application server, in which case it is used to build web-based applications, such as online shops or project management tools. Of course, Zope is also suitable for regular websites.

Zope can also be employed as a reliable back-end server, to help manage the logistics of a company's operations. In fact, bluedynamics.com in Austria built a logistic software program based on Zope 2 ZClasses and a relational database that was able to handle hundreds of thousands of transactions each day, from taking credit card information and billing the customer to ordering products from the warehouse, using XML-RPC. This is the true strength of Zope because it allows Zope to work with not only web-familiar protocols but also any other network protocol you can imagine. Zope 3, with its component architecture, excels even more in this area, because third-party add-on packages can be easily plugged in or even replace some of the existing defaults. For example, the Twisted framework can replace all of ZServer (the Zope server components).

Now that you know about some of the uses of Zope, we can use the following more formal definition of Zope: *Zope is an application and back-end server framework that allows developers to quickly implement protocols, build applications (usually web-based), and function as glue among other Internet-enabled services.*

Before it developed Zope, Zope Corporation reviewed many possible programming languages for developing the framework, such as Java, C/C++, Perl, and Python. After extensive research, the developers of Zope found that only Python would give them a competitive advantage compared to the other large framework providers, such as IBM and BEA.

Powerful Python

Python is a high-level, object-oriented scripting language that produces—by design—clean code through mandatory indentation. Although Perl is also an interpreted scripting language, it lacks the cleanness and object-orientation of Python. Java, on the other hand, provides a nice object-oriented approach, but it fails to provide powerful tools to build applications quickly. So it is not surprising that Python is used in a wide variety of real-world situations, such as by NASA, which uses Python to interpret simulation data and connect various small C/C++ programs. Also, Mailman, the well-known mailing list manager, was developed using Python. Academics use this easy-to-learn language for their introductory programming courses.

Because Python is such an integral part of the understanding of Zope, you should know it well. If you are looking for some introductory documentation, you should start with the tutorial that is available at the Python home page, `www.python.org/doc/current/tut/tut.html`. Also, there are a wide variety of books on Python, including *Python Web Programming* by Steve Holden, *Python Programming Patterns* by Thomas Christopher, and *Python How to Program* by Harvey Deitel, et al.

In the Beginning There Was...

Zope's is a classic open-source story, and knowing this story gives some background on why the software behaves the way it does.

Before Zope was born, Zope Corporation (which was originally named Digital Creations) developed and distributed three separate products, called Bobo, Principia, and Aqueduct. Bobo was an object publisher written in Python, which allowed a developer to publish objects as pages on the Web. It also served as an object database and an object request broker (ORB), converting URLs into object paths. Most of this base was implemented by Jim Fulton in 1996, after he gave a frustrating Python CGI tutorial at the International Python Conference. Even though Bobo was licensed under a "free" license, it was not totally open-source, and Principia was its commercial big brother.

In 1998, Hadar Pedhazur, a well-known venture capitalist, convinced Digital Creations to open up its commercial products and publish them as open source under the name Zope. Zope stands for "Z Object Publishing Environment." The first Zope release was 1.7, and it came out in December 1998. Paul Everitt, former CEO, and all the other people at Zope Corporation, converted their product company into a successful consultant firm.

In the summer of 1999, Zope Corporation published version 2.0, which is currently the stable release, expected to be replaced by Zope 3.0 in the next year. Zope gained a lot of popularity with the 2.x series; it is now included in all major Linux distributions, and many books have been written about it. Originally this was going to be a book on the Zope 2.x API, but with the beginning of the Zope 3.x development in late 2001, it seemed much more useful to do the documentation right and write an API book parallel to the development itself. In fact, when these words were originally written (in

2001), there was no Zope Management Interface (ZMI), and the initial security had just been recently implemented. Currently, the first stable version of Zope 3, X3.0.0, has just been released, and by the time you read this book, Zope X3.1 might already exist.

Zope 3 Components

Zope 3 makes use of many of the latest and hottest development patterns and technologies, with "a twist," as Jim Fulton likes to say. But Zope 3 also reuses some of the parts that were developed for previous versions. Users will be glad to find that Acquisition (but in a very different form) is available again, as are Zope page templates (ZPT) and Document Template Markup Language (DTML), although with less emphasis. Also, Zope 3 contains a ZMI, but this ZMI has been completely developed from scratch in a modular fashion so that components can be reused and the entire GUI can also be altered as desired.

But DTML, ZPT, and Acquisition are not the only components to receive a new face in Zope 3; external data handling has also been totally reworked to make external data play better together with the internal persistence framework, so that the system can take advantage of transactions and event channels. Furthermore, the various external data sources are now handled much more generically and are therefore more transparent to the developer. But which external data sources are supported? By default, Zope 3 comes with a database adapter for Gadfly; additional adapters for PostGreSQL and other databases already exist, and many others will follow. Data sources that support XML-RPC, such as the very scalable XML database Tamino, could also be seamlessly integrated. However, any other imaginable data source can be connected to Zope 3 by developing a couple Python modules, as described in various chapters throughout this book.

During the past five years (during the age of Zope 2), not only was Zope developed and improved, but many third-party products were written by members of the very active Zope community for their everyday need. These products range from hot fixes, database adapters, and Zope objects to a wide range of end-user software, such as e-commerce, content management, and e-learning systems. Some of these products have turned out to be very useful to a wide variety of people—so much so that their concepts have been incorporated into the Zope 3 core. The prime examples are the two localization and internationalization tools Localizer (by Juan David Ibáñez Palomar) and ZBabel (by Andrew K. Milton and Stephan Richter), whose existence significantly shaped the implementation of the localization and internationalization support of Zope 3. Another great product that has made it into the Zope 3 core, Formulator, was originally written by Martijn Faassen. Formulator allows the developer to define fields (representing some metadata of a piece of content) that represent data on the one side and HTML fields on the other. The developer can then combine fields in a form and have it displayed on the Web. Formulator was also provides a validator, which validates user-entered data on the server side. Formulator's concepts were modularized into schemas and forms/widgets and incorporated into Zope 3.

Altogether, the Zope framework is much cleaner now (and more Pythonic), and features that failed to make it into the Zope 2 core have been incorporated.

The Goals of This Book

The main target audience for this book is developers who would like to develop on top of the Zope 3 framework; this book refers to these people as *Zope developers*. Python programmers will also find many of the chapters of this book interesting because they introduce concepts that could be used in other Python applications besides Zope. Python programmers could also use this book as an introduction to Zope.

In general, this book is arranged in such a way that you can easily understand the Zope 3 structure. Part I, "Zope 3 from a User's Point of View," gets you set up so that you can evaluate and develop with Zope 3. Part II, "The Ten-Thousand-Foot View," consists of chapters that are meant as introductions to various important concepts of Zope 3. If you are a hands-on developer, you might want to skip this part until you have done some development. Parts III, "Content Components—The Basics," and IV, "Content Components—Advanced Techniques," are the heart of the book, where you develop a new content component that implements many features over the course of 12 chapters. When you understand how to develop content components, you can face Part V, "Other Components," which introduces other components that might be important for your projects. Part VI, "Advanced Topics," is intended for people who want to use Zope technologies outside Zope 3. Part VII, "Writing Tests," is dedicated to various ways to write tests. The emphasis on testing is one of the most important philosophical transitions the Zope 3 development team has undergone.

This book should encourage you to start helping in the development of Zope 3. You might want to help enhance the Zope 3 core itself, or you might want to develop third-party packages, reaching from new content objects to entire applications, such as an e-commerce system. This book covers all the modules and packages required for you to start developing.

I

Zope 3 from a User's Point of View

This part concentrates on getting Zope 3 set up on your computer.

Chapter 1: Installing Zope 3

Before you can try all the code snippets provided by the following chapters, you need to install Zope 3 on your system. This introduction chapter covers only the basic installation and leaves advanced setups for the following chapters.

Chapter 2: The New Web-Based Zope User Interface

Although the GUI interface doesn't have much to do with Python development, you must be comfortable with it so you can test the features of the new code effectively. This chapter familiarizes you with the GUI interface and briefly introduces the through-the-Web (TTW) development interface.

Chapter 3: Installing New Zope Packages

This is a simple chapter on installing packages in your Zope 3 installation.

Chapter 4: Setting Up Virtual Hosting

This chapter describes how to set up virtual hosting in Zope 3, as is required for using Apache in front of Zope 3.

Installing Zope 3

Difficulty

Newcomer

Skills

- You should know how to use the command line of your operating system. (For Windows releases, the Installer is provided.)
- You need to know how to successfully install the latest version of Python on your system.

Problem/Task

Before you can develop anything for Zope 3, you should, of course, install it.

Zope 3 Installation Requirements

Zope 3 usually requires the latest stable Python version. For the Zope X3 3.0.0 release, this is Python 2.3.4 or better. Note that you should always use the latest bug-fix release. Zope 3 does not require you to install or activate any special packages; the stock Python is fine. This has the great advantage that you can use a prepackaged Python distribution (for example, RPM, deb, Windows Installer) for your favorite operating system.

> **Note**
>
> While distutils is part of the standard Python distribution, packagers often treat it as a separate installation package. In order to install Zope 3, your Python must have distutils installed as well.

The only catch is that Zope 3's C modules must be compiled with the same C compiler as Python. For example, if you install the standard Python distribution on Windows, which is compiled with Visual C++ 7, you cannot compile Zope 3's modules with Cygwin. However, this problem is not as bad as it seems. The Zope 3 binary distributions are always compiled with the same compiler as the standard Python distribution for the operating system. Furthermore, if you want to compile everything yourself, you are likely to use only one compiler anyway.

On Unix/Linux, your best bet is gcc. All Zope 3 developers are using gcc, so it will always be supported. Furthermore, all Linux Python distribution packages are compiled using gcc. In Windows, the standard Python distribution is compiled using Visual C++ 7, as mentioned previously. Therefore, the Zope 3 binary Windows release is also compiled with that compiler. However, people have also successfully used gcc by using Cygwin, which comes with Python. Finally, you can run Zope 3 on MacOS X as well. All you need are gcc and the make program. With these, both Python and Zope 3 compile just fine.

Python is available at the Python Web site (www.python.org).

Installing Zope from SVN

In order to check out Zope 3 from SVN, you need to have a SVN client installed on your system. If you do not have an SVN account, you can use the anonymous user to check out a sandbox:

```
svn co svn://svn.zope.org/repos/main/Zope3/trunk Zope3
```

After the checkout is complete, you enter the Zope 3 directory:

```
cd Zope3
```

From there you run make (so you need to have make installed, and it should be available for all mentioned environments). If your Python executable is not called python2.3 and/or your Python binary is not in the path, you need to edit the first line of the makefile to contain the correct path to the Python binary. Then you just run make, which builds/compiles Zope 3:

```
make
```

Next, you copy sample_principals.zcml to principals.zcml and add a user with manager rights, as follows:

```
01 <principal
02     id="zope.userid" title="User Name Title"
03     login="username" password="passwd" />
04
05 <grant role="zope.Manager" principal="zope.userid" />
```

In the preceding code block, note the following:

- Line 2: Notice that you do not need zope. as part of your principal ID, but the ID *must* contain at least one dot (.) because that signals a valid ID.

- Line 3: The login and password strings can be any random value, but they must be correctly encoded for XML.
- Line 5: If you do not use the default security policy, you might not be able to use this `zope:grant` directive because it might not support roles. However, if you use the plain Zope 3 checkout, roles are available by default.

During development, you often do not want to worry about security. In such a case, you can simply give `anybody` the `Manager` role:

```
<grant role="zope.Manager" principal="zope.anybody" />
```

The fundamental application server configuration can be found in `zope.conf`. If `zope.conf` is not available, `zope.conf.in` is used instead. In this file, you can define the types and ports of the servers you would like to activate, set up the ZODB storage type, and specify logging options. The configuration file is very well documented, and making the desired changes should be easy.

Now you are ready to start Zope 3 for the first time:

```
./bin/runzope
```

The following output text should appear:

```
01 ------
02 2003-06-02T20:09:13 INFO PublisherHTTPServer zope.server.http (HTTP) started.
03         Hostname: localhost
04         Port: 8080
05 ------
06 2003-06-02T20:09:13 INFO PublisherFTPServer zope.server.ftp started.
07         Hostname: localhost
08         Port: 8021
09 ------
10 2003-06-02T20:09:13 INFO root Startup time: 5.447 sec real, 5.190 sec CPU
```

After Zope comes up, you can test the servers by typing the following URL in your browser: `http://localhost:8080/`. You can test FTP by using `ftp://username@localhost:8021/`. Even WebDAV is available, using `webdav://localhost:8080/` in Konqueror.

An XML–RPC server is also built in to Zope by default, but most objects do not support any XML–RPC methods, so you cannot test this functionality right away. Chapter 23, "Availability of Content via XML–RPC," provides detailed instructions on how to use the XML–RPC server.

Installing the Source Distribution

The following sections describe how to use the source TAR ball to compile and install a Zope 3 distribution.

Before installing Zope 3, you need to install Python 2.3.4 or higher. In Windows NT/2000/XP, the extension .py is automatically associated with the Python executable, so you do not need to specify the Python executable when running a script.

After you unpack the distribution, you enter the directory. You build the software by using this:

```
install.py -q build
```

When the build process is complete, you can run the tests with this:

```
test.py -v
```

This should give you the same output as under Unix/Linux. After the tests are verified, you install the distribution by using the following command:

```
install.py -q install
```

You have now completed the installation of Zope 3. Now you can follow the final steps in the previous section to create an instance and start up Zope.

Note

When you install Zope 3 in Windows without using make, it's really hard to uninstall it later because you have to manually delete files and directories from various locations, including your Python's Lib\ site-packages\ and Scripts\ directories. You also have to completely remove the zopeskel\ directory. If you use Windows Installer instead, an uninstallation program is provided and registered in the Control Panel's Add/Remove Programs applet.

Installing the Binary Distribution of Zope

Currently, binary releases of Zope are available only for Windows. These releases assume that you have the standard Windows Python release installed. The Windows binary release is an executable that automatically executes Windows Installer. The first task is to make sure that you have the correct Python version installed. Zope X3.0 is released to work with Python 2.3. Thus, you need to install the latest Python 2.3 bug fix release. You can get the Windows binary installer at www.python.org/download.

If you already have a previous version of Zope X3, you need to remove it by using Add/Remove Programs from the Control Panel. Then you can install the Zope X3.0 release, which you can find at dev.zope.org/Zope3/Downloads. After you download it, you simply execute the installer and follow its instructions.

When the install is complete, you need to open a Windows command prompt and change to the root Python 2.3 directory, usually c:\python23\. Then you execute the instance creation script by using this:

```
.\python .\Scripts\mkzopeinstance -u username:password -d c:\path\to\instance
```

Unpacking the Package

The latest release of Zope 3 can be found at `www.zope.org/Products/ZopeX3`. First, you need to download the latest Zope 3 release by clicking the file that is available for all platforms: `ZopeX3-VERSION.tgz`. You can use `tar` or WinZip to extract the archive, like this:

```
tar xzf ZopeX3-3.0.0.tgz
```

Building Zope

For Zope 3 releases, distribution makers provided the well-known `configure/make` procedure. So you can start the configuration process by using the following after you have entered the newly created directory:

```
./configure
```

If you want to place the binaries of the distribution somewhere other than `/usr/local/ZopeX3-VERSION`, you can specify the `--prefix` option. Also, if you have Python installed at a nonstandard location, you can specify the Python executable by using `--with-python`. A full configuration statement could look like this:

```
./configure --prefix=/opt/Zope3 -with-python=/opt/python2.3/bin/python2.3
```

The following output is immediately returned:

```
01 Configuring Zope X3 installation
02
03 Using Python interpreter at /opt/python2.3/bin/python2.3
```

Now that the source has been configured, you can build it by using `make`. After you enter the `make` command, the following line is returned:

```
/opt/pythcn2.3/bin/python2.3 install.py -q build
```

The hard drive is busy for several minutes, compiling the source. When the command line returns, you can run the tests by using the following:

```
make check
```

Here, both the unit and functional tests are executed. For each executed test, you have one dot on the screen. The check takes between 5 and 10 minutes, depending on the speed and free cycles on your computer. The final output should look as follows:

```
01 Python2.3 install.py -q build
02 Python2.3 test.py -v
03 Running UNIT tests at level 1
04 Running UNIT tests from /path/to/ZopeX3-VERSION/build/lib.linux-i686-2.3
05 [some 4000+ dots]
06 -------------------------------------------------------------------
07 Ran 3896 tests in 696.647s
08
09 OK
```

The exact number of tests run depends on the version of Zope, the operating system, and the host platform. If the last line displays OK, you know that all tests passed. After you have verified the check, you can install the distribution as follows:

```
make install
```

> **Note**
> You have to have the correct permissions to create the installation directory and copy the files into it. Thus, it might be useful to become root to execute the command.

Creating a Zope Instance

When the installation is complete, Zope is available in the directory you specified in `--prefix` or under `/usr/local/ZopeX3-VERSION`. However, Zope will not yet run because you have not created an instance yet. You use *instances* when you want to host several Zope-based sites, using the same base software configuration.

Creating a new instance is easy. You enter the Zope 3 installation directory and enter the following command:

```
./bin/mkzopeinstance -u username:password -d path/to/instance
```

This creates a Zope 3 instance in `path/to/instance`. A user who has the login username and password `password` is created for you, and the `zope.manager` role is assigned to it. All the configuration for the created instance are available in the `path/to/instance/etc` directory. You need to review all the information in there to ensure that it fits your needs.

Running Zope

You execute Zope by calling

```
./bin/runzope
```

from the instance directory. The startup output is equal to that of the source Zope SVN installation.

You are all done now! When the server is up and running, you can test it via you favorite browser, as described earlier in this chapter.

Installing the Source Distribution in Windows Without Using make

Installing the source distribution on Windows is possible even without `make`. However, you need a supported C compiler to build the package. If you do not have a C compiler or Cygwin installed, you can use Windows Installer to install Zope 3. (See the next section for more details.)

This completes the installation. You can now run Zope 3 by using this:

```
.\python c:\path\to\instance\bin\runzope
```

The instance's `bin` directory also contains some other useful scripts, such as the test runner.

You can later use the Control Panel's Add/Remove Programs applet to uninstall Zope 3.

The New Web-Based Zope User Interface

Difficulty

Newcomer

Skills

- You need to have some high-level object-oriented skills in order for the examples in this chapter to make sense.
- Familiarity with the component architecture would be useful because some of the vocabulary would make more sense. Optional.

Problem/Task

At this point, you might say, "I have installed Zope 3, but now what?" This is a good question, especially if you have never seen any version of Zope before. After Zope starts with the bootstrap configuration, it starts up HTTP and FTP servers. The HTTP server provides a web user interface in which the site manager can not only configure the server further but also develop through-the-Web (TTW) software. After introducing the basic elements and concepts of the Web interface, which is known as the Zope Management Interface (ZMI), this chapter gives a couple simple demonstrations. The Zope X3 3.0.0 release concentrates mainly on filesystem-based development—which this book is about—so TTW is still very immature and not even available via the Zope distribution.

AFTER ZOPE 3 STARTS, YOU CAN ENTER the ZMI via the Manage screen. The full URL is then `http://localhost:8080/manage`. After you enter your username and password, you should see a screen similar to Figure 2.1.

Figure 2.1   The initial Contents view of the Zope root folder.

Zope 3 has very flexible skinning support, which allows you to alter the look and, to some extent, the feel of the ZMI. You can reach other skins by using the ++skin++ URL namespace. One nice skin is ZopeTop, which is excluded from the Zope X3 3.0.0 release but is available in the repository. To see the initial contents screen of the ZopeTop skin, as shown in Figure 2.2, you use `http://localhost:8080/++skin++ZopeTop/ manage`.

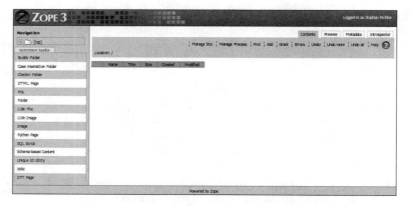

Figure 2.2   The initial Contents view, using the ZopeTop skin.

Note

This book exclusively uses the default skin to describe the user interface (UI).

Getting Comfortable with the ZMI

The ZMI is basically a classic two-column layout, with one horizontal bar at the top. The bar at the top is used for branding and some basic user information. The thin left column is known as the *Navigators column*. The first box of this column is usually the navigation tree, which is a hierarchical view of the object database structure. This works well because the two main object categories are normal objects and containers. Note that the tree uses JavaScript to load the contents and may not work well in all browsers, including Konqueror. If your browser does not support the JavaScript-based tree, you can use the `StaticTree` skin to get a pure HTML-based version of the tree. Below the tree can be a wide range of other boxes, including Add.

The main part of the screen is the wide right column, known as the *workspace*. The workspace specifically provides functionality related to the accessed object. At the top of the workspace is the full path of the object, in "breadcrumbs" form, which provides a link to each element in the path.

Below the location is a tab-box. The tabs, known as *ZMI views*, are various views that have been defined for the object. You can think of these views as different ways of looking at an object. A good example is the Contents view of a `Folder` object.

Below the tabs is a list of actions, known as *ZMI actions*. ZMI actions are also object specific, but they are usually available in a lot of different objects. Common actions that are available on all objects include Undo, Find, Grant, and Help.

Below the actions is the *viewspace*, which may contain several elements. All views have the Content column, which contains the information and forms of the selected tab. On the right side of the viewspace, there can be an optional column called Context Information. It is sometimes used to display view-specific help or metadata.

Figure 2.3 shows an overview of all the functional sections of the ZMI.

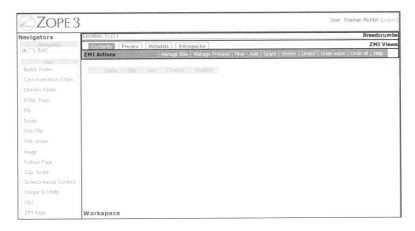

Figure 2.3   The sections of the ZMI.

The ZMI is built to contain common elements for consistency.

To see how the ZMI works, you can try to create a folder and create a ZPT page that displays the title of the folder:

1. Add a new object to the root by clicking the ZMI action Add. You are presented with a list of all available content objects.

2. Select Folder and insert the name `folder` in the input box on the bottom. Finalize the addition by clicking the Add button. The system returns you to the root folder's Contents view.

3. To add a sensible title to the new folder, click the empty cell of the Title column. An input field appears, and in it you can add the title *Some Cool Title*. Then press Enter.

4. Enter the folder and add a ZPT page called `showTitle.html` in the same way you added the folder. You are then presented with an Add page, which allows you to enter the source code.

5. Add the following ZPT source code to the Source text area field:

```
01 <html>
02   <body>
03     <h4>Folder Title</h4>
04     <br/>
05     <h1 tal:content="context/zope:title">title here</h1>
06   </body>
07 </html>
```

The strange `tal` namespace on line 5 is the first appearance of Zope's powerful scripting language, Page Templates. The `content` attribute replaces `title here` with the title of the folder when the template is executed, which is accessed by using `context/zope:title`.

6. After you enter the code, click the Add button at the bottom of the form. You can safely ignore the other two options for now. You are forwarded to the folder's Contents view again.

7. Click the template to open it. Then click the page's Preview tab, and you see the title of the folder being displayed. You can open the page directly by using `http://localhost:8080/folder/showTitle.html`.

Help and Documentation

Zope 3 comes with a simple online help system. Generally, you can reach this help system via the Help link in the ZMI actions list. If a particular help page is registered for the currently displayed view, then the Help link will directly forward you to this help page. The default is to show you the help system introduction page. Figure 2.4 shows Zope's online help system.

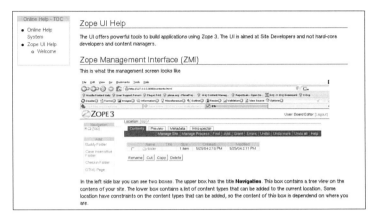

Figure 2.4   Zope's online help, with a table of contents on the left.

Another helpful feature is the Introspector view (see Figure 2.5). You might have noticed the Introspector ZMI tab that is available for all objects. It provides a list of all interfaces that the object provides and base classes that the object extends.

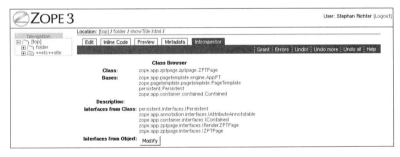

Figure 2.5   The Introspector view for an object.

The interfaces and classes listed in the Introspector view are actually linked to the API documentation, which is the third major dynamic documentation tool in Zope 3. The API doc tool (see Figure 2.6) is commonly accessed via `http://localhost:8080/++apidoc++`, and it provides dynamically generated documentation for interfaces, classes, the component architecture, and ZCML.

The tools provided by the API doc tool are not just useful for scripters and users of the Web interface; they are also useful for Python developers, who can use them to get a fast overview of how components are connected to each other and the functionality they provide.

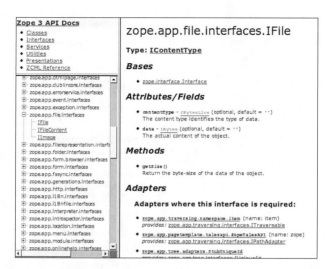

Figure 2.6 The API doc tool, showing the
Interfaces menu and the IFile details.

The Scripter's World

Although Zope 3 is truly an object- and component-oriented application server, it tries
to accommodate the scripter—someone who is a high-level developer but is not very
familiar with advanced programming concepts. Several tools that have been developed
for scripters are available in the Zope 3 source repository. However, the Zope X3 3.0.0
release concentrates on providing the Python developer with a solid framework to work
with. The focus of the upcoming releases will be providing facilities that help scripters to
switch from PHP, ColdFusion, and ASP to Zope 3. Furthermore, Zope helps a scripter
become a developer.

The Content Space Versus the Software Space

Zope 2 makes a great mistake by allowing software and content to live in the same
place. Zope's developers did not want to repeat the same mistake in version 3. Therefore,
they developed a content space and a software space. So far in this book you have only
worked in the content space.

The Content Space

As the name implies, the content space only stores content. Whereas simple DTML and
ZPT scripts are dynamic content, Python scripts are clearly software and are therefore
not available in the content space. The only type of programming that is supported there

is scripter support. However, being a scripter in this sense is not desirable, and Zope's developers want to provide a way to help a scripter become a TTW developer.

The Software Space

Every `Site` object has a software space, which can be accessed via the Manage Site action. You can see the link when you're looking at the contents of the root folder because the root folder is always a site. But because it is not on the list of addable types, how do you create a `Site` object? To create a site, you create a folder and click the Make a Site action item. That's it! Any folder can be upgraded to a site.

After the site is created and you click Manage Site, you are presented with an overview of possible tasks to do. Each site consists of several packages, including the `default` package, which is always defined. Packages are used to later pack up and distribute software. An involved registration and constraint system ensures the integrity of the setup.

If you now click the Visit Default Folder action link, you end up in the Contents view of the package. The goal is to add local components here that act as software. Because this looks and behaves very similar to the folder's content space's Contents view, the added components are called metacontent.

Let's look at how all this hangs together. The simplest example is to create a local Translation Domain utility and use it to translate a silly message:

1. In the Contents view of the default package, click Add, select Translation Domain, and enter Translations as the name. Then press the Add button to submit the request. You are then prompted to register the component.

2. Create a registration by clicking Register.

3. Register the domain under the name silly (which will be the official domain name). The provided interface should be `ILocalTranslationDomain,` and the registration status should be set to Active. Finish the request by clicking the Add button. Now you have an active Translation Domain utility.

4. Click the Translate tab to enter the translation environment.

5. In the translation environment, add some languages. Enter `en` under New Language and click the Add button. Do the same for `de`. Then select both English (en) and German (de) from the list on the left and click Edit. The table further down the page grows by two columns, each representing a language.

6. To add a new translation, look at the first row. For the message ID, enter `greeting`, and for the de and en columns add `Hallo Welt!` and `Hello World!`, respectively.

7. To save the new translation, press the Edit Messages button at the bottom of the screen. You now have a translation of the greeting into English and German.

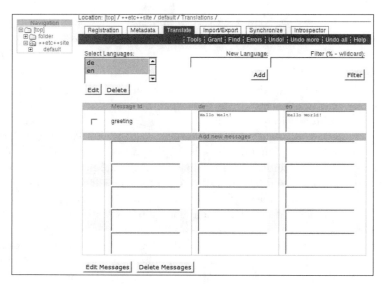

Figure 2.7   The Translate screen of the Translation Domain utility.

Now that you have defined the software—the Translation Domain utility—it is time to go back to the content space and use the new software. In the root folder, you need to create a new ZPT page called `i18n.html` and add the following content to it:

```
01 <html>
02    <body i18n:domain="silly">
03       <h1 i18n:translate="">greeting</h1>
04    </body>
05 </html>
```

When you save these lines and click the Preview tab, with English as the preferred language, you see a big Hello World! onscreen. If you change the language to German (de), Hallo Welt! should appear.

> **Note**
>
> In Mozilla you can change the preferred language by selecting Edit, Preferences, Navigator, Languages. Then you simply add German (de) and move it to the top of the list.

You have seen how simple it is to develop software in a site and then use it in the content space. As Zope 3 matures, it will offer much more impressive features, such as new views and TTW development of content components using schemas.

This concludes our brief trip into the land of TTW development. After talking a little bit more about setting up Zope, we will turn to filesystem-based development and start take a more formal look at the concepts in Zope 3.

3

Installing New Zope Packages

Difficulty

Newcomer

Skills

- You should know how to use the command line of your operating system.
- You should know how to install Python and Zope 3 (and do so before reading this chapter).

Problem/Task

After having installed Zope 3, there is only so much you can do with it. However, there are a bunch of interesting third-party add-on packages, such as relational database adapters and a Wiki implementation. A *Wiki* consists of a collection of pages that can be edited by any party visiting the page. The pages are connected via *Wiki links*, which are references to other Wiki pages via name. This chapter demonstrates how to install these packages, especially the ones maintained in the Zope repository.

INSTALLING THIRD-PARTY PACKAGES IN ZOPE 3 is much more explicit and similar to doing so in Python than in Zope 2. You can put a Zope 3 add-on package anywhere in your Python path, as you can any other Python package. This means that you can use the `distutils` package to distribute your add-on.

However, after you install the package, the Zope 3 framework does not know about it, and no magical package detection is used to find available packages. The Zope 3 framework is configured using Zope Configuration Markup Language (ZCML). Zope-specific Python packages also use ZCML to register their components with Zope 3. Therefore, you have to register a package's root ZCML file with the startup mechanism.

This chapter demonstrates how to install the Wiki application for Zope 3. If you are using the repository version of Zope 3, Wiki will already be installed, but the steps shown in this chapter are the same for all other packages.

Step 1: Determining the Installation Directory

Determining where to install a package can be a difficult challenge because packages can be located anywhere in the path hierarchy. For example, the Wiki application is a top-level Python package and the Jobboard Example lives in `zope.app.demo`.

You usually want to place third-party packages in the common Zope 3 directory structure because that makes it easiest to find the packages later. After you have determined the Zope 3 package root, you are all set. For the repository distribution, the package root is `Zope3/src`, where `Zope3` is the directory that you checked out from the repository (for example, `svn://svn.zope.org/repos/main/Zope3/trunk`). For distributions, the package root is `Zope3/lib/python`, where `Zope3` is `/usr/local/ZopeX3-VERSION` by default or the directory specified using the `--prefix` option of `configure`. An alternative is to use the `zope` instance as package root—for example, `Zope3-Instance/lib/python`, where `Zope3-Instance` is the path to the Zope 3 instance directory you provided during the `mkzopeinstance` call. The remainder of the book assumes that you are working with the distribution.

To install the Wiki application, you have to go to the `Zope3-Instance/lib/python` directory, which should be available in a Zope 3 instance.

Step 2: Fetching the Wiki Application from SVN

The next step in installing a new Zope package is to get the package. You generally just download a TAR or ZIP archive and unpack it in the directory. However, for the Wiki application, there is no archive, and you have to fetch the package from SVN.

If you have the SVN client installed on your computer, you can use the following command to do an anonymous checkout of the `wiki` package from the Zope X3 3.0 branch:

```
svn co \
  svn://svn.zope.org/repos/main/Zope3/branches/ZopeX3-3.0/src/zwiki \
  zwiki
```

Although SVN allows you to name the created directory any way you want to, it is necessary to name the directory `zwiki` because imports in the package assume this name. When the command line returns, the package should be located at `Zope3-Instance/lib/python//zwiki`.

Step 3: Registering the Package

The next step in installing a new Zope package is to register the package's new components with the Zope 3 framework. To do that, you have to place a file in the `package-`

includes directory. In a repository hierarchy, this directory is found in `Zope3`. In the distribution installation, it is located in `Zope3/etc`. You should enter the `package-includes` directory now and add a file called `zwiki-configure.zcml`, which contains the following:

```
<include package="zwiki" />
```

The `package-includes` directory is special in that all files ending with `-meta.zcml` will be executed when all meta directives are initiated and all files ending with `-configure.zcml` are evaluated after all other configuration is complete. However, there is no magic involved in finding this directory because the behavior is explicitly defined in `Zope3/etc/site.zcml`.

When you save the file, Zope will be able to execute the Wiki package's configuration.

Step 4: Confirming the Installation

If Zope 3 is running, you should stop it at this point. Then you should start Zope 3 and read the messages it prints during startup. If it starts without any error messages, your package has been installed successfully.

Note that unlike Zope 2, Zope 3 has no way to show you which products have been successfully installed because there is no formal concept of a Zope 3 add-on. However, you can usually tell immediately whether an installation was successful by entering the ZMI. If the `Wiki` object is available as a new content type, you know the configuration was loaded correctly.

Step 5: Adding a Sample Wiki Instance

To add a sample Wiki instance via a web browser, you need to visit the Zope 3 web UI by entering the URL `http://localhost:8080/`. Then you need to click the top folder in the Navigation column (at the upper left of the UI).

To add a sample Wiki, you follow these steps:

1. Click Add in the actions list.
2. Select Wiki from the list of content types.
3. Type `wiki` in the text field and click the Add button.
4. Because the Wiki object provides a custom adding screen, you have to confirm the addition once more by clicking the Add button.

You should now see a Wiki entry in the list of objects. To experiment with the object, you simply click Wiki.

As you can see, installing a Zope 3 add-on package is similar to adding an add-on in Python, with the addition that you have to point Zope 3 to the ZCML file of the package.

4

Setting Up Virtual Hosting

Difficulty

Newcomer

Skills

- You should have a basic understanding of the namespace syntax in Zope URLs.
- You should be familiar with the Apache configuration file.

Problem/Task

One of the most common tasks in the Zope world is to hide Zope behind the Apache web server in order to make use of all the nice features Apache provides, especially SSL encryption.

APACHE AND OTHER WEB SERVERS ARE commonly connected to Zope via rewrite rules specified in virtual hosts. Zope needs to interpret these requests correctly and provide meaningful output. You might think this is easy because you just have to point to the right URL of the Zope server. But this is only half the story. What about a URL that points to another object? To handle that situation, you need to tell Zope what the true virtual hosting address is. In Zope 3 you do this by using a special namespace called vh, which specifies the public address.

Before you can start setting up a virtual hosting environment on your server, you need to do the following:

1. Make sure Zope 3 is running at `http://localhost:8080/site/` or, more generically, at `http://destination_url:port/path-to-site/`.

2. Make sure Apache is running at `http://www.example.com:80/` or, more generically, at `http://public_url:port/`.

Zope 3 uses its URL namespace capability to allow virtual hosting, so that no special component or coding practice is required, which means virtual hosting is always available. Generally, namespaces are specified using *++namespace++* as one element of the URL. For the vh namespace, for example, you have *++vh++Public-URL++*. The *++* at the end of the URL is specific to the vh namespace. It signals the end of the public URL.

The namespace approach has the advantage that you can never lock yourself out due to misconfiguration. Some Zope 2 virtual hosting solutions have this problem and cause unnecessary headaches. In Zope 2 you also have to add an additional object. Zope 3 does not use any service or utility for this task, which makes virtual hosting support a very core functionality.

However, from an Apache 1.3 point of view, the setup of Zope 3 is very similar to that of Zope 2. In the `httpd.conf` file—usually found somewhere in `/etc` or `/etc/httpd`—you insert the following lines:

```
01 LoadModule proxy_module /path/to/apache/1.3/libproxy.so
02
03 Listen 80
04
05 NameVirtualHost *:80
06
07 <VirtualHost *:80>
08   SSLDisable
09   ServerName www.example.com
10   RewriteEngine On
11   RewriteRule ^/site(/?.*) \
12 http://localhost:8080/site/++vh++http:www.example.com:80/site/++$1 \
13 [P,L]
14   CustomLog /var/log/apache/example.com/access.log combined
15   ErrorLog /var/log/apache/example.com/error.log
16 </VirtualHost>
```

In the preceding code block, note the following:

- Line 1: You load the module that allows rewriting and redirecting of the URL.
- Line 3: You set up the Apache server for the default port 80.
- Line 5: You declare all incoming requests on port 80 as virtual hosting sites.
- Lines 7–16: These are all specific configuration instructions for the virtual host at port 80.
- Line 8: This specifies to not use SSL encryption for communication. You are allowing only normal HTTP connections. Note that you need this line only if SSL is enabled (that is, if mod_ssl is installed). If SSL is not installed, having this line will actually cause a configuration error during startup.
- Line 9: The virtual host is known as www.example.com to the outside world.
- Line 10: You turn on the Rewrite Engine, basically telling Apache that this virtual host will rewrite and redirect requests.

- Lines 11–13: The code in these lines should really appear on one line. It defines the actual rewrite rule, which says "If you find the URL after the hostname and port to begin with `/site`, then rewrite this URL to `http://localhost:8080/site/++vh++http:www.example.com: 80/site/++` plus whatever was behind `/site`." For example, `www.example.com:80/site/hello.html` is rewritten to `http://localhost:8080/site/++vh++http:www.example.com:80/site/++/hello.html`.

  Note that the part after ++vh++ must strictly be of the form `<protocol>:<host>:<port>/<path>`. Even if the port is 80 (the default), you have to specify it.

- Line 14: You define the location of the access log. This assumes that you have write access to the logfile directory, and you need to make sure the directory exists before you start Apache.

- Line 15: You define the location of the error log.

> **Note**
> The preceding configuration steps have also been verified for Apache 2.0.

At this point you are done setting up Apache. It's easy, isn't it? All you need to do now is restart Apache so that the changes in configuration will take effect.

Nothing special needs to be configured on the Zope 3 side. Zope is actually totally unaware of the virtual hosting setup. Note that you do not have to map the URL `www.example.com/site` to `localhost:8080/site`; you can choose any location on the Zope server you like.

You can now combine the preceding setup with all sorts of other Apache configurations as well (for example, SSL). You just use port 443 instead of 80 and enable SSL.

> **Note**
> One of the current problems in Zope 3 is that the XML navigation tree in the management interface does not work with virtual hosting because of the way it treats a URL.

The Ten-Thousand-Foot View

This part of the book provides an overview over some of the fundamental ideas in Zope 3. It doesn't jump into the technical details. You might prefer to read these chapters after reading some of the more hands-on parts, such as Parts III, IV, and V.

Chapter 5: The Zope 3 Development Process

This chapter briefly introduces the process that is used to develop and fix components for Zope 3.

Chapter 6: An Introduction to Interfaces

Because interfaces play a special role in Zope 3, it is important that you understand what they are used for and what they offer to developers.

Chapter 7: The Component Architecture: An Introduction

This chapter provides an overview of components and their possible interactions.

Chapter 8: Zope Schemas and Forms

One of the powerful features that comes up over and over in Zope 3 is schemas. Schemas are an extension to interfaces, and they allow attributes to be specified in more detail, which in turn allows autogeneration of forms as well as the conversion and validation of the inputted data.

Chapter 9: Introduction to Zope Configuration Markup Language (ZCML)

Although you are probably familiar with ZCML by now, this chapter provides a comprehensive introduction.

Chapter 10: Introduction to Zope's I18n and L10n Support

This introduction presents the new I18n and L10n features of Zope 3 and demonstrates how you can completely internationalize a Zope application. This chapter discusses I18n in ZPT, DTML, ZCML, and Python code.

Chapter 11: Metadata and the Dublin Core

The Dublin Core: Everyone knows about it, everyone talks about it, but few know the details. This chapter discusses the fields of the Dublin Core, as well as how you can and should use them.

Chapter 12: Porting Applications from Zope 2 to Zope 3

For many developers, it is very important to have a migration path from Zope 2 applications to Zope 3. This chapter concentrates on the technical aspects of this type of porting and discusses the design changes that have to be applied to make an old Zope application fit the new model. The porting of ZWiki is used as an example.

The Zope 3 Development Process

Difficulty

Newcomer

Skills

- You need to be familiar with Python's general coding style.

Problem/Task

The simple question this chapter answers is, "How can I participate in the development of Zope 3?" In addition, this chapter encourages you to adopt the same high standard of code quality and stability that the Zope 3 developers have used for Zope 3 itself.

BECAUSE ZOPE 3 WAS DEVELOPED FROM SCRATCH, there was much opportunity, not only in the sense of the software, but also in terms of processes, organization, and everything else related to a software project.

Very early on, Zope 3's developers decided that the Zope 3 project would provide a great opportunity to implement some of the methods suggested by the eXtreme Programming development paradigm. The concept of sprints was introduced in the Zope development community. *Sprints* are designed to boost the development and introduce the new framework to community members. The developers also established a style guide and a unique development process. The latter is discussed in this chapter because it is especially important to Zope developers.

From Idea to Implementation

With a big software project, it is necessary to have some sort of formal process that controls the development. Such a process stops developers from hacking and checking in half-baked code, and this requires a lot of discipline among free software developers because they generally don't receive any compensation. The developers of Zope 3 tried to implement a flexible process that can be adjusted to the task at hand.

When a developer has an idea about a desired feature, he or she usually presents the idea on the Zope 3 developer's mailing list or on IRC. The developer can figure out whether his or her feature already exists and whether the task the feature seeks to complete can be accomplished otherwise. If the idea is a good one, then one of the core Zope developers usually suggests that the submitter write a formal proposal that will be available in the Zope 3 Proposals Wiki. After the developer has written a proposal, he or she announces it to the mailing list for discussion. Comments to the proposals are usually made via email or directly as comments on the Wiki page. The discussion often requires changes to be made to the proposal through adjustment of the design or thinking of further use-cases. After a draft is approved by the other developers—silence is consent, though Jim Fulton normally likes to have the last say—it can be implemented. Although the developers of Zope 3 tried hard not to make the proposal writer the implementer, it works out that the proposal writer almost always has to implement his or her proposal.

How can you get developer status for Zope 3? Besides community acceptance, there are a couple of formal steps you must take to receive check-in rights. The first step is to sign the "Zope Contributor Agreement," which can be found at `http://dev.zope.org/Subversion/Contributor.pdf`. After you have signed and sent this document to Zope Corporation, you can deposit your SSH key online for secure access. All this is described in much more detail on the `http://dev.zope.org/Subversion/` Wiki pages.

As a developer, you can usually check in new features (components) or bug fixes. As described in the following sections, these two processes are slightly different from one another.

Implementing New Components

Let's say you want to implement a new component and integrate it into Zope 3. For the development of new software, Extreme Programming provides a nice method, which the developers of Zope 3 adopted and which is outlined in the following paragraphs.

Starting with your proposal, you develop the interface(s) for your component. Often, you will have already written the interfaces in the proposal because it helps in explaining the functionality. If you have not, you can use the text of the proposal for documenting your interfaces and its methods. For information on the formal aspects of writing interfaces, see Chapter 6, "An Introduction to Interfaces."

Next, you should write the tests that check the implementation and the interfaces themselves. When testing against interfaces, you can use so-called stub-implementations of the interfaces (see Chapter 44, "Writing Tests Against Interfaces"). If you are not certain about implementation, you can use prototype code that is thrown away afterward. (This step usually requires the most understanding of Zope 3, so that most of the learning process happens at this point. However, it is also the point where most new developers get frustrated. See Part VII, "Writing Tests," for an extended discussion of tests.) At this point, you are ready to write the implementation of the interfaces. There is a nice little tool called `pyskel` (found in *Zope3-Instance*/bin for releases and in *ZOPE3*/utilities for SVN checkouts) that helps you get a skeleton for a class that is implementing a specified interface. You can get hands-on experience with this tool in Part III, "Content Components—The Basics."

The final step is to run the tests. You start out by running the new tests only and, after everything passes those tests, running all the Zope 3 tests as confirmation. When all of Zope 3's tests pass, you can check in the code. It is a good idea to ask the other developers to update their checkouts and review your code and functionality.

Fixing Bugs

In order to effectively fix bugs, you need to have supporter status for the Zope 3 Bug and Feature Collector, so that you can change the status of the various issues you are trying to solve. You can also ask an existing supporter, of course, although that is much more cumbersome. You can contact the Zope 3 mailing list (`zope3-dev@zope.org`) to get this status.

When you have access to the Zope 3 Bug and Feature Collector, you can accept an issue by assigning it to yourself in the Collector. At this point, no one else will claim the issue. At this point you need to create tests that clearly point out the bug and failures due to the bug. Then you can try to fix the bug. While fixing, you might discover other untested functionality and side effects, so it is common to write more tests during the fixing process.

Finally, similarly to when you develop new components, you should run the new/local tests first, see whether they pass, and then run the global tests. It sometimes happens that you will not be able to solve a bug because tests of other packages fail and you do not understand why. At that stage, you should create a branch and ask other developers for help. When you are done with the code and all tests pass, you can check in the changes and ask people to have a look. When you are more experienced, a code review will not be necessary anymore.

Zope 3 Naming Rules

Zope 2 is a big mess in terms of the naming of classes, methods, and files. It is almost impossible to find a method in the API. The Java API, on the other hand, is well organized and consistent, and you can often just guess a method name without looking it up. To make Zope as organized and consistent as Java, the Zope 3 developers introduced a strict naming style guide that is maintained as part of the Zope 3 development Wiki. The guide has brought us a lot of cleanliness to the code base and has made it much easier to remember Zope 3's APIs.

The following subsections provide an overview of the Zope 3 naming conventions. See `http://dev.zope.org/Zope3/CodingStyle` for the detailed and up-to-date guide.

Directory Hierarchy Conventions

In Zope 3, package and module names are all lowercase. They should also be kept short, so that two consecutive words should be rare. If two consecutive words are used, howeverer, you should just put them together, without using an underscore (_). Note that any distributed packages outside zope are not maintained by the Zope 3 community and thus might not follow the same style guide.

The top-level directories are considered packages (for example, ZODB, zope.i18n). A special package called zope.app contains the Zope 3 application server. This package is special because it contains application-server–specific subpackages, which can be distributed separately. Each distribution package contains an interfaces module; depending on your needs, this can be implemented as a file-based module or as a package. This interfaces module should capture all externally available interfaces. A local interface that will be implemented only once can live in the same module with its implementation.

Usually, presentation-specific code lives in a separate module in the package; therefore, you often see a browser directory or a browser.py file in the package. If the package defines only a few small views, a file is preferred, as is usually the case for XML-RPC views, because you usually have only a couple classes for the XML-RPC support.

There are no rules on where a third-party package must be placed, as long as it is found in the Python path. The recommended place for Zope 3 distributions, however, is the lib/python directory of the Zope 3 instance directory.

Python Naming and Formatting Conventions

While the generic Python style guide allows you to use *either* spaces or tabs as indentation, Zope uses four spaces for indentation because otherwise the code base might be corrupted, and that can cause a lot of grief.

For method and variable naming, Zope uses exclusively camel-case naming (like Java) throughout the public API. Private attribute names can contain underscores. For other usages of the underscore character (_), see PEP 8 (www.python.org/peps/pep-0008.html), the Python style guide. The underscore character is mainly used in method and variable names to signify private and protected attributes and methods (including built-in ones, such as __init__). Classes always start with uppercase, with the exception of ZCML directives, which are a special case. Attribute and method names always begin with a lowercase letters, and a method should always start with a verb. Here is an example of these rules:

```
01 class SimpleExample:
02
03    def __init__(self, text):
04        self.text = text
05
06    def getText(self):
07        return self.text
```

In addition, for legal reasons and to protect the developers' rights, the Zope 3 community requires a file header in every Python file. Excluded are empty __init__.py files. Here is the standard Zope Public License (ZPL) file header:

```
00  ############################################################################
01  #
02  # Copyright (c) 2004 Zope Corporation and Contributors.
03  # All Rights Reserved.
04  #
05  # This software is subject to the provisions of the Zope Public License,
06  # Version 2.1 (ZPL).  A copy of the ZPL should accompany this distribution.
07  # THIS SOFTWARE IS PROVIDED "AS IS" AND ANY AND ALL EXPRESS OR IMPLIED
08  # WARRANTIES ARE DISCLAIMED, INCLUDING, BUT NOT LIMITED TO, THE IMPLIED
09  # WARRANTIES OF TITLE, MERCHANTABILITY, AGAINST INFRINGEMENT, AND FITNESS
10  # FOR A PARTICULAR PURPOSE.
11  #
12  ############################################################################
13  """A one line description of the content of the module.
14
15  If necessary, one can write a longer description here. This is also a
16  good place to include usage notes and requirements.
17
18  $Id$
19  """
```

In the preceding code block, note the following:

- Line 3: The copyright notice should always contain all the years that this file has been worked on. At the beginning of each year, you use a script to add the new year to the file header.

- Lines 1–13: You should use this header only if you are the only author of the code or you have the permission of the original author to use this code and publish it under the ZPL 2.1. Just to be on the safe side, you should always ask Jim Fulton about checking in code that you did not develop yourself. Of course, you must yourself be willing to publish your code under the ZPL. Note that you do *not* need to sign a contributor agreement to add this header, unless you want to add the code in the zope.org source repository. Also, the ZPL 2.1 does not automatically make Zope Corporation a copyright owner of the code, as is the case for ZPL 2.0.

- Line 19: Id is a placeholder for the source code repository to insert file revision information, which can be extremely useful.

- Lines 14–20: The module documentation string should always be in a file. The first line of the doc string is a short description of the module. Next, an empty line is inserted, after which you can give more detailed documentation of the module. For example, in executable files, you usually store all the help in this doc string.

In general, you should document your code well, so that others can quickly understand what it does. You should feel free to refer to the interface documentation.

Interfaces have a couple more naming constraints. The name of an interface should always start with a capital I, so that it can be easily distinguished from a class. Also, interface declarations are used for documenting the behavior and everything around a component, so you should have almost all your documentation there. Zope 3's API documentation tool mainly uses the interface doc strings for providing information to the reader.

ZCML Naming and Formatting Conventions

ZCML is a dialect of XML, so the usual good naming practices of XML apply.

ZCML subelements are indented by using two spaces; again, you should not use tab characters because their width is ambiguous. Each attribute of an element should be on a separate line, with an indentation of four spaces. Here is an example:

```
01 <configure
02     namespace="http://namespaces.org/my-namespace">
03
04   <namespace:directive
05       attr="value">
06
07     <namespace:sub-directive
08         attr1="value"
09         attr2="This is a long value that
10                 spans over two lines."
11         />
12
13   </namespace:directive>
14
15 </configure>
```

Although it is possible to specify any number of ZCML namespaces inside a configure element, you should declare only the namespaces you actually use, just as you only import objects in Python that the code in the module actually uses. As for all source code in Zope, you should try to avoid long lines greater than 80 characters. However, sometimes that is not possible because the dotted Python identifiers and IDs can become very long. In these rare cases, it is permissible to have lines longer than 80 characters.

Page Template Naming and Formatting Conventions

Page templates were designed, as their name suggests, to provide presentation templates. Unfortunately, it is possible to supply Python-based logic via the Template Attribute Language Expression Syntax (TALES) expressions as well. In Zope 3 templates, you should avoid Python code completely because the necessary logic can be provided by an HTML presentation component, as shown in Chapter 14, "Adding Views for Content

Objects." In general, even if you have complex non-Python logic in a template, you should try to think about a way to move your logic into the Python-based presentation class.

Finally, XHTML is a dialect of XML, which means that all contents of double tags should be indented by two spaces (as for ZCML). For tag attributes, you use four spaces as indentation. Remember that it is very hard to read and debug incorrectly indented XHTML code.

Test Writing Conventions

Although not necessary for the standard Python `unittest` package, the Zope 3 test runner expects unit tests to be in a module called `tests`. If `tests` is a directory (that is, package), you should not forget to have an empty `__init__.py` file in the directory. Similarly, you should have an `ftests` module for functional tests.

Usually you have several testing modules in a `tests` directory. Each of these modules' names should begin with the prefix `test_`. Note that this is one of the few acceptable violations of the rule that you shouldn't use the underscore character in a module name. The prefix is very helpful in detecting the actual tests because sometimes supporting files are also located in the `tests` directory.

The testing methods inside a `TestCase` class do not have doc strings because the test runner would use the doc strings instead of the method names for reporting, which makes it much harder to find failing tests. Instead, you should choose an instructive method name—do not worry if it is long—and write detailed comments if necessary. Finally, if a test case tests a particular component, you should always include an interface verification test, like the following:

```
01 def test_interface(self):
02     self.assert_(IExample.providedBy(SimpleExample()))
```

This is probably the most trivial test you can write, but it's also a very important one because it tells you whether you fully implemented the interface.

The Importance of Having and Following Conventions

Earlier text in this chapter addresses some of the motivations for strict naming conventions, and this section describes some more reasons. First, many people work on Zope 3. Everybody has an idea of an ideal style for his or her code, but in a project such as Zope, only one style can be adopted. If no one style were created, people would constantly correct others' code, and we would end up with a colorful mix of styles and unmaintainable code.

Naming conventions also make the API more predictable and consequently more usable. For example, if you only remember the name of a class, such as "simple example," you will always know what the spelling of the class will look like (that is, `SimpleExample`). There is no ambiguity in the name at all.

A lot of time has been spent on developing the Zope directory structure. The goal is to have a well-thought-out and flat tree so that the imports of the corresponding modules can stay manageable. For this reason, the developers eventually adopted the Java design. The development team also wanted to be able to separate contract, implementation, and presentation in order to address the different development roles (for example, developer, scripter, graphic designer, information architect, translator) of the individuals contributing to the project.

Ultimately, the development team hopes that these conventions are followed by all ZPL code in the `zope.org` source code repository.

For more information on coding style, see the Zope 3 development Wiki page, at `http://dev.zope.org/Zope3/CodingStyle`.

6

An Introduction to Interfaces

Difficulty

Newcomer

Skills

- You should know Python well, which is a requirement for all the following chapters.
- You should have some knowledge about the usage of formal interfaces in software design. Optional.

Problem/Task

Every chapter in this book deals with interfaces in one way or another. Hence it is very important that you understand the purpose of interfaces.

I N VERY LARGE SOFTWARE PROJECTS, especially where the interaction with a lot of other software is expected and desired, it is necessary to develop well-specified application programming interfaces (APIs). You can think of APIs as standards of the framework, such as the RFC or POSIX standards. After an interface is defined and made public, it should be very difficult to change it. But an API is also useful inside a single piece of software; this is known as an internal API.

Interfaces (in the sense the term is used in this book) provide a programmatic way to specify an API in a programming language.

Whereas other modern programming languages, such as Java, use interfaces as a native language feature, Python did not even have the equivalent of a formal interface until recently. Interfaces are specified in PEP 245, though not all syntax is provided by the language yet. In Python the API is usually defined by the class that implements it, and it is up to the documentation to create a formal representation of the API. This approach has many problems. Often, developers change the API of a class without realizing that they have broken many other people's code. Programmed interfaces can completely resolve this problem because alarm bells can be rung (via tests) as soon as an API break-age occurs. Here is a simple example of a Python interface (as used by the Zope project):

```
01 from zope.interface import Interface, Attribute
02
03 class IExample(Interface):
04     """This interface represents a generic example."""
05
06     text = Attribute("The text of the example")
07
08     def setText(text):
09         "This method writes the passed text to the text attribute."
10
11     def getText():
12         "This method returns the value of the text attribute."
```

In the preceding code block, note the following:

- Line 1: You import the only two important objects from `zope.interface`: the metaclass `Interface` and the class `Attribute`.

- Line 3: You "misuse" the `class` declaration to declare interfaces. Note, though, that interfaces are *not* classes and do not behave as such! Using `Interface` as the base class makes this object an interface.

- Line 4: In Zope 3, interfaces are the main source for API documentation, so it is necessary to always write very descriptive doc strings. The interface doc string gives a detailed explanation as to how objects implementing this interface are expected to function.

- Line 6: The `Attribute` class is used to declare attributes in an interface. The con-structor of this class takes only one string argument: the documentation of this attribute. You might say now that there is much more metadata that an attribute could have, such as the minimum value of an integer or the maximum length of a string. These types of extensions to the `Attribute` class are provided by another module, called `zope.schema`, which is described in Chapter 8, "Zope Schemas and Forms."

- Line 8–9 and 11–12: Methods are declared using the `def` keyword, as usual. However, the first argument is not `self`. You only list all the common arguments. The doc string is again used for documentation. Otherwise, methods can contain anything you like, yet Zope does not use anything else of the method content. If you use the `zope.interface` package apart from Zope 3, you could use the method body to provide formal descriptions of pre- and postconditions, argument types, and return types.

The preceding is a typical but not practical example of an interface. Because you are using Python, it is not necessary to specify both the attribute and the setter/getter methods. In this case, you would usually just specify the attribute as part of the interface and implement it as a Python property if necessary.

Advanced Usages of Interfaces

When you have Python-based interfaces, many new possibilities develop. You can use interfaces as objects that can define contracts. For example, you can say that there is a class `AllText` that converts `IExample` to `IAllText`, where the latter interface has a method `getAllText()` that returns all human-readable text from `IExample`. Such a class is known as an *adapter*. More formally, adapters use one interface (for example, `IExample`) to provide another interface (for example, `IAllText`).

Even more commonly, interfaces are used for identification. Zope 3's utility registry often executes queries in the form "Give me all utilities that implement interface `I1`." Interfaces are even used to classify other interfaces. For example, you might declare your `IExample` interface to be an `IContentType`. You can then go to the utility registry and say, "Give me all interfaces that represent a content type (`IContentType`)." When you know these content type interfaces, you can figure out which classes are content types.

You can see that interfaces provide a solution to a wide range of use-cases.

> **Note**
>
> It is very common to create empty interfaces purely for identification purposes; these interfaces are known as *marker interfaces*.

Using Interfaces

In objects, interfaces are used as follows:

```
01 from zope.interface import implements
02 from interfaces import IExample
03
04 class SimpleExample:
05     implements(IExample)
```

The `implements()` method tells the system that *instances* of the class provide `IExample`. But, of course, modules and classes themselves can implement interfaces as well. For modules you can use `moduleProvides(*interfaces)`. For classes you can insert `classImplements(*interfaces)` directly in the class definition or use `classProvides(cls, *interfaces)` for an existing class. Also, you can use `directlyProvides(instance, *interfaces)` for any object (including instances of classes).

The `Interface` object itself has some nice methods. The most common one is `providedBy(ob)`, which checks whether the passed object implements the interface:

```
01 >>> ex = SimpleExample()
02 >>> IExample.providedBy(ex)
03 True
```

Similarly, you can pass in a class and test whether instances of that class implement the interface by calling `IExample.implementedBy(SimpleExample)`.

Another useful method is `isOrExtends(interface)`. This method checks whether the passed interface equals the interface or whether the passed interface is a base of the interface (that is, whether it extends the interface).

When you're creating classes from an interface, you might want to use the helpful script `pyskel`, which creates a class skeleton from an interface. Before using the script, you have to make sure that `Zope3-Instance/lib/python` (or the directory to your package) is in your Python path. Here's how you use `pyskel`:

```
bin/pyskel dotted.path.ref.to.interface
```

This call creates a skeleton of the class in your console, which saves you a lot of typing. The order of the attributes and methods, as they appear in the interface, is preserved.

Some interfaces are part of the `zope.interface` package because they have implementations in the built-in Python types. They can be found in `zope.interface.common`.

This overview of interfaces should be sufficient to get you started with the following chapters. Many of the concepts will become much clearer as you work through the hands-on examples of the following parts of the book.

7

The Component Architecture: An Introduction

Difficulty

Newcomer

Skills

- You should be familiar with object-oriented programming.
- You should be knowledgeable about interfaces (for example, by reading the previous chapter on interfaces).
- Knowledge of component-oriented programming is preferable. Optional.

Problem/Task

When the component architecture for Zope was first imagined, it was intended as an extension to Zope 2, not a replacement, as it ended up becoming. The issue was that the existing Zope 2 API was too bloated and inconsistent, due to constant feature additions, bug fixes, and coding inconsistencies. Developers used the extremely bad practice of "monkey patching" to overcome the limitations of the API and to fix bugs. (Monkey patching is a method of overwriting library functions and class methods after importing them, and it is a powerful, but dangerous, side effect of loosely typed scripting languages.)

Another motivation was to incorporate the lessons learned from consulting jobs and building large web applications, which demonstrated the practical limits of simple object inheritance. The need for a more loosely connected architecture arose, with many objects having rather tiny interfaces in contrast to Zope 2's few, large objects. This type of framework was also desired to drastically reduce the learning curve because a developer would need to learn fewer APIs to accomplish a given task.

All these requirements pointed to a component-oriented framework that is now known as the component architecture of Zope 3. Many large software projects have already turned to component-based systems. Some of the better-known projects include the following:

- COM (Microsoft's object model)
- Corba (an open-source object communication protocol)
- KParts (from the KDE project)
- Mozilla API (which is in some ways very similar to Zope 3's component architecture)
- JMX (Sun's Java Management Extensions, which manages Beans)

However, although Zope 3 has many similarities with these architectures, thanks to Python, with Zope 3, certain flexibilities are possible that compiled languages do not allow.

THIS CHAPTER PROVIDES A HIGH-LEVEL introduction to all component types. Throughout the book there are concrete examples on developing most of the component types introduced here.

Services

Services provide fundamental functionality, without which the application server would fail to function. They correspond to tools in Zope 2's Content Management Framework (CMF), by which some of the semantics were also inspired.

Services do not depend on other components at all. You only interact with other components by passing them as arguments to the constructor or the methods of the service. Any given application should have only a few services that cover the most fundamental functionality. When dealing with locality, services should always delegate requests upward—up to the global version of the service—if a request cannot be answered locally.

The most fundamental services are the registries of the components themselves. Whenever you register a class as a utility using ZCML, for example, the class is registered in the utility service and can be retrieved later, using the service. And yes, there is also a service service that manages all registered services.

Another service is the error reporting service, which records all errors that occur during the publication process of a page. It allows a developer to review the details of the error and the state of the system/request at the time the error occurred. Figure 7.1 shows a UML diagram of the service.

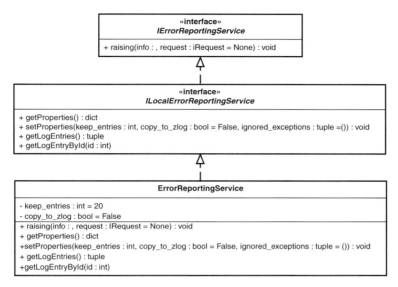

Figure 7.1   A UML diagram of the error reporting service.

A convention for service interfaces is that they only contain accessor methods. Mutator methods are usually implementation specific and are provided by additional interfaces. A consequence of this pattern is that services are usually not modified after the system is running. Please note, though, that developers are strongly discouraged from writing services for applications; they should use utilities instead.

Services make use of acquisition by delegating a query if it cannot be answered locally. For example, if you want to find a utility named "hello 1," providing the interface `IHello`, and it cannot be found at my local site, the local utility service delegates the request to the parent site. This goes all the way up to the global utility service. If the global utility service cannot provide a result, an error is returned. For more details about local and global components, see the section "Global Versus Local," later in this chapter.

Adapters

Adapters could be considered the glue components of the Zope architecture because they connect one interface with another and allow various advanced programming techniques, such as aspect-oriented programming. An adapter uses a component implementing one interface to provide another interface.

This allows the developer to split up the functionality into small API pieces and keep the functionality manageable. For example, you could write an adapter that allows an `IExample` content component to be represented as a file in FTP (see Figure 7.2). This can be done by implementing the `IReadFile` and `IWriteFile` interface for the content component. Instead of adding this functionality directly to the `SimpleExample` class by implementing the interfaces in the class, you can create an adapter that adapts IExample to IReadFile and IWriteFile. An adapter can be registered programmatically, but the more common use is to use the ZCML adapter directive. When the adapter is registered for both interfaces (usually through ZCML), it can be used as follows:

```
read_file = zapi.getAdapter(example, IreadFile, name='')
write_file = IWriteFile(example)
```

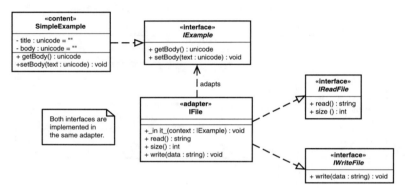

Figure 7.2   A UML diagram of an adapter adapting
IExample to IReadFile and IWriteFile.

The getAdapter() method finds an adapter that maps any of the interfaces that are implemented by example (which is a SimpleExample instance) to IReadFile. The name of the adapter must always be specified. If no name was provided, then an empty string must be passed as the name. An optional argument named context can be passed as a keyword argument, specifying the place to look for the adapter. None causes the system to look only for global adapters. The default is the site from which the request was made.

For the second adapter call, you use some syntactic sugar by calling the interface to create the adapter. The first argument is the object that is being adapted to the called interface. An optional second argument specifies the alternative result if no adapter was found. The semantics of this function are based on those of the PEP 246 adapt() function. Note that for simple adaptations, this is the preferred way to get an adapter.

In the preceding two cases, you adapted from one interface to another. But adapters can also adapt from several interfaces to another. These are known as *multi-adapters*. While multi-adapters were first thought of as unnecessary, they are now used in a wide range of situations.

The best side effect of using adapters is that it is not necessary to touch the original implementation (SimpleExample, in the preceding example) at all. This means you can use any Python package in Zope 3 by integrating it, using adapters and ZCML.

Utilities

Utilities are similar to services, but they do not provide vital functionality, so applications should not be broken if utilities are missing. This statement should be clarified by an example.

In pre-alpha development of Zope 3, SQL connections to various relational databases were managed by a service. The SQL connection service would manage SQL connections, and the user could then ask the service for SQL connections by name. If a connection was not available, the service would give a negative answer. Then the Zope 3 developers realized the role of utilities, and they were able to be rid of the SQL connection service and implement SQL connections as utilities. Now you can ask the utility service to give you an object that implements ISQLConnection and has a specified name. Many services that merely acted as registries were thrown out, and the objects they managed became utilities. This greatly reduced the number of services and the complexity of the system.

The lesson here is that before you develop a service, you should evaluate whether it would just act as a container, in which case the functionality is better implemented using utilities.

Factories (Object Classes/Prototypes)

Factories, as the name suggests, exist merely to create other components and objects. Factories can be methods, classes, or even instances that are callable. You encounter them directly only when dealing with content objects (because ZCML creates factories for you automatically) if you specify the factory directive. The functionality and usefulness of factories is best described by an example.

Let's consider the SimpleExample content component once more. A factory has to provide two methods. The obvious one is the __call__() method, which creates and returns a SimpleExample instance. The second method, called getInterfaces(), returns a list of interfaces that the object created by calling __call__ will provide.

Factories are simply named utilities that provide IFactory. Using a special subdirective, you can register a factory by using an ID, such as example.SimpleExample. When the factory is registered, you can use the component architecture's createObject() method to create SimpleExample components by using the factory (implicitly):

```
ex = zapi.createObject(None, 'example.SimpleExample')
```

The first argument is the place to look for the factory; passing None causes a global lookup only. The second argument is simply the factory ID.

> **Note**
>
> A factory ID must be unique in the entire system, and the low-level functionality of factories is mostly hidden by high-level configuration.

One of the bug advantages of factories is that they are independent of the location of the object. Clearly, you could simply use the Python class itself to create objects, but that would mean that you need to import the class. If the location of the class changes, your code will break. This is not true for factories; as long as the ID remains the same, the `createObject()` call will not fail.

Also note that a factory often can do much more than just instantiate an object instance; often the factory will also ensure that the created object is security proxied and might even notify other components of the system about the creation of the object. However, the ZCML-generated factories will not notify the system about the created object; they leave it to the developer to send out an event.

Presentation Components: Views, Resources, Skins, and Layers

Presentation components, especially views, are very similar to adapters, except that they take into account additional parameters, such as layers and skins. In fact, in future versions of Zope 3, the presentation service will be removed, and presentation components will become adapters. Presentation components are used for providing presentation for other components in various output formats (that is, presentation types), such as HTML, FTP, and XML-RPC.

In order to make a view work, two pieces of information have to be provided. First, the view must know for which object it is providing a view. This object is commonly known as the `context` of the view. Second, you need to know some protocol-specific information, which is stored in a `Request` object that is always accessible under the variable name `request` in the view. For HTML, for example, the request contains all cookies, form variables, and HTTP header values, but also the authenticated user and the applicable locale. The return values of the methods of a view depend on the presentation type and the method itself. For example, HTTP views usually return the HTML body, and FTP might return a list of filenames.

Resources are presentation components in their own right. In comparison to views, they do not provide a presentation of another component, but they provide some presentation output that is independent of any other component. HTML is a prime example. Stylesheets and images used for the layout of a site are often not considered content and also do not depend on any content object, yet they are presentation for the HTTP presentation type. However, not all presentation types require resources; both FTP and XML-RPC do not have such independent presentation components.

Next, views and resources are grouped by layers, which are usually used for grouping similar look and feel. In Zope 2's CMF, layers are the folders contained by the `portal_skins` tool. An example for a layer is `debug`, which simply inserts Python tracebacks into exception HTML pages.

Multiple layers can then be stacked together to become a skin. Currently, the Zope 3 core has several skins: rotterdam (the default), Basic, Debug, and ZopeTop (which is excluded from the 3.0 distribution). You can change the skin simply by typing ++skin++*SKINNAME* after the root of your URL. Here's an example:

```
http://localhost: 8080/++skin++ZopeTop/folder1
```

When you develop an end-user website, you definitely want to create your own layer and incorporate it as a new skin. You want to avoid writing for your site views that each enforce the look and feel. Instead, you can use skins to create a look and feel that will work for all new and existing templates.

Global Versus Local Components

Zope 3 consciously separates local and global components. Global components have no place associated with them and are therefore always reachable and present. They are always initialized and registered at Zope 3 startup via ZCML, as mentioned previously. Therefore, global components are *not* persistent, which means they are not stored in the Zope Object Database (ZODB) at all. Their state is destroyed (and should be) upon server shutdown.

Local components, on the other hand, are stored in the ZODB at the place in the object tree where they were defined. Local components always only add and overwrite previous settings; they can never remove existing ones. You can create new local components through the Web interface by clicking Manage Site. This leads you into the configuration namespace, which is always marked by ++etc++site in the URL.

Every folder can be promoted to become a site. When you declare a local site manager for a folder by clicking Make Site, you call this object/folder a *site*.

As mentioned earlier in this chapter, local components use an explicit acquisition process when looking up information. For example, you may want to get the factory for SimpleExample.

When looking for any component, the original site of the publication is chosen. However, sometimes you want to start looking for a component from a different site. In such a case, you simply specify the context in the call, as in this example:

```
01 from zope.component.interfaces import IFactory
02 factory = zapi.getUtility(IFactory, 'example.SimpleExample',
context=other_site)
```

If a local utility service exists and an IFactory utility with the name example.SimpleExample is found, then the factory is returned. Otherwise, the local utility service delegates the request to the next site. Requests can be delegated all the way up to the global utility service, at which point an answer must be given. If the global Utility Service does not know the answer either, a ComponentLookupError error is raised.

You can see that there are slight semantic differences between global and local implementations of a service, besides the differences in data storage and accessibility. The global service never has to worry about place or the delegation of the request. The net effect is that global components are often easier to implement than their local equivalents. Furthermore, local components usually have writable APIs in addition to the readable ones because they have to allow runtime management.

8

Zope Schemas and Forms

Difficulty

Newcomer

Skills

- You should be familiar with the various built-in Python types.
- You should be familiar with HTML forms and CGI.
- Knowledge about the Zope 2 Formulator is advantageous. Optional.

Problem/Task

Early on, the Zope 3 developers decided that it would be cumbersome to manually write HTML forms and to manually validate the input. They realized that if they extended interfaces, they could create autogenerating HTML forms and also cause any input to be automatically validated. This chapter gives some background information and formally introduces the `zope.schema` and `zope.app.form` packages.

O RIGINALLY, THE ZOPE 3 DEVELOPMENT TEAM simply wanted to port Formulator, a very successful Zope 2 product that autogenerated and validated forms, to Zope 3. In Formulator, you could create various input fields (such as integers or text lines) in a form and provide some metadata about the fields, such as the maximum and minimum length of a string. You could then tell the form to simply render itself. (For more details, see `http://zope.org/Members/infrae/Formulator`.)

Even though Formulator tried to split application logic and presentation, various parts were still not sufficiently separated, mainly due to the limitations of Zope 2. Therefore, the original port remained a hack in Zope 3 until the idea of schemas was developed by

Jim Fulton and Martijn Faassen (the original author of Formulator) during the Berlin BBQ Sprint (April 2002), when trying to combine Zope 3's version of Formulator and class properties. After all the presentation logic was removed, Formulator fields felt a lot like interface specifications for attributes. So the team realized that if they supplied more metadata to the attribute declarations in the interfaces, it could accomplish autogeneration and validation of HTML forms. These extended attributes are still known as *fields*. If an interface contains any fields, then that interface is conventionally called a *schema*.

The following are the three main goals of developing schemas:

- Full specification of properties on an API level

- Data input validation and conversion

- Automated GUI form generation (mainly for web browsers)

Schemas Versus Interfaces

As mentioned earlier, schemas are just an extension to interfaces and therefore depend on the `zope.interface` package. Fields in schemas are equivalent to methods in interfaces. They are complementary to one other because they describe different aspects of an object. The methods of an interface describe the functionality of a component, and a schema's fields represent the state.

It is thus not necessary to develop a new syntax for writing schemas, and you can simply reuse the interface declaration:

```
01 from zope.interface import Interface
02 from zope.schema import Text
03
04 class IExample(Interface):
05
06     text = Text(
07         title=u"Text",
08         description=u"The text of the example.",
09         required=True)
```

In the preceding code block, note the following:

- Line 2: You can simply import all the default fields from `zope.schema`.

- Lines 7–8: For form generation, you use the title and description as human-readable text. Of course, the title and description also serve as documentation of the field itself.

- Line 9: Various fields support several other metadata fields. The `required` option is actually available for all fields and specifies whether an object implementing `IExample` must provide a value for `text`.

The Core Schema Fields

Now that you have seen a simple example of a schema, let's look at all the basic fields and their properties.

All fields support the following properties:

- **title (type: `TextLine`)**—The title of the attribute is used as the label when displaying the field widget.

- **description (type: `Text`)**—The description of the attribute is used for ToolTips and advanced help.

- **required (type: `Bool`)**—This field specifies whether an attribute is required to have a value. In add forms, required attributes are equivalent to required constructor arguments.

- **readonly (type: `Bool`)**—If a field is read-only, then the value of this attribute can be set only once and can then only be displayed. Often a unique ID for some object is a good candidate for a `readonly` field.

- **default (type: depends on field)**—This field uses the default value given to the attribute, if no initialization value is provided. This value is often specified if a field is required.

- **missing_value (type: `object`)**—If no input was provided for this field, this value is used to represent the unset field. It differs from the default value in that it represents a non-assigned state versus the initial state. For example, if you have an integer and it is not set, you might want to use `None` to describe it. You could not use a valid integer, such as zero, because then you would have assigned a value to the field.

- **order (type: `Int`)**—Fields are often grouped in some logical order. The `order` value specifies a relative position in that order. You usually do not set this value manually because it is automatically assigned when an interface is initialized. The order of the fields in a schema is, by default, the same as the order of the fields in the Python code.

The following basic fields are available in the `zope.schema` package:

- **Bytes and BytesLine**—`Bytes` and `BytesLine` only differ in that `BytesLine` cannot contain a newline character. `Bytes` behaves identically to the Python type `str`. The `Bytes` and `BytesLine` fields can be iterated. The following additional properties are available:

    - **min_length (type: `Int`)**—After the whitespace has been normalized, there cannot be fewer than this number of characters in the byte string. The default is `None`, which means no minimum.

    - **max_length (type: `Int`)**—After the whitespace has been normalized, there cannot be more than this number of characters in the byte string. The default is `None`, which means no maximum.

- **Text and TextLine**—These two fields only differ in that TextLine cannot contain a newline character. Text fields contain Unicode, meaning that they are intended to be human-readable strings/text. Text and TextLine fields can be iterated. The following additional properties are available:
  - **min_length (type: Int)**—After the whitespace has been normalized, there cannot be fewer than this number of characters in the text string. The default is None, which means no minimum.
  - **max_length (type: Int)**—After the whitespace has been normalized, there cannot be more than this number of characters in the text string. The default is None, which means no maximum.
- **SourceText**—SourceText is a special field derived from Text, and it contains source code of any type. It is more or less a marker field for a form's machinery, so that special input fields can be used for source code.
- **Password**—Password is a special derivative for the TextLine field and is treated separately for presentation reasons. However, you might at times want more fine-grained validation for passwords.
- **Bool**—The Bool field, which has no further attributes, maps directly to Python's bool object.
- **Int**—Int fields directly map to Python's int type. The following additional properties are available:
  - **min (type: Int)**—This field specifies the smallest acceptable integer. This is useful in many ways; for example, you can allow only positive values by making this field 0.
  - **max (type: Int)**—This field specifies the largest acceptable integer, which excludes the value itself. It can be used to specify an upper bound, such as the current year if you are interested in the past only.

  You can use these two attributes to specify ranges of acceptable values.
- **Float**—Float fields directly map to Python's float type. The following additional properties are available:
  - **min (type: Float)**—This field specifies the smallest acceptable floating-point number. This is useful in many ways; for example, you can allow only positive values by making this field 0.0.
  - **max (type: Float)**—This field specifies the largest acceptable floating-point number, which excludes the value itself. (This is a typical computer programming pattern.) It can be used to specify an upper bound, such as 1.0, if you are interested only in probabilities.

  You can use these two attributes to specify ranges of acceptable values.
- **Datetime**—Similar to Int and Float, Datetime has min and max fields that specify the boundaries of the possible values. Acceptable values for these fields must be instances of the built-in datetime type.

- **Tuple and List**—The reason both of these fields exists is so you can easily map them to the Python types tuple and list, respectively. The Tuple and List fields can be iterated. The following additional properties are available:
  - **min_length (type: Int)**—There cannot be fewer than this number of items in the sequence. The default is None, which means there is no minimum.
  - **max_length (type: Int)**—There cannot be more than this number of items in the sequence. The default is None, which means there is no maximum.
  - **value_type (type: Field)**—Values contained by these sequence types must conform to this field's constraint. Most commonly, a Choice field (described later in this list) is specified here, which allows you to select from a fixed set of values.
- **Dict**—Dict is a mapping field that maps from one set of fields to another. Dict fields can be iterated. The following additional properties are available:
  - **min_length (type: Int)**—There cannot be fewer than this number of items in the dictionary. The default is None, which means there is no minimum.
  - **max_length (type: Int)**—There cannot be more than this number of items in the dictionary. The default is None, which means there is no maximum.
  - **key_type (type: Field)**—Every dictionary item key has to conform to the specified field.
  - **value_type (type: Field)**—Every dictionary item value has to conform to the specified field.
- **Choice**—The Choice field allows you to select a particular value from a provided set of values. You can either provide the values as a simple sequence (list or tuple) or specify a vocabulary (by reference or name) that will provide the values. Vocabularies provide a flexible list of values; in other words, the set of allowed values can change as the system changes. Because they are so complex, they are covered in detail in Chapter 31, "Vocabularies and Related Fields/Widgets." The following additional properties are available:
  - **vocabulary (type: Vocabulary)**—This vocabulary instance is used to provide the available values. This attribute is None if a vocabulary name was specified and the field has not been bound to a context.
  - **vocabularyName (type: TextLine)**—This is the name of the vocabulary that is used to provide the values. The vocabulary for this name can only be looked up when the field is bound (that is, when the field has a context). Upon binding, the vocabulary is automatically looked up, using the name and the context.

The constructor also accepts a values argument that specifies a static set of values. These values are immediately converted to a static vocabulary.

- **Object**—This field specifies an object that must implement a specific schema. Only objects that provide the specified schema are allowed. The following additional properties are available:
  - **schema (type: Interface)**—This field provides a reference to the schema that must be provided by objects that want to be stored in the described attribute.
- **DottedName**—Derived from the BytesLine field, the DottedName field represents valid Python-style dotted names (object references). This field can be used when it is desirable that a valid and resolvable Python dotted name be provided. This field has no further attributes.
- **URI**—Derived from the BytesLine field, the URI field makes sure that the value is always a valid URI. This is particularly useful when you want to reference resources (such as RSS feeds or images) on remote computers. This field has no further attributes.
- **Id**—Both the DottedName and URI fields make up the Id field. Any dotted name or URI represent a valid ID in Zope. IDs are used for identifying many types of objects, such as permissions and principals, but also for providing annotation keys. This field has no further attributes.
- **InterfaceField**—The Interface field has no further attributes. Its value must be an object that provides zope.interface.Interface; in other words, it must be an interface.

For a complete listing of the schema/field API, see the API documentation tool at http://localhost:8080/++apidoc++ or see the zope.schema.interfaces module.

Autogenerated Forms Using the `forms` Package

Forms are much more Zope specific than schemas, and they can be found in the zope.app.forms package. The views of schema fields are called *widgets*. Widgets are responsible for data display and conversion in their specific presentation types. Currently, widgets exist mainly for HTML (that is, for web browsers).

Widgets fall into two groups: display and input widgets. Display widgets are often very simple and show only a text representation of the Python object. Input widgets are more complex, and they display a greater variety of choices. The following sections describe all the available browser-based input widgets (found in zope.app.form.browser).

Text Widgets

Text-based widgets always require some sort of keyboard input. A string representation of a field is then converted to the desired Python object, such as an integer or a date.

Here is a list of the base text widgets:

- **TextWidget**—Being probably the simplest widget, TextWidget displays the text input element and is mainly used for the TextLine field, which is expected to be Unicode. It also serves as the base widget for many of the following widgets.

- **TextAreaWidget**—As the name suggests, this widget displays a text area and assumes its input to be some Unicode string. (Note that the publisher already takes care of the encoding issues.)

- **BytesWidget and BytesAreaWidget**—Direct descendents of TextWidget and TextAreaWidget, the only difference between those widgets and BytesWidget and BytesAreaWidget is that these widgets expect bytes as input and not a Unicode string, which means they must be valid ASCII encodable.

- **ASCIIWidget**—This widget, based on BytesWidget, ensures that only ASCII characters are part of the inputted data.

- **PasswordWidget**—Almost identical to TextWidget, this widget displays a password element instead of a text element.

- **IntWidget**—A derivative of TextWidget, this widget overwrites the conversion method to ensure the conversion to an integer.

- **FloatWidget**—Derivative of TextWidget, this widget overwrites the conversion method to ensure the conversion to a floating-point number.

- **DatetimeWidget**—You might expect a smart and complex widget at this point, but for now, it is just a simple TextWidget widget with a String-to-Datetime converter. There is also a DateWidget widget that only handles dates.

Boolean Widgets

Boolean widgets' only responsibility is to convert some binary input to the Python values True or False. Here are the ones provided by Zope:

- **CheckBoxWidget**—This widget displays a single check box widget that can be either checked or unchecked, representing the state of the Boolean value.

- **BooleanRadioWidget**—Two radio buttons are used to represent the Boolean true and false states. You can pass the textual values for the two states in the constructor. The default is on and off (or their translations for languages other than English).

- **BooleanSelectWidget and BooleanDropdownWidget**—Similar to BooleanRadioWidget, with these widgets, textual representations of the true and false states are used to select the value. See SelectWidget and DropdownWidget, in the following section, for more details.

Single-Selection Widgets

Widgets that allow a single item to be selected from a list of values are usually views of a field, a vocabulary, and the request, instead of just the field and request pair. Therefore, *proxy–widgets* are used to map from field/request pairs to field/vocabulary/request groups. For example, ChoiceInputWidget, which takes a Choice field and a request object, simply looks up another widget that is registered for the Choice field, its vocabulary, and the request. The following is a list of all the available widgets that require the latter three inputs:

- **SelectWidget**—This widget provides a multiply sized selection element where the options are populated through the vocabulary terms. If the field is not required, a "no value" option is available as well. The user is allowed to only select one value, though, because the Choice field is not a sequence–based field.

- **DropdownWidget**—As a simple derivative of SelectWidget, DropdownWidget has its size set to 1, which makes it a drop-down box. Drop-down boxes have the advantage that they always show just one value, which can make them more user friendly for single selections.

- **RadioWidget**—This widget displays a radio button for each term in the vocabulary. Radio buttons have the advantage that they always show all choices and are therefore suitable for small vocabularies.

Multiple-Selections Widgets

The multiple-selection widgets are used to display input form collection–based fields, such as List or Set. As with the single-selection widgets, two proxy-widgets are used to look up the correct widget. The first step is to map from field/request to field/value_type/request, using a widget called CollectionInputWidget. This allows you to use different widgets when the value type is an Int or Choice field, for example. Optionally, a second proxy/widget is used to convert the field/value_type/request group to a field/vocabulary/request group, as is the case when the value type is a choice field.

The following is a list of all the widgets that come with Zope 3:

- **MultiSelectWidget**—This widget creates a select element with the multiple attribute set to true. This creates a multiselection box. This is especially useful for vocabularies with many terms. Note that if a vocabulary supports a query interface, you can even filter the selectable items by using queries.

- **MultiCheckBoxWidget**—Similarly to MultiSelectWidget, this widget allows multivalue selections of a given list, but it uses check boxes instead of a list. This widget is useful for small vocabularies.

- **TupleSequenceWidget**—This widget is used for all cases where the value type is not a Choice field. It uses the widget of the value type field to add new values to the tuple. Other input elements are used to remove items.

- **ListSequenceWidget**—This widget is equivalent to TupleSequenceWidget, except that it generates lists instead of tuples.

Miscellaneous Widgets

The widgets listed in this section deal in one way or another with nontextual data:

- **FileWidget**—This widget displays a file input element and makes sure the received data is a file. This field is ideal for quickly uploading byte streams, as required for the Bytes field.

- **ObjectWidget**—ObjectWidget is the view for an object field. It uses the schema of the object to construct an input form. The object factory, which is passed in as a constructor argument, is used to build the object from the input afterward.

Using Widgets

The following simple interactive example demonstrates the rendering and conversion functionality of a widget:

```
01 >>> from zope.publisher.browser import TestRequest
02 >>> from zope.schema import Int
03 >>> from zope.app.form.browser import IntWidget
04 >>> field = Int(__name__='number', title=u'Number', min=0, max=10)
05 >>> request = TestRequest(form={'field.number': u'9'})
06 >>> widget = IntWidget(field, request)
07 >>> widget.hasInput()
08 True
09 >>> widget.getInputValue()
10 9
11 >>> print widget().replace(' ', '\n  ')
12 <input
13   class="textType"
14   id="field.number"
15   name="field.number"
16   size="10"
17   type="text"
18   value="9"
19
20   />
```

In the preceding code block, note the following:

- Lines 1 and 5: For views, including widgets, you always need a request object. Using the `TestRequest` class is the quick and easy way to create a request without much hassle. For each presentation type there exists a `TestRequest` class. The class takes a `form` argument, which is a dictionary of values contained in the HTML form. The widget will later access this information.

- Line 2: You import an integer field.

- Lines 3 and 6: You import the widget that displays and converts an integer from the HTML form. Initializing a widget only requires a field and a request.

- Line 4: You create an integer field with the constraint that the value must lie between 0 and 10. The __name__ argument must be passed here because the field has not been initialized inside an interface, where the __name__ argument would be automatically assigned.

- Lines 7–8: This method checks whether the form contains a value for this widget.

- Lines 9–10: If the form contains a value for the widget, you can use the `getInputValue()` method to return the converted and validated value (an integer, in this case). If you chose an integer outside this range, a `WidgetInputError` exception would be raised.

- Lines 11–20: You display the HTML representation of the widget. The `replace()` call is included for better readability of the output.

Note that you usually do not have to deal with these methods manually because the form generator and data converter do all the work for you. The only method you commonly overwrite is `_validate()`, which you use to validate custom values.

There are two ways of customizing widgets. For small adjustments to some parameters (for example, properties of the widget), you can use the `browser:widget` subdirective of the `browser:addform` and `browser:editform` directives. For example, to change the widget for a field called name, you can use the following ZCML code:

```
01 <browser:addform
02   ... >
03
04   <browser:widget
05       field="name"
06       class="zope.app.form.browser.TextWidget"
07       displayWidth="45"
08       style="width: 100%"/>
09
10 </browser:addform>
```

In this case, you force the system to use the `TextWidget` field for the name, set the display width to 45 characters, and add a style attribute that should try to set the width of the input box to the available width. Note that this procedure works only for attributes that are supported by the widget. Because these attributes are not captured via an interface, you must inspect the code to find out about these attributes at this point.

The second possibility for changing the widget of a field is to write a custom view class. In it, custom widgets are easily realized, using the `CustomWidget` wrapper class. Here is a brief example:

```
01 from zope.app.form.widget import CustomWidget
02 from zope.app.form.browser import TextWidget
03
04 class CustomTextWidget(TextWidget):
05     ...
06
07 class SomeView:
08     name_widget = CustomWidget(CustomTextWidget)
```

In the preceding code block, note the following:

- Line 1: Because `CustomWidget` is presentation type independent, it is defined in `zope.app.form.widget`.

- Lines 4–5: You simply extend an existing widget. Here you can overwrite everything, including the `_validate()` method.

- Lines 7–8: You can hook in the custom widget by adding an attribute called *name*_widget, where *name* is the name of the field. The value of the attribute is a `CustomWidget` instance. `CustomWidget` has only one required constructor argument: the custom widget for the field. Other keyword arguments can be specified as well, and they will be set as attributes on the widget.

You can find more information about schemas in the `README.txt` file of the `zope.schema` package. The Zope 3 development website, `http://dev.zope.org/Zope3`, also contains some additional material.

This concludes this book's introduction to schemas and forms. For examples of schemas and forms in practice, see Chapters 13, "Writing New Content Objects," and 14, "Adding Views for Content Objects."

Introduction to the Zope Configuration Markup Language (ZCML)

Difficulty

Newcomer

Skills

- You should be familiar with the previous chapters of this section, specifically Chapter 7, "The Component Architecture: An Introduction."
- Some basic familiarity with XML is advantageous. Optional.

Problem/Task

Developing components alone does not make a framework. There must be a configuration utility that tells the system how the components work together to create the application server framework. In Zope, this is done using Zope Configuration Markup Language (ZCML) for all filesystem-based code. Therefore, it is very important that you know how to use ZCML to hook up your components to the framework.

WITH ZOPE, IT BECAME NECESSARY to develop a method to set up and configure the components that make up the application server. Although it might seem otherwise, it is not that easy to develop an effective configuration system because several requirements must be satisfied. Over time, the following high-level requirements caused revisions of the implementation and coding styles to be created:

- Although the developer is certainly the one who writes the initial cut of the configuration, that user is not the real target audience. After the product is written, you expect a system administrator to interact frequently with the configuration, adding and removing functionality or adjusting the configuration of the server setup. System administrators are often not developers, so it would be unfortunate to write the configuration in the programming language (in this case, Python). But an administrator is familiar with configuration scripts, shell code, and XML to some extent. Therefore, an easy-to-read syntax that is similar to other configuration files is advantageous.

- Because the configuration is not written in Python, it is very important that it be tightly integrated with Python. For example, it must be very simple to refer to the components in the Python modules and to internationalize any human-readable strings.

- The configuration mechanism should be declarative and not provide any facilities for logical operations. If the configuration supported logic, it would become very hard to read, and the initial state of the entire system would be unclear. This is another reason Python was not suited for this task.

- Developing new components sometimes requires you to extend the configuration mechanism. Therefore, it must be easy for developers to extend the configuration mechanism without much hassle.

Using XML

To satisfy the first requirement, the Zope development team decided to use an XML-based language (as the name ZCML suggests). The advantage of XML is that it is a "standard format," which increases the likelihood that people will be able to read it right away. Furthermore, you can use standard Python modules to parse the format, and XML namespaces help you to group the configuration by functionality.

A single configuration step is called a *directive*. Each directive is an XML tag, and therefore the tags are grouped by namespaces. Directives come in two flavors: simple and complex. Complex directives can contain other subdirectives. They are usually used to provide a set of common properties but do not generate an action immediately.

The following is an example of a typical configuration file:

```
01 <configure
02     xmlns="http://namespaces.zope.org/zope">
03
04 <adapter
05     factory="product.FromIXToIY"
06     for="product.interfaces.IX"
07     provides="product.interfaces.IY" />
08
09 </configure>
```

The configure tag

All configuration files are wrapped by the `configure` tag, which represents the beginning of the configuration. In the opening of this tag, you always list the namespaces you want to use in the configuration file. In this example you only want to use the generic Zope 3 namespace, which is used as the default. Then you register an adapter with the system on lines 4–7. The interfaces and classes are referred to by a proper Python dotted name. The `configure` tag might also contain an `i18n_domain` attribute that contains the domain that is used for all the translatable strings in the configuration.

As everywhere in Zope 3, there are several naming and coding conventions for ZCML inside a package. By default, you should name the configuration file `configure.zcml`. Inside the file, you should declare only namespaces that you are actually going to use. When writing the directives, you need to make sure to logically group directives together and use comments as necessary.

> **Note**
>
> Comments are written using the common XML syntax: `<!-- ... -->`. For more information on comments, see Steve Alexander's detailed ZCML Style Guide at `http://dev.zope.org/Zope3/ZCMLStyleGuide`.

To satisfy the fourth requirement, it is possible to easily extend ZCML by utilizing the `meta` namespace. A directive can be completely described by four components—its name, the namespace it belongs to, the schema, and the directive handler—as shown in the following example:

```
01 <meta:directives namespace="http://namespaces.zope.org/zope">
02   <meta:directive
03      name="adapter"
04      schema=".metadirectives.IAdapterDirective"
05      handler=".metaconfigure.adapterDirective" />
06 </meta:directives>
```

These meta-directives are commonly placed in a file called `meta.zcml`.

The schema of a directive, which commonly lives in a file called `metadirectives.py`, is a simple Zope 3 schema whose fields describe the available attributes for the directive. The configuration system uses the fields to convert and validate the values of the configuration for use. For example, dotted names are automatically converted to Python objects. There are several specialized fields specifically for the configuration machinery:

- **`PythonIdentifier`**—This field describes a Python identifier (for example, a simple variable name).

- **`GlobalObject`**—This field describes an object that can be accessed as a module global, such as a class, function, or constant.

- **`Tokens`**—This field describes a sequence that can be read from a whitespace-separated string. The `value_type` of the field describes `token type`.

- **Path**—This field describes a file pathname, which may be input as a relative path. Input paths are converted to absolute paths and normalized.

- **Bool**—This field describes an extended Boolean value. Values may be input (in uppercase or lowercase) as yes, no, y, n, true, false, t, or f.

- **MessageID**—This field describes a text string that should be translated. Therefore, the directive schema is the only place that needs to deal with internationalization. This satisfies part of the second requirement

The handler, which commonly lives in a file called metaconfigure.py, is a function or another callable object that knows what needs to be done with the given information of the directive. Here is a simple example (simplified to the actual code):

```
01 def adapter(_context, factory, provides, for_, permission=None, name='',
02          trusted=False):
03
04    _context.action(
05        discriminator = ('adapter', for_, provides, name),
06        callable = provideAdapter,
07        args = (for_, provides, name, factory, _context.info),
08        )
```

The context Variable

The first argument of the handler is always the _context variable, which has a similar function to self in classes. It provides some common methods that are necessary for handling directives. The following arguments are the attributes of the directive (and their names must match). If an attribute name equals a Python keyword, such as for in the example, an underscore is appended to the attribute name.

The handler should also not directly execute an action because the system should first go through all of the configuration and detect possible conflicts and overrides. Therefore, the _context object has a method called action that registers an action to be executed at the end of the configuration process. The first argument is discriminator, which uniquely defines a specific directive. callable is the function that is executed to provoke the action, the args argument is a list of arguments that is passed to callable, and kw contains callable's keywords.

As you can see, there is nothing inherently difficult about ZCML. Still, people coming to Zope 3 often think ZCML is the most difficult part to understand. This has created huge discussions about the format of ZCML. However, the problem lies not within ZCML itself but with the task it tries to accomplish. The components themselves always seem so clean in implementation—and then you get to the configuration. There you have to register this adapter and that view, make security assertions, and so on. And this in itself seems overwhelming at first. When I look at a configuration file after a long time I often have this feeling, too, but reading directive for directive often helps me to get a quick overview of the functionality of the package. In fact, the configuration files can help you understand the processes of the Zope 3 framework without reading the code because all the interesting interactions are defined right there. Another advantage of using an XML dialect is that there are many syntax verification tools available, and it would be relatively easy to create a graphical configuration tool, which could allow you to quickly see the dependencies between components.

Furthermore, ZCML is well documented in many places, including the Zope 3 API documentation tool, at `http://localhost:8080/++apidoc++/`, where all ZCML namespaces are referenced. The following are the most important namespaces:

- **zope**—This is the most generic and fundamental namespace of all because it allows you to register all basic components with the component architecture.

- **browser**—This namespace contains all the directives that deal with HTML output, including managing skins and layers, declaring new views (pages) and resources, and setting up autogenerated forms.

- **meta**—As discussed previously, you can use this namespace to extend ZCML's available directives.

- **xmlrpc**—This is the equivalent to `browser`, except that it allows you to specify methods of components that should be available via XML-RPC.

- **i18n**—This namespace contains all internationalization- and localization-specific configuration. By using `registerTranslations`, you can register new message catalogs with a translation domain.

- **help**—By using the `register` directive, you can register new help pages with the help system. This gives you context-sensitive help for the Zope Management Interface (ZMI) screens of your packages.

- **mail**—By using the directives of this namespace, you can set up mailing components that your application can use to send out emails.

This concludes this basic introduction to ZCML. Starting in the next part of the book, you will be using ZCML all the time to register and configure your components.

10

Introduction to Zope's I18n and L10n Support

Difficulty

Newcomer

Skills

- You should be familiar with the previous chapters in this part, specifically Chapter 7, "The Component Architecture: An Introduction."
- You should be familiar with common tasks and problems that arise when developing translatable software.
- It is helpful to know about the gettext and/or ICU tools. Optional.

Problem/Task

Often it is not acceptable to provide an application in just one language and it must be possible to provide the software in many languages. But the problem is not solved there. Besides simple text, one must also deal with date/time and number formats, for example, because they are specific to regions and languages as well. This chapter provides an overview of the utilities that Zope 3 provides to solve these problems.

ONE OF THE MOST SEVERE PROBLEMS with Zope 2 is its lack of multilanguage support. This problem significantly limits the adoption of Zope 2 outside English-speaking regions. Multilanguage support was partially added to Zope 2 through add-on products such as Localizer and ZBabel, which allow translation of DTML and Python code (and therefore ZPT). However, these solutions cannot overcome the great limitation that

Zope 2 is not Unicode aware. Several workarounds to the problem have been provided, but they do not provide a solid solution.

When the Zope developers initiated their internationalization effort and developed the i18n page template namespace for Zope 3, this namespace was backported to Zope 2, and the Placeless Translation Service product was provided by the community (see www.zope.org/Members/efge/TranslationService).

> **Note**
>
> Zope 3 now uses translation domain utilities instead of translation services. If this does not make sense at this point, you can safely ignore this bit of information.

When Zope 3 development was opened to the community, it was realized that internationalization is a very important feature because Zope has a large market in Latin America, Asia, and especially in Europe. Therefore, the first public Zope 3 sprint in January 2002 was dedicated to this subject.

Diving into I18n and L10n

What do the terms *internationalization* and *localization* mean?

Internationalization, often abbreviated *I18n*, is the process of making a software product translatable. This includes preparing and marking strings for translation, providing utilities to represent data (such as dates/times and numbers) in regional formats, and enabling the software to recognize the user's region/language setting. The last section of this chapter deals in detail with how to internationalize the various components of Zope 3 code.

Localization, often abbreviated *L10n*, is the process of translating software to a particular language/region. For this task, you need one tool to extract all translatable strings and another tool to aid the translation process. Localization data for number formatting, currencies, time zones, and much more are, luckily, already compiled in large volumes of XML locale files.

The Zope 3 I18n support aims to accomplish three goals:

- The support will only deal with the translation of software, not with content. Internationalizing and localizing content requires custom software that implements very specific workflows.

- Because Zope 3 is a network application server, rather than a simple application, the I18n solution should be flexible enough to support changing locale settings among different users. This is appreciably more difficult to implement than I18n for an application that runs on a client.

- It should be very simple and transparent to internationalize third-party add-on packages.

In the open-source world, there are two established solutions for providing I18n libraries and L10n utilities: GNU gettext and ICU. gettext is the de facto standard for the Free Software world (for example, KDE and Gnome), but it has some major shortcomings. gettext only does a so-so job of translating messages (human-readable strings). On the other hand, many translation tools support the gettext format, such as KBabel, which is a true power tool for translating message catalogs. Therefore, it is important to support the gettext message catalog format, even if it is only through import and export facilities.

ICU, in contrast, is a very extensive and well-developed framework that builds on the experience of the Java I18n libraries. (It was primarily developed to replace the original Java I18n support.) ICU provides objects for everything you could ever imagine, including locales, object formatting, and transliteration rules. Best of all, the information of more than 220 locales is available in XML files. These files contain complete translations of all countries and languages, date/time formatting/parsing rules for three different formats (following the standard specification)—including all month/weekday names/abbreviations, time zone specifications (city names inclusive)—and number formatting/parsing rules for decimal, scientific, monetary, percent, and per-mile numbers.

The Zope 3 development team decided to make all human-readable text Unicode, so that it would not run into the same issues as with Zope 2. Only the publisher would convert the Unicode to bytes (using UTF-8 or other encodings). The discussion and decision of this subject are immortalized in the proposal at
`http://dev.zope.org/Zope3/UnicodeForText`.

Because the ICU framework is simply too massive to be ported to Python for Zope 3, the Zope 3 development team decided to adopt the locales support from ICU (using the XML files as data) and support the gettext message catalogs for translation, simply because the gettext tools are available as standard libraries in Python. From the XML locale files, Zope mainly uses the date/time and number patterns for formatting and parsing these data types. Two generic pattern-parsing classes have been written and can be used independently of Zope 3's I18n framework. On top of these pattern-parsing classes are the formatter and parser class for each corresponding data type. But all this is hidden behind the `Locale` object, which makes all the locale data available and provides some convenience functions.

Locales

The `Locale` instance for a user is available via the `request` object, which is always available from a view. However, you can easily test the functionality of `Locale` instances by using the interactive Python prompt. To do so, you go to the directory *Zope3-Installation*/lib/python and start Python. You can then use the following code to get a locale:

```
01 >>> from zope.i18n.locales import LocaleProvider
02 >>> provider = LocaleProvider('./zope/i18n/locales/data')
03 >>> locale = provider.getLocale('en', 'US')
```

As you can see, the locale data is located in *Zope3-Installation*/lib/python/zope/i18n/locales/data.

You can then, for example, retrieve the currency that is used in the United States and get the symbol and name of the currency:

```
01 >>> numbers = locale.numbers
02 >>> currency = numbers.currencies['USD']
03 >>> currency.symbol
04 u'$'
05 >>> currency.type
06 u'USD'
07 >>> currency.displayName
08 u'US Dollar'
```

More interesting tasks are formatting and parsing dates/times. You can choose from four predefined date/time formatters: short, medium, full, and long. Here is an example of short:

```
01 >>> formatter = locale.dates.getFormatter('dateTime', length='short')
02 >>> formatter.parse(u'1/25/80 4:07 AM')
03 datetime.datetime(1980, 1, 25, 4, 7)
04 >>> from datetime import datetime
05 >>> dt = datetime(1980, 1, 25, 4, 7, 8)
06 >>> formatter.format(dt)
07 u'1/25/80 4:07 AM'
```

For numbers you can choose between decimal, percent, scientific, and currency:

```
01 >>> formatter = locale.numbers.getFormatter('decimal')
02 >>> formatter.parse(u'4,345.03')
03 4345.0299999999997
04 >>> formatter.format(34000.45)
05 u'34,000.45'
```

Messages and Message Catalogs

Although object formatting is a more interesting task, a more common task is the markup and translation of message strings. In order to manage translations better, message strings are categorized in domains. There is currently only one domain for all of the Zope core: zope. Add-on packages use a different domain; for example, Bugtracker uses the domain bugtracker. Translatable messages are particularly marked in the code (see the section "Internationalizing Message Strings," later in this chapter) and are translated before their final output.

All message translations for a particular language of one domain are stored in a message catalog. Therefore, you have a message catalog for each language and domain pair. You differentiate between filesystem (global) and ZODB (local) product development. Global message catalogs are standard gettext PO files. The PO files for the zope domain are located in ZOPE3/src/zope/app/locales/<REGION>/LC_MESSAGES/zope.po, where REGION can be de, en, or pt_BR.

Local message catalogs, on the other hand, are managed via the ZMI through local translation domains. In such a utility, you can create new languages, domains, and message strings; search through existing translations and make changes (see Figure 10.1); import/export external message catalogs—for example, gettext PO files (see Figure 10.2); and synchronize a translation domain with another one (see Figure 10.3). The synchronization between translation domain utilities is especially very powerful because it allows easy translation upgrades between development and production environments.

Figure 10.1 shows the main translation screen. It allows you to add to the domain languages that can be edited. After a language is created, you need to select it for modification. You can then add new messages or edit existing messages in the languages you selected. The filter option helps you to filter the message IDs so that you can find messages faster.

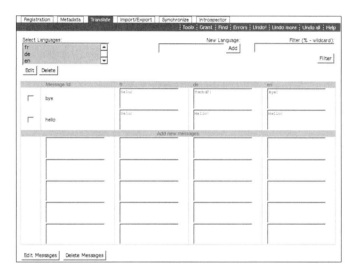

Figure 10.1   The main Zope translation screen.

Figure 10.2   The screen for importing gettext PO files or exporting the existing translations to gettext PO files.

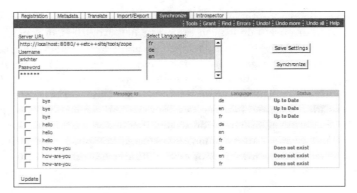

Figure 10.3   The Synchronization screen, for synchronizing
translations across remote domains.

Now you know how to manage translatable strings, but how can you tell the system
which strings are translatable? Translatable strings can occur in ZPT, DTML, ZCML, and
Python code. The Zope 3 development team noticed, however, that almost all Python-
based translatable strings occur in views, which led the team to the conclusion that message strings outside views are usually a sign of bad programming; there are only a few
exceptions to this rule (for example, interface declarations). This leads to a very important rule: Translations of human-readable strings should be done very late in the publication process, preferably just before the final output.

The next section goes into more detail on how to mark up the code in each language.

Internationalizing Message Strings

Now let's have a look at how strings are marked up in the various programming languages.

Python Code

As mentioned earlier in this chapter, Zope is not a simple application, and therefore you
cannot translate a text message directly in the Python code (because you do not know
the user's locale), but you must mark it as a translatable string, which is known as a *message ID*. Message IDs are created using `MessageId` factories. The factory takes the
domain as an argument to the constructor:

```
01 from zope.i18nmessageid import MessageIDFactory
02 _ = MessageIDFactory('demo')
```

You can simply mark up translatable strings by using the _ function:

```
01 title = _('This is the title of the object.')
```

But this is a simple case. What if you want to include some data? Then you can use this:

```
01 text = _('You have $x items.')
02 text.mapping = {'x': x}
```

In this case, the number is inserted after the translation. This way, you can avoid having a translation for every different value of x.

ZPT

For ZPT, or page templates in general, the Zope 3 development team came up with a special i18n namespace that can be used to translate messages. The namespace is well documented at http://dev.zope.org/Zope3/ZPTInternationalizationSupport, and some examples are available at
http://dev.zope.org/Zope3/ZPTInternationalizationExamples.

DTML

There is no DTML tag defined for doing translations yet, but the Zope 3 development team thinks it will be very similar to the ZBabel and Localizer versions because they are almost the same.

ZCML

Chapter 9, "Introduction to the Zope Configuration Markup Language (ZCML)," briefly describes ZCML's way of internationalizing text. In the schema of each ZCML directive, you can declare translatable attributes simply by making them MessageId fields. The domain for the message strings is provided by the i18n_domain attribute in the configure tag. Therefore, the user only has to specify this attribute to do the I18n in ZCML.

Extracting Message Strings

When the code is marked up, you must extract these strings from the code and compile message catalogs. For this task, there is a tool called Zope3-Instance/bin/i18nextract. Its functionality and options are discussed in Chapter 18, "Internationalizing Packages."

11

Metadata and the Dublin Core

Difficulty

Newcomer

Skills

- You should be familiar with the previous chapters in this part, specifically Chapter 7, "The Component Architecture: An Introduction."
- You should be familiar with the term *metadata* and what it implies.
- It is helpful to be knowledgeable about the Dublin Core standard. Optional.

Problem/Task

Any advanced system has the need to specify metadata for various artifacts of its system, especially for objects that represent content. For a publishing environment such as Zope 3, it is important to have a standard set of metadata fields for all content objects. Already in Zope 2's CMF, the Dublin Core was used to provide such a set of fields.

EVEN THOUGH YOU PROBABLY KNOW what the term *metadata* means, it can be useful to do a quick review because people use the term in a very broad sense. *Data* in general is the information an object inherently carries. It represents the state and is necessary to identify the object. *Metadata*, on the other hand, is information *about* the object and its content. Metadata is not required in order for the object to function in itself (that is, object methods should not depend on metadata), but it might be important in order for an object to function inside a larger framework, providing additional information for identification, cataloging, indexing, integration with other systems, and so on.

The Dublin Core

One standard set of metadata is called the Dublin Core (see `http://dublincore.org`). The Dublin Core provides additional information about content-centric objects, such as the title, description (summary or abstract), and author of an object. As mentioned previously, the Dublin Core was very successful in Zope 2's CMF and Plone.

In the Dublin Core, all elements are lists, which means they can have multiple values. The Dublin Core elements are useful because they cover the most common metadata items, such as the creation date, title, and author. This data is useful in the context of most objects, and with it, at least their high-level meaning is easily understood. But there are some issues with the Dublin Core. There is a temptation for developers to interpret some deep meaning into the Dublin Core elements because it is such a well-established standard. As Ken Manheimer pointed out, even the Dublin Core designers succumbed to that temptation and tried to be a bit too ambitious with some of the fields.

A good example here is the contributor element. It is not clear what is meant by a contributor. Is it an editor, a translator, or an additional content author? And how does this information help you if you want to find the person who last modified the object or publication? It is therefore important to specify the meaning of the various elements (and the items in a particular element) for each specific implementation, such as Zope 3. All the elements and how they are implemented are well documented by the interfaces found in `ZOPE3/src/zope/app/interfaces/dublincore.py` and in the following section.

The Dublin Core Elements

The following Dublin Core element list was taken from `http://dublincore.org/documents/2003/02/04/dces`, and it includes some additional comments with regard to Zope 3's implementation.

Title

Label: Title
Definition: A human-readable name given to the resource.

> **Note**
>
> In Dublin Core lingo, *resource* is the generic term for an object. On the other hand, Zope 3 uses the term *resource* for a presentation component that does not require a context. You can read *content component* instead of *resource* for all occurrences of the term in this chapter.

Comment: In Zope 3, the name of a resource is a unique string within its container (it used to be called `id` in Zope 2). However, names of objects are often not presented to the end user. The title is used to represent an object instead.

Creator

Label: Creator

Definition: An entity primarily responsible for making the content of the resource.

Comment: A creator in Zope is a special example of a principal, which can take a lot of forms, but it is typically a user of the application. Zope 3 stores the user ID in this field.

Subject

Label: Subject and Keywords

Definition: A topic of the content of the resource.

Comment: Typically, Subject is expressed as keywords, key phrases, or classification codes that describe a topic of the resource. The recommended best practice is to select a value from a controlled vocabulary or formal classification scheme. Note that this is ideal for cataloging.

Description

Label: Description

Definition: An account of the content of the resource.

Comment: Examples of Description include, but are not limited to, an abstract, a table of contents, a reference to a graphical representation of the content, and a free-text account of the content. In Zope 3 you usually use Description to give more details about the semantics of the object/resource, so that the user gains a better understanding about its purpose.

Publisher

Label: Publisher

Definition: An entity responsible for making the resource available.

Comment: It is unlikely that this entity will be used heavily in Zope 3, but it might be useful for workflows of news sites and other publishing applications. Publisher is the name/ID of a principal.

Contributor

Label: Contributor

Definition: An entity responsible for making contributions to the content of the resource.

Comment: Examples of Contributor include a person, an organization, and a service. Typically, the name of a Contributor should be used to indicate the entity. As mentioned previously, the term *contributor* is incredibly vague and needs some additional policy; Zope 3 has not made up such a policy yet. Contributor is the name/ID of a principal.

Date

Label: Date

Definition: A date of an event in the life cycle of the resource.

Comment: Typically, Date is associated with the creation or availability of the resource. The recommended best practice for encoding the Date value is defined in a profile of ISO 8601 [W3CDTF] and includes (among others) dates of the form YYYY-MM-DD. Note that time often matters to people as well; of course, instead of saving text, we store Python datetime objects. Also note that the definition is very vague and needs some more policy to be useful.

Type

Label: Resource Type

Definition: The nature or genre of the content of the resource.

Comment: Type includes terms describing general categories, functions, genres, or aggregation levels for content. The recommended best practice is to select a value from a controlled vocabulary (for example, the DCMI Type Vocabulary [DCT1]). To describe the physical or digital manifestation of the resource, you use the Format element. For content objects, the resource type is clearly Content Type. For other objects, it might be simply the registered component name. However, Zope 3 is not using this element yet.

Format

Label: Format

Definition: The physical or digital manifestation of the resource.

Comment: Typically, Format may include the media type or dimensions of the resource. Format may be used to identify the software, hardware, or other equipment needed to display or operate the resource. Examples of dimensions include size and duration. The recommended best practice is to select a value from a controlled vocabulary (for example, the list of Internet Media Types [MIME] defining computer media formats). The Zope 3 development team has not used this element so far, even though it could use some of the existing framework for this.

Identifier

Label: Resource Identifier

Definition: An unambiguous reference to the resource within a given context.

Comment: The recommended best practice is to identify the resource by means of a string or number conforming to a formal identification system. Formal identification systems include, but are not limited to, the uniform resource identifier (URI) (including the uniform resource locator [URL]), the digital object identifier (DOI), and the international standard book number (ISBN). In Zope 3's case, this could be either the object's path or unique ID (as assigned by some utility).

Source

Label: Source
Definition: A reference to a resource from which the present resource is derived.
Comment: The present resource may be derived from the Source resource in whole or in part. The recommended best practice is to identify the referenced resource by means of a string or number conforming to a formal identification system. This is not generically useful to Zope components, although it could be applicable in specific applications written in Zope.

Language

Label: Language
Definition: A language of the intellectual content of the resource.
Comment: The recommended best practice is to use RFC 3066, which, in conjunction with ISO 639, defines two and three primary language tags with optional subtags. Examples include en or eng for English, akk for Akkadian, and en-GB for English used in the United Kingdom. Note that there is a system in place to describe locales; see Chapter 10, "Introduction to Zope's I18n and L10n Support."

Relation

Label: Relation
Definition: A reference to a related resource.
Comment: The recommended best practice is to identify the referenced resource by means of a string or number conforming to a formal identification system. This is another vague element because it does not specify what sort of relation is meant; it could be containment, for example, in which case the parent object would be a good candidate. However, more policy is required to make this field useful in Zope.

Coverage

Label: Coverage
Definition: The extent or scope of the content of the resource.
Comment: Typically, Coverage includes spatial location (a place name or geographic coordinates), temporal period (a period label, date, or date range), or jurisdiction (such as a named administrative entity). The recommended best practice is to select a value from a controlled vocabulary (for example, *Thesaurus of Geographic Names*) and to use, where appropriate, named places or time periods rather than numeric identifiers such as sets of coordinates or date ranges. This seems to not be useful to Zope generically.

Rights

Label: Rights Management
Definition: Information about rights held in and over the resource.
Comment: Typically, Rights contains a rights management statement for the resource or references a service providing such information. Rights information often encompasses intellectual property rights, copyrights, and various property rights. If the Rights element is absent, no assumptions may be made about any rights held in or over the resource. Zope 3 could use this element to show its security settings on this object—in other words, who has read and modification access to the resource. It makes little sense to use this element to generically define a copyright or license entry. Again, specific applications might have a better use for this element.

Further Readings

To see how the Dublin Core fields can be accessed for an object, see Chapter 14, "Adding Views for Content Objects." You might also find the following sites useful:

- www.xml.com/pub/a/2000/10/25/dublincore/
- www.lub.lu.se/cgi-bin/nmdc.pl
- www.sics.se/~preben/DC/DC_guide.html

Porting Applications from Zope 2 to Zope 3

Difficulty

Sprinter

Skills

- You should have some understandings of Zope 3 and know how to develop filesystem-based products for it. If necessary, you should read Part III, "Content Components—The Basics," and Part IV, "Content Components—Advanced Techniques," of this book first.
- You should know how to develop Zope 2 products.
- It is useful to know about the ZWiki for Zope 2 product and its purpose.
- It is useful to be familiar with the Zope 2 implementation of ZWiki. Optional.

Problem/Task

Porting applications from an older to a new version of a framework is always tricky, especially if the new version is a total rewrite and based on a totally different software model. Zope 3 is not only a complete rewrite of Zope 2, but it's also a complete shift in philosophy and development style.

THERE ARE TWO METHODS TO APPROACH porting an application. The first one is to completely redesign the existing Zope 2 application in light of the Zope 3 framework. The second method is to use various compatibility layers and conversion scripts to allow the existing code to run under Zope 3.

Porting an Application by Redesign

The great advantage of redesigning and reimplementing an application is that you can make use of all the new tools and gadgets available under the new framework. In the case of Zope 3, this tends to make the new implementation much cleaner and to consist of less code. The disadvantage here is that this solution will take a lot of time because all the logic must usually be written from scratch. However, the GUI templates are commonly less affected and are reusable.

> **Note**
>
> This section is based on my experience with porting the core functionality of the ZWiki product for Zope 2 to Zope 3, for which I had some help from Simon Michael, the original author of ZWiki. It turns out that this section also serves well as a comparison between the development models of Zope 2 and 3.

Wikis are easily editable web pages that are linked through keywords. If a word in a Wiki page is identical to the name of another Wiki page, then a *Wiki link* is inserted at that position, making a connection to the other Wiki page. If a mixed-case term is found in a Wiki Page (for example, Zope3Book), a question mark is placed after it. If you click the question mark, you are able to create a new Wiki page with the name Zope3Book. Every user of the Wiki can usually update and add new content and Wiki pages. These properties make Wikis a great tool for interactive and networked technical documentation and communication.

In the Zope 2 implementation, most of the ZWiki functionality is in a 121KB file called `ZWikiPage.py`, which includes core and advanced functionality, Zope 2 presentation logic, and documentation. It is almost impossible to understand what's going on, and the code does not seem very Pythonic. For example, all possible source-to-output converters (for example, STX to HTML, plain text to HTML, STX with DTML to HTML) are hard-coded into this one massive class, and new converters can only be added through monkey patching. The code is so massive that the core functionality code had to be extracted for the new implementation. However, I do not think that the messy code is Simon's fault; it is a classic example of the breakdown of the Zope 2 development model. Zope 2 encourages development of extensions through inheritance, and old applications often consist of massive classes that eventually become unmanagable.

But where do you start with the refactoring? The first task is to (re)identify the core functionality of the object you try to port. For the `ZWikiPage` class, the main purpose is to store the source of the page and maybe the type of the source (for example, plain text, STX, ReST). Note that the object itself has no knowledge whatsoever about how to convert from the various source types to HTML, for example, because these converters are presentation specific. The Zope 3 implementation of the `WikiPage` object is now only 26 lines long! All additional, non-core features will be added through adapters and views later.

Okay, Zope 3 has a nice, compact content object, but now it needs some presentation logic. Because schemas are used to define the attributes of the `WikiPage` object, you can create, add, and edit screens purely using ZCML directives, which means no further Python or ZPT code. The tricky part is to get the converters right. For example, you could have an `ISource` interface, which would serve as a base for all possible source types (for example, plain text, STX, ReST) and an `ISourceRenderer` interface, which would serve as a base to render a particular source type to a particular presentation type (for example, browser, XUL). This means that renderers are simply views of `ISource` objects. To ease the implementation of new source renderers for other developers, new ZCML directives were developed to hide the low-level management of source types and renderers. The renderer code was later placed in a separate package (that is, `zope.app.renderer`) because it is useful for many other applications as well. (See the interfaces in `zope.app.renderer.interfaces` for details.)

The result is very nice. With some abstraction and new configuration code, you can make the content object totally agnostic of the rendering mechanism. Furthermore, it is easy to add new third-party source types and renderers without altering or monkey patching the original package. Add-on features, such as a page hierarchy and email notification support, can be implemented, using adapters and annotations. See the chapters in Parts III and IV for more details on how to develop a product from scratch and extend it without touching the original code.

The Zope 3 Wiki implementation is part of the Zope 3 core and can be found at `ZOPE3/src/zwiki`.

Porting Using Compatibility Layers and Scripts

The advantage of using conversion scripts and compatibility layers for porting an application is that it is usually fast and easy. However, although this method saves a lot of initial development time, such a solution does not facilitate the use of the new features of the framework, and you might keep a lot of unnecessary code around.

There are currently no compatibility scripts available for porting Zope 2 applications to Zope 3. The current plan is that they will be written after Zope X3.0 ships.

A final alternative for porting applications is to use Zope 2 and 3 at the same time and convert features as slowly as you can. The Five project, initiated by Martijn Faassen, is a Zope 2 product that makes Zope 3 available under Zope 2 and allows you to use ZCML to configure Zope 2. `http://codespeak.net/z3/five/` is the project's home page.

Content Components—The Basics

This part deals with the creation and basic functionality of content objects. So that the chapters flow well, they are all guided by the creation of a simple message board application.

Chapter 13: Writing New Content Objects

This chapter describes how to implement a new simple content component/object.

Chapter 14: Adding Views for Content Objects

This chapter demonstrates various methods of creating browser-specific views for a component.

Chapter 15: Custom Schema Fields and Form Widgets

This chapter basically tells you how to implement your own field and corresponding widget. It then demonstrates how this field and widget can be used in a content object.

Chapter 16: Securing Components

Zope 3 comes with an incredible security system, but the best system is only as good as the end developer using it. This chapter gives some hands-on tips and tricks on how to make your code secure.

Chapter 17: Changing Size Information

This chapter describes a small interface for content objects that allows you to display them and compare their size. The interface is implemented as an adapter for the content components.

Chapter 18: Internationalizing Packages

This chapter gives step-by-step instructions on how to internationalize the application you developed in the previous chapters and how to create a German translation for it.

Writing New Content Objects

Difficulty

Newcomer

Skills

- You should be familiar with Python and some object-oriented concepts. Component-based programming concepts are a plus.
- Some understanding of the schema and interface packages is helpful. Optional.

Problem/Task

It is essential for any serious Zope 3 developer to know how to implement new content objects. Using the example of a message board, this chapter outlines the main steps required to implement and register a new content component in Zope 3.

I N THIS CHAPTER YOU BEGIN THE development of the MessageBoard content type and everything that is related to it. This serves very well as the first hands-on task because it does not assume anything other than that you have Zope 3 installed, you know some Python, and are willing to invest some time in learning the Zope 3 framework.

Step 1: Preparing to Write the Content Object

Before you start writing the MessageBoard content object, you need to install Zope 3, create a principal.zcml file, and successfully start Zope. If you have already done those things, you can get started!

In contrast to Zope 2 products, Zope 3 does not require you to place add-on packages in a special directory, and you are free to choose where to put them. The most convenient place is inside Zope3-Instance/lib/python because it does not require you to mess with PYTHONPATH. To clearly signal that the application you're working with in this chapter is a demo from this book, you can place all the code in a package called book. To create that package, you add a directory by using the following on a Unix system:

```
mkdir Zope3-Instance/lib/python/book
```

To make this directory a package, you place an empty __init__.py file in the new directory. In Unix you can do something like this:

```
echo "# Make it a Python package" >> Zope3-Instance/lib/python/book/__init__.py
```

But of course you can also just use a text editor and save a file with this name. You just need to make sure that there is valid Python code in the file. The file should at least contain some whitespace because empty files confuse some archive programs.

Next, you create another package inside book, called messageboard, in a similar manner (do not forget to create the __init__.py file). From now on, you are only going to work inside this messageboard package, which should be located at Zope3-Instance/lib/python/book/messageboard.

> **Note**
>
> The source code, which you can download for every chapter in this book from http://svn.zope.org/book/trunk/messageboard, contains a license header. However, we omit license headers throughout the book to save typing and space. Even so, the copyright as stated in the source files still applies.

Step 2: Creating the Initial Design

As stated earlier in this chapter, the goal of this chapter is to develop a fully functional, though not great-looking, web-based message board application. The root object is MessageBoard, which can contain postings, or in other words Message objects, from various users. Because you want to allow people to respond to various messages, you need to allow messages to contain replies, which are in turn just other Message objects.

That means you have two container-based components. MessageBoard contains only messages and can be added to any folder or container that wants to be able to contain it. To make the message board more interesting, it also has a description, which briefly introduces the subject/theme of the discussions hosted. Message objects, on the other hand, should be contained only by message boards and other messages. Each should have a title and a body.

This setup should contain all the essential things you need in order to make the object usable. Later on, you will associate a lot of other metadata with these components to integrate them even better into Zope 3 and add additional functionality.

Step 3: Writing the Interfaces

The very first step of the coding process is always to define your interfaces, which represent your external API. You should be aware that software that is built on top of your packages expects the interfaces to behave exactly the way you specify them. This is often not too much of an issue for attributes and arguments of a method, but developers often forget to specify what the expected return value of a method or function is or which exceptions it can raise or catch.

Interfaces are commonly stored in an `interfaces` module or package. Because the `messageboard` package is not that big, you are going to use a file-based module; therefore, you can start editing a file called `interfaces.py` in your favorite editor.

At this point, you are only interested in defining one interface for the message board itself and one for a single message. You should add the following interfaces to the file `interfaces.py`:

```
01 from zope.interface import Interface
02 from zope.schema import Text, TextLine, Field
03
04 from zope.app.container.constraints import ContainerTypesConstraint
05 from zope.app.container.constraints import ItemTypePrecondition
06 from zope.app.container.interfaces import IContained, IContainer
07 from zope.app.file.interfaces import IFile
08
09
10 class IMessage(Interface):
11     """A message object. It can contain its own responses."""
12
13     title = TextLine(
14         title=u"Title/Subject",
15         description=u"Title and/or subject of the message.",
16         default=u"",
17         required=True)
18
19     body = Text(
20         title=u"Message Body",
21         description=u"This is the actual message. Type whatever you wish.",
22         default=u"",
23         required=False)
24
25
26 class IMessageBoard(IContainer):
27     """The message board is the base object for our package. It can only
28     contain IMessage objects."""
29
30     def __setitem__(name, object):
31         """Add a IMessage object."""
32
```

```
33        __setitem__.precondition = ItemTypePrecondition(IMessage)
34
35    description = Text(
36        title=u"Description",
37        description=u"A detailed description of the content of the board.",
38        default=u"",
39        required=False)
40
41
42 class IMessageContained(IContained):
43    """Interface that specifies the type of objects that can contain
44    messages."""
45    __parent__ = Field(
46        constraint = ContainerTypesConstraint(IMessageBoard, IMessage))
47
48
50 class IMessageContainer(IContainer):
51    """We also want to make the message object a container that can contain
52    responses (other messages) and attachments (files and images)."""
53
54    def __setitem__(name, object):
55        """Add a IMessage object."""
56
57    __setitem__.precondition = ItemTypePrecondition(IMessage, IFile)
```

In the preceding code block, note the following:

- Line 1: You import the base Interface class. Any object that has this metaclass in its inheritance path is an interface and *not* a regular class.

- Line 2: The attributes and properties of an object are described by fields. Fields hold the metadata about an attribute and are used, among other things, to validate values and create autogenerated input forms. Most fields are defined in the zope.schema package. For more details and a complete list of fields, see Chapter 8, "Zope Schemas and Forms."

- Line 4: ContainerTypesConstraint conditions allow you to tell the system to which type of containers an object can be added. For example, a message may only want to be contained by the message board and another message (when it is a reply to the parent message). See the description of lines 45–49 for information on how it is used.

- Line 5: ItemTypePrecondition is the opposite of ContainerTypesConstraint in that it specifies the object types that can be contained by a container. See the description of lines 33–36 for information on its usage.

- Line 6: Objects providing the IContained interface can be included in the Zope object tree. You also import IContainer here, and it is used as a base interface in Lines 26 and 49. IContainer defines all the necessary methods for this object to be recognized as a container by Zope 3.

Note that you do not need to inherit `Interface` directly because `IContainer` already inherits it, which automatically makes `IMessageBoard` also an interface.

- Line 10: You might have noticed the `I` in front of all the interfaces; this simply stands for *interface*, as you might have guessed. It is a convention in Zope that helps you not confuse interfaces and classes because these two different object types cannot be used in the same way.

  In general, a message is simply an object that has a title and a body—nothing more. You'll later declare more semantics through additional interfaces and metadata.

- Lines 13–17: You need a simple title/subject headline for the message. Note that this is a `TextLine` field instead of a `Text` field; this is so no newline characters can be inserted. This way, the title will be relatively short and will be perfect for the title display, where desired.

- Lines 19–23: The body is the actual message content. Note that you make no restriction to its size here, but you might want to do that if you are afraid of spam filling your message board.

- Lines 30–33: You do not want to allow any content type to be added to the message board. In fact, you just want to be able to add `IMessage` objects. Therefore, you declare a precondition on the `__setitem__()` method of the message board interface. You simply list all allowed interfaces as arguments of the `ItemTypePrecondition` constructor.

  Even though `IContainer` already defines `__setitem__()`, you have to declare it again here so that it is in the scope of the interface and specific to `IMessageBoard`; otherwise, all `IContainer` objects will have this precondition.

- Lines 35–39: You declare a property on the interface that will contain the description of the message board. It is a typical `Text` field with the usual options (see Chapter 8 for details). One note, though: Notice that you *always* use Unicode strings for human-readable text; this is a required convention throughout Zope 3. One of the major focus points of Zope 3 is internationalization, and Unicode strings are the first requirement to support multilingual applications.

- Lines 42–46: This interface describes via field constraints which other content types can contain a message. Clearly, message boards can contain messages, but also, messages can contain other messages—known as replies to a message. You usually specify this constraint on the parent on the main content type interface (that is, `IMessage`) directly, but because this constraint refers explicitly to `IMessage`, you have to wait until the interface is defined. Also, the split between the message properties and the containment constraints allows you to use the `Imessage` interface in other contexts with different semantics.

- Lines 49–56: You want the message to be a container so that it can contain responses and attachments. However, you do not want any object to be able to be added to messages, so you add a precondition, as you did for the `IMessageBoard` interface. Again, you have to do this in a separate interface here because you reference `IMessage` in the condition.

Step 4: Writing Unit Tests

There are two ways unit tests can be written in Zope 3. The first one is through special `TestCase` classes, using the `unittest` package, which is modeled after JUnit. The second technique is to write tests inside doc strings, which are commonly known as *doc tests*.

Late in the development of Zope 3, using doc tests became the standard way of writing tests. (For philosophical and technical differences between the two approaches, see Part VII, "Writing Tests," especially Chapter 40, "Writing Basic Unit Tests," and Chapter 41, "Doc Tests: Example-Driven Unit Tests.")

Using common unit tests, however, is advantageous when it is desirable to reuse abstract tests, as is the case for various container tests. Therefore, this book uses unit tests for the container tests, and it uses doc tests for everything else.

First, you need to create a package called `tests` inside the `messageboard` package. Note that calling the test module `tests` (file-based test modules would be called `tests.py`) is a convention throughout Zope 3, and it allows the automated test runner to pick up the tests.

Next, you need to begin editing a file called `test_messageboard.py` and insert the following in it:

```
01 import unittest
02 from zope.testing.doctestunit import DocTestSuite
03
04 from zope.app.container.tests.test_icontainer import TestSampleContainer
05
06 from book.messageboard.messageboard import MessageBoard
07
08
09 class Test(TestSampleContainer):
10
11     def makeTestObject(self):
12         return MessageBoard()
13
14 def test_suite():
15     return unittest.TestSuite((
16         DocTestSuite('book.messageboard.messageboard'),
17         unittest.makeSuite(Test),
18         ))
19
20 if __name__ == '__main__':
21     unittest.main(defaultTest='test_suite')
```

A lot of cool stuff happens in this code, including providing your first 12 unit tests. Let's have a closer look:

- Line 1: The `unittest` module comes with stock Python and is used to create the test suite.

- Line 2: Zope provides a specialized `DocTestSuite` class that integrates doc tests into the common `unittest` framework and allows the doc tests to be run via the test runner.

- Line 4: There are some basic tests for containers, and you should import them. Freebie tests are always good.

- Lines 9–13: You define the `Container` tests. You only have to provide an instance of the container you would like to be tested as the return value of the `makeTestObject()` method.

- Lines 15–19: The `test_suite()` method collects all the defined test cases and compiles them into one test suite. This method must always be named that way so that the test runner picks up the suite. Besides defining the container test, you also register the doc tests.

- Lines 21–23: You need to allow any test module to be executable by itself. Here you just tell the test runner to execute all tests of the test suite returned by `test_suite()`. These lines are common boilerplate material for any test module in Zope 3.

Now it is time to do the second test module for the `IMessage` component. To start, you simply copy `test_messageboard.py` to `test_message.py` and modify the new file so that it looks like this:

```
01 import unittest
02 from zope.testing.doctestunit import DocTestSuite
03
04 from zope.app.container.tests.test_icontainer import TestSampleContainer
05
06 from book.messageboard.message import Message
07
08
09 class Test(TestSampleContainer):
10
11     def makeTestObject(self):
12         return Message()
13
14 def test_suite():
15     return unittest.TestSuite((
16         DocTestSuite('book.messageboard.message'),
17         unittest.makeSuite(Test),
18         ))
19
20 if __name__ == '__main__':
21     unittest.main(defaultTest='test_suite')
```

There is not really any difference between the two testing modules.

Note that none of the tests deal with implementation details yet, simply because you do not know what the implementation details will be. These tests could be used by other packages, similarly to how you used the `SampleContainer` base tests, because these tests only depend on the API. In general, however, tests should cover implementation-specific behavior.

Step 5: Implementing Content Components

Now you are finally ready to implement the content components of the package. This is the heart of this chapter. But how do you know which methods and properties you have to implement? There is a neat tool called `pyskel` in *Zope3-Instance*/bin that generates a skeleton. The tool inspects the given interface and creates the skeleton of an implementing class. It also recurses into all base interfaces to get their methods. Go to *Zope3-Instance*/lib/python and type this:

```
01 python2.3 ../../bin/pyskel \
02          book.messageboard.interfaces.IMessageBoard
```

Here's the expected result:

```
01 from zope.interface import implements
02 from book.messageboard.interfaces import IMessageBoard
03
04 class MessageBoard:
05     __doc__ = IMessageBoard.__doc__
06
07     implements(IMessageBoard)
08
09
10     def __setitem__(self, name, object):
11         "See book.messageboard.interfaces.IMessageBoard"
12
13     # See book.messageboard.interfaces.IMessageBoard
14     description = None
15
16     def __getitem__(self, key):
17         "See zope.interface.common.mapping.IItemMapping"
18
19     def get(self, key, default=None):
20         "See zope.interface.common.mapping.IReadMapping"
21
22     def __contains__(self, key):
23         "See zope.interface.common.mapping.IReadMapping"
24
25     def __getitem__(self, key):
26         "See zope.interface.common.mapping.IItemMapping"
27
```

```
28    def keys(self):
29        "See zope.interface.common.mapping.IEnumerableMapping"
30
31    def __iter__(self):
32        "See zope.interface.common.mapping.IEnumerableMapping"
33
34    def values(self):
35        "See zope.interface.common.mapping.IEnumerableMapping"
36
37    def items(self):
38        "See zope.interface.common.mapping.IEnumerableMapping"
39
40    def __len__(self):
41        "See zope.interface.common.mapping.IEnumerableMapping"
42
43    def get(self, key, default=None):
44        "See zope.interface.common.mapping.IReadMapping"
45
46    def __contains__(self, key):
47        "See zope.interface.common.mapping.IReadMapping"
48
49    def __getitem__(self, key):
50        "See zope.interface.common.mapping.IItemMapping"
51
52    def __setitem__(self, name, object):
53        "See zope.app.container.interfaces.IWriteContainer"
54
55    def __delitem__(self, name):
56        "See zope.app.container.interfaces.IWriteContainer"
```

This result is good, but some parts are unnecessary; for example, you can simply inherit the BTreeContainer base component, so that you do not have to implement the methods from the IReadMapping, IEnumerableMapping, IReadMapping, IItemMapping, and IWriteContainer interfaces.

Next, you need to open a new file called messageboard.py for editing. The implementation of the message board, including doc tests, looks like this:

```
01 from zope.interface import implements
02 from zope.app.container.btree import BTreeContainer
03
04 from book.messageboard.interfaces import IMessageBoard
05
06 class MessageBoard(BTreeContainer):
07     """A very simple implementation of a message board using B-Tree Containers
08
09     Make sure that the ``MessageBoard`` implements the ``IMessageBoard``
10     interface:
11
```

```
12      >>> from zope.interface.verify import verifyClass
13      >>> verifyClass(IMessageBoard, MessageBoard)
14      True
15
16      Here is an example of changing the description of the board:
17
18      >>> board = MessageBoard()
19      >>> board.description
20      u''
21      >>> board.description = u'Message Board Description'
22      >>> board.description
23      u'Message Board Description'
24      """
25      implements(IMessageBoard)
26
27      # See book.messageboard.interfaces.IMessageBoard
28      description = u''
```

In the preceding code block, note the following:

- Line 1: You use the `implements()` method to declare that a class implements one or more interfaces. See Chapter 6, "An Introduction to Interfaces," for more details.

- Line 2: Everything that has to do with containers is located in `zope.app. container`. `BTreeContainer` components are a very efficient implementation of the `IContainer` interface and are commonly used as base classes for other container-type objects, such as the message board.

- Lines 7–24: The class doc string's purpose is to document the class. To follow Python documentation standards, all doc strings should use the restructured text format. And doc tests are considered documentation, so they should be written in a narrative style.

  On lines 12–14 you verify that the `MessageBoard` component really implements `IMessageBoard`. The `verifyClass` function actually checks the object for the existence of the specified attributes and methods.

  Lines 18–23 demonstrate the default `description` value and how it can be set. The test seems trivial, but at some point you might change the implementation of the `description` attribute to using properties, and the test should still pass.

- Line 25: Here you tell the class that it implements `IMessage`. This function call might seem like magic because you might wonder how the function knows to which class to assign the interface.

- Lines 27–28: You make the description a simple attribute.

> **Note**
>
> Python is unique in that it commonly deals with attributes directly. In almost any other object-oriented language (for example, Java), you would write an accessor (for example, `getDescription()`) and a mutator (for example, `setDescription(desc)`) method. However, Python's attribute and property support makes this unnecessary, which in turn makes the code cleaner.

The next task is to write the `Message` object, which is pretty much the same code as the `MessageBoard` class. Therefore, the code is not listed here but is available at `http://svn.zope.org/book/trunk/messageboard/step01/message.py`. The only difference is that in this case the `Message` component must implement `IMessage`, `IMessageContained`, and `IMessageContainer`.

Step 6: Running Unit Tests Against the Implementation

Now that you have finished the implementation, you need to make sure all the tests pass. A script called `test.py` runs all or only specified tests for you. To run a test against your implementation, you execute the following line from the Zope 3 instance directory:

```
python2.3 bin/test -vpu --dir lib/python//book/messageboard
```

The `-v` option cases the currently running test to be displayed, `-p` allows you to see the progress of the tests being run, and `-u` tells the test runner to just run the unit tests. For a list of all available options, you can run the script with the `-h` (help) option.

You should see 26 tests pass. The output of the test run should look like this:

```
Configuration file found.
Running UNIT tests at level 1
Running UNIT tests from /opt/zope/Zope3/Zope3-Cookbook
  26/26 (100.0%): test_values (....messageboard.tests.test_messageboard.Test)
------------------------------------------------------------------
Ran 26 tests in 0.346s

OK
```

It is very likely that some tests will fail or that the test suite will not run due to syntax errors. This is totally normal and exactly the reason you write tests in the first place. In these cases, you should keep fixing the problems until all tests pass.

Step 7: Registering the Content Components

Now that you have developed your components, it is necessary to tell Zope 3 how to interact with them. This is commonly done using Zope's own configuration language, called ZCML. By convention, the configuration is stored in a file called `configure.zcml`. You should start to edit this file by adding the following ZCML code:

```
01 <configure
02    xmlns="http://namespaces.zope.org/zope">
03
04  <interface
05      interface=".interfaces.IMessageBoard"
06      type="zope.app.content.interfaces.IContentType"
07      />
08
09  <content class=".messageboard.MessageBoard">
10    <implements
11        interface="zope.app.annotation.interfaces.IAttributeAnnotatable"
12        />
13    <implements
14        interface="zope.app.container.interfaces.IContentContainer"
15        />
16    <factory
17        id="book.messageboard.MessageBoard"
18        description="Message Board"
19        />
20    <require
21        permission="zope.ManageContent"
22        interface=".interfaces.IMessageBoard"
23        />
24    <require
25        permission="zope.ManageContent"
26        set_schema=".interfaces.IMessageBoard"
27        />
28  </content>
29
30  <interface
31      interface=".interfaces.IMessage"
32      type="zope.app.content.interfaces.IContentType"
33      />
34
35  <content class=".message.Message">
36    <implements
37        interface="zope.app.annotation.interfaces.IAttributeAnnotatable"
38        />
39    <implements
40        interface="zope.app.container.interfaces.IContentContainer"
41        />
42    <require
43        permission="zope.ManageContent"
44        interface=".interfaces.IMessage"
45        />
46    <require
47        permission="zope.ManageContent"
```

```
48          interface=".interfaces.IMessageContainer"
49          />
50      <require
51          permission="zope.ManageContent"
52          set_schema=".interfaces.IMessage"
53          />
54      </content>
55
56  </configure>
```

In the preceding code block, note the following:

- Lines 1–2 and 65: As the file extension promises, configuration is done using XML. All configuration in a ZCML file must be surrounded by the `configure` element. At the beginning of the `configure` element, you list all the ZCML namespaces you are going to use and define the default one. In this case, you only need the generic `zope` namespace. You will get to know many more namespaces as you develop new functionality in the following chapters.

- Lines 4–7: It is sometimes necessary to categorize interfaces. For example, you may need to specify which interface provides a content type for Zope 3. The `zope:interface` directive is used to assign these types on interfaces. Another way to think about it is that interfaces are just components, and components can provide other interfaces.

- Lines 9–28: The `zope:content` directive registers the `MessageBoard` class as a content component. The element always has only one attribute, `class`, that points to the component's class, using a dotted Python path.

  Lines 10–12: In order for the object to have a creation and modification date as well as other metadata (for example, the Dublin Core), you need to tell the system that this object can have annotations associated with it. This is not necessarily required, but it is a good habit.

  Annotations store add-on data, which is also commonly known as *metadata* because it is data that is not necessary for the correct functioning of the object itself. However, metadata allows an object to be better integrated in the system. Annotations are heavily used in Zope 3.

  In general, the `zope:implements` subdirective allows you to assert new implemented interfaces on a class. It is totally equivalent to `classImplements(Class, ISomeInterface)` in Python. So why would you want to declare interfaces in ZCML instead of in Python? For one thing, declaring interfaces in Python clutters the Python code and distracts from the actual functionality of the component. Also, when dealing with third-party Python packages, you do not want to touch this code, but you still want to be able to make assertions about objects so that they can be used inside Zope 3 without modification.

Note that usually only *marker interfaces*—that is, interfaces that have no methods and/or properties—are declared via ZCML because no additional Python code for the implementation of the interface is required.

Lines 13–15: The `IContentContainer` interface is another example of a marker interface. It simply declares that this container contains ordinary content in content space, which is clearly the case for your message board.

Lines 16–19: The `zope:factory` subdirective allows you to register a factory named `book.messageboard.MessageBoard` for the `MessageBoard` component.

Every factory needs an `id` argument (that is, a first directive argument) through which the factory can be accessed and executed. However, you are not required to specify an `id` argument; if you don't, the literal string value of `zope:content`'s `class` attribute is used; it is `.messageboard.MessageBoard` in this case.

The `zope:factory` directive also supports two human-readable information strings, `title` and `description`, that can be used for user interfaces.

Lines 20–27: In Zope 3 you differentiate between trusted and untrusted environments. Trusted environments have no security or can easily circumvent security. An example is file-based Python code, which is always trusted. The opposite is true for untrusted environments; in that case, security should apply everywhere and should not be avoidable. All Web and FTP transactions are considered untrusted.

Of course, you want to use your message board via the Web because it is the default user interface of Zope 3. To make it usable, you have to declare the minimal security assertions for the properties and methods of the component. You create security assertions by using the `zope:require` and `zope:allow` directives.

The `zope:require` directive usually starts out by specifying a `permission`. Then you have to decide what you want to protect with this declaration. Here are your choices:

- The `attributes` attribute allows you to specify attributes and methods that can be *accessed* if the user has the specified permission. (Note that methods are just callable attributes.)

- `set_attributes` allows you to specify individual attributes that can be modified or mutated. Note that you should not list any methods here because otherwise someone could override a method and insert malicious code.

- If you specify one or more interfaces by using the `interface` attribute, the directive automatically extracts all declared methods and properties of the interfaces and grants access rights to them.

- When you specify a set of schemas by using the `set_schema` attribute, all the defined properties in it are granted modification rights. Methods listed in the schema are ignored.

> **Note**
> In ZCML, tokens of a list are separated by simple whitespace and not commas, as you might expect.

A somewhat different option from the preceding choices is the `like_class` attribute, which must be specified without any permission. If used, it simply transfers all the security assertions from the specified class to the class specified in the `zope:content` directive that encloses the security assertions. In this case, this is your `MessageBoard` component. The usage of the directive looks like this:

```
<require like_class=".message.Message" />
```

Here `MessageBoard` would simply inherit the security assertions made for the `Message` component.

The second security directive, `zope:allow`, either takes a set of attributes or interfaces. All attributes specified are publicly available for everyone to access. This is equivalent to requiring someone to have the `zope.Public` permission, which every principal accessing the system automatically possesses.

At this point, it is easy to decipher the meaning of your two security assertions. You basically give read and write access to the `IMessageBoard` interface (which includes all `IContainer` methods and the `description` attribute) if the user has the `zope.ManageContent` permission.

- Lines 30–54: This is the same as the previous `zope:content` directive, except that it is for the `Message` content component.

Step 8: Configuring Some Basic Views

Even though the content components are registered now, nothing interesting can happen yet because there exists only a programmatic way of adding and editing the new components. Thus, you need to define some very basic browser views to make the content components accessible via the browser-based user interface.

First, you need to create a package called `browser` (do not forget the `__init__.py` file) inside the `messageboard` package. Then you need to add a new configuration file, `configure.zcml`, inside `browser` and insert the following content:

```
01 <configure
02     xmlns="http://namespaces.zope.org/browser">
03
04   <addform
05       label="Add Message Board"
06       name="AddMessageBoard.html"
07       schema="book.messageboard.interfaces.IMessageBoard"
08       content_factory="book.messageboard.messageboard.MessageBoard"
09       fields="description"
```

```
10          permission="zope.ManageContent"
11          />
12
13      <addMenuItem
14          class="book.messageboard.messageboard.MessageBoard"
15          title="Message Board"
16          description="A Message Board"
17          permission="zope.ManageContent"
18          view="AddMessageBoard.html"
19          />
20
21      <editform
22          schema="book.messageboard.interfaces.IMessageBoard"
23          for="book.messageboard.interfaces.IMessageBoard"
24          label="Change Message Board"
25          name="edit.html"
26          permission="zope.ManageContent"
27          menu="zmi_views" title="Edit"
28          />
29
30      <containerViews
31          for="book.messageboard.interfaces.IMessageBoard"
32          index="zope.View"
33          contents="zope.View"
34          add="zope.ManageContent"
35          />
36
37      <addform
38          label="Add Message"
39          name="AddMessage.html"
40          schema="book.messageboard.interfaces.IMessage"
41          content_factory="book.messageboard.message.Message"
42          fields="title body"
43          permission="zope.ManageContent"
44          />
45
46      <addMenuItem
47          class="book.messageboard.message.Message"
48          title="Message"
49          description="A Message"
50          permission="zope.ManageContent"
51          view="AddMessage.html"
52          />
53
54      <editform
55          schema="book.messageboard.interfaces.IMessage"
56          for="book.messageboard.interfaces.IMessage"
```

```
57        label="Change Message"
58        fields="title body"
59        name="edit.html"
60        permission="zope.ManageContent"
61        menu="zmi_views" title="Edit"
62        />
63
64    <containerViews
65        for="book.messageboard.interfaces.IMessage"
66        index="zope.View"
67        contents="zope.View"
68        add="zope.ManageContent"
69        />
```

```
</configure>
```

In the preceding code block, note the following:

- Line 2: In this configuration file, you do not use the zope namespace; rather, you use the browser namespace because you want to configure browser-specific functionality. Also note that browser is the default namespace, so your directives do not need the namespace prefix.

  Namespaces for ZCML commonly start with http://namespaces.zope.org/, followed by the short name of the namespace, which is commonly used in this book to refer to namespaces.

- Lines 4–11: You register an autogenerated Add view for the message board.

  Line 5: The label is in small text and is shown on top of the screen.

  Line 6: You specify the name of the view. The name is the string that is actually part of the URL.

  Line 7: You define the schema that will be used to generate the form. The fields of the schema are used to provide all the necessary metadata to create meaningful form elements.

  Line 8: The content factory is the class/factory used to create the new content component.

  Line 9: You add a list of field names that are displayed in the form. This allows you to create forms for a subset of fields in the schema and to change the order of the fields in the form.

  Line 10: You specify the permission required to be able to create and add the new content component.

- Lines 13–19: After creating a view for adding the message board, you have to register it with the Add menu, which you do by using the browser:addMenuItem directive. You use title to display the item in the menu. The important attribute is view, which must match the name of the Add view.

- Lines 21–28: Declaring an Edit view is very similar to defining an Add view, and several of the options/attributes are the same. The main difference is that you do not need to specify a content factory because the content component already exists.

  The `for` attribute specifies the interface for the type of component that the Edit view is for. All view directives (except `browser:addform`) require the `for` attribute. If you would like to register a view for a specific implementation, you can also specify the class in the `for` attribute.

  You also commonly specify the menu for edit views directly in the directive by using the `menu` and `title` attributes, as shown on line 27. The `zmi_views` menu is the menu that creates the tabs on the default web user interface. It contains all views that are specific to the object.

- Lines 30–35: The message board is a container, and a quick way to register all necessary container-specific views is to use the `browser:containerViews` directive. Note, though, that this directive is not very flexible, and you should later replace it by writing regular views.

- Lines 37–69: You specify exactly the same directives over again, this time just for the `IMessage` interface.

In order for the system to know about the view configuration, you need to reference the configuration file in `messageboard/configure.zcml`. To include the view configuration, you add the following line:

```
01 <include package=".browser" />
```

Step 9: Registering the Message Board with Zope

At this stage, you have a complete package. However, unlike in Zope 2, you have to register a new package explicitly. That means you have to hook up the components to Zope 3. You do this by creating a new file, called `messageboard-configure.zcml`, in `Zope3-Instance/etc/package-includes`. The name of the file is not arbitrary, and it must be in the form `name-configure.zcml`. The file should just contain one directive:

```
01 <include package="book.messageboard" />
```

When Zope 3 boots, it walks through each file of this directory and executes the ZCML directives inside each file. Usually, the files just point to the configuration of a package.

Step 10: Testing the Content Component

Congratulations! You have finished your first little Zope 3 application, which is quite a bit more than what would minimally be required, as you will see in a moment. It is time now to harvest the fruits of your labor.

You should start your Zope 3 server now, by using `make run` from the Zope 3 root. If you get complaints about the Python version being used, you can edit the makefile and enter the correct path to Python's executable. Other errors that might occur are due to typos or misconfigurations. The ZCML interpreter will give you the line and column number of the failing directive in Emacs-friendly format. You should try to start Zope 3 again and again until you have fixed all the errors and Zope 3 has this output at the end of its startup:

```
------
2003-12-12T23:14:58 INFO PublisherHTTPServer zope.server.http (HTTP) started.
      Hostname: localhost
      Port: 8080
------
2003-12-12T23:14:58 INFO PublisherFTPServer zope.server.ftp started.
      Hostname: localhost
      Port: 8021
------
2003-12-12T23:14:58 INFO root Startup time: 11.259 sec real, 5.150 sec CPU
```

Note that you also get some internationalization warnings, which you can safely ignore for now.

When the server is up and running, you should go to your favorite browser and enter the following URL:

`http://localhost:8080/@@contents.html`.

At this point, an authentication box should pop up and ask you for your username and password; users are listed in `principals.zcml`. If you have not added any special user, you should use `gandalf` as the login name and `123` as password. After the authentication is complete, you should be taken to the Zope 3 web user interface. Under Add: you can now see a new entry, Message Board.

You should feel free to add and edit a message board object.

After you create a message board, you can click it and enter it. You will then notice that you are only allowed to add message objects here. The choice is limited due to the conditions you specified in the interfaces. The default view will be the Edit view, which allows you to change the description of the board. The second view is Contents, which you can use to manage the messages of the message board.

You should add a message now. After you add a message, it appears in the Contents view. You can then click the message, and you are allowed to modify the data about the message and add new messages (replies) to it. With the code you have written so far, you are now able to create a complete message board tree and access it via the web user interface.

Note that you still might get errors, and if you do, you need to fix them. Most often, you have security problems, which narrows the range of possible issues tremendously. Unfortunately, `NotFoundError` is usually converted to `ForbiddenAttributeError`, so be careful if you see this problem.

Another common trap is that standard error screens do not show the traceback. However, for these situations, the `Debug` skin comes in handy—instead of `http://localhost:8080/@@contents.html`, you can use `http://localhost:8080/++skin++Debug/@@contents.html`, and the traceback is shown.

Note

If you make data-structural changes in your package, it might become necessary to delete old instances of the objects/components. Sometimes even this is not enough, and you have to either delete the parent folder or delete the `Data.fs` (ZODB) file. There are ways to upgrade gracefully to new versions of objects, but during development, the listed methods are simplest and fastest.

The code for this chapter is available in the Zope SVN, at `http://svn.zope.org/book/trunk/messageboard/step01`.

Adding Views for Content Objects

Difficulty

Newcomer

Skills

- You need to have a firm grasp of the information contained in Chapter 13, "Writing New Content Objects."
- It would be helpful to have some understanding of the presentation components. Optional.

Problem/Task

Now that you have two fully functional content objects, you have to make the functionality available to the user because there are currently only three very simple views: Add, Edit, and Contents. In this chapter you will create a nice message details screen, as well as a threaded subbranch view for both messages and the message board.

THIS CHAPTER REVOLVES AROUND BROWSER-BASED view components for the `MessageBoard` and `Message` classes. Views, which are mainly discussed here, are secondary adapters. They adapt `IRequest` and a context object to some output interface (often just `zope.interface.Interface`).

There are several ways to write a view. These are some of the dominant ones:

- You have already learned about using the `browser:addform`, `browser:editform`, and `browser:containerViews` directives. These directives are high-level directives that hide a lot of the details about creating and registering appropriate view components.

You can easily configure forms via ZCML, as you did in Chapter 13, "Writing New Content Objects." Forms are incredibly flexible and allow you any degree of customization.

- The browser:page and browser:pages directives are the most commonly used directives for easily creating browser views and groups of views. You will use these two directives in this chapter for your new views.

- The zope:view directive is very low level, and it provides functionality for registering multi-views, which the other directives are not capable of doing. However, for the average application developer, the need to use this directive might never arise.

Step 1: Creating the Message Details View

In the following sections you'll create two new browser views. Although you are already able to edit a message, you currently have no view for simply viewing the message, which is important because not many people will have access to the edit screen.

The view that displays the details of a message should contain the following data of the message: the title, the author, the creation date/time, the parent title (with a link to the message), and the body.

Writing a view usually consists of writing a page template, some supporting Python view class, and some ZCML to insert the view into the system. You can start by creating the page template.

Creating the Page Template

You need to create a file called details.pt in the browser package of messageboard and fill it with the following content:

```
01 <html metal:use-macro="views/standard_macros/view">
02   <body>
03     <div metal:fill-slot="body">
04
05       <h1>Message Details</h1>
06
07         <div class="row">
08             <div class="label">Title</div>
09             <div class="field" tal:content="context/title" />
10         </div>
11
12         <div class="row">
13             <div class="label">Author</div>
14             <div class="field" tal:content="view/author"/>
15         </div>
16
```

```
17          <div class="row">
18              <div class="label">Date/Time</div>
19              <div class="field" tal:content="view/modified"/>
20          </div>
21
22          <div class="row">
23              <div class="label">Parent</div>
24              <div class="field" tal:define="info view/parent_info">
25                <a href="../details.html"
26                    tal:condition="info"
27                    tal:content="info/title" />
28              </div>
29          </div>
30
31          <div class="row">
32              <div class="label">Body</div>
33              <div class="field" tal:content="context/body"/>
34          </div>
35
36      </div>
37    </body>
38 </html>
```

In the preceding code block, note the following:

- Lines 1–3 and 36–38: This is some standard boilerplate code for a Zope page template that will embed the displayed data inside the common Zope 3 user interface. This ensures that all the pages have a consistent look and feel, which allows the developer to concentrate on the functional parts of the view.

- Line 9: You can retrieve title directly from the content object (the Message instance), which is available as context.

- Lines 14 and 19: The author and the modification date/time are not directly available because they are part of the object's metadata (Dublin Core). Therefore, you need to make them available via the Python-based view class, which is provided to the template under the name view. The sole purpose of a Python-based view class is to retrieve and prepare data to be in a displayable format.

- Lines 24–27: Although you probably could get to the parent via a relatively simple TALES path expression, it is customary in Zope 3 to make that the responsibility of the view class, so that the template contains as little logic as possible. In the next step you will see how this information is collected.

Creating the Python-Based View Class

You need the following methods (or attributes/properties) in your view class: author(), modified(), and parent_info(). First, you need to create a new file called message.py in the `browser` package. Note that you will place all browser-related Python code for `IMessage` in this module.

Here is the Python class you should implement:

```
01 from zope.app import zapi
02 from zope.app.dublincore.interfaces import ICMFDublinCore
03
04 from book.messageboard.interfaces import IMessage
05
06
07 class MessageDetails:
08
09     def author(self):
10         """Get user who last modified the Message."""
11         creators = ICMFDublinCore(self.context).creators
12         if not creators:
13             return 'unknown'
14         return creators[0]
15
16     def modified(self):
17         """Get last modification date."""
18         date = ICMFDublinCore(self.context).modified
19         if date is None:
20             date = ICMFDublinCore(self.context).created
21         if date is None:
22             return ''
23         return date.strftime('%d/%m/%Y %H:%M:%S')
24
25     def parent_info(self):
26         """Get the parent of the message"""
27         parent = zapi.getParent(self.context)
28         if not IMessage.providedBy(parent):
29             return None
30         return {'name': zapi.name(parent), 'title': parent.title}
```

In the preceding code block, note the following:

- Line 1: Many of the fundamental utilities that you need are available via the `zapi` module. The `zapi` module provides all the crucial component architecture methods, such as `getParent()`. All the core service names are also available. Furthermore, you can access traversal utilities as well. See `ZOPE3/src/zope/app/interfaces/zapi.py` for a complete list of methods that are available via the `zapi` module.

- Line 2: You use the `ICMFDublinCore` interface to store the Dublin Core metadata. By using this interface, you can get to the desired information.

- Line 7: Note that the view class has no base class and that it does not specify any implementing interface. The reason for this is that the ZCML directive will take care of that later on, by adding the `BrowserView` class as a base class of the view.

  In some parts of Zope 3, you might still see the view class inheriting from `BrowserView`.

- Lines 09–14: The code tries to get a list of `creators` principal IDs (referred to as authors) from the Dublin Core metadata. If no creator is found, you return the string `"unknown"`; otherwise, you return the first `creator` in the list, which is the owner or the original author of the object. Note that you should usually have only one entry because messages are not edited (as of this stage of the message board's development).

- Lines 16–23: Finding the modification date is a bit tricky because during the creation, only the `created` field is populated, and the `modified` field is not. Therefore, you first try to grab the `modified` field, and if that fails, you get the `created` field. If the `created` field date/time does not exist, you return an empty string.

  Finally, if a date object is found, you convert it to a string and return it.

- Lines 25–30: Getting the parent is easy: You just use the `getParent()` method. But then you need to make sure that the parent is also an `IMessage` object; if it is not, you have a root message, and you return `None`. The `name` and the `title` attributes of the parent are stored in an information dictionary so that the data can be easily retrieved in a page template.

Registering the View

The final task in creating the Message Details view is to register the new view by using ZCML. You need to open the configuration file in the `browser` subpackage and add the following lines:

```
01  <page
02      name="details.html"
03      for="book.messageboard.interfaces.IMessage"
04      class=".message.MessageDetails"
05      template="details.pt"
06      permission="zope.Public"
07      menu="zmi_views" title="Preview"/>
```

In the preceding code block, note the following:

- Line 1: The `browser:page` directive registers a single page view.
- Line 2: The `name` attribute specifies the name by which the view will be accessible in the URL `http://localhost:8080/`*board-name*`/`*message-name*`/@@details.html`. The `name` attribute is required.

- Line 3: The `for` attribute tells the system that this view is for `IMessage` objects. If this attribute is not specified, the view is registered for `Interface`, which means for all objects.
- Lines 4–5: You use the just-created `MessageDetails` class and `details.pt` page template for the view; for this page, `details.pt` is rendered, and it uses an instance of `MessageDetails` as its view.

Note

Not all views need to have supporting view classes; therefore, the `class` attribute is optional.

Although you usually specify a page template for regular pages, there are situations in which you might prefer to use a view on an attribute of the Python view class. In these cases, you can specify the `attribute` attribute instead of `template`. The specified attribute/method should return a Unicode string that is used as the final output.

- Line 6: The `permission` attribute specifies the permission that is required to see this page. At this stage, you want to open up the details pages to any user of the site, so you assign the `zope.Public` permission, which is special because every user, whether authenticated or not, has this permission.
- Line 7: In order to save yourself from having to include a separate menu entry directive, you can use the `menu` and `title` attributes to tell the system under which menu the page will be available. In this case, you should make it a tab (`zmi_views` menu), which will be called Preview.

All you need to do now is to restart Zope, add a `Message` content object (if you have not done so yet), and click it. The Preview tab should be available now. Note that you should have no Parent entry because the message is not inside another one.

To see a Parent entry, you can add another message inside the current message by using the Contents view. After you add the new message, you can click it and go to the Details view. You should now see a Parent entry with a link back to the parent message.

Testing the View

Before moving to the next item on the list, you should develop some functional tests to ensure that the view works correctly. Functional tests are usually straightforward because they resemble the steps a user would take with the user interface. The only possibly tricky part is to get all the form variables set correctly.

To run the functional tests, you need to bring up the entire Zope 3 system so that you can test all side effects and behavior of an object inside its natural environment. Oftentimes, very simple tests suffice to determine bugs in the user interface and also in ZCML because all of it is executed during the functional test startup.

The functional tests you need to create can ensure that messages can be properly added and that the all the message details information is displayed in the Preview tab. By convention, all functional tests are stored in a submodule called `ftests`. Because you plan to write many of these tests, you should make this module a package by creating the directory and adding an __init__.py file.

At this point you need to create a file called `test_message.py` and add the following testing code to it:

```
01 import unittest
02 from zope.app.tests.functional import BrowserTestCase
03
04 class MessageTest(BrowserTestCase):
05
06     def testAddMessage(self):
07         response = self.publish(
08             '/+/AddMessageBoard.html=board',
09             basic='mgr:mgrpw',
10             form={'field.description': u'Message Board',
11                   'UPDATE_SUBMIT': 'Add'})
12         self.assertEqual(response.getStatus(), 302)
13         self.assertEqual(response.getHeader('Location'),
14                          'http://localhost/@@contents.html')
15         response = self.publish(
16             '/board/+/AddMessage.html=msg1',
17             basic='mgr:mgrpw',
18             form={'field.title': u'Message 1',
19                   'field.body': u'Body',
20                   'UPDATE_SUBMIT': 'Add'})
21         self.assertEqual(response.getStatus(), 302)
22         self.assertEqual(response.getHeader('Location'),
23                          'http://localhost/board/@@contents.html')
24
25     def testMessageDetails(self):
26         self.testAddMessage()
27         response = self.publish('/board/msg1/@@details.html',
28                                 basic='mgr:mgrpw')
29         body = response.getBody()
30         self.checkForBrokenLinks(body, '/board/msg1/@@details.html',
31                                  basic='mgr:mgrpw')
32
33         self.assert_(body.find('Message Details') > 0)
34         self.assert_(body.find('Message 1') > 0)
35         self.assert_(body.find('Body') > 0)
36
37
38 def test_suite():
39     return unittest.TestSuite((
40         unittest.makeSuite(MessageTest),
```

```
41          ))
42
43 if __name__ == '__main__':
44     unittest.main(defaultTest='test_suite')
```

In the preceding code block, note the following:

- Line 2: In order to simplify writing browser-based functional tests, you can use `BrowserTestCase` as a test case base class. The most important convenience methods are utilized, and thus introduced, in the body of the class.

- Lines 6–23: Before you can test views on a message, you have to create a message. Although it is possible to create a message by using a lower-level API, this is a perfect chance to write tests for adding views as well.

  Lines 7–11: You use the `publish()` method to publish a request with the publisher. The first argument is the URL (excluding the server and port) to be published. You might also include the `basic` argument, which specifies the username and password. The system knows only about the user `zope.mgr` with username `mgr` and password `mgrpw`. The role `zope.Manager` has been granted for this user, so that all possible screens should be available.

  In the `form` argument, you specify a dictionary of all variables that are submitted via the HTTP form mechanism. The values of the entries can be already-formatted Python objects and do not have to be just raw Unicode strings. Note that the adding view requires a field named `UPDATE_SUBMIT` for the object to be added. Otherwise, it just thinks this is a form reload.

  Lines 12–14: The adding view always returns a redirect (HTTP code 302). You can also verify the destination by looking at the Location HTTP header.

  Lines 15–23: Here you repeat the same procedure as in lines 7–11, this time by adding a message named `msg1` to the message board.

- Lines 25–35: After creating the message object (line 26), you simply request the Details view and store the HTML result in `body` (lines 27–29).

  One of the nice features of `BrowserTestCase` is a method called `checkForBrokenLinks()` that parses the HTML, looking for local URLs, and then tries to verify that they are good links. The second argument of the method is the URL of the page that generated the body. This is needed to determine the location correctly. You should also specify the same authentication parameters as used during the publication process because certain links are available only if the user has the permission to access the linked page.

  In the last part the test (lines 33–35), you simply check that some of the expected information is somewhere in the HTML, which is usually efficient because a faulty view usually causes a failure during the publishing process.

- Lines 38–44: As always, you have to have the usual boilerplate code.

Now that you have developed the tests, you can run them as you run the unit tests, except that instead of using the -u option (which is for unit tests only), you now specify the -f option (which is for functional tests only):

```
python2.3 bin/test -vpf --dir lib/python/book/messageboard
```

Because you already looked at the pages before, all tests should pass easily, unless you have a typo in your test case. When the tests pass, you can feel free to go on to the next step.

Step 2: Specifying the Default View

If you try to view a message by using http://localhost:8080/*board-name*/*message-name* at this point, you get the standard container index.html view. This is rather undesirable because your default view should show the contents of the message.

There is a special directive for declaring a default view. You simply need to add the following lines to your browser package configuration file:

```
01 <defaultView
02    for="book.messageboard.interfaces.IMessage"
03    name="details.html"/>
```

In the preceding code block, note the following:

- Line 2: Here you tell the system that you are adding a default view for the components implementing IMessage.
- Line 3: You make the Preview tab the default view. However, you can choose whatever view you like. Naturally, these views are usually views that display data instead of asking for input. It is also advisable to make the least restrictive and most general view the default, so that users with only a few permissions can see something about the object.

Step 3: Adding the Threaded Subtree View

Creating a nice and extensible thread view is difficult because the problem is recursive in nature. You would also like to have all HTML generation occur in page templates because it allows you to enhance the functionality of the view later; however, page templates do not like recursion.

The Main Thread Page Template

You need to create the main view template for thread.html, which you can call thread.pt:

```
01 <html metal:use-macro="views/standard_macros/view">
02   <body>
03     <div metal:fill-slot="body">
04
```

```
05        <h1>Discussion Thread</h1>
06
07        <div tal:replace="structure view/subthread" />
08
09    </div>
10    </body>
11 </html>
```

Almost all of this is boilerplate code, but there is opportunity here to add some more functionality later, if you desire to do so.

In the preceding code block, note the following:

- Line 7: Being blind about implementation, you simply assume that the Python-based view class will have a `subthread()` method that can magically generate the desired subthread for this message or even the message board.

The Thread Python View Class

Next, you have to build a Python view class. You start by editing a file called `thread.py` and insert the following code in it:

```
01 from zope.app.pagetemplate.viewpagetemplatefile import ViewPageTemplateFile
02 from book.messageboard.interfaces import IMessage
03
04 class Thread:
05
06    def __init__(self, context, request, base_url=''):
07        self.context = context
08        self.request = request
09        self.base_url = base_url
10
11    def listContentInfo(self):
12        children = []
13        for name, child in self.context.items():
14            if IMessage.providedBy(child):
15                info = {}
16                info['title'] = child.title
17                url = self.base_url + name + '/'
18                info['url'] = url + '@@thread.html'
19                thread = Thread(child, self.request, url)
20                info['thread'] = thread.subthread()
21                children.append(info)
22        return children
23
24    subthread = ViewPageTemplateFile('subthread.pt')
```

In the preceding code block, note the following:

- Line 1: The `ViewPageTemplateFile` class is used to allow page templates to be attributes/methods of a Python class. This is very handy.

- Line 2: You import the `IMessage` interface because you'll need it for object identification later.

- Line 24: Here is the promised `subthread()` method, which is simply a page template that knows how to render the thread. Note that you might want to read the section "The Subthread Page Template" before proceeding.

- Lines 11–22: This method provides all the information necessary for the subthread page template to do its work. For each child, it generates an `info` dictionary. The interesting elements of the dictionary include the `url` and `thread` values. The URL is built up in every iteration of the recursive process. You could also use the `zope.app.traversing` framework to generate the URL, but it is much simpler this way.

  The second interesting component of the info, the `thread` value, should contain a string with the HTML describing the subthread. This is where the recursion comes in. First, you create a `Thread` instance (view) for each child. Then you ask the view to return the subthread of the child, which is certainly one level deeper, which in turn creates deeper levels, and so on. Therefore, the `thread` value contains a threaded HTML representation of the branch.

The Subthread Page Template

The subthread page template, named `subthread.pt`, as required by the view class, is only responsible for creating an HTML presentation of the nested message children, using the information provided; therefore, the template is very simple (because it contains no logic):

```
01 <ul>
02   <li tal:repeat="item view/listContentInfo">
03     <a href=""
04        tal:attributes="href item/url"
05        tal:content="item/title">Message 1</a>
06     <div tal:replace="structure item/thread"/>
07   </li>
08 </ul>
```

In the preceding code block, note the following:

- Lines 1 and 8: Unordered lists are always good for creating threads or trees.

- Line 2: Thanks to the `Thread` view class, you simply need to iterate over the child information.

- Lines 3–5: You need to make sure you show the title of the message and link it to the actual object.
- Line 6: You insert the subthread for the message.

Registering the Thread View

Registering the thread view works just like registering any other page:

```
01 <page
02     name="thread.html"
03     for="book.messageboard.interfaces.IMessage"
04     class=".thread.Thread"
05     template="thread.pt"
06     permission="zope.View"
07     menu="zmi_views" title="Thread"/>
```

You should be familiar with the page directive already, so this code should be easy to understand.

You also have to register the same view for IMessageBoard so that you can get the full thread of the entire message board as well.

The Message Board Default View

Because the message board does not have a default view yet, you need to make the thread view the default:

```
01 <defaultView
02     for="book.messageboard.interfaces.IMessageBoard"
03     name="thread.html"/>
```

This is, of course, very similar to the default view you registered earlier for IMessage.

Step 4: Adding Icons

Now that you have some text-based views, you need to look into registering custom icons for the message board and message. Icons are just views on objects—in this case, your content components. However, to make life easier, the browser namespace provides a convenience directive called icon to register icons.

You need to simply add the following directive for each content type in the browser package configuration file:

```
01 <icon
02     name="zmi_icon"
03     for="book.messageboard.interfaces.IMessage"
04     file="message.png" />
```

The code should be self-explanatory at this point. Instead of a template, you are specifying a file as the view, which is expected to be binary image data and not just ASCII text.

Step 5: Final Testing

Now you should be all set. You can restart Zope 3 and see whether the new features are working as expected.

The code of this chapter is available in the Zope SVN, under `http://svn.zope.org/book/trunk/messageboard/step02`.

15

Custom Schema Fields and Form Widgets

Difficulty

Sprinter

Skills

- You should be familiar with the results achieved in Chapters 13, "Writing New Content Objects," and 14, "Adding Views for Content Objects."
- You should be comfortable with presentation components (views), as introduced in the Chapter 14.

Problem/Task

So far you have created fairly respectable content components and some nice views for them. In this chapter you'll look at the fine print; currently, it is possible that anything can be written into the message fields, including malicious HTML and JavaScript. Therefore, it would be useful to develop a special field (and corresponding widget) that strips out disallowed HTML tags.

CREATING CUSTOM FIELDS AND WIDGETS is a common task for end-user applications because those systems often have very specific requirements. The Zope 3 schema/form subsystem is designed to be as customizable as possible, so it should be no surprise that it is very easy to write your own field and widget in Zope.

Step 1: Creating a Field

The goal of the special field that you're going to add to your form should be to verify input based on allowed or forbidden HTML tags. If the message body contains HTML tags other than the ones allowed or contains any forbidden tags, the validation of the value should fail. Note that only one of the two attributes can be specified at once.

It is often not necessary to write a field from scratch because Zope 3 ships with a respectable collection already. These fields commonly also serve as base classes for custom fields. For your HTML field, the Text field seems to be the most appropriate base because it provides most of the functionality for you already.

You will extend the Text field by using two new attributes: allowed_tags and forbidden_tags. Then you are going to modify the _validate() method to reflect the constraint made by the two new attributes.

The Interface of the Field

As always, the first step in developing a new feature is to define the interface. In the messageboard package's interfaces module, you need to add the following lines:

```
01 from zope.schema import Tuple
02 from zope.schema.interfaces import IText
03
04 class IHTML(IText):
05     """A text field that handles HTML input."""
06
07     allowed_tags = Tuple(
08         title=u"Allowed HTML Tags",
09         description=u"""\
10         Only listed tags can be used in the value of the field.
11         """,
12         required=False)
13
14     forbidden_tags = Tuple(
15         title=u"Forbidden HTML Tags",
16         description=u"""\
17         Listed tags cannot be used in the value of the field.
18         """,
19         required=False)
```

In the preceding code block, note the following:

- Line 1: The Tuple field requires a value to be a Python tuple.
- Lines 2 and 4: You extend the IText interface and schema.
- Lines 7–12 and 14–19: You define the two additional attributes by using the field Tuple.

Implementation of the Field

As previously mentioned, you will use the Text field as the base class because it provides most of the functionality you need. The main task of the implementation is to rewrite the validation method.

You need to start by editing a file called fields.py in the messageboard package and inserting the following code in it:

```
01 import re
02
03 from zope.schema import Text
04 from zope.schema.interfaces import ValidationError
05
06 forbidden_regex = r'</?(?:%s).*?/?>'
07 allowed_regex = r'</??(?!%s[ />])[a-zA-Z0-9]*? ?(?:[a-z0-9]*?=?".*?")*/??>'
08
09 class ForbiddenTags(ValidationError):
10     __doc__ = u"""Forbidden HTML Tags used."""
11
12
13 class HTML(Text):
14
15     allowed_tags = ()
16     forbidden_tags = ()
17
18     def __init__(self, allowed_tags=(), forbidden_tags=(), **kw):
19         self.allowed_tags = allowed_tags
20         self.forbidden_tags = forbidden_tags
21         super(HTML, self).__init__(**kw)
22
23     def _validate(self, value):
24         super(HTML, self)._validate(value)
25
26         if self.forbidden_tags:
27             regex = forbidden_regex %'|'.join(self.forbidden_tags)
28             if re.findall(regex, value):
29                 raise ForbiddenTags(value, self.forbidden_tags)
30
31         if self.allowed_tags:
32             regex = allowed_regex %'[ />]|'.join(self.allowed_tags)
33             if re.findall(regex, value):
34                 raise ForbiddenTags(value, self.allowed_tags)
```

In the preceding code block, note the following:

- Line 1: You import the Regular Expression module (re); you will use regular expressions to do the validation of the HTML.

- Line 3: You import the Text field that you will use as the base class for the HTML field.

- Lines 4 and 10–11: The validation method of the new HTML field will be able to throw a new type of validation error when an illegal HTML tag is found.

  Usually, errors are defined in the interfaces module, but because doing so there would cause a recursive import between the interfaces and fields module, you define it here.

- Lines 7—9: These strings define the regular expression templates for detecting forbidden and allowed HTML tags, respectively. Note that these regular expressions are quite a bit more restrictive than what the HTML 4.01 standard requires, but they are a good enough demonstration.

- Lines 16—19: In the constructor, you are extracting the two new arguments and sending the rest to the constructor of the Text field (line 21).

- Line 22: Here you delegate validation to the Text field. The validation process might already fail at this point, in which case further validation is unnecessary.

- Lines 24–27: If forbidden tags were specified, then you try to detect them. If a forbidden tag is found, a ForbiddenTags error is raised, attaching the faulty value and the tuple of forbidden tags to the exception.

- Lines 29–32: Similarly to the previous block, this block checks whether all used tags are in the collection of allowed_tags; if they are not, a ForbiddenTags error is raised.

You have an HTML field, but it does not implement IHTML interface. Why? Doing so would cause a recursive import when you use the HTML field in your content objects. To make the interface assertion, you add the following lines to the interfaces.py module:

```
01 from zope.interface import classImplements
02 from fields import HTML
03 classImplements(HTML, IHTML)
```

At this point you should have a working field, but you need to write some unit tests to verify the implementation.

Unit Tests for the Field

Because you will use the Text field as a base class, you can also reuse the Text field's tests. Other than that, you simply have to test the new validation behavior.

In the messageboard/tests directory, you add the file test_fields.py, to which you add the following base tests:

Note

Note that the code is not complete (abbreviated sections are marked with . . .). You can find the complete code in the source repository, though. The code of this chapter is available in the Zope SVN, at http://svn.zope.org/book/trunk/messageboard/step03.

```
01 import unittest
02 from zope.schema.tests.test_strfield import TextTest
03
04 from book.messageboard.fields import HTML, ForbiddenTags
05
06 class HTMLTest(TextTest):
07
08     _Field_Factory = HTML
09
10     def test_AllowedTagsHTMLValidate(self):
11         html = self._Field_Factory(allowed_tags=('h1','pre'))
12         html.validate(u'<h1>Blah</h1>')
13         ...
14         self.assertRaises(ForbiddenTags, html.validate,
15                           u'<h2>Foo</h2>')
16         ...
17
18     def test_ForbiddenTagsHTMLValidate(self):
19         html = self._Field_Factory(forbidden_tags=('h2','pre'))
20         html.validate(u'<h1>Blah</h1>')
21         ...
22         self.assertRaises(ForbiddenTags, html.validate,
23                           u'<h2>Foo</h2>')
24         ...
25
26 def test_suite():
27     return unittest.TestSuite((
28         unittest.makeSuite(HTMLTest),
29         ))
30
31 if __name__ == '__main__':
32     unittest.main(defaultTest='test_suite')
```

In the preceding code block, note the following:

- Line 2: Because you use the `Text` field as the base class, you can also use its test case as base, which means you get some freebie tests in return.

- Line 8: The `TextTest` base comes with some rules by which you have to abide. Specifying the `fieldFactory` attribute is required, to ensure that the correct field is tested.

- Lines 10–16: These are tests of the validation method, using the `allowed_tags` attribute. Some text has been removed in this area to conserve space. You can look at the code repository to see the full test suite.

- Lines 18–24: Here you are testing the validation method, using the `forbidden_tags` attribute.

Step 2: Creating a Widget

Widgets are simply views of a field. Therefore, you place the widget code in the browser subpackage.

HTMLSourceWidget will use TextAreaWidget as a base, and only the converter method _toFieldValue(input) has to be reimplemented, so that it will remove any undesired tags from the input value. (Yes, this means that the validation of values coming through these widgets will always pass.)

Implementation of the HTML Source Widget

Because there is no need to create a new interface, you can start right away with the implementation. You get started by adding a file called widgets.py and inserting the following content in it:

```
01 import re
02 from zope.app.form.browser import TextAreaWidget
03 from book.messageboard.fields import forbidden_regex, allowed_regex
04
05 class HTMLSourceWidget(TextAreaWidget):
06
07   def _toFieldValue(self, input):
08       input = super(HTMLSourceWidget, self)._toFieldValue(input)
09
10       if self.context.forbidden_tags:
11           regex = forbidden_regex %'|'.join(
12               self.context.forbidden_tags)
13           input = re.sub(regex, '', input)
14
15       if self.context.allowed_tags:
16           regex = allowed_regex %'[ />]|'.join(
17               self.context.allowed_tags)
18           input = re.sub(regex, '', input)
19
20       return input
```

In the preceding code block, note the following:

- Line 2: As mentioned previously, you can use TextAreaWidget as a base class.

- Line 3: There is no need to redefine the regular expressions for finding forbidden and non-allowed tags again, so you use the field's definitions. This also prevents the widget converter and field validator from getting out of sync.

- Line 8: You still want to use the original conversion because it takes care of weird line endings and some other routine cleanups.

- Lines 10–13: If you find a forbidden tag, you simply remove it by replacing it with an empty string. Notice that you get the `forbidden_tags` attribute from the context (which is the field itself) of the widget.
- Lines 15–18: If you find a tag that is not in the allowed tag's tuple, you remove it as well.

Overall, this a very nice and compact way of converting the input value.

Unit Tests for the Widget

Although you usually do not write *unit* tests for high-level view code, widget code—particularly the converter—should be tested. You need to open `test_widgets.py` in `browser/tests` and insert the following in it:

```
01 import unittest
02 from zope.app.form.browser.tests.test_textareawidget import TextAreaWidgetTest
03 from book.messageboard.browser.widgets import HTMLSourceWidget
04 from book.messageboard.fields import HTML
05
06 class HTMLSourceWidgetTest(TextAreaWidgetTest):
07
08     _FieldFactory = HTML
09     _WidgetFactory = HTMLSourceWidget
10
11
12     def test_AllowedTagsConvert(self):
13         widget = self._widget
14         widget.context.allowed_tags=('h1','pre')
15         self.assertEqual(u'<h1>Blah</h1>',
16                          widget._toFieldValue(u'<h1>Blah</h1>'))
17         ...
18         self.assertEqual(u'Blah',
19                          widget._toFieldValue(u'<h2>Blah</h2>'))
20         ...
21
22     def test_ForbiddenTagsConvert(self):
23         widget = self._widget
24         widget.context.forbidden_tags=('h2','pre')
25
26         self.assertEqual(u'<h1>Blah</h1>',
27                          widget._toFieldValue(u'<h1>Blah</h1>'))
28         ...
29         self.assertEqual(u'Blah',
30                          widget._toFieldValue(u'<h2>Blah</h2>'))
31         ...
32
```

```
33 def test_suite():
34     return unittest.TestSuite((
35         unittest.makeSuite(HTMLSourceWidgetTest),
36         ))
37
38 if __name__ == '__main__':
39     unittest.main(defaultTest='test_suite')
```

In the preceding code block, note the following:

- Line 2: Of course, you reuse `TextAreaWidgetTest` to get some freebie tests.
- Lines 8–9: Fulfilling the requirements of the `TextAreaWidgetTest` test case, you need to specify the field and widget you are using, which makes sense because the widget must have the field (context) in order to fulfill all its duties.
- Lines 12–31: Similarly to testing the fields, you need to test the converter. In this case, however, you compare the output because it can differ from the input, based on whether forbidden tags were found.

Step 3: Using the HTML Field

Now you have all the pieces you need for using the HTML field in the message board. All that's left is to integrate them with the rest of the package. There are a couple of steps involved. First, you register `HTMLSourceWidget` as a widget for the HTML field. Next, you need to change the `IMessage` interface declaration to use the HTML field.

Registering the Widget

To register the new widget as a view for the HTML field, you use the `zope` namespace `view` directive. Therefore, you have to add the `zope` namespace to the configuration file's namespace list by adding the following line in the opening `configure` element:

```
01 xmlns:zope="http://namespaces.zope.org/zope"
```

Then you add the following directive:

```
01 <zope:view
02     type="zope.publisher.interfaces.browser.IBrowserRequest"
03     for="book.messageboard.interfaces.IHTML"
04     provides="zope.app.form.interfaces.IInputWidget"
05     factory=".widgets.HTMLSourceWidget"
06     permission="zope.Public"
07     />
```

In the preceding code block, note the following:

- Line 2: Because the `zope:view` directive can be used for any presentation type (for example, HTTP, WebDAV, FTP), it is necessary to state that the registered widget is for browsers (that is, HTML).

- Line 3: You specify that this widget will work for all fields implementing IHTML.

- Line 4: In general, presentation components, like adapters, can have a specific output interface. Usually this interface is just zope.interface.Interface, but here you specifically want to say that this is a widget that is accepting *input* for the field. The other type of widget is IDisplayWidget.

- Line 5: You specify the factory or class that will be used to generate the widget.

- Line 6: You make this widget publicly available, meaning that everyone using the system can use the widget.

Adjusting the IMessage Interface

The final step for the integration is to use the field in the IMessage interface. You need to go to the interfaces module to decide which property is going to become an HTML field. The field is already imported.

Next, you definitely want to make the body property of IMessage an HTML field. You could also do that for description of IMessageBoard, but you can keep things simple and not do that now. Here are the changes that need to be made to the body property declaration (starting at line 24):

```
01 body = HTML(
02     title=u"Message Body",
03     description=u"This is the actual message. Type whatever!",
04     default=u"",
05     allowed_tags=('h1', 'h2', 'h3', 'h4', 'h5', 'h6', 'img', 'a',
06                   'br', 'b', 'i', 'u', 'em', 'sub', 'sup',
07                   'table', 'tr', 'td', 'th', 'code', 'pre',
08                   'center', 'div', 'span', 'p', 'font', 'ol',
09                   'ul', 'li', 'q', 's', 'strong'),
10     required=False)
```

In the preceding code block, note the following:

- Lines 5—9: You added this new attribute in the IHTML interface. This is just an example of valid tags, and you can feel free to add or remove whatever tags you like.

And that's it! You're done implementing and integrating the new HTML field. To try the result of your work, you can restart Zope 3, start editing a new message, and see if it will accept tags such as html or body. You should notice that these tags will be silently removed from the message body when you save the message.

16

Securing Components

Difficulty

Sprinter

Skills

- You should be knowledgeable about topics covered in the previous chapters in Part III, "Content Components—The Basics."
- You should be familiar with interfaces, ZCML, and security concepts, such as permissions, roles, and principals.

Problem/Task

Although you have made some basic security assertions in order to get your message board to work, it does not really represent a secure system at this point. Some end-user views require the `zope.ManageContent` permission, and there are no granular permissions and roles defined for the message board.

Z OPE 3 HAS A FLEXIBLE security mechanism. The two fundamental concepts of this mechanism are permissions and principals. *Permissions* are like keys to doors that open to a particular functionality. For example, you might need the permission `zope.View` to look at a message's detail screen. *Principals*, on the other hand, are agents of the system that execute actions. The most common example of a principal is a user of the system. The goal is to grant permissions to principals, which is the duty of another subsystem, known as the *security policy*.

Zope 3 does not enforce any particular security policy. On the contrary, it encourages site administrators to carefully choose a security policy that fits their needs best. The default Zope 3 distribution comes with a default security policy (`zope.app.securitypolicy`) that supports the concept of roles. Roles are like hats people wear, and they can be seen as a collection of permissions. A single user can have several hats but can wear only one at a time. Examples of roles include editor and administrator. Therefore, the default security policy supports mappings from permissions to principals, permissions to roles, and roles to principals. This chapter is mostly independent of the security policy in use; sections that are security policy specific are clearly marked. In the latter case, it is assumed that the default security policy is used.

The first task in this chapter is to define a sensible set of permissions and change the existing directives to use those new permissions. This can be a bit tedious, but it is important that you do it carefully because the quality of your security depends on this task. While adjusting the permissions, you are likely to discover that you have missed a permission, so you should not hesitate to add permissions as the need arises. That is something a programmer should always do.

Next, the site administrator, who uses the default security policy, is the one who normally defines roles and grants permissions to them. Finally, users need to have roles granted to them for testing.

Securing an object does not require any modification to the existing Python code, as you will see in this chapter, because all interactions with the Zope 3 system are configured via ZCML. Therefore, you can configure security completely by using ZCML, leaving the Python code untouched; this is another advantage of using Zope 3 (in comparison to Zope 2, for example).

Step 1: Declaring Permissions

In contrast to Zope 2, Zope 3 permissions have to be explicitly defined. For your message board, it will suffice to define the following four basic permissions:

- `View`—This permission allows users to access the data for message boards and messages. Every regular message board `User` is going to have this permission.

- `Add`—This permission allows someone to create (that is, post) a message and add it to the message board or another message. Note that every regular `User` is allowed to do this because posting and replying should be publicly available by default.

- `Edit`—You want to allow only the message board `Editor` to edit content (for the purpose of moderation) because you would not want a regular user to be able to manipulate posts after creation.

- `Delete`—The `Editor` must be able to get rid of messages, of course. Therefore, the `Delete` permission is assigned to the `Editor`. Note that this permission does not allow the `Editor` to delete `MessageBoard` objects from folders or other containers.

Now you need to define these permissions. Note that they must appear at the very beginning of the configuration file, so that they will be defined by the time the other directives (which will use the permissions) are executed. Here are the four directives you should add to your main `configure.zcml` file in the `messageboard` package:

```
01 <permission
02     id="book.messageboard.View"
03     title="View Message Board and Messages"
04     description="View the Message Board and all its content."
05     />
06 <permission
07     id="book.messageboard.Add"
08     title="Add Message"
09     description="Add Message."
10     />
11 <permission
12     id="book.messageboard.Edit"
13     title="Edit Messages"
14     description="Edit Messages."
15     />
16 <permission
17     id="book.messageboard.Delete"
18     title="Delete Message"
19     description="Delete Message."
20     />
```

The zope:permission directive defines and creates a new permission in the global permission registry. The id attribute should be a unique name for the permission, so it is a good idea to give the name a dotted prefix, such as book.messageboard. in this case. Note that the id attribute must be a valid URI or a dotted name; if there is no dot in the dotted version, a ValidationError exception will be raised. The id attribute is used as an identifier in the following configuration steps. The title attribute of the permissions is a short description that will be used in GUIs to identify the permission, and the description attribute is a longer explanation that serves more or less as documentation. Both id and title are required attributes.

Step 2: Using the Permissions

Now that you have defined permissions, you also have to use them. You can start with the main message board configuration file (messageboard/configure.zcml). In the following walk-through, you are only going to use the last part of the permission name to refer to the permission, leaving off book.messageboard. However, the full id attribute has to be specified for the configuration to execute.

You have to make the following changes in the configuration file:

- Change the first require statement in the MessageBoard content directive to use the View permission (line 42). This makes the description attribute and the items accessible to all message board users. Similarly, change line 64 for the Message object.

- Change the permission of line 46 to Edit because only the message board administrator should be able to change any of the properties of the MessageBoard object.

- All the container functionality will only require the view permission, so change the permission on line 68 to `View`. This is not secure because it includes read and write methods, but it will suffice for this demonstration.

- For the `Message` object, you need to be able to set the attributes with the `Add` permission, so change line 72 to specify this permission.

Now you need to go to the `browser` configuration file (`messageboard/browser/configure.zcml`) and fix the permissions there:

- The permissions for the message board's add form (line 11), add menu item (line 18), and edit form (line 27) stay unchanged because only an administrator should be able to manage the board.

- Because you want every user to see the messages in a message board, the permission on line 33 should become `View`. Because the `contents` view is meant for management, only principals with the `Edit` permission should be able to see it (line 34). Finally, you need the `Add` permission to actually add new messages to the message board (line 35). The same is true for the message's container views permissions (lines 84–86).

- Because all users should be able to see the message thread and the message details, the permissions on lines 43, 94, and 106 should become `View`.

- On line 61 you should change the permission to `Add` because you allow messages to be added to the message board only if the user has this permission. The same is true for the message board's add menu item on line 68.

- On line 78, make sure that a user can only access the edit screen if he or she has the `Edit` permission.

That's it. If you restarted Zope 3 at this point, you would not even be able to access the `MessageBoard` and/or `Message` instances. Therefore, you need to create some roles and assign permissions to them.

Step 3: Declaring Roles

The declaration of roles is specific to Zope 3's default security policy. Another security policy might not even have the concept of roles. Therefore, the role declaration and grants to the permissions should not even be part of your package. For simplicity and to keep it all in one place, you are going to store the policy-specific security configuration in `security.zcml`. For the `messageboard` package, you really need only two roles— `User` and `Editor`—which are declared as follows:

```
01 <role
02     id="book.messageboard.User"
03     title="Message Board User"
04     description="Users that actually use the Message Board."/>
05
```

```
06 <role
07     id="book.messageboard.Editor"
08     title="Message Board Editor"
09     description="The Editor can edit and delete Messages."/>
```

Equivalently to the `zope:permission` directive, the `zope:role` directive creates and registers a new role with the global role registry. Again, the `id` attribute must be a unique identifier that is used throughout the configuration process to identify the role. Both the `id` attribute and the `title` attribute are required.

Next, you need to grant the new permissions to the new roles (that is, create a permission-role map). The user should be able only to add and view messages, and the editor should be allowed to execute all permissions. Here is the ZCML that is needed to realize the map:

```
01 <grant
02     permission="book.messageboard.View"
03     role="book.messageboard.User"
04     />
05 <grant
06     permission="book.messageboard.Add"
07     role="book.messageboard.User"
08     />
09 <grant
10     permission="book.messageboard.Edit"
11     role="book.messageboard.Editor"
12     />
13 <grant
14     permission="book.messageboard.Delete"
15     role="book.messageboard.Editor"
16   />
```

The `zope:grant` directive is fairly complex because it permits all three different types of security mappings. It allows you to assign a permission to a principal, a role to a principal, and a permission to a role. Therefore, the directive has three optional arguments: `permission`, `role`, and `principal`. Exactly two of the three arguments have to be specified to make it a valid directive. All three security objects are specified by their `id` attributes.

Finally, you have to include the `security.zcml` file in your other configuration. You do this by simply adding the following inclusion directive in the *Zope3-Instance*/etc/principals.zcml file:

```
01 <include package="book.messageboard" file="security.zcml" />
```

The reason you put the directive here is to make it obvious that this file depends on the security policy. Also, when assigning permissions to roles, you want all possible permissions the system can have to be defined. Because the `principals.zcml` file is the last ZCML to be evaluated, this is the best place to put the declarations.

Step 4: Assigning Roles to Principals

To make the messageboard package work again, you now have to connect the roles to some principals. You are going to create two new principals called boarduser and boardeditor. To do that, you go to the Zope 3 instance etc/ directory and add the following lines to principals.zcml:

```
01 <principal
02     id="book.messageboard.boarduser"
03     title="Message Board User"
04     login="boarduser" password="book"
05     />
06 <grant
07     role="book.messageboard.User"
08     principal="book.messageboard.boarduser"
09     />
10
11 <principal
12     id="book.messageboard.boardeditor"
13     title="Message Board Editor"
14     login="boardeditor" password="book"
15     />
16 <grant
17     role="book.messageboard.User"
18     principal="book.messageboard.boardeditor"
19     />
20 <grant
21     role="book.messageboard.Editor"
22     principal="book.messageboard.boardeditor"
23     />
```

The zope:principal directive creates and registers a new principal/user in the system. As for all security object directives, the id and title attributes are required. You could also specify a description attribute. In addition to these three attributes, you *must* specify a login and password (plain text) for the user, for authentication.

Note that you might want to grant the book.messageboard.User role to the zope.anybody principal so that everyone can view and add messages.

The zope.anybody principal is an unauthenticated principal, which is defined using the zope:unauthenticatedPrincipal directive. This directive has the same three basic attributes the zope:principal directive, but it does not accept the login and password attributes.

Now your system should be secure and usable. If you restart Zope 3 now, you will see that only the message board's Editor can freely manipulate objects. (Of course, you have to log in as an Editor.)

Changing Size Information

Difficulty

Newcomer

Skills

- You should be familiar with the previous chapters in Part III, "Content Components—The Basics."

Problem/Task

Currently, when looking at the Contents View of a message, you see the number of items in the message, which includes reply messages and attachments (for example, files, images). It would be nice if the size field would say "x replies, y attachments."

THE SIZE OUTPUT IS HANDLED by a very simple adapter that adapts from IMessage to ISized. An adapter is a component that creates a bridge from one interface to another. In this case, you want to be able to *provide* the ISized interface for components implementing the IMessage interface. The adapter can use the IMessage API to collect information to provide to the ISized API.

Step 1: Implementing the Adapter

An adapter is usually a simple class, which is marked by the fact that it takes one object as the constructor argument. This object must provide the "from" interface that is often also listed in the used_for attribute of the class. You need to add the following code in your message.py file:

```
01 from zope.app.size.interfaces import ISized
02
03 class MessageSized(object):
04
05     implements(ISized)
06     __used_for__ = IMessage
07
08     def __init__(self, message):
09         self._message = message
10
11     def sizeForSorting(self):
12         """See ISized"""
13         return ('item', len(self._message))
14
15     def sizeForDisplay(self):
16         """See ISized"""
17         messages = 0
18         for obj in self._message.values():
19             if IMessage.providedBy(obj):
20                 messages += 1
21
22         attachments = len(self._message)-messages
23
24         if messages == 1: size = u'1 reply'
25         else: size = u'%i replies' %messages
26
27         if attachments == 1: size += u', 1 attachment'
28         else: size += u', %i attachments' %attachments
29
30         return size
```

The ISized interface specifies two methods:

- Lines 11–13: sizeForSorting() must return a tuple, with the first element being a unit and the second the value. This format provides a generic comparable representation of the size.

- Lines 15–30: sizeForDisplay() can return any sort of Unicode string that represents the size of the object in a meaningful way. The output should not be too long. As promised, it displays responses and attachments separately.

Step 2: Writing and Running Unit Tests

Now you need to write some doc tests for the adapter. You should add the following tests in the doc string of the sizeForSorting() method:

```
01 Create the adapter first.
02
03 >>> size = MessageSized(Message())
```

```
04
05 Here are some examples of the expected output.
06
07 >>> size.sizeForSorting()
08 ('item', 0)
09 >>> size._message['msg1'] = Message()
10 >>> size.sizeForSorting()
11 ('item', 1)
12 >>> size._message['att1'] = object()
13 >>> size.sizeForSorting()
14 ('item', 2)
```

The test is straightforward because you add an object and check whether it increases the size of items by one. In the `sizeForDisplay()` doc string, you add the following:

```
01 Create the adapter first.
02
03 >>> size = MessageSized(Message())
04
05 Here are some examples of the expected output.
06
07 >>> size.sizeForDisplay()
08 u'0 replies, 0 attachments'
09 >>> size._message['msg1'] = Message()
10 >>> size.sizeForDisplay()
11 u'1 reply, 0 attachments'
12 >>> size._message['msg2'] =  Message()
13 >>> size.sizeForDisplay()
14 u'2 replies, 0 attachments'
15 >>> size._message['att1'] = object()
16 >>> size.sizeForDisplay()
17 u'2 replies, 1 attachment'
18 >>> size._message['att2'] = object()
19 >>> size.sizeForDisplay()
20 u'2 replies, 2 attachments'
```

The doc tests are already registered because the `message.py` file already contains some doc tests. However, adding an object to a container requires some of the component architecture to be up and running. There is a testing convenience module called `zope.app.tests.placelesssetup`. It contains two functions, `setUp()` and `tearDown()`, that can be passed in the doc test suite as positional arguments. Therefore, the test suite declaration in `tests/test_message.py` changes from this:

```
01 DocTestSuite('book.messageboard.message')
```

to this:

```
01 DocTestSuite('book.messageboard.message',
02               setUp=setUp, tearDown=tearDown)
```

In addition, you have to import the `setUp` and `tearDown` functions:

```
01 from zope.app.tests.placelesssetup import setUp, tearDown
```

You can now run the tests the usual way:

```
python2.3 bin/test -vpu --dir lib/python/book/messageboard
```

Step 3: Registering the Adapter

Now you need to register the adapter in `messageboard/configure.zcml`, using the following ZCML directive:

```
01 <adapter
02     factory=".message.MessageSized"
03     provides="zope.app.size.interfaces.ISized"
04     for=".interfaces.IMessage"
05     />
```

Using the `zope:adapter` directive is the way to register global adapters via ZCML. The `factory` attribute allows you to specify a list of factories (usually only one is specified) that are responsible for creating an adapter instance; the adapter instance takes an object that provides the interface specified in the `for` attribute and provides the interface specified in `provides`. All three of these attributes are mandatory.

In this case, you basically say that an instance of the `MessageSized` class provides an `ISized` interface for objects implementing `IMessage`.

The directive also supports three optional arguments: *trusted*, *permission*, and *name*. By default, the API of an adapter is publicly available, but because its context is security-proxied, the availability of the API depends on the security declarations of the context. When the trusted attribute is specified, the adapter is considered to be trusted code, and the context object passed into it is never security-proxied. This means that the adapter always has access to all attributes and methods of the context object. However, when an adapter is declared trusted, it will itself always be security-proxied. Thus it becomes necessary to specify the *permission* attribute, which causes the adapter API to be available only to principals that have been granted the specified permission. Of course, you can also specify the *permission* attribute by itself to create security assertions on the adapter API.

The third optional argument of the directive is the name attribute, which specifies the name of the adapter. By using names, you can specify multiple adapters from one interface to another.

That's it! You can now restart Zope 3 and see for yourself. You can click the Contents tab of the message board to see the new size information of messages. Note that you did not need to touch any existing Python code to provide this functionality.

Internationalizing Packages

Difficulty

Sprinter

Skills

- You should be familiar with the preceding chapters in Part III, "Content Components—The Basics."
- You should be familiar with page templates.
- Basic knowledge of the gettext format and tools is a plus. Optional.

Problem/Task

Now that you have a working messageboard package, it is time to think about the fact that not everyone in the world can speak English. Therefore, it is your task now to internationalize and localize the code to another language—let's say German.

BEFORE YOU CAN START CODING, you need to know some of the basics. If you are not familiar with common terminology used in regard to this subject, please read Chapter 10, "Introduction to Zope's I18n and L10n Support."

This chapter has little to do with Python development, but the information here is still useful because all Zope 3 core components are required to be internationalized.

Step 1: Internationalizing Python Code

There should be only a few spots where internationalizing is necessary because translatable strings are used for views, which are usually coded in page templates. One of the big exceptions is schemas because in them you always define human-readable titles, descriptions, and default text values for the declared fields.

Zope uses message IDs to mark strings as translatable. A translatable string must always carry a domain, so that you know which translation domain to pick.

You use message ID factories to create message IDs:

```
01 from zope.i18n import MessageIDFactory
02 _ = MessageIDFactory('messageboard')
```

In the preceding code block, note the following:

- Lines 1–2: Every Python file containing translatable strings must contain this small bit of boilerplate code. Note that for Zope 3 core code, there is a shortcut:

  ```
  from zope.app.i18n import ZopeMessageIDFactory as _
  ```

  This import creates a message ID factory that uses the zope domain.

- Line 2: The underscore character is commonly used to represent the translation function (from gettext). In this case, it is used as a message ID constructor/factory. The argument of the MessageIDFactory factory is the domain, which in this case is messageboard.

But why do we need domains in the first place? An example that explains the need of domains is the word *sun*. This word really represents three different meanings in English: (1) earth's closest star, (2) an abbreviation for Sunday, and (3) the company Sun Microsystems. All these meanings have different translations in German, for example. So you can distinguish between them by specifying domains, such as astronomy, calendar, and companies, respectively. Domains also allow you to organize and reuse translations; they are almost like libraries. For example, not every package needs to collect its own calendar translations, but all packages could benefit from one cohesive domain.

Another way of categorizing translations is by creating somewhat abstract message strings. So, for example, the value of an add button becomes add-button instead of the usual Add, and translations for this string would then insert a human-readable string, such as Add for English or Hinzufügen for German. (You will see this usage specifically in page templates in the next section of this chapter.) These abstract message strings are known as explicit message IDs.

You might wonder why you have to use the message ID concept instead of using a translation function directly, as other desktop applications do. Recall that Zope is an application server that serves multiple users over the network. So when a piece of code is called, you often do not know anything about the user or the desired language. Only views (whether in Python code or in page templates) have information about the user and therefore the desired locale, which contains the language, so the translation has to be prolonged as long as possible. As a rule of thumb, translating is the last task the application should do before providing the final end-user output. Zope 3 honors this rule in every aspect.

Let's get back to translating Python code. Because the interfaces have the most translatable strings, let's start with them. You need to open the interfaces.py module and add the previously mentioned boilerplate code. Next, you internationalize each field. For example, you change the IMessageBoard schema's description field from this:

```
01 description = Text(
02     title=u"Description",
03     description=u"A detailed description of the content of the board.",
04     default=u"",
05     required=False)
```

to this:

```
01 description = Text(
02     title=_("Description"),
03     description=_("A detailed description of the content of the board."),
04     default=u"",
05     required=False)
```

Note that the underscore message ID factory simply functions like a translating message. You need to do the same transformation for all schemas in the interfaces module. Also, you should note that whereas title and description require Unicode strings, you can simply pass a regular string into the message ID factory because the message ID uses unicode as its base class, which makes the message ID look like a unicode object. Another minor translation markup is required in the __doc__ attribute of the ForbiddenTags class of the fields module. You need to make sure to internationalize that one as well, in the same manner.

Another interesting case of marking message strings is found in message.py in the MessageSized class's sizeForDisplay() method. The original code looks like this:

```
01 if messages == 1: size = u'1 reply'
02 else: size = u'%i replies' %messages
03
04 if attachments == 1: size += u', 1 attachment'
05 else: size += u', %i attachments' %attachments
```

This usage causes a problem with this example's simplistic usage of message IDs because you now have variables in the string, and something like 'messages' + _(" replies") will not work, unlike in gettext applications, because the underscore object will not actually do the translation. The lookup for the translation would simply fail because the system would look for translations such as "2 replies," "3 replies," and so on. This means that the actual variable values need to be inserted into the text *after* the translation. For exactly this case, the MessageId object has a mapping attribute that can store all variables, and it inserts them after the translation is completed. This means, of course, that you also have to mark up your text string in a different way, so that the new code becomes this:

```
01 if messages == 1 and attachments == 1:
02     size = _('1 reply, 1 attachment')
03 elif messages == 1 and attachments != 1:
```

```
04    size = _('1 reply, ${attachments} attachments')
04 elif messages != 1 and attachments == 1:
05    size = _('${messages} replies, 1 attachment')
06 else:
07    size = _('${messages} replies, ${attachments} attachments')
08
09 size.mapping = {'messages': `messages`, 'attachments': `attachments`}
```

And don't forget the preceding boilerplate code. In the preceding code block, note the following:

- Lines 1–8: Here you handle the four different cases you could possibly have. Although this might not be the most efficient way of doing it, it allows you to list all four combinations separately, so that the message string extraction tool will be able to find them. This tool looks for strings that are enclosed by _().

  Note that the %i occurrences have been replaced by ${messages} and ${attachments}, which is the translation domain way of marking a variable that is to be inserted later.

- Line 10: After the message ID is constructed, you add the mapping with the two required variable values.

Because you have tests written for the size adapter, you need to correct them at this point, as well. You might try to fix the tests yourself before reading on. To do so, you change the doc string of the sizeForDisplay() method to this:

```
01 Creater the adapter first.
02
03 >>> size = MessageSized(Message())
04
05 Here are some examples of the expected output.
06
07 >>> str = size.sizeForDisplay()
08 >>> str
09 u'${messages} replies, ${attachments} attachments'
10 >>> 'msgs: %(messages)s, atts: %(attachments)s' %str.mapping
11 'msgs: 0, atts: 0'
12 >>> size._message['msg1'] = Message()
13 >>> str = size.sizeForDisplay()
14 >>> str
15 u'1 reply, ${attachments} attachments'
16 >>> 'msgs: %(messages)s, atts: %(attachments)s' %str.mapping
17 'msgs: 1, atts: 0'
18 >>> size._message['att1'] = object()
19 >>> str = size.sizeForDisplay()
20 >>> str
21 u'1 reply, 1 attachment'
```

```
22 >>> 'msgs: %(messages)s, atts: %(attachments)s' %str.mapping
23 'msgs: 1, atts: 1'
24 >>> size._message['msg2'] = Message()
25 >>> str = size.sizeForDisplay()
26 >>> str
27 u'${messages} replies, 1 attachment'
28 >>> 'msgs: %(messages)s, atts: %(attachments)s' %str.mapping
29 'msgs: 2, atts: 1'
30 >>> size._message['att2'] = object()
31 >>> str = size.sizeForDisplay()
32 >>> str
33 u'${messages} replies, ${attachments} attachments'
34 >>> 'msgs: %(messages)s, atts: %(attachments)s' %str.mapping
35 'msgs: 2, atts: 2'
```

In the preceding code block, note the following:

- Lines 7–11: The sizeForDisplay() method returns a message ID object. The message ID uses its text part for representation. In the following lines, you check that the mapping exists and that it contains the correct values.

- Line 12–35: You repeat the test as before, using different numbers of replies and attachments.

One last location where you have to internationalize some Python code output is in browser/message.py. The string 'unknown' must be wrapped in a message ID factory call. Also, the string returned by the modified() method of the MessageDetails view class must be adapted to use the user's locale information because it returns a formatted date/time string. Because MessageDetails is a *view* class, you have the user's locale available, so you can easily change the old version:

```
01 return date.strftime('%d/%m/%Y %H:%M:%S')
```

to the internationalized version:

```
01 formatter = self.request.locale.dates.getFormatter('dateTime', 'short')
02 return formatter.format(date)
```

Every BrowserRequest instance has a locale object, which represents the user's regional settings. The getFormatter() method returns a formatter instance that can format a datetime object to a string, based on the locale. (You can refer to the API reference at http://localhost:8080/++apidoc++ or to Chapter 10 to see all of the locale's functionality.)

You have already done everything that needs to be done in the Python code. You should feel free to check the other Python modules for translatable strings; you will not find any. As promised, Python code contains only a human-readable strings, and that is a good thing.

Step 2: Internationalizing Page Templates

Internationalizing page templates is more interesting than Python code in many ways. You do not have to worry only about finding the correct tags to internationalize; because you can also have heavy nesting, the complexity can become overwhelming. It's a good idea to keep the content of translatable tags as flat as possible; that is, you should try to have translatable text that does not contain much HTML and TAL code.

To achieve internationalization support in Zope 3's page templates, the Zope 3 developers designed a new `i18n` namespace, which is well documented at `http://dev.zope.org/Zope3/ZPTInternationalizationSupport`. The three most common attributes are `i18n:domain`, `i18n:translate`, and `i18n:attributes`. Note that the `i18n` namespace has been back-ported to Zope 2 as well, so you might be familiar with it already.

The cleanest page template in the `browser` package is `details.pt`, so let's internationalize it first:

```
01 <html metal:use-macro="context/@@standard_macros/page">
02   <body>
03     <div metal:fill-slot="body" i18n:domain="messageboard">
04
05       <h1 i18n:translate="">Message Details</h1>
06
07       <div class="row">
08           <div class="label" i18n:translate="">Title</div>
09           <div class="field" tal:content="context/title" />
10       </div>
11
12       <div class="row">
13           <div class="label" i18n:translate="">Author</div>
14           <div class="field" tal:content="view/author"/>
15       </div>
16
17       <div class="row">
18           <div class="label" i18n:translate="">Date/Time</div>
19           <div class="field" tal:content="view/modified"/>
20       </div>
21
22       <div class="row">
23           <div class="label" i18n:translate="">Parent</div>
24           <div class="field" tal:define="info view/parent_info">
25             <a href="../"
26                 tal:condition="info"
27                 tal:content="info/title" />
28           </div>
29       </div>
30
```

```
31            <div class="row">
32                <div class="label" i18n:translate="">Body</div>
33                <div class="field" tal:content="structure context/body"/>
34            </div>
35
36        </div>
37    </body>
38 </html>
```

In the preceding code block, note the following:

- Line 3: The best place for the domain specification is this `div` tag because it is inside a specific slot and will not influence other template files' domain settings.
- Lines 8, 13, 18, 23, and 32: `i18n:translate=""` just causes the content of the `div` tag to be translated.

Note that there is no need here to use `i18n:attributes`. However, when you deal with buttons, you use this instruction quite often. Here is an example:

```
01 <input type="submit" value="Add" i18n:attributes="value add-button" />
```

Similarly to `tal:attributes`, the `value` attribute value is replaced by the translation of `add-button`, or it can remain as the default string (`Add`) if no translation is found.

This is really everything that is needed for page templates.

Step 3: Internationalizing ZCML

Internationalizing ZCML is a one-time, one-step process. All you need to do is to add a `i18n_domain="messageboard"` attribute assignment to your `configure` tag in the main `configure.zcml` file. The directive author needs to specify which attribute values should be converted to message IDs, so you should not have to worry about anything else. All this might seem a bit magical, but it is explicit and an incredibly powerful feature of Zope 3's translation system because it minimizes the overhead of internationalizing ZCML code.

Setting the `i18n_domain="messageboard"` attribute gets rid of all the warnings you have experienced until now when you start up Zope 3.

Step 4: Creating Language Directories

The directory structure of the translations has to follow a strict format because the Zope 3 developers have tried to keep it gettext compatible. By convention, you keep all message catalogs and message catalog templates in a directory called `locales`, which you should create now. This directory typically contains the message catalog template file (with the extension `.pot`) and the various language directories, such as `en`. Because you want to create a translation for English and German, you should create the directories `en` and `de`.

Now comes the part that might not make sense at first. The language directories do not contain the message catalog directly, but they contain another directory, called `LC_MESSAGES`. You should create this directory in each of the language directories.

Because English is the default language, you always want it to use the default value. Therefore, the message catalog can be totally empty (or just contain the metadata). You should create a file called `messageboard.po` in the `locales/en/LC_MESSAGES` directory and add the following comment and metadata to it:

```
01 # This file contains no message ids because the messageboard's default
02 # language is English
03 msgid ""
04 msgstr ""
05 "Project-Id-Version: messageboard\n"
06 "MIME-Version: 1.0\n"
07 "Content-Type: text/plain; charset=UTF-8\n"
08 "Content-Transfer-Encoding: 8bit\n"
```

Now you are done with the preparations. Before you can localize the message board, you need to create the message catalogs, as described in the next section.

Step 5: Extracting Translatable Strings

Zope provides a very powerful extraction tool for grabbing all translatable text strings from Python, page template and ZCML files. With each translatable string, the file and line number are recorded, and then they are later added as a comment in the message catalog template file.

After all strings are collected and duplicates are merged into single entries, the tool saves the strings in a message catalog template file called *domain*.pot. This is the beginning of localization. From this point on, you are only concerned about using the template to create translations.

You can find the extraction tool, called `i18nextract`, in the *Zope3-Instance*/bin directory. Before you execute the tool, you should add your Zope 3 source directory to `PYTHONPATH` so that all necessary modules are found. In `bash`, you can set `PYTHONPATH` by using this:

```
export PYTHONPATH=$PYTHONPATH:Zope3-Instance/lib/python
```

To execute the tool, you need to go to the `messageboard` directory and enter the following command, making sure that you enter the absolute path for *Zope3-Instance* because the tool does not work well with symlinks:

```
python2.3 Zope3-Instance/bin/i18nextract -d messageboard -p ./ -o ./locales
```

This extracts all translatable strings from the `messageboard` package and stores the template file as `messageboard/locales/messageboard.pot`.

As you can see, the tool supports three options plus a help option:

- **-h / --help**—This option prints the help information for the i18nextract tool on the screen and exits.

- **-d / --domain** *<domain>*—This option specifies the domain—in this case, messageboard—that is supposed to be extracted.

- **-p / --path** *<path>*—<path> specifies the package that is searched for translatable strings. In this case, you just use ./ because you are already in the package.

- **-o** *<dir>*—This option specifies a directory, relative to the package in which to put the output translation template, which is commonly ./locales in add-on packages.

If you want to update the Zope 3 core message catalog template file, you simply run the extraction tool without specifying any options.

Step 6: Translating Message Strings

Now that you have a message catalog template file, you can finally create a translation. Because you do not have existing message catalogs, you can simply copy the .pot template file to the language you want to localize. In Unix you can just use the following from the locales directory:

```
cp messageboard.pot de/LC_MESSAGES/messageboard.po
```

You need to open de/LC_MESSAGES/messageboard.po in your favorite translation tool or a text editor. However, it is strongly recommended that you use a gettext-specific translation tool because that will guarantee format integrity. Some of the choices include KBabel and the Vim/Emacs gettext modes.

KBabel seems to be the most advanced tool and is becoming a standard application for localization of free software. It has many functions that make it easy for translators to do their job efficiently. KBabel is a fantastic tool that allows you, for example, to walk only through all untranslated or fuzzy strings and helps in managing the message strings by providing message numbers and statistics.

When you are done with the translations, you can save the changes, and you should be all set.

Now you have a translation, but what happens if you develop new code and you need to update the template and catalog files? For creating the template, you do nothing different because a template can be created over and over from scratch. But creating an actual catalog isn't so easy because you do not want to lose existing translations. The gettext utilities that come with every Linux system have a nice command-line tool called msgmerge (for Windows, you can use Cygwin's version of the gettext packages). msgmerge merges all changes of the .pot file into the message catalog, keeping all comments and existing translations intact and even marking changed translations as fuzzy.

Here is how you can use the tool from the locales directory:

```
msgmerge -U de/LC_MESSAGES/messageboard.po ./messageboard.pot
```

Step 7: Compiling and Registering Message Catalogs

Before you can use your new translations, you need to compile the message catalogs into a more efficient binary format and then register the `locales` directory as a message catalog container.

To compile the catalogs, you go to the directory and type this:

```
msgfmt messageboard.po -o messageboard.mo
```

The `msgfmt` program is part of the gettext tools, which you need to have installed (as for the `msgmerge` tool) to successfully execute the preceding command.

> **Note**
>
> If you have trouble keeping the extensions `.po` and `.mo` in mind, here is a tip: The *p* of the `.po` extension can stand for people comprehensible, and the *m* in `.mo` can stand for machine comprehensible.

To register the `locales` directory as a translation container, you open the main `configure.zcml` file for the message board and register the `i18n` namespace as follows in the `configure` tag:

```
01 xmlns:i18n="http://namespaces.zope.org/i18n"
```

Now you register the directory by using the following:

```
01 <i18n:registerTranslations directory="locales" />
```

The `i18n:registerTranslations` directive is smart enough to detect the directory structure and extract all the message catalogs for all the available languages.

> **Note**
>
> In the last few steps, keep in mind that the filename of the message catalog *must* be the domain name. The `registerTranslations` directive uses the filename to determine the domain, which is completely in line with the gettext standard.

Step 8: Trying the Translations

To test the translations, you need to restart Zope 3. Different languages are best tested with Mozilla because it allows you to quickly change the accepted languages of the browser itself. You can change the language in the preferences under Navigator Languages. You should put `German [de]` at the top of the list. The best view to test is the Preview view which you can reach with a URL similar to

```
http://localhost:8080/board-name/message-name/@@details.html.
```

You should now see all the attribute names (such as `Title`, which becomes `Titel`) in German (see Figure 18.1). You should also notice that the date is formatted in the German standard way, using *day.month.year* and 24-hour time.

Figure 18.1   The Message Details view in German.

Step 9: Updating Translations on-the-Fly

While you're translating a package, it might be cumbersome to restart Zope 3 just to update translations. For this reason, a process control called the Translation Domain control (`http://localhost:8080/++etc++process/@@TranslationDomain.html`) was created that allows you to update message catalogs at runtime, without needing to restart the server (see Figure 18.2). You should see the new `messageboard` domain for German (`de`) on this screen.

Figure 18.2   Translation domain control.

Content Components—Advanced Techniques

Having a well-working basic message board is great, but it certainly isn't the greatest invention ever. This part presents some more advanced APIs.

Chapter 19: Events and Subscribers

Events and subscribers are a very powerful idea. This chapter explains how to write your own event subscribers by implementing a mail subscription feature for messages.

Chapter 20: Approval Workflow for Messages

This chapter shows how to integrate an editorial workflow for a content component.

Chapter 21: Providing Online Help Screens

Every good application should have online help screens; in this chapter you'll learn how to implement them.

Chapter 22: Object-to-Filesystem Mapping, Using FTP as an Example

Although there are standard hooks for content objects to be handled by FTP, it is often useful to write your own FTP handlers so that the file-to-object conversion (and vice versa) seems more natural.

Chapter 23: Availability of Content via XML–RPC

If you want to make XML–RPC calls on your content objects, you must write a view that declares the methods and define how their output is mapped to a type that XML–RPC understands.

Chapter 24: Developing New Skins

This chapter gives instructions on how to implement a new skin, so that you can develop sites that do not look like the Zope Management Interface but still allow you to make use of the autogeneration of forms.

19

Events and Subscribers

Difficulty

Contributor

Skills

- You should be comfortable with the topics covered in Part III, "Content Components—The Basics."
- You should feel comfortable with the component architecture.
- You should be familiar with annotations. Optional.

Problem/Task

Events are a powerful programming tool, and they are primary citizens in Zope 3. In this chapter you'll learn about the subscription of existing events by implementing a mail subscription system for messages. With this system, whenever a message is modified, subscribed users will receive an email message about the change. This will also demonstrate how annotations can be added to an object. The last part of this chapter talks about the theory of triggering events.

Y OU NEED TO DEVELOP TWO MAIN components in this chapter. The first is the mail subscription adapter for the message, which manages the subscription emails. The second component is the event subscriber, which listens for incoming events and starts the mailing process, if appropriate.

Step 1: Developing the Mail Subscription Interface

You need to have an interface for managing the subscriptions for a particular message (that is, adding, deleting, and getting email addresses). Therefore, you need to add the following interface to the `interfaces` module:

```
01 class IMailSubscriptions(Interface):
02     """This interface allows you to retrieve a list of E-mails for
03     mailings. In our context these are messages."""
04
05     def getSubscriptions():
06         """Return a list of E-mails."""
07
08     def addSubscriptions(emails):
09         """Add a bunch of subscriptions; one would be okay too."""
10
11     def removeSubscriptions(emails):
12         """Remove a set of subscriptions."""
```

This code is simple enough that no further explanation is needed at this point.

Step 2: Implementing the Mail Subscription Adapter

The `MailSubscriptions` implementation should be straightforward. The subscriptions are implemented as a simple tuple data structure, and they are accessible via the annotations adapter. Note that the implementation makes no assumption about the type of annotation that is going to be used; that is, you might use the `AttributeAnnotations` out of pure convenience, but the data could just as well be stored in LDAP without having any effect on the `MailSubscriptions` implementation.

Because there is no need to create a new module, you should add the following code to the `message.py` file:

```
01 from zope.app.annotation.interfaces import IAnnotations
02 from book.messageboard.interfaces import IMailSubscriptions
03
04 SubscriberKey='http://www.zope.org/messageboard#1.0/MailSubscriptions/emails'
05
06
07 class MailSubscriptions:
08     """Message Mail Subscriptions."""
09
10     implements(IMailSubscriptions)
11     __used_for__ = IMessage
12
```

```
13    def __init__(self, context):
14        self.context = self.__parent__ = context
15        self._annotations = IAnnotations(context)
16        if not self._annotations.get(SubscriberKey):
17            self._annotations[SubscriberKey] = ()
18
19    def getSubscriptions(self):
20        "See book.messageboard.interfaces.IMailSubscriptions"
21        return self._annotations[SubscriberKey]
22
23    def addSubscriptions(self, emails):
24        "See book.messageboard.interfaces.IMailSubscriptions"
25        subscribers = list(self._annotations[SubscriberKey])
26        for email in emails:
27            if email not in subscribers:
28                subscribers.append(email.strip())
29        self._annotations[SubscriberKey] = tuple(subscribers)
30
31    def removeSubscriptions(self, emails):
32        "See book.messageboard.interfaces.IMailSubscriptions"
33        subscribers = list(self._annotations[SubscriberKey])
34        for email in emails:
35            if email in subscribers:
36                subscribers.remove(email)
37        self._annotations[SubscriberKey] = tuple(subscribers)
```

In the preceding code block, note the following:

- Line 4: This is the fully qualified subscriber annotation key that will uniquely identify this annotation data. In this case, a URL is used, but dotted names are also common.

- Line 11: Although this declaration is not needed, it clearly signifies that this implementation is an adapter for IMessage objects.

- Line 14: Because this adapter will use annotations, it will be a trusted adapter, meaning that it will be a proxied object. Each proxied object must provide a location (at least through a __parent__ attribute) so that permission declarations can be found. Otherwise, only global permission settings would be available.

- Line 15: Here you get the Annotations adapter that will provide you with a mapping object in which you will store the annotations. Note that this statement says nothing about the type of annotation you are about to get.

- Lines 16–17: You make sure an entry for your subscriber key exists. If not, you create an empty one.

- Lines 19–37: There is nothing interesting going on here. The only fact worth mentioning is the use of tuples instead of lists. Tuples make the code a bit more complex, but they are not mutable, so they are automatically saved in the ZODB if you have AttributeAnnotations.

This is pretty much everything there is to the subscription part of this step. You can now register the new component via ZCML, using the adapter directive:

```
01 <adapter
02    factory=".message.MailSubscriptions"
03    provides=".interfaces.IMailSubscriptions"
04    for=".interfaces.IMessage"
05    permission="book.messageboard.Add"
06    trusted="true" />
```

In the preceding code block, note the following:

- Lines 2–4: As for the ISized adapter, you specify the necessary adapter registration information.
- Line 6: If an adapter is declared trusted, then its context (the object being passed into the adapter constructor) will *not* be security proxied. This is necessary so that the Annotations adapter can use the __annotations__ attribute to store the annotations. If the adapter is not trusted and the context is security proxied, then a ForbiddenAttribute error will be raised whenever you try to access the annotations.
- Line 5: When an adapter is trusted, the adapter itself is security proxied. Therefore, you need to define a permission that is required to use the adapter.

Step 3: Testing the Adapter

The MailSubscriptions tests are as straightforward as the implementation. In the doc string of the MailSubscriptions class, add the following documented testing code:

```
01 Verify the interface implementation
02
03 >>> from zope.interface.verify import verifyClass
04 >>> verifyClass(IMailSubscriptions, MailSubscriptions)
05 True
06
07 Create a subscription instance of a message
08
09 >>> msg = Message()
10 >>> sub = MailSubscriptions(msg)
11
12 Verify that we have initially no subscriptions and then add some.
13
14 >>> sub.getSubscriptions()
15 ()
16 >>> sub.addSubscriptions(('foo@bar.com',))
17 >>> sub.getSubscriptions()
18 ('foo@bar.com',)
```

```
19 >>> sub.addSubscriptions(('blah@bar.com',))
20 >>> sub.getSubscriptions()
21 ('foo@bar.com', 'blah@bar.com')
22 >>> sub.addSubscriptions(('doh@bar.com',))
23 >>> sub.getSubscriptions()
24 ('foo@bar.com', 'blah@bar.com', 'doh@bar.com')
25
26 Now let's also check that we can remove entries.
27
28 >>> sub.removeSubscriptions(('foo@bar.com',))
29 >>> sub.getSubscriptions()
30 ('blah@bar.com', 'doh@bar.com')
```

When you construct a new mail subscription adapter instance, the values should still be there:

```
01 >>> sub1 = MailSubscriptions(msg)
02 >>> sub1.getSubscriptions()
03 ('blah@bar.com', 'doh@bar.com')
```

In the preceding code block, note the following:

- Lines 3–5: You do a very detailed analysis to ensure that the `MailSubscriptions` class implements the `IMailSubscriptions` interface.

- Lines 7–10: In doc tests, it helps very much if you emphasize how you set up the test case. Here, you make that very explicit by creating a separate section and adding some explanation to it.

- Lines 12–24: You check that you can retrieve the list of subscribers and add new ones as well.

- Lines 26–30: You make sure deleting subscriptions works as well.

- Lines 32–37: When you create a new adapter that uses the same message, the subscriptions should still be available. This ensures that the data is not lost when the adapter is destroyed. An even stronger test would be that persistence also works.

Note that there is no check for the case that the annotation is not there. This is because the `MailSubscriptions` constructor should make sure the annotation is available, even though it means simply creating an empty storage, so you have definitely covered this case in the implementation.

Because the adapter uses annotations, you need to do some setup of the component architecture to run the tests. You already bring the services up for the tests, but now you also have to register an adapter to provide the annotations. Therefore, you have to write a custom `setUp()` method and use it. The testing code in `tests/test_message.py` changes to this:

```
01 from zope.interface import classImplements
02
03 from zope.app.annotation.attribute import AttributeAnnotations
```

```
04 from zope.app.annotation.interfaces import IAnnotations
05 from zope.app.annotation.interfaces import IAttributeAnnotatable
06 from zope.app.tests import placelesssetup
07 from zope.app.tests import ztapi
08
09 def setUp(test):
10     placelesssetup.setUp()
11     classImplements(Message, IAttributeAnnotatable)
12     ztapi.provideAdapter(IAttributeAnnotatable, IAnnotations,
13                          AttributeAnnotations)
14
15 def test_suite():
16     return unittest.TestSuite((
17         DocTestSuite('book.messageboard.message',
18                      setUp=setUp, tearDown=placelesssetup.tearDown),
19         unittest.makeSuite(Test),
20         ))
```

In the preceding code block, note the following:

- Line 7: The `ztapi` module contains some very useful convenience functions to set up the component architecture for a test, such as view and adapter registration.

- Line 9: Note that the `setUp()` function expects a `test` argument, which is an instance of `DocTest`. You can use this object to provide global test variables.

- Line 11: You usually use ZCML to declare that `Message` implements `IAttributeAnnotatable`. Because ZCML is not executed for unit tests, you have to do it manually here.

- Lines 12–13: You set up the adapter that allows you to look up an annotation adapter for any object that claims to provide the `IAttributeAnnotatable` interface.

You should now run the tests and ensure that they pass.

Step 4: Providing a View for the Mail Subscription

The last piece you have to provide is a view to manage the subscriptions via the Web. The page template (`browser/subscriptions.pt`) could look like this:

```
01 <html metal:use-macro="context/@@standard_macros/view">
02   <body>
03     <div metal:fill-slot="body" i18n:domain="messageboard">
04
05       <form action="changeSubscriptions.html" method="post">
06
07         <div class="row">
```

```
08                    <div class="label"
09                        i18n:translate="">Current Subscriptions</div>
10                    <div class="field">
11                  <div tal:repeat="email view/subscriptions">
12                        <input type="checkbox" name="remails:list"
13                            value="" tal:attributes="value email">
14                        <div tal:replace="email">zope3@zope3.org</div>
15                    </div>
16                    <input type="submit" name="REMOVE" value="Remove"
17                        i18n:attributes="value remove-button">
18                </div>
19            </div>
20
21            <div class="row">
22                <div class="label" i18n:translate="">
23                  Enter new Users (separate by 'Return')
24                </div>
25                <div class="field">
26                <textarea name="emails" cols="40" rows="10"></textarea>
27                </div>
28            </div>
29
30                <div class="row">
31                  <div class="controls">
32                    <input type="submit" value="Refresh"
33                    i18n:attributes="value refresh-button" />
34                    <input type="submit" name="ADD" value="Add"
35                        i18n:attributes="value add-button" />
36                  </div>
37                </div>
38
39        </form>
40
41      </div>
42    </body>
43 </html>
```

In the preceding code block, note the following:

- Lines 7–19: You list the existing subscriptions, and then you can select them for removal.
- Lines 21–37: You provide a text area for adding new subscriptions. Each email address should be separated by a newline (that is, there should be one email address per line).

The supporting view Python class then simply needs to provide a subscriptions() method (see line 11 in the preceding code block) and a form action. You place the following code in browser/message.py:

```
01 from book.messageboard.interfaces import IMailSubscriptions
02
03 class MailSubscriptions:
04
05     def subscriptions(self):
06         return IMailSubscriptions(self.context).getSubscriptions()
07
08     def change(self):
09         if 'ADD' in self.request:
10             emails = self.request['emails'].split('\n')
11             IMailSubscriptions(self.context).addSubscriptions(emails)
12         elif 'REMOVE' in self.request:
13             emails = self.request['remails']
14             if isinstance(emails, (str, unicode)):
15                 emails = [emails]
16             IMailSubscriptions(self.context).removeSubscriptions(emails)
17
18         self.request.response.redirect('./@@subscriptions.html')
```

In the preceding code block, note the following:

- Lines 9 and 12: You simply use the name of the submit button to decide which action the user intended.

The rest of the code should be pretty straightforward. You can register the view as follows:

```
01 <pages
02     for="book.messageboard.interfaces.IMessage"
03     class=".message.MailSubscriptions"
04     permission="book.messageboard.Edit"
05     >
06   <page
07       name="subscriptions.html"
08       template="subscriptions.pt"
09       menu="zmi_views" title="Subscriptions"
10       />
11   <page
12       name="changeSubscriptions.html"
13       attribute="change"
14       />
15 </pages>
```

In the preceding code block, note the following:

- Line 1: The `browser:pages` directive allows you to register several pages for an interface, using the same view class and permission at once. This is particularly useful for views that provide a lot of functionality.
- Lines 6–10: This page uses a template for creating the HTML.

- Lines 11–14: This view, on the other hand, uses an attribute of the view class. Usually, methods on the view class do not return HTML but redirect the browser to another page.

- Line 9: You make sure the `Subscriptions` view becomes a tab for the `Message` object.

It is amazing how compact the `browser:pages` and `browser:page` directives make the registration. In the early development stages, the Zope 3 development team did not have this directive, and everything had to be registered via `browser:view`, which required a lot of repetitive boilerplate ZCML and Python code.

Step 5: Writing an Event Subscriber

Until now, you have not heard a word about events. But that is about to change because the next task is to implement the subscriber object. The generic event system is very simple: It consists of a list of subscribers and a `notify(event)` function. You can subscribe event subscribers to the event system by appending them to the list. To unsubscribe an object, you must remove it from the list. Subscribers do not have to be any special type of objects; they merely have to be callable. The `notify(event)` function takes an object (the event) as a parameter; it then iterates though the list of subscribers and calls each subscriber with the event as argument.

This means you have to implement a `__call__(event)` method as part of your message mailer API in order to make it a subscriber. The entire `MessageMailer` class, which you should put in the `message` module, should look like this:

```
01 from zope.app import zapi
02 from zope.app.container.interfaces import IObjectAddedEvent
03 from zope.app.container.interfaces import IObjectRemovedEvent
04 from zope.app.event.interfaces import IObjectModifiedEvent
05 from zope.app.mail.interfaces import IMailDelivery
06
07 class MessageMailer:
08     """Class to handle all outgoing mail."""
09
10     def __call__(self, event):
11         """Called by the event system."""
12         if IMessage.providedBy(event.object):
13             if IObjectAddedEvent.providedBy(event):
14                 self.handleAdded(event.object)
15             elif IObjectModifiedEvent.providedBy(event):
16                 self.handleModified(event.object)
17             elif IObjectRemovedEvent.providedBy(event):
18                 self.handleRemoved(event.object)
19
20     def handleAdded(self, object):
21         subject = 'Added: '+zapi.getName(object)
```

```
22           emails = self.getAllSubscribers(object)
23           body = object.body
24           self.mail(emails, subject, body)
25
26       def handleModified(self, object):
27           subject = 'Modified: '+zapi.getName(object)
28           emails = self.getAllSubscribers(object)
29           body = object.body
30           self.mail(emails, subject, body)
31
32       def handleRemoved(self, object):
33           subject = 'Removed: '+zapi.getName(object)
34           emails = self.getAllSubscribers(object)
35           body = subject
36           self.mail(emails, subject, body)
37
38       def getAllSubscribers(self, object):
39           """Retrieves all email subscribers."""
40           emails = ()
41           msg = object
42           while IMessage.providedBy(msg):
43               emails += tuple(IMailSubscriptions(msg).getSubscriptions())
44               msg = zapi.getParent(msg)
45           return emails
46
47       def mail(self, toaddrs, subject, body):
48           """Mail out the Message Board change message."""
49           if not toaddrs:
50               return
51           msg = 'Subject: %s\n\n\n%s' %(subject, body)
52           mail_utility = zapi.getUtility(IMailDelivery, 'msgboard-delivery')
53           mail_utility.send('mailer@messageboard.org' , toaddrs, msg)
54
55 mailer = MessageMailer()
```

In the preceding code block, note the following:

- Lines 2–4: You want the subscriber to handle add, edit, and delete events. You import the interfaces of these events so that you can differentiate among them.

- Lines 10–18: This is the heart of the subscriber and this chapter. When an event occurs, the __call__() method is called. First, you need to check whether the event was caused by a change of an IMessage object; if so, you need to check which event was triggered. Based on the event that occurred, a corresponding handler method is called.

- Lines 20–36: You specify the three handler methods that handle the various events. Note that the modified event handler should really generate a nice diff instead of sending the entire message again.

- Lines 38–45: You retrieve all the subscriptions of the current message and all its ancestors. This way, someone who subscribed to the message `Hello Everyone` will also get emailed about all responses to `Hello Everyone`.

- Lines 47–53: Here you get a quick introduction to the Mail Delivery utility. Note how simple the `send()` method of the Mail Delivery utility is; it is the same API as for `smtplib`. The policy and configuration on how the mail is sent is fully configured via ZCML. The mail delivery is configured in the next code snippet.

- Lines 60: You can only subscribe *callable* objects to the event system, so you need to instantiate the `MessageMailer` component.

Finally, you need to register the message mailer component to the event service and set up the mail utility correctly. To do these things, you need to go to your configuration file and register the following namespace in the `configure` element:

```
01 xmlns:mail="http://namespaces.zope.org/mail"
```

Next, you set up the mail utility:

```
01 <mail:smtpMailer name="msgboard-smtp" hostname="localhost" port="25" />
02
03 <mail:queuedDelivery
04     name="msgboard-delivery"
05     permission="zope.SendMail"
06     queuePath="./mail-queue"
07     mailer="msgboard-smtp" />
```

In the preceding code block, note the following:

- Line 1: Here you decide to send the mail via an SMTP server from `localhost` on the standard port 25. You could instead send the mail via the command-line tool `sendmail`.

- Lines 3–7: The Queued Mail Delivery utility does not send mail out directly; rather, it schedules mail to be sent out independently of the current transaction. This has huge advantages because the request does not have to wait until the mail is sent. However, this version of the mail utility requires a directory to store email messages until they are sent. Here, you specify the `mail-queue` directory inside the `messageboard` package. `MessageMailer` uses the value of the attribute `name` to retrieve the Queued Mail Delivery utility. Another mail utility is the Direct Mail Delivery utility, which blocks the request until the email messages are sent.

Now you register your message mailer object for the events you want to observe:

```
01 <subscriber
02     factory=".message.mailer"
03     for="zope.app.event.interfaces.IObjectModifiedEvent" />
04
05 <subscriber
```

```
06        factory=".message.mailer"
07        for="zope.app.container.interfaces.IObjectAddedEvent" />
08
09 <subscriber
10        factory=".message.mailer"
11        for="zope.app.container.interfaces.IObjectRemovedEvent" />
```

The `subscriber` directive adds a new subscriber (specified via the `factory` attribute) to the subscriber list. The `for` attribute specifies the interface the event must implement for this subscriber to be called. You might be wondering at this point why such strange attribute names are used. In the Zope 3 application server, event subscriptions are realized via a special kind of adapter, called a *subscription adapter*. So internally, you registered an adapter from `IObjectModifiedEvent` to `None`, for example. See the section "The Theory behind Events" at the end of this chapter for more details.

You should be careful before you try the new code: You should write some unit tests before testing the code practically.

Step 6: Testing the Message Mailer

So far in Part III, you have not written any complicated tests. That changes now. First of all, you have to bring up quite a bit more of the Zope 3 framework to do the tests. The `test_message.py` module's `setUp()` function needs to register the location adapters and the message mail subscription adapter. So it should look like this:

```
01 from zope.app.location.traversing import LocationPhysicallyLocatable
02 from zope.app.location.interfaces import ILocation
03 from zope.app.traversing.interfaces import IPhysicallyLocatable
04
05 from book.messageboard.interfaces import IMailSubscriptions
06 from book.messageboard.interfaces import IMessage
07 from book.messageboard.message import MailSubscriptions
08
09 def setUp(test):
10        ...
11        ztapi.provideAdapter(ILocation, IPhysicallyLocatable,
12                             LocationPhysicallyLocatable)
13        ztapi.provideAdapter(IMessage, IMailSubscriptions, MailSubscriptions)
```

In the preceding code block, note the following:

- Lines 1–3 and 11–12: This adapter allows you to use the API to access parents of objects or even the entire object path.
- Lines 5–7 and 13: You simply register the mail subscription adapter that you just developed so that the mailer can find the subscribers in the messages.
- Line 10: The three dots stand for the existing content of the function.

Now all the preparations are made, and you can start writing the doc tests. Let's look at the `getAllSubscribers()` method tests. You basically want to produce a message and add a reply to it. Each of these two messages will have one subscriber. When the `getAllSubscribers()` method is called, using the reply message, the subscribers for the original message and the reply should be returned. Here is the test code, which you should place in the `getAllSubscribers()` doc string:

```
01 Here a small demonstration of retrieving all subscribers.
02
03 >>> from zope.interface import directlyProvides
04 >>> from zope.app.traversing.interfaces import IContainmentRoot
05
06 Create a parent message as it would be located in the message
07 board. Also add a subscriber to the message.
08
09 >>> msg1 = Message()
10 >>> directlyProvides(msg1, IContainmentRoot)
11 >>> msg1.__name__ = 'msg1'
12 >>> msg1.__parent__ = None
13 >>> msg1_sub = MailSubscriptions(msg1)
14 >>> msg1_sub.context.__annotations__[SubscriberKey] = ('foo@bar.com',)
15
16 Create a reply to the first message and also give it a subscriber.
17
18 >>> msg2 = Message()
19 >>> msg2_sub = MailSubscriptions(msg2)
20 >>> msg2_sub.context.__annotations__[SubscriberKey] = ('blah@bar.com',)
21 >>> msg1['msg2'] = msg2
22
23 When asking for all subscriptions of message 2, we should get the
24 subscriber from message 1 as well.
25
26 >>> mailer.getAllSubscribers(msg2)
27 ('blah@bar.com', 'foo@bar.com')
```

In the preceding code block, note the following:

- Lines 3–4: You import some of the general functions and interfaces you are going to use for the test.

- Lines 6–14: You create the first message. Note that the message must provide the `IContainmentRoot` interface (line 10). This signals the traversal lookup to stop looking any further when this message is found. Using the mail subscription adapter (lines 13–14), you now register a subscriber for the message.

- Lines 16–21: Here you create the reply to the first message. The parent and name of the second message will be automatically added during the __setitem__() call.

- Lines 23–27: The mailer should now be able to retrieve both subscriptions. If the test passes, all subscribers were retrieved correctly.

Finally, you test the __call__() method directly; this method is the heart of this object and the only *public* method. For the notification to work properly, you have to create and register an IMailDelivery utility with the name msgboard-delivery. Because you do not want to actually send out mail during a test, it is wise to write a stub implementation of the utility. Therefore, you should start your doc tests for the __call__() method by adding the following mail delivery implementation to the doc string of the method:

```
01 >>> mail_result = []
02
03 >>> from zope.interface import implements
04 >>> from zope.app.mail.interfaces import IMailDelivery
05
06 >>> class MailDeliveryStub(object):
07 ...     implements(IMailDelivery)
08 ...
09 ...     def send(self, fromaddr, toaddrs, message):
10 ...         mail_result.append((fromaddr, toaddrs, message))
11
12 >>> from zope.app.tests import ztapi
13 >>> ztapi.provideUtility(IMailDelivery, MailDeliveryStub(),
14 ...                      name='msgboard-delivery')
```

In the preceding code block, note the following:

- Line 1: The mail requests are stored in this *global* variable, so you can make test assertions about the mail that was supposedly sent.
- Lines 6–10: Luckily, the mail utility requires only the send() method to be implemented, and in it you simply store the data.
- Lines: 12–14: Using the ztapi API, you can quickly register the utility. You need to be careful that you get the name right; otherwise, the test will not work.

So far, so good. As for the previous test, you now have to create a message and add a subscriber:

```
01 Create a message.
02
03 >>> from zope.interface import directlyProvides
04 >>> from zope.app.traversing.interfaces import IContainmentRoot
05
06 >>> msg = Message()
07 >>> directlyProvides(msg, IContainmentRoot)
08 >>> msg.__name__ = 'msg'
09 >>> msg.__parent__ = None
10 >>> msg.title = 'Hello'
11 >>> msg.body = 'Hello World!'
12
```

```
13 Add a subscription to message.
14
15 >>> msg_sub = MailSubscriptions(msg)
16 >>> msg_sub.context.__annotations__[SubscriberKey] = ('foo@bar.com',)
```

This is equivalent to what you did earlier in this chapter. Finally, you create a modification event that uses the message and send it to the __call__() method. You then probe the global mail_result variable for the correct functioning of the method.

Now, you create an event and send it to the message mailer object:

```
01 >>> from zope.app.event.objectevent import ObjectModifiedEvent
02 >>> event = ObjectModifiedEvent(msg)
03 >>> mailer(event)
04
05 >>> from pprint import pprint
06 >>> pprint(mail_result)
07 [('mailer@messageboard.org',
08   ('foo@bar.com',),
09   'Subject: Modified: msg\\n\\n\\nHello World!')]
```

In the preceding code block, note the following:

- Lines 1–2: In this particular test, you use the object modification event. You can initiate any IObjectEvent event by passing the affected object as an argument to the constructor of the event.

- Line 3: Here you notify the mailer that an object has been modified. Note that the mailer object is an instance of the MessageMailer class and is initialized at the end of the module.

- Lines 5–9: You use the pretty print (pprint) module, which comes in very handy when outputting complex data structures.

You are finally done now. You should run the tests to verify your implementation and then head to the next section to see how you can give this code a real run.

Step 7: Using the New Mail Subscription System

Before you can use the new system, you have to restart Zope and make sure in boots up properly. Then you can go to the management interface and view a particular message. As you might notice, you have a new tab called Subscriptions, which you should click.

In the Subscriptions view is a text area in which you can enter subscription email addresses, which will receive email messages when the message or any children are changed. When you add a test email address, you need to make sure that the email address exists and is your own, so you can verify the message's arrival. You need to click the Add button to add the email message to the subscriber list. When the screen returns, you see this email message appear under Current Subscriptions, with a check box before it, so you can delete it later, if you wish.

Next, you need to switch to the Edit view, where you should modify the message body a bit and submit the change. You should notice that the screen returns almost immediately, but your message has not necessarily arrived yet. This is because the Queued Mail Delivery utility sends the email messages on separate threads. However, depending on the speed of your email server, a few moments later you should receive an appropriate email message.

The Theory Behind Events

Although this chapter has demonstrated a classical use of events from an application developer point of view, it is not quite the whole story. So far, you have discovered the use of the basic event system.

This chapter has not explained how Zope 3 uses this system. As mentioned before, the `subscriber` directive does not append the message mailer instance to the subscription list directly, as you may expect. Instead, it registers the message mailer as a "subscription adapter" that adapts an event by providing some event interface, such as `IObjectModifiedEvent`, to `None`, because it explicitly does not provide any special interface. The difference between regular and subscription adapters is that you can register several subscription adapters that have the same required and provided interfaces. When requested, all matching adapters are returned. This allows you to have multiple subscribers for an event.

The Zope application server adds a special dispatch subscriber (`zope.app.event.dispatching`) that forwards the notification to all adapter-based subscriptions. Figure 19.1 shows how an event flows through the various parts of the system to the subscriber that will make use of the event. This example is based on the code developed in this chapter.

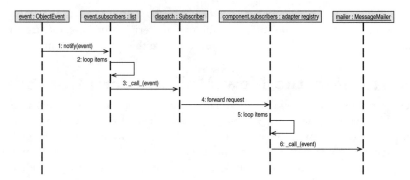

Figure 19.1   An event being distributed to its subscribers.

A special kind of subscriber is an event channel, which changes an event and redistributes it or serves it as an event filter. You could think of event channels as middlemen.

This chapter could have been written using event channels, with a subscriber that forwards an event only if the object provides IMessage. An implementation could look as follows:

```
01 def filterEvents(event):
02     if IMessage.providedBy(event.object):
03         zope.event.notify(event.object, event)
```

The actual mailer would then be a multi-adapter that adapts from both the message and the event:

```
01 class MessageMailer:
02
03     __call__(self, message, event):
04         ...
```

Multi-subscription-adapters are registered in ZCML as follows:

```
01 <subscriber
02   factory = ".message.mailer"
03   for = ".interface.IMessage
04           zope.app.event.interface.IObjectEvent" />
```

Figure 19.2 shows the modified sequence diagram.

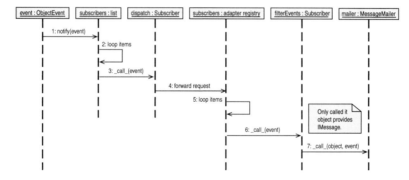

Figure 19.2   Modification of the even publication, using an event channel.

Note that sometimes events are hard to debug. In such cases, it is extremely helpful to write a small subscriber that somehow logs all events. In the simplest case, this can be a one-line function that prints the string representation of the event in the console. To subscribe a subscriber to all events, you simply specify for="*" in the zope:subscriber directive.

Approval Workflow for Messages

Difficulty

Contributor

Skills

- You need to have a good understanding of the component architecture and ZCML.
- You need to be familiar with the `messageboard` package so that you can easily follow the new extensions.
- Some familiarity with workflows and various solutions is helpful. Optional.

Problem/Task

Workflows are important in any company. Therefore, it is not surprising that software-based workflows have become a primary requirement for many computer systems, especially for content management systems (CMSs). In this chapter you'll add a publication workflow to the `messageboard` package.

ALTHOUGH THIS CHAPTER DOES NOT DEAL WITH every aspect of the `zope.app.workflow` package—for example, it does not explain how to create process definitions—it demonstrates the most common use cases by integrating a workflow into an existing content object package. The realization of the workflow is amazingly simple. Behind the simple front end, however, are a maze of interfaces, their implementations, and their presentation. Therefore, the goal of the last section of this chapter is to explain the framework from an architectural point of view.

Step 1: Making a Message Workflow-Aware

In order to make a content object workflow-aware, you simply have to tell the message that it can store workflow data. The simplest way is to add the following interface declaration to the `Message` content directive in the main configuration file:

```
01 <implements interface=
02    "zope.app.workflow.interfaces.IProcessInstanceContainerAdaptable"/>
```

Appropriate adapters for storing workflow data are already defined for objects that implement `IAnnotable`. Your message object does this already by implementing `IAttributeAnnotable`, as you can see in the content directive.

Now the object can contain workflows, and when you restart your browser, you should notice that `Message` instances now also have a Workflow tab, which is still totally empty.

Step 2: Creating a Workflow and Its Supporting Components via a Browser

At this point you need to create the workflow components themselves. As a first attempt, you are going to create all the components by hand because that process provides some enlightenment on how the entire workflow mechanism works.

After you start Zope 3, you need to go to the folder you want to add (or have already added) your messageboard. Then you go to Site Manager by clicking Manage Site; if the folder is not yet a site, you click Make a Site first. In the site manager, you then click the Tools tab.

If you just created the site, you next have to create a local utility service. You can accomplish this by clicking the Service Tool link. Then you click the Add button, select Utility Service on the next screen, enter a name (such as `utilities`), and confirm all this by clicking Add. When you're done with this process, you have a fully configured and activated a local utility service.

At this point you should go back to the tools overview screen. The next step is to define an actual workflow in terms of a process that contains states and transitions. Therefore, you need to click the Workflows link. Next, you add a workflow by clicking the Add button. For this workflow, you want to select Stateful Process Definition (which is likely to be your only choice); then you name the workflow `publish-message`. Next, you click the Add button, and the workflow is created and activated.

Because the stateful process definition component supports a nice XML import and export filter, it is best to define the process in XML. For later reference, you are going to store the workflow XML in a file and make it part of your package. Therefore, you need to open a new file called `workflow.xml` in the `messageboard` package and add the following process definitions to the file:

```
01 <?xml version="1.0"?>
02 <workflow type="StatefulWorkflow" title="Message Publication Review">
03    <schema name=""/>
```

```
04    <states>
05      <state name="INITIAL" title="initial" />
06      <state name="private" title="Private" />
07      <state name="pending" title="Pending Publication" />
08      <state name="published" title="Public" />
09    </states>
10    <transitions>
11
12      <transition
13          sourceState="published"
14          destinationState="private"
15          name="published_private"
16          title="Unpublish Message"
17          permission="book.messageboard.PublishContent"
18          triggerMode="Manual" />
19
20      <transition
21          sourceState="private"
22          destinationState="pending"
23          name="private_pending"
24          title="Submit Message"
25          permission="book.messageboard.Edit"
26          triggerMode="Manual" />
27
28      <transition
29          sourceState="INITIAL"
30          destinationState="private"
31          name="initial_private"
32          title="Make Private"
33          triggerMode="Automatic" />
34
35      <transition
36          sourceState="pending"
37          destinationState="published"
38          name="pending_published"
39          title="Publish Message"
40          permission="book.messageboard.PublishContent"
41          triggerMode="Manual" />
42
43      <transition
44          sourceState="pending"
45          destinationState="private"
46          name="pending_private"
47          title="Retract Message"
48          permission="book.messageboard.Edit"
49          triggerMode="Manual" />
50
```

```
51    <transition
52        sourceState="pending"
53        destinationState="private"
54        name="pending_private_reject"
55        title="Reject Message"
56        permission="book.messageboard.PublishContent"
57        triggerMode="Manual" />
58
59   </transitions>
60
61 </workflow>
```

In the preceding code block, note the following:

- Line 2: You define the workflow to be a stateful workflow—the only type that is currently implemented. `title` is the string under which the workflow will be known.

- Line 3: You do not have a particular data schema, so you can skip that. These schemas allow you to add additional workflow-relevant (object-specific) data to the workflow instances.

- Lines 4–9: You define the states in which a message can be. Again, `title` serves as a human-readable presentation of the state.

- Lines 10–59: This is a list of all possible transitions the object can undergo. The attributes of the transition directive are self-explanatory and do not need any further explanation.

After you save the XML file, you can click the newly created workflow (in the Workflows tool overview) and then click the Import/Export tab. Next, you copy the XML from the file and paste it into the text area of the screen. Then you click the Import button. The Import/Export screen returns, with a message saying "Import was successful!". You should also see the XML (probably formatted differently) at the bottom of the screen. If you now click Manage States, you should see the four states you just added via the XML import. The same is true for the Manage Transitions view.

You might have already noticed that the workflow requires a new permission named `book.messageboard.PublishContent` to be defined. Therefore, you need to go to the `messageboard` package's configuration file and add this permission:

```
01 <permission
02     id="book.messageboard.PublishContent"
03     title="Publish Message"
04     description="Publish Message."/>
```

In the `security.zcml` configuration file, you grant Editor the permission to publish content:

```
01 <grant
02     permission="book.messageboard.PublishContent"
03     role="book.messageboard.Editor"/>
```

Now you are finished creating a workflow and its supporting components and you should restart Zope 3. In the following section you'll see whether everything works.

Step 3: Assigning a Workflow

Now that your message is workflow-aware and a workflow has been created, you have to assign the workflow to `IMessage` objects. You do this via the Content Workflow Manager, which maps workflows to content objects.

Go to the site's `tools` site management folder. To do that, you go to the site's overview and select the Software tab. You can then enter the `tools` folder. When you are there, you should add a content workflow manager named `ContentWorkflows`. When you are done with that, you are automatically forwarded to the Registration view because the manager is just another utility. Next, you click the Register button, register the utility as `ContentWorkflows`, and click the Add button. You have now successfully registered and activated the utility.

The next step is to declare the workflow-to-interface mapping. To do so, you go to the Content/Process Registry tab of the Content Workflow Manager. On this page you should now see a list of many interfaces and a list of process definition names that contains only one entry—the name of the previously created workflow. You need to select the `book.messageboard.interface.IMessage` interface and select `publish-message` and click Add Mappings. The previous page should return, but this time with an entry below Available Mappings.

But how does the workflow get appended to a message object? The Content Workflow Manager is a subscriber to `IObjectCreated` events. If the created object implements an interface for which you have a workflow, then a process instance of that workflow is added to the object as an annotation. Note that you can assign many different workflows to an object. The Content Workflow Manager is subscribed as soon as you make it active as a utility, which you already did when you registered it.

Step 4: Testing the Workflow

The workflow you've created in this chapter will only work with new messages, of course. So, in the folder in which you created the workflow components, create a new message board and add a new message to it. If you now click the Workflows tab, you see that the tab is not empty anymore. In the selection box, you can see all the available workflows; currently, there should be only one, called Message Publication Review (remember the workflow title in the XML?). You can choose this workflow.

Below the selection box you can see the current status of the message, which is private at this point; remember, the transition from `initial` to `private` is automatic, based on the workflow definition. In the last entry, you now see the possible transitions you can execute from this state. Currently, you can only use Submit Message to submit the message for review. So you should select that transition and then click Make Transition.

The status switches to Pending Publication (pending), and now you have three transition choices. You might have noticed already that this workflow is not very safe or useful because every editor (and only editors) can cause transitions.

In your application, you might want the message to automatically switch from private to pending when it is created. You can easily accomplish this by changing the Submit Message transition's trigger mode to automatic. To do that, you go to your workflow's definition, click Manage Transitions, select the Submit Message transition, and adjust the trigger mode in the Edit view.

Step 5: Creating a Review Messages View for Message Boards

Now that you have a basic workflow working, you can look at an example of how you can make use of the workflow mechanism. The first task is to provide the editor with a nice overview of all pending messages in the message board.

You basically need a view class that recursively walks through the tree and picks out the pending messages. To accomplish this task, it is extremely helpful to write a convenience function that simply checks whether a message has a certain status. The implementation could be something like the following, which you simply place in browser/messageboard.py:

```
01 from zope.app import zapi
02 from zope.app.workflow.interfaces import IProcessInstanceContainer
03
04 def hasMessageStatus(msg, status, workflow='publish-message'):
05     """Check whether a particular message matches a given status"""
06     adapter = IProcessInstanceContainer(msg)
07     if adapter:
08         # No workflow is defined, so the message is always shown.
09         if not adapter.keys():
10             return True
11         for item in adapter.values():
12             if item.processDefinitionName != workflow:
13                 continue
14             if item.status == status:
15                 return True
16
17     return False
```

In the preceding code block, note the following:

- Lines 2 and 6: The returned adapter provides access to the message's workflows (that is, process instances). In this case, you expect to find only one workflow.
- Lines 8–10: You need to provide some backward compatibility for the messages that were created before you added the workflow feature.

- Lines 11–15: You look through all the workflows (that is, process instances) and try to find the one you are looking for. If the status matches the state you are checking for, you can return a positive result. If not, you will eventually return `False` (line 16).

Next you need to implement the view class, which should provide the method `getPendingMessagesInfo()`; this method returns a list of information structures for pending messages, where each structure contains the title and the URL of the workflow view of the message. You need to place the following view in `brower/messageboard.py`:

```
01 from book.messageboard.interfaces import IMessage
02
03 class ReviewMessages:
04     """Workflow: Review all pending messages"""
05
06     def getPendingMessages(self, pmsg):
07         """Get all pending messages recursively."""
08         msgs = []
09         for name, msg in pmsg.items():
10             if IMessage.providedBy(msg):
11                 if hasMessageStatus(msg, 'pending'):
12                     msgs.append(msg)
13                 msgs += self.getPendingMessages(msg)
14         return msgs
15
16     def getPendingMessagesInfo(self):
17         """Get all the display info for pending messages"""
18         msg_infos = []
19         for msg in self.getPendingMessages(self.context):
20             info = {}
21             info['title'] = msg.title
22             info['url'] = zapi.getView(
23                 msg, 'absolute_url', self.request)() + '/@@workflows.html'
24             msg_infos.append(info)
25         return msg_infos
```

In the preceding code block, note the following:

- Lines 6–14: This is the recursive method that searches for all the pending messages.

  Line 8: This is the resulting flat list of pending messages.

  Line 10: Because you can find replies (messages) and attachments (files) in a message, you have to make sure that you deal with an `IMessage` object.

  Lines 11–12: If the message is `pending`, then you add it to the list of pending messages.

  Line 13: Whatever message it is, you definitely want to look at its replies to see whether there are pending messages lying around.

- Lines 16–25: This method creates a list of info structures about the messages, using the list of pending messages (line 20). This is actually the method that will be called from the page template.

Next, you create a template named `review.pt` that will display the pending messages:

```
01 <html metal:use-macro="context/@@standard_macros/view">
02   <body>
03     <div metal:fill-slot="body" i18n:domain="messageboard">
04
05       <h1 i18n:translate="">Pending Messages</h1>
06
07       <div class="row" tal:repeat="msg view/getPendingMessagesInfo">
08         <div class="field">
09           <a href="" tal:attributes="href msg/url"
10                tal:content="msg/title" />
11         </div>
12       </div>
13
14     </div>
15   </body>
16 </html>
```

In the preceding code block, note the following:

- Lines 7–12: You iterate over all message entries and create links to each pending message, displaying its title.

Finally, you have to register the new view by using the following:

```
01 <page
02     name="review.html"
03     for="book.messageboard.interfaces.IMessageBoard"
04     class=".messageboard.ReviewMessages"
05     permission="book.messageboard.PublishContent"
06     template="review.pt"
07     menu="zmi_views" title="Review Messages"/>
```

Now you can restart your Zope 3 server and enjoy the new view. You could do much more with this view, but you should now have an idea of the framework's functionality.

Step 6: Adjusting a Message Thread

Now you have a working workflow, a way for the message writer to request publication, and a view for the editor to approve or reject messages. But the workflow does not impinge on the interaction of the user with the message board at all yet. Therefore, you need to modify the message thread view to show only published messages.

The change requires only two more lines in `browser/thread.py`. First, you import the `hasMessageStatus()` function:

```
01 from messageboard import hasMessageStatus
```

Second, you extend the condition that checks whether an object implements `IMessage` to also make sure it is published:

```
01 if IMessage.providedBy(child) and \
02       hasMessageStatus(child, 'published'):
```

And that's it! You can now restart Zope and ensure that this works!

Step 7: Automating the Creation of Workflow and Friends

Now that you have your workflow support completed, you should direct your attention to one last quirk. Remember earlier in this chapter, when you created the workflow by hand in several steps? You certainly do not want to require your users to add all those objects by hand. It would be neat if the workflow code could be added after the message board is created and added. That is actually not hard to make happen. You only have to create a custom template and an Add view and insert it in the `browser:addform` directive.

You should start with the template, which should provide an option for the user to choose whether the workflow objects should be generated. You need to create a new file called `messageboard_add.pt` and insert the following content in it:

```
01 <html metal:use-macro="context/@@standard_macros/page">
02   <body>
03     <div metal:fill-slot="body" i18n:domain="messageboard">
04
05       <div metal:use-macro="views/form_macros/addform">
06
07         <div metal:fill-slot="extra_bottom" class="row">
08           <div class="field">
09             <h3><input type="checkbox" name="workflow:int"
10                   value="1" checked=""/>
11               <span i18n:translate="">Create Workflow</span>
12             </h3>
13             <span i18n:translate="">Without the workflow you will
14               not be able to review messages before they are
15               published. Note that you can always modify the
16               messageboard workflow later to make all transitions
17               automatically.</span>
18           </div>
19         </div>
20
```

```
21        </div>
22
23      </div>
24    </body>
25 </html>
```

There's nothing surprising here; if you find the `workflow` attribute in the request, you know the option was set. Next, you write the custom Create and Add view for the message board, which you simply place in `browser/messageboard.py`:

```
00 import os
01
02 from zope.security.proxy import removeSecurityProxy
03
04 from zope.app.registration.interfaces import ActiveStatus
05 from zope.app.site.interfaces import ISite
06 from zope.app.site.service import SiteManager, ServiceRegistration
07 from zope.app.utility.utility import LocalUtilityService, UtilityRegistration
08 from zope.app.workflow.interfaces import IProcessDefinitionImportHandler
09 from zope.app.workflow.stateful.contentworkflow import ContentWorkflowsManager
10 from zope.app.workflow.stateful.definition import StatefulProcessDefinition
11 from zope.app.workflow.stateful.interfaces import IContentWorkflowsManager
12 from zope.app.workflow.stateful.interfaces import IStatefulProcessDefinition
13
14 import book.messageboard
15
16
17 class AddMessageBoard(object):
18     """Add a message board."""
19
20     def createAndAdd(self, data):
21         content = super(AddMessageBoard, self).createAndAdd(data)
22
23         if self.request.get('workflow'):
24             folder = removeSecurityProxy(zapi.getParent(content))
25             if not ISite.providedBy(folder):
26                 sm = SiteManager(folder)
27                 folder.setSiteManager(sm)
28             default = zapi.traverse(folder.getSiteManager(), 'default')
29
30             # Create Local Utility Service
31             default['Utilities'] = LocalUtilityService()
32             rm = default.getRegistrationManager()
33             registration = ServiceRegistration(zapi.servicenames.Utilities,
34                                                'Utilities', rm)
35             key = rm.addRegistration(registration)
36             zapi.traverse(rm, key).status = ActiveStatus
37
```

```
38              # Create the process definition
39              default['publish-message'] = StatefulProcessDefinition()
40              pd_path = zapi.getPath(default['publish-message'])
41              registration = UtilityRegistration(
42                  'publish-message', IStatefulProcessDefinition, pd_path)
43              pd_id = rm.addRegistration(registration)
44              zapi.traverse(rm, pd_id).status = ActiveStatus
45
46              import_util = IProcessDefinitionImportHandler(
47                  default['publish-message'])
48
49              xml = os.path.join(
50                  os.path.dirname(book.messageboard.__file__), 'workflow.xml')
51
52              import_util.doImport(open(xml, mode='r').read())
53
54              # Create Content Workflows Manager
55              default['ContentWorkflows'] = ContentWorkflowsManager()
56              cm_path = zapi.getPath(default['ContentWorkflows'])
57              registration = UtilityRegistration(
58                  'wfcontentmgr', IContentWorkflowsManager, cm_path)
59              cm_id = rm.addRegistration(registration)
60              zapi.traverse(rm, cm_id).status = ActiveStatus
61
62              contentmgr = default['ContentWorkflows']
63              contentmgr.register(IMessage, 'publish-message')
64
65          return content
```

In the preceding code block, note the following:

- Lines 1–14: You must do a huge number of imports so that all components are available. (This alone shows what a mess simple configuration objects and ZCML usually save you from.)

- Lines 20–21: The `createAndAdd()` method is the only one you have to override and extend. It is the method that is called during the execution of the add form. The good part is that the original method returns the added message board instance itself, so you can store it and make use of it. After line 21, the message board is already created and added.

- Line 23: If the user wants you to autogenerate the workflow objects, you do it here.

- Line 24: You grab the folder that contains the message board.

- Lines 25–27: You make sure that the folder is a site. If it is not, you make it one.

- Line 28: Now you just get the `default` site management folder, into which you will place all the local component.

- Lines 30–36: You create a new local utility service so that you can register the local utilities you are about to create. Note that both the Content Workflow Manager and the Stateful Process Definition are local utilities.

- Lines 38–44: You add the a new process definition and register it to be usable (active).

- Lines 46–52: Here comes the tricky part. You have to create the workflow states and transitions from your saved `workflow.xml` file. But where do you get the directory? The easiest way is to import the package itself, get the path, and then truncate the `__init__.py` part; then you should be left with the directory path. You then simply add the workflow XML filename at the end and open it for import. The reason you want to use the `os` module everywhere is that you want to keep Zope packages platform independent.

- Lines 54–63: You create the Content Workflow Manager, which gets notified when `IObjectCreatedEvent` events occur, so it can add process instances to the event. On line 63 you tell the system that the `publish-message` workflow (created earlier in this chapter) should be used only for `IMessage` components.

Now you need to register the Add view class and template with the `addform` directive in ZCML. The `addform` directive for the message board therefore becomes this:

```
01 <addform
02     label="Add Message Board"
03     name="AddMessageBoard.html"
04     template="messageboard_add.pt"
05     class=".messageboard.AddMessageBoard"
06     schema="book.messageboard.interfaces.IMessageBoard"
07     content_factory="book.messageboard.messageboard.MessageBoard"
08     fields="description"
09     permission="zope.ManageContent"
10     />
```

In the preceding code block, note the following:

- Lines 3–4: See how easy it is to incorporate custom templates and classes for an Add view? (The same is true for edit forms.)

After restarting Zope, you should be able to enjoy the changes. You need to create a new folder and in it a new message board. You should then see the new option, and after the message board is successfully created, the workflow components should be available in the parent folder.

There are some limitations to the preceding implementation. When you allow for the workflow to be created automatically, it is assumed that your site does not yet have a local utility service. This means that you cannot use this option in the root folder. Note that this limitation can be overcome by inserting some conditional statements in the code before creating the service.

Also, the automated code creates all the workflow-related components in the `default` software management folder, whereas during the manual process, you added all components to the `tools` software management folder. This is because the `default` folder is guaranteed to exist.

The Theory Behind Workflows

Now that you have completed the practical part of the chapter, it is time to look a bit more carefully at the framework that supports all this functionality. The workflow framework is designed to support any type of generic workflow implementation. The Zope community itself has produced two workflow implementations: the activity and entity models.

Activity-based workflows implement workflow in a transition-centric fashion, where an object is moved in a graph of workflow states and transitions outside its physical hierarchy. This type of model was developed by the Workflow Management Coalition (WfMC) and is implemented in the Zope 2 OpenFlow/CMFFlow product. The advantage of this model is that it has a high degree of flexibility and scalability, and it is well established, thanks to the WfMC.

Entity-based workflows, on the other hand, store the current workflow state of the object as metadata in the object itself, so no real workflow graph exists; the workflow is only defined by a set of states and transitions. This model was implemented by `DCWorkflow` in Zope 2 and is known as "stateful" workflow in Zope 3. One of its advantages is the simplicity of implementation and its flatter learning curve. This workflow type is used in this chapter.

You should know the following terms related to workflows:

- **Process definition**—This component defines in what states a content object can be and what the possible transitions between them are. It is basically a blueprint of the actual workflow.

- **Process instance**—If the process definition is the blueprint, then the process instance is the workflow itself; it is the realization of the process definition, which is used to actually manage the workflow for *one* particular object (that is, there is one process instance per workflow per content component instance). Note that one object can have several workflows associated with it.

- **Process instance container**—This object is used to store actual process instances and is usually the component that is tagged to an object via an annotation.

- **Content Workflow Manager (stateful)**—This utility is responsible to add the correct workflows to a content object upon creation.

One of the powerful features of the stateful workflow implementation is that every process instance can have workflow-relevant data associated with it. The specifics of this data are specified via a schema in the process definition. When an instance of a process is appended to an object, placeholders for that data are created as well. The workflow-relevant data can be useful for transition conditions, comments, and the like.

21

Providing Online Help Screens

Difficulty

Newcomer

Skills

- Although this chapter has almost no direct prerequisites, you should still be familiar with at least Chapters 19, "Events and Subscribers," and 20, "Approval Workflow for Messages." Optional.
- Some ZCML knowledge is advantageous. Optional.

Problem/Task

Offering help to the user at any point in a GUI is an important feature for all applications. The `messageboard` package you have been working on while reading this book does a really bad job of providing help up to this point. In this chapter you'll change that by using Zope 3's online help package. This doesn't have much to do with Python programming, but it is part of the Zope 3 development process.

T HIS IS A VERY BRIEF CHAPTER BECAUSE there are only two tasks. First, you need to write the actual help screens (which can be either pain text, STX, ReST, or HTML) and then you simply register them.

Creating Help Files

Because the help will be for browser views, you can place the help files in a `help` directory inside `messageboard/browser`.

First, you create a file called `package_intro.rst` and enter the following content in it:

```
01 ===========================
02 Message Board Demo Package
02 ===========================
03
04 This package demos various features of the Zope 3 Framework. If you
05 have questions or concerns, please let me know.
```

Then you create a file called `board_review.rst` that contains the following:

```
01 This view lists all messages in the board that are pending for
02 publication. Each listed method is a link that brings you to the
03 message's "Workflow" view where you can initiate a transition.
```

Finally, you add the file `msg_edit.rst`, which contains the following text:

```
01 This screen allows you to edit the data (i.e. the subject and body) of
02 the Message object.
03
04 title - A one line unicode text string that briefly describes the
05         purpose/subject of the message.
06
07 body - A multiple line unicode text string that is the actual content of
08        the message. It is accepting HTML, but restricts the user to a
09        couple of selected tags. Feel free to type anything you wish.
```

Notice that there are not any titles for the text itself here. You will define titles in the configuration, which is displayed as a header on the website, so there is no need for another title.

Registering the Online Help Topics

All that's left to do is to register the new help screens. Help topics can be organized in a hierarchical manner. In order to keep all the `messageboard` package screens together in one subtree, you can make the `package_info.rst` help topic the parent of all the other help screens. To make this happen, you need to first open your configuration file (`messageboard/browser/configure.zcml`). Then you need to add the `help` namespace in the `zope:configure` element, using the following declaration:

```
01 xmlns:help="http://namespaces.zope.org/help"
```

Now you can add the following directives:

```
01 <help:register
02     id="messageboard"
03     title="Message Board Help"
04     parent="ui"
```

```
05      for="book.messageboard.interfaces.IMessageBoard"
06      doc_path="./help/package_intro.rst"/>
07
08  <help:register
09      id="board.review"
10      title="Publication Review"
11      parent="ui/messageboard"
12      for="book.messageboard.interfaces.IMessageBoard"
13      view="review.html"
14      doc_path="./help/board_review.rst"/>
15
16  <help:register
17      id="message.edit"
18      title="Change Message"
19      parent="ui/messageboard"
20      for="book.messageboard.interfaces.IMessage"
21      view="edit.html"
22      doc_path="./help/msg_edit.rst"/>
```

In the preceding code block, note the following:

- Line 2: You specify the ID of the help topic, as it will be available in the URL.

- Line 3: You specify the title of the help topic that is displayed above the topic's content.

- Line 4: You specify the path of the parent help topic. The ui help topic comes by default with Zope 3, and you should attach all your screen help to it.

- Line 5: You register the help topic as the default context help for MessageBoard objects. This is an optional attribute.

- Line 6: You specify the relative path to the help file. Zope 3 recognizes file endings and creates the appropriate filters for the output. Possible endings include txt, rst, html, and stx.

- Lines 12–13: You register a topic specifically for the review.html view of a message in the messageboard.

- Lines 11 and 19: You need to be careful to use URI-like syntax to specify the parent.

Now all you need to do is restart Zope and go to a message board's Review Messages view. Like all management pages, there is a Help link on the right side, below the tabs. Usually this link just brings you to the generic online help screen, but if you click it from the message board's review screen, the help for this particular view appears (see Figure 21.1). Another possibility would be to create special Message and MessageBoard object introduction screens, but that would be overkill in this situation.

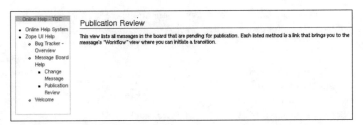

Figure 21.1   The help screen for the message board's Review Messages tab.

Object-to-Filesystem Mapping, Using FTP as an Example

Difficulty

Newcomer

Skills

- You should be familiar with the `messageboard` package up to this point.
- You need to have a good understanding of the component architecture, especially adapters.
- You should feel comfortable with writing ZCML-based configurations.
- A basic knowledge of the filesystem interfaces is beneficial. Optional.

Problem/Task

By default, Zope provides an FTP server, which is a filesystem-based protocol. So how are objects mapped to the filesystem representation and back? To accomplish the mapping in a flexible and exchangeable way, there is a set of interfaces that can be implemented as adapters to provide a representation that the FTP publisher understands. This chapter shows how to implement some of the interfaces for a custom filesystem representation.

ᴀT THIS POINT, YOU MIGHT WONDER, "Why in the world would I have to write my own filesystem support? Does Zope not provide any implementations by default?" Well, to answer the latter question: yes and no. There is an adapter registered for `IContainer` to `IReadDirectory` and `IWriteDirectory`. However, these adapters are not very useful because the `MessageBoard` and `Message` objects are not only containers, but they also contain content that is not represented anywhere. You can start Zope 3 and check it out yourself. The goal of this chapter is to create a representation that handles the containment and the content at the same time.

Because the Zope 3 core already has a lot of code presenting `IContainer` implementations as directories, you should reuse that part of the framework. The content of an object could be simply represented by a virtual file called `contents`, which contains all relevant data, normalized as simple plain text. Note also that you do not need to have a complete mapping between the object and the filesystem representation because you do not need or want to expose annotations, for example. The `contents` file of the `MessageBoard` object should simply contain the data of the `description` attribute, and the `Message` component's `content` file should have the following format:

```
Title: <message title>

<message body>
```

This way, you can also easily parse the title when new contents are submitted because you want to implement the read *and* write interfaces of the filesystem representation. The functionality of accessing and mutating the virtual `contents` file will be managed by a class called `VirtualContentsFile`. A goal of the implementation is to keep the `VirtualContentsFile` class as generic as possible so that you can use it for both message boards and messages. To do that, the virtual file must delegate the request to create the plain-text representation to a component that knows about the specifics of the respective content object. For this task, you can use a simple `IPlainText` adapter that provides the plain-text representation of each content component's contents.

Step 1: `IPlainText` Adapters

As mentioned at the beginning of this chapter, `IPlainText` adapters will be responsible for returning and accepting the plain-text representation of the object's content and for just doing the right thing with the data. They are very simple objects; each has two methods—one for providing and one for processing the text.

The `IPlainText` Interface

The `IPlainText` interface is simple; it defines a `getText()` method and a `setText()` method:

```
01 class IPlainText(Interface):
02     """This interface allows you to represent an object's content in plain
03     text."""
04
05     def getText():
06         """Get a pure text representation of the object's content."""
07
08     def setText(text):
09         """Write the text to the object."""
```

This interface should be placed in the `interfaces` module of the `messageboard` package. In the doc strings, you refer to the object's content without further qualifying it. *Content* in this case refers to all data (that is, property values) that should be represented via the plain-text representation.

The `setText()` method could in theory become quite complex, depending on how many properties you want to map and how you represent them. In the two cases you'll deal with in this chapter, the method will be fairly simple.

The Plain-Text Adapter Implementation

You need two implementations: one for the `Message` class and one for the `MessageBoard` class. At this point you don't need to write tests because the functionality of these adapters is carefully tested in the following code.

First, you need to write the message board adapter, so open the `messageboard.py` file and add the following code to it:

```
00 from book.messageboard.interfaces import IPlainText
01
02 class PlainText:
03
04     implements(IPlainText)
05
06     def __init__(self, context):
07         self.context = context
08
09     def getText(self):
10         return self.context.description
11
12     def setText(self, text):
13         self.context.description = unicode(text)
```

This is an extremely simple implementation of the `IPlainText` interface because you map only one attribute.

In the preceding code block, note the following:

- Line 14: You need to make sure that the incoming text is Unicode. This is very important for the system's integrity.

The implementation for the `Message` component, which you should put in `message.py`, looks like this:

```
01 from book.messageboard.interfaces import IPlainText
02
03 class PlainText:
04
05     implements(IPlainText)
06
```

```
07    def __init__(self, context):
08        self.context = context
09
10    def getText(self):
11        return 'Title: %s\n\n%s' %(self.context.title,
12                                   self.context.body)
13
14    def setText(self, text):
15        text = unicode(text)
16        if text.startswith('Title: '):
17            title, text = text.split('\n', 1)
18            self.context.title = title[7:]
19
20        self.context.body = text.strip()
```

This implementation is more interesting than the first one because you map two properties to the plain text.

In the preceding code block, note the following:

- Lines 11–12: In typical MIME-header style, you define a field with the pattern *name*: *value* for the title and place the body as content. Note that the Zope 3 standard requires an empty line after the headers, too.

- Line 15: You have to ensure again that the incoming text is Unicode.

- Lines 16–20: You need to check whether a title was specified in the upload. If it was, you extract the title from the data and store the title; if it was not, you just ignore the title altogether. Finally, you store the rest of the text as the body.

The Configuration of the Adapters

The last step in providing the plain-text adapters is to register them with the component architecture. You just add the following two `adapter` directives to `configure.zcml`:

```
01 <adapter
02     factory=".messageboard.PlainText"
03     provides=".interfaces.IPlainText"
04     for=".interfaces.IMessageBoard" />
05
06 <adapter
07     factory=".message.PlainText"
08     provides=".interfaces.IPlainText"
09     for=".interfaces.IMessage" />
```

You are now done. Even though you have two new fully functional components at this point, you have gained no new functionality yet because these adapters are not used anywhere. You have to complete the next two sections to see any results.

Step 2: The Virtual Contents File Adapter

How you implement the virtual `contents` file is fully up to you. However, you can do less work if you choose one way over another. The best method is to create a new interface, `IVirtualContentsFile`, which extends `zope.app.file.interfaces.IFile`. The advantage of doing this is that there are already filesystem-specific adapters (implementing `zope.app.filerepresentation.interfaces.IReadFile` and `zope.app.filerepresentation.interfaces.IWriteFile`) for the `IFile` interface. `IFile` might not be the best and most concise interface for your needs, but the advantages of using it are very convincing.

The Virtual Contents File Interface

When you look through the Zope 3 source code, you should notice that the `IFile` and `IFileContent` interfaces go hand-in-hand with each. Thus, your virtual contents file interface will extend both of these interfaces:

```
01 from zope.app.file.interfaces import IFileContent
02
03 class IVirtualContentsFile(IFile, IFileContent):
04     """Marker Interface to mark special Message and Message Board
05     Contents files in FS representations."""
```

As usual, the interface should be placed in the `interfaces.py` module.

The Implementation

Now the fun begins. First, you note that `IFile` requires two properties, `contentType` and `data`, as well as the method `getSize()`. Whereas `data` and `getSize()` are obvious, you need to think a bit about `contentType`. Because you really just want to always return `text/plain`, the accessor should statically return `text/plain`, and the mutator should just ignore the input.

To make a long story short, here is the code, which you should place in a new file called `filerepresentation.py`:

```
01 from zope.interface import implements
02 from interfaces import IVirtualContentsFile, IPlainText
03
04 class VirtualContentsFile(object):
05
06     implements(IVirtualContentsFile)
07
08     def __init__(self, context):
09         self.context = context
10
11     def setContentType(self, contentType):
12         '''See interface IFile'''
```

```
13          pass
14
15    def getContentType(self):
16        '''See interface IFile'''
17        return u'text/plain'
18
19    contentType = property(getContentType, setContentType)
20
21    def edit(self, data, contentType=None):
22        '''See interface IFile'''
23        self.setData(data)
24
25    def getData(self):
26        '''See interface IFile'''
27        adapter = IPlainText(self.context)
28        return adapter.getText() or u''
29
30    def setData(self, data):
31        '''See interface IFile'''
32        adapter = IPlainText(self.context)
33        return adapter.setText(data)
34
35    data = property(getData, setData)
36
37    def getSize(self):
38        '''See interface IFile'''
39        return len(self.getData())
```

In the preceding code block, note the following:

- Lines 11–13: As promised, the mutator ignores the input totally and is really just an empty method.
- Lines 15–17: You need to make sure to *always* return text/plain.
- Lines 25–28 and 30–33: Now you are making use of the previously created PlainText adapters. You simply use the two available API methods.

This is pretty straightforward; there are really no surprises here.

The Tests for the VirtualContentsFile Class

Because even the coding step you took in the preceding section did not provide a functional piece of code, it is especially important that you write some careful tests for the VirtualContentsFile class. Another requirement of the tests is that this adapter be tested with both MessageBoard and Message instances. To accomplish this, you write a base test and then realize this test for each component. So in the tests folder, you create a new file called test_filerepresentation.py and add the following content to it:

```
01 import unittest
02 from zope.interface.verify import verifyObject
03 from zope.app import zapi
04 from zope.app.tests import ztapi
05 from zope.app.tests.placelesssetup import PlacelessSetup
06
07 from book.messageboard.interfaces import \
08      IVirtualContentsFile, IPlainText, IMessage, IMessageBoard
09 from book.messageboard.message import \
10      Message, PlainText as MessagePlainText
11 from book.messageboard.messageboard import \
12      MessageBoard, PlainText as MessageBoardPlainText
13 from book.messageboard.filerepresentation import VirtualContentsFile
14
15 class VirtualContentsFileTestBase(PlacelessSetup):
16
17     def _makeFile(self):
18         raise NotImplemented
19
20     def _registerPlainTextAdapter(self):
21         raise NotImplemented
22
23     def setUp(self):
24         PlacelessSetup.setUp(self)
25         self._registerPlainTextAdapter()
26
27     def testContentType(self):
28         file = self._makeFile()
29         self.assertEqual(file.getContentType(), 'text/plain')
30         file.setContentType('text/html')
31         self.assertEqual(file.getContentType(), 'text/plain')
32         self.assertEqual(file.contentType, 'text/plain')
33
34     def testData(self):
35         file = self._makeFile()
36
37         file.setData('Foobar')
38         self.assert_(file.getData().find('Foobar') >= 0)
39         self.assert_(file.data.find('Foobar') >= 0)
40
41         file.edit('Blah', 'text/html')
42         self.assertEqual(file.contentType, 'text/plain')
43         self.assert_(file.data.find('Blah') >= 0)
44
45     def testInterface(self):
46         file = self._makeFile()
47         self.failUnless(IVirtualContentsFile.providedBy(file))
```

```
48            self.failUnless(verifyObject(IVirtualContentsFile, file))
49
50
51 class MessageVirtualContentsFileTest(VirtualContentsFileTestBase,
52                                      unittest.TestCase):
53
54     def _makeFile(self):
55         return VirtualContentsFile(Message())
56
57     def _registerPlainTextAdapter(self):
58         ztapi.provideAdapter(IMessage, IPlainText, MessagePlainText)
59
60     def testMessageSpecifics(self):
61         file = self._makeFile()
62         self.assertEqual(file.context.title, '')
63         self.assertEqual(file.context.body, '')
64         file.data = 'Title: Hello\n\nWorld'
65         self.assertEqual(file.context.title, 'Hello')
66         self.assertEqual(file.context.body, 'World')
67         file.data = 'World 2'
68         self.assertEqual(file.context.body, 'World 2')
69
70
71 class MessageBoardVirtualContentsFileTest(
72         VirtualContentsFileTestBase, unittest.TestCase):
73
74     def _makeFile(self):
75         return VirtualContentsFile(MessageBoard())
76
77     def _registerPlainTextAdapter(self):
78         ztapi.provideAdapter(IMessageBoard, IPlainText,
79                              MessageBoardPlainText)
80
81     def testMessageBoardSpecifics(self):
82         file = self._makeFile()
83         self.assertEqual(file.context.description, '')
84         file.data = 'Title: Hello\n\nWorld'
85         self.assertEqual(file.context.description,
86                          'Title: Hello\n\nWorld')
87         file.data = 'World 2'
88         self.assertEqual(file.context.description, 'World 2')
89
90 def test_suite():
91     return unittest.TestSuite((
92         unittest.makeSuite(MessageVirtualContentsFileTest),
93         unittest.makeSuite(MessageBoardVirtualContentsFileTest),
```

```
94         ))
95
96 if __name__ == '__main__':
97     unittest.main(defaultTest='test_suite')
```

In the preceding code block, note the following:

- Line 5: Because you are going to make use of adapters, you need to bring up the component architecture by using the `PlacelessSetup`.

- Lines 7–13: You import all the relevant interfaces and components for this test. There is a lot to import at this point because you have to register the components by hand (instead of by using ZCML).

- Lines 17–18: The implementation of this method should create a `VirtualContentsFile` adapter that has the correct object as `context`. Because the context varies, the specific test case class has to take care of its implementation.

- Lines 20–21: Because there is a specific adapter registration required for each case (board and message), you have to leave that up to the test case implementation as well.

- Lines 27–32: You need to make sure that the `plain/text` setting can never be overwritten.

- Lines 34–43: You can make only some marginal tests here because the storage details depend on the `IPlainText` implementation. Later in this code block, there are stronger tests in the specific test cases for the message board and message (see the `testMessageSpecifics()` and `testMessageBoardSpecifics()` methods).

- Lines 45–48: You need to always make sure that the interface is completely implemented by the component.

- Line 51: This is the beginning of a concrete test case that implements the base test. Note that you should only make the concrete implementation a `TestCase`-derived class.

- Lines 54–55: You just stick a plain, empty `Message` instance in the adapter.

- Lines 60–68: Here you test whether the written contents of the virtual file are correctly passed and the right properties are set.

- Lines 71–88: Here you do pretty much the same as you did for the `Message` test in lines 51–68.

- Lines 90–97: Here you include the usual test boilerplate.

You can now run the test and verify the functionality of the new adapters.

The Configuration of the `VirtualContentsFile` Class

Although you do not need to register the file representation component, you are required to make some security assertions about the object's methods and properties.

You need to place the following content component configuration directives in your main configuration file, `configure.zcml`:

```
01 <content class=".filerepresentation.VirtualContentsFile">
02
03   <implements interface="
04       zope.app.annotation.interfaces.IAttributeAnnotatable" />
05
06   <require
07       permission="book.messageboard.View"
08       interface="zope.app.filerepresentation.interfaces.IReadFile" />
09
10   <require
11       permission="books.messageboard.Edit"
12       interface="zope.app.filerepresentation.interfaces.IWriteFile"
13       set_schema="zope.app.filerepresentation.interfaces.IReadFile" />
14
15 </content>
```

In the preceding code block, note the following:

- Lines 3–4: You need the virtual file to be annotatable so that it can reach the Dublin Core for dates/times and owner information.

Step 3: The `IReadDirectory` Implementation

You are finally ready to give your content components, `MessageBoard` and `Message`, a cool filesystem representation.

The Directory Implementation

You need to realize that `zope.app.folder.filerepresentation.ReadDirectory` already has a nice implementation, except for the superfluous `SiteManager` class support and the missing `contents` file. So you simply subclass this class and overwrite `keys()`, `get(key, default=None)`, and `len()`. All the other methods depend on these three. So your code for the `ReadDirectory` class, which you should place in `filerepresentation.py`, looks like this:

```
01 from zope.app.filerepresentation.interfaces import IReadDirectory
02 from zope.app.folder.filerepresentation import \
03     ReadDirectory as ReadDirectoryBase
04
05 class ReadDirectory(ReadDirectoryBase):
06     """An special implementation of the directory."""
07
08     implements(IReadDirectory)
09
```

```
10    def keys(self):
11        keys = self.context.keys()
12        return list(keys) + ['contents']
13
14    def get(self, key, default=None):
15        if key == 'contents':
16            return VirtualContentsFile(self.context)
17        return self.context.get(key, default)
18
19    def __len__(self):
20        l = len(self.context)
21        return l+1
```

In the preceding code block, note the following:

- Lines 10–12: When you are asked for a list of names available for this container, you get the list of keys plus the virtual `contents` file.

- Lines 14–17: All objects except the `contents` file are simply found in the context (`MessageBoard` or `Message`) itself. When the system asks for the `contents` file, you simply give it the `VirtualContentsFile` instance that you prepared in the previous section, and you do not have to worry about anything because you know the system knows how to handle `zope.app.file.interfaces.IFile` objects.

- Lines 19–21: Obviously, you pretend to have one more object than you actually have.

Now you are done with the `ReadDirectory` implementation. You write some unit tests to ensure its functionality and then register the filesystem components.

The Directory Tests

To test the `ReadDirectory` implementation, you again need to test it with the `MessageBoard` and `Message` components. So, similarly to the previous tests, you have a base test with specific implementations. Also note that it is not necessary to test all `IReadDirectory` methods because they are already tested in the base class tests. Therefore, you just need to test the methods you have overridden:

```
01 from book.messageboard.filerepresentation import ReadDirectory
02
03 class ReadDirectoryTestBase(PlacelessSetup):
04
05     def _makeDirectoryObject(self):
06         raise NotImplemented
07
08     def _makeTree(self):
09         base = self._makeDirectoryObject()
10         msg1 = Message()
```

```
11          msg1.title = 'Message 1'
12          msg1.description = 'This is Message 1.'
13          msg11 = Message()
14          msg11.title = 'Message 1-1'
15          msg11.description = 'This is Message 1-1.'
16          msg2 = Message()
17          msg2.title = 'Message 1'
18          msg2.description = 'This is Message 1.'
19          msg1['msg11'] = msg11
20          base['msg1'] = msg1
21          base['msg2'] = msg2
22          return ReadDirectory(base)
23
24      def testKeys(self):
25          tree = self._makeTree()
26          keys = list(tree.keys())
27          keys.sort()
28          self.assertEqual(keys, ['contents', 'msg1', 'msg2'])
29          keys = list(ReadDirectory(tree['msg1']).keys())
30          keys.sort()
31          self.assertEqual(keys, ['contents', 'msg11'])
32
33      def testGet(self):
34          tree = self._makeTree()
35          self.assertEqual(tree.get('msg1'), tree.context['msg1'])
36          self.assertEqual(tree.get('msg3'), None)
37          default = object()
38          self.assertEqual(tree.get('msg3', default), default)
39          self.assertEqual(tree.get('contents').__class__,
40                           VirtualContentsFile)
41
42      def testLen(self):
43          tree = self._makeTree()
44          self.assertEqual(len(tree), 3)
45          self.assertEqual(len(ReadDirectory(tree['msg1'])), 2)
46          self.assertEqual(len(ReadDirectory(tree['msg2'])), 1)
47
48
49 class MessageReadDirectoryTest(ReadDirectoryTestBase,
50                               unittest.TestCase):
51
52      def _makeDirectoryObject(self):
53          return Message()
54
55
```

```
56 class MessageBoardReadDirectoryTest(ReadDirectoryTestBase,
57                                     unittest.TestCase):
58
59     def _makeDirectoryObject(self):
60         return MessageBoard()
```

In the preceding code block, note the following:

- Lines 5–6: You return an instance of the object to be tested.

- Lines 8–22: You create an interesting message tree on top of the base. This allows some more detailed testing.

- Lines 24–31: You make sure this `contents` file and the submessages are correctly listed.

- Lines 33–40: You make sure that the objects you get are the right ones.

- Lines 42–46: You run a simple test for the number of contained items (including `contents`).

- Lines 49–60: You provide the concrete implementations of the base test.

After you are done writing the tests, you need to add the two new `TestCase` classes to the test suite.

The Directory Configuration

At this point, you simply register your new components properly, using the following ZCML directives:

```
01 <adapter
02     for=".interfaces.IMessageBoard"
03     provides="zope.app.filerepresentation.interfaces.IReadDirectory"
04     factory=".filerepresentation.ReadDirectory"
05     permission="zope.View"/>
06
07 <adapter
08     for=".interfaces.IMessage"
09     provides="zope.app.filerepresentation.interfaces.IReadDirectory"
10     factory=".filerepresentation.ReadDirectory"
11     permission="zope.View"/>
```

You can now restart Zope and test the filesystem representation with an FTP client of your choice. Figure 22.1 is a sequence diagram that shows how a request is guided to find its information and return it properly.

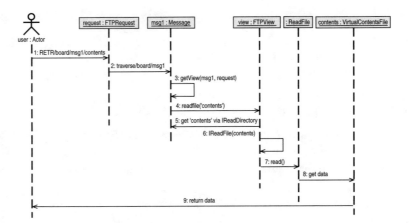

Figure 22.1   The inner working of publishing FTP requests, from requesting the contents file to receiving the actual data.

Step 4: Putting the Icing on the Cake: A Special Directory Factory

While you were playing around with the new filesystem support, you might have tried to create a directory to see what happened, and it probably just caused a system error because no adapter was found from IMessage/IMessageBoard to IDirectoryFactory. Because such behavior is undesirable, you should create a custom adapter that provides IDirectoryFactory. The IWriteDirectory adapter of any container object will then know how to make use of this factory adapter. You should therefore add the following trivial factory to the filerepresentation module:

```
01 from zope.app.filerepresentation.interfaces import IDirectoryFactory
02 from message import Message
03
04 class MessageFactory(object):
05     """A simple message factory for file system representations."""
06
07     implements(IDirectoryFactory)
08
09     def __init__(self, context):
10         self.context = context
11
12     def __call__(self, name):
13         """See IDirectoryFactory interface."""
14         return Message()
```

Registering the factory is just a matter of using two adapter directives (one for each content component):

```
01  <adapter
02      for=".interfaces.IMessageBoard"
03      provides="zope.app.filerepresentation.interfaces.IDirectoryFactory"
04      factory=".filerepresentation.MessageFactory"
05      permission="zope.View" />
06
07  <adapter
08      for=".interfaces.IMessage"
09      provides="zope.app.filerepresentation.interfaces.IDirectoryFactory"
10      factory=".filerepresentation.MessageFactory"
11      permission="zope.View" />
```

Now you have finally completed the filesystem representation support. The filesystem support should be very smooth and usable at this point. You should be able to view all relevant content, upload new data, using the virtual contents file, and create new messages. The only problem that might remain is that some FTP clients (such as KDE's FTP support) might try to upload the contents file as contents.part and then rename it to contents. Because your filesystem code does not support such a feature, this will cause an error.

Availability of Content via XML-RPC

Difficulty

Sprinter

Skills

- You should be familiar with the `messageboard` package up to this point.
- You should feel comfortable with writing ZCML-based configuration.
- Some insight into the publisher framework is advantageous. Optional.

Problem/Task

A very common way to communicate with remote systems is via XML-RPC, which is a very lightweight protocol that runs on top of HTTP. By default, Zope's HTTP server comes with an XML-RPC component. If you want to allow other systems to communicate with your message board, then you need to declare the methods that will be available via XML-RPC.

Y OU MIGHT WONDER AT THIS POINT why you can't simply map all the existing methods to XML-RPC and be done with it. There are three reasons for not doing this. First, XML-RPC handles only a limited number of data types. The following is a mapping of Python data types to XML-RPC data type elements:

Python Data Type	XML-RPC Data Type
integer	<int>
float	<double>
string	<string>
list	<array>
dict/struct	<dict>
bool	<boolean>
xmlrpclib.Binary	<binary>
xmlrpclib.DateTime	<dateTime>

As you can see, XML-RPC provides no support for None and Unicode, which is a huge drawback.

Second, XML-RPC lacks keyword arguments. XML-RPC understands only regular positional arguments and arguments that have default values. Third, because by default Python returns None for methods, any method that does not have a return value is doomed.

Now that you have taken a brief look at the shortcomings of XML-RPC, you need to know that XML-RPC is still a very powerful tool that you can use without much hassle.

Step 1: Creating Methods: XML-RPC Presentation Components

Obviously, you have to create a view component for each of the content objects, MessageBoard and Message. However, both can contain and manage submessages, so you want to factor out this functionality into a common base class, MessageContainerMethods. Because you want to keep the XML-RPC code separate from other code, you should create a new module called xmlrpc.py in the messageboard directory and add the following content:

```
01 from zope.event import notify
02 from zope.app.publisher.xmlrpc import MethodPublisher
03
04 from zope.app.event.objectevent import ObjectCreatedEvent
05
06 from book.messageboard.message import Message
07
08 class MessageContainerMethods(MethodPublisher):
09
10     def getMessageNames(self):
11         """Get a list of all messages."""
12         return list(self.context.keys())
13
```

```
14    def addMessage(self, name, title, body):
15        """Add a message."""
16        msg = Message()
17        msg.title = title
18        msg.body = body
19        notify(ObjectCreatedEvent(msg))
20        self.context[name] = msg
21        return name
22
23    def deleteMessage(self, name):
24        """Delete a message. Return True, if successful."""
25        self.context.__delitem__(name)
26        return True
```

In the preceding code block, note the following:

- Line 8: You make the class a subclass of the `MethodPublisher` class, which is similar to a `BrowserView` class. Its constructor will expect a `context` object and a `XMLRPCRequest` instance.

- Lines 10–12: You return a list of all message names. Remember that you implemented the containment with BTrees (see Chapter 13, "Writing New Content Objects,"), so `keys()` will not return a list or tuple as a result but will return a BTree-items object. Therefore, you need to implicitly cast the result to become a list, so that XML-RPC is able understand it.

- Line 19: Because you want to play nice with the system, you need to let it know that you created a new content object.

- Lines 21 and 26: You need to make sure you return something so that XML-RPC will not be upset with us. As mentioned previously, if no return value is specified, `None` is implicitly returned, which XML-RPC does not understand.

The two actual views for the content objects are now also implementing accessor and mutator methods for their properties. The following two views should be added to the `xmlrpc.py` module:

```
01 from zope.app.event.objectevent import ObjectModifiedEvent
02
03 class MessageMethods(MessageContainerMethods):
04
05    def getTitle(self):
06        return self.context.title
07
08    def setTitle(self, title):
09        self.context.title = title
10        notify(ObjectModifiedEvent(self.context))
11        return True
12
```

```
13    def getBody(self):
14        return self.context.body
15
16    def setBody(self, body):
17        self.context.body = body
18        notify(ObjectModifiedEvent(self.context))
19        return True
20
21
22 class MessageBoardMethods(MessageContainerMethods):
23
24    def getDescription(self):
25        return self.context.description
26
27    def setDescription(self, description):
28        self.context.description = description
29        notify(ObjectModifiedEvent(self.context))
30        return True
```

In the preceding code block, note the following:

- Lines 10, 18, and 29: When modifying a message board or message, you have to explicitly send out a modification notification event. You haven't had to deal with this until now because for browser forms, these events are created automatically by the form machinery.

- Lines 11, 19, and 30: Again, you need to make sure you do not return None from a method.

You have finished the XML-RPC presentation components from a coding perspective. But before you hook up the code in the component architecture, you need to do some testing.

Step 2: Testing the XML-RPC Views

Of course, the testing code is many times more complex than the implementation of the feature because you have to bring up the component architecture and the event service manually. As in the implementation, you can place the container-related tests in a base class (the code should be located in tests/test_xmlrpc.py):

```
01 from zope.app.tests.placelesssetup import PlacelessSetup
02
03 class MessageContainerTest(PlacelessSetup):
04
05    def _makeMethodObject(self):
06        return NotImplemented
07
08    def _makeTree(self):
09        methods = self._makeMethodObject()
```

```
10          msg1 = Message()
11          msg1.title = 'Message 1'
12          msg1.description = 'This is Message 1.'
13          msg2 = Message()
14          msg2.title = 'Message 1'
15          msg2.description = 'This is Message 1.'
16          methods.context['msg1'] = msg1
17          methods.context['msg2'] = msg2
18          return methods
19
20      def test_getMessageNames(self):
21          methods = self._makeTree()
22          self.assert_(isinstance(methods.getMessageNames(), list))
23          self.assertEqual(list(methods.context.keys()),
24                          methods.getMessageNames())
25
26      def test_addMessage(self):
27          methods = self._makeTree()
28          self.assertEqual(methods.addMessage('msg3', 'M3', 'MB3'),
29                          'msg3')
30          self.assertEqual(methods.context['msg3'].title, 'M3')
31          self.assertEqual(methods.context['msg3'].body, 'MB3')
32
33      def test_deleteMessage(self):
34          methods = self._makeTree()
35          self.assertEqual(methods.deleteMessage('msg2'), True)
36          self.assertEqual(list(methods.context.keys()), ['msg1'])
```

In the preceding code block, note the following:

- Lines 5–6: The implementation of the `makeMethodObject()` method should return a valid XML-RPC method publisher.

- Lines 8–18: You create an interesting message tree so that you have something to test with.

- Lines 20–24: You make sure the names list is converted to a Python list and that all elements are contained in it.

- Lines 26–31: You test the adding capability. You need to just try to make sure that the correct attributes are assigned to the message.

- Lines 33–36: You simply check that a message is really deleted.

Now that you have the base class, you can implement the real test cases and add tests for the property accessors and mutators:

```
01 import unittest
02
03 from zope.publisher.xmlrpc import TestRequest
04
```

```
05 from book.messageboard.message import Message
06 from book.messageboard.messageboard import MessageBoard
07 from book.messageboard.xmlrpc import MessageBoardMethods, MessageMethods
08
09 class MessageBoardMethodsTest(MessageContainerTest, unittest.TestCase):
10
11     def _makeMethodObject(self):
12         return MessageBoardMethods(MessageBoard(), TestRequest())
13
14     def test_description(self):
15         methods = self._makeTree()
16         self.assertEqual(methods.getDescription(), '')
17         self.assertEqual(methods.setDescription('Board 1') , True)
18         self.assertEqual(methods.getDescription(), 'Board 1')
19
20 class MessageMethodsTest(MessageContainerTest, unittest.TestCase):
21
22     def _makeMethodObject(self):
23         return MessageMethods(Message(), TestRequest())
24
25     def test_title(self):
26         methods = self._makeTree()
27         self.assertEqual(methods.getTitle(), '')
28         self.assertEqual(methods.setTitle('Message 1') , True)
29         self.assertEqual(methods.getTitle(), 'Message 1')
30
31     def test_body(self):
32         methods = self._makeTree()
33         self.assertEqual(methods.getBody(), '')
34         self.assertEqual(methods.setBody('Body 1') , True)
35         self.assertEqual(methods.getBody(), 'Body 1')
36
37
38 def test_suite():
39     return unittest.TestSuite((
40         unittest.makeSuite(MessageBoardMethodsTest),
41         unittest.makeSuite(MessageMethodsTest),
42         ))
43
44 if __name__ == '__main__':
45     unittest.main(defaultTest='test_suite')
```

In the preceding code block, note the following:

- Lines 11–12 and 22–23: You create an XML-RPC method publisher for the message board and the message, respectively. To do that, you need an object instance (which is no problem) and an XML-RPC request. Luckily, like for the browser publisher, the XML-RPC publisher provides a `TestRequest` class, which was written to be easy to use in unit tests such as these.

- Lines 38–45: Again, you need to include the usual unit test boilerplate code.

The rest of the code is not very interesting, and its purpose should be obvious. You should run these tests now and make sure that everything passes.

Step 3: Configuring the New Views

To register the XML-RPC views, you need to import the `xmlrpc` namespace into your main configuration file by using this in the `zope:configure` element:

```
01 xmlns:xmlrpc="http://namespaces.zope.org/xmlrpc"
```

Now you simply add the following two directives to the configuration:

```
01 <xmlrpc:view
02     for=".interfaces.IMessageBoard"
03     permission="book.messageboard.Edit"
04     methods="getMessageNames addMessage deleteMessage
05             getDescription setDescription"
06     class=".xmlrpc.MessageBoardMethods" />
07
08 <xmlrpc:view
09     for=".interfaces.IMessage"
10     permission="book.messageboard.Edit"
11     methods="getMessageNames addMessage deleteMessage
12             getTitle setTitle getBody setBody"
13     class=".xmlrpc.MessageMethods" />
```

In the preceding code block, note the following:

- Line 2: You specify that this view is for `IMessageBoard` objects.
- Line 3: XML-RPC views require the `book.messageboard.Edit` permission, which means that someone has to authenticate before using these methods.
- Lines 4–5: You specify the list of methods that will be available as XML-RPC methods on the message board.
- Line 6: The method publisher class is `.xmlrpc.MessageBoardMethods`, which provides the previously defined methods.
- Lines 8–13: You repeat the previous directive for `IMessage` components.

Now you can restart Zope 3 and give your XML-RPC methods a run. But how do you test this? Certainly, a browser will not get you very far.

Step 4: Testing XML-RPC Features in Action

Python has a really nice XML-RPC module that you can use as an XML-RPC client and that also provides some extra help with basic authentication. To save the reader some typing, a module called `xmlrpc_client.py` is included in the `messageboard` package at `http://svn.zope.org/book/trunk/messageboard/step11/`. You can call it from the command line as follows:

```
# ./xmlrpc_client.py
```

You are asked for the URL to your `messageboard` object and for your username and password. After you have entered those correctly, you are presented with a normal Python prompt, except that there is a local variable called `board` available, and it represents your XML-RPC connection. You can now use the available methods to manipulate the board to your heart's content.

The following is a sample XML-RPC session, using the provided client:

```
# ./messageboard/xmlrpc_client.py
Message Board URL [http://localhost:8080/board/]:
Username: srichter
Password: ........
The message board is available as 'board'
Python 2.3 (#2, Aug 31 2003, 17:27:29)
[GCC 3.3.1 (Mandrake Linux 9.2 3.3.1-1mdk)] on linux2
Type "help", "copyright", "credits" or "license" for more information.
(InteractiveConsole)
>>> board.getDescription()
'First Message Board'
>>> board.getMessageNames()
['msg1', 'msg2']
>>> board.msg1.getMessageNames()
['msg11']
>>> board.msg1.msg11.getTitle()
'Message 1-1'
>>> board.msg1.msg11.getBody()
'This is the first response to Message 1.'
>>> board.msg1.addMessage('msg12', 'Message 1-2', 'Second response!')
'msg12'
>>> board.msg1.getMessageNames()
['msg11', 'msg12']
>>> board.msg1.msg12.getTitle()
'Message 1-2'
>>> board.msg1.deleteMessage('msg12')
True
>>> board.msg1.getMessageNames()
['msg11']
>>>
```

The code for this chapter can be found at `http://svn.zope.org/book/trunk/messageboard/step11/`.

Developing New Skins

Difficulty

Newcomer

Skills

- You should be familiar with the `messageboard` package up to this point.
- Feeling comfortable with writing ZCML-based view configuration would be advantageous. Optional.

Problem/Task

Until now you have only enhanced the `messageboard` package with features, but you have not done much to improve the user interface. In fact, you are still using the ZMI to do all your message board management, which is totally inappropriate to the end user. Therefore, this chapter concentrates on developing a skin specifically designed for the message board that implements a user interface like those typically seen in real-world message board applications. Although this package has little to do with Python development, it is a good final task for Parts III, "Content Components—The Basics," and IV, "Content Components—Advanced Techniques."

BY USING SKINS (THE EQUIVALENCE OF CMF skins in Zope 2), you can implement a custom look and feel for existing views. This is very similar to HTML and CSS (Cascading Style Sheets), where the HTML codes are equivalent to views (page templates, view classes) and the CSS style sheets are the skin over the HTML structural elements. However, there is another abstraction layer beneath a skin.

A skin is really just a stack of layers. Each layer can contain any number of views and resources. This allows particular views and resources to be overridden. For example, the

CSS style sheet for the `messageboard` package might have been defined in the `default` layer. However, that style sheet is really simplistic and inappropriate for your needs. You can instead create a new layer called `board` and place a new style sheet in it. When that is done, you can define a skin that places the `board` layer after the `default` layer, and all the new style definitions will be adopted.

Step 1: Preparing for a New Skin

Before you can create a new skin, you need to make some preparations. In order to not confuse the original views and resources with the new ones, you create a package called `skin` in the `messageboard/browser` directory; you need a `__init__.py` file to make the `skin` directory a package. Then you create an empty `configure.zcml` file:

```
01 <configure
02     xmlns="http://namespaces.zope.org/browser">
03
04 </configure>
```

Now you hook up this configuration file from the browser's `configure.zcml` by using this:

```
01 <include package=".skin" />
```

Step 2: Creating a New Skin

Creating a new skin is very easy and can be accomplished purely with ZCML configuration directives. The `browser` namespace has a special directive called `skin` that lets you do this, so you just have to add the following directive to the configuration file of the `skin` package:

```
01 <layer name="board"/>
02
03 <skin name="board" layers="board rotterdam default" />
```

The first directive creates a new layer, in which you will place all the new templates and which will make the skin unique. The second directive creates a skin named `board` that consists of a three-layer stack. The lowest layer is `default`, which is overridden by `rotterdam`, which is overridden by `board`. Every browser presentation directive supports a `layer` attribute, which defines the layer in which a view or resource is placed. If no layer is specified, the presentation component is placed in the default layer.

You might wonder why the `rotterdam` layer is placed here. The `rotterdam` layer contains some nice definitions, such as the favicon and some other view code that is useful for you here as well. Other than that, you will not be using this layer actively.

Step 3: Customizing the Base Templates

The first task in customizing a base template is always to override the skin macros and the dialog macros. Usually the skin macros are defined in a file called `template.pt`, and the dialog macros are defined in `dialog_macros.pt`. Macros are a technology for page templates that allow inserting dynamic code segments during runtime. By modifying macros, you can completely manipulate the look and feel of the existing pages without needing to implement their functionality from scratch.

Your new `template.pt` file for the `board` layer might look something like this:

```
01 <metal:block define-macro="page">
02   <metal:block define-slot="doctype">
03     <!DOCTYPE html PUBLIC "-//W3C//DTD XHTML 1.0 Transitional//EN"
04         "http://www.w3.org/TR/xhtml1/DTD/xhtml1-transitional.dtd">
05   </metal:block>
06
07 <html xmlns="http://www.w3.org/1999/xhtml" xml:lang="en" lang="en">
08
09   <head>
10     <title metal:define-slot="title">Message Board for Zope 3</title>
11
12     <style type="text/css" media="all"
13       tal:content=
14       "string: @import url(${context/++resource++board.css});">
15       @import url(board.css);
16     </style>
17
18     <meta http-equiv="Content-Type"
19         content="text/html;charset=utf-8" />
20
21     <link rel="icon" type="image/png"
22         tal:attributes="href context/++resource++favicon.png" />
23   </head>
24
25   <body>
26
27     <div id="board_header" i18n:domain="messageboard">
28       <img id="board_logo"
29         tal:attributes="src context/++resource++logo.png" />
30       <div id="board_greeting"> 
31         <span i18n:translate="">Zope 3 Message Board</span>
32       </div>
33     </div>
34
35     <div id="workspace">
36
37       <div metal:define-slot="message" id="message"></div>
38
39       <div id="content">
40         <metal:block define-slot="body">
41        This is the content.
```

```
42            </metal:block>
43         </div>
44
45     </div>
46
47     <div id="footer">
48
49       <div id="actions">
50         <metal:block define-slot="actions" />
51       </div>
52       <div id="credits" i18n:domain="messageboard">
53         Powered by Zope 3.<br>
54         Stephan Richter in 2003
55       </div>
56     </div>
57
58   </body>
59
60 </html>
61
62 </metal:block>
```

In the preceding code block, note the following:

- Lines 12–16: Instead of the standard `zope3.css`, you use a new `board.css` style sheet.
- Lines 21–22: This favicon is provided by the `rotterdam` skin.
- Lines 27–33: Do you see how simple the header is? A couple styles, a logo, and a simple title will do in this case.
- Lines 47–56: The footer consists of a placeholder (slot) into which you can later drop actions and a tiny credits section.

There is not really much to this template. Notice how much simpler this is than, for example, the `rotterdam` equivalent, which can be found at `src/zope/app/rotterdam`. Similarly simple is the `dialog_macros.pt` page template, which you can find at `http://svn.zope.org/book/trunk/messageboard/step12/browser/skin/`.

In the preceding template you refer to two new resources—`logo.png` and `board.css`. Both are configured as follows:

```
01 <resource
02     name="board.css" file="board.css" layer="board" />
03
04 <resource
05     name="logo.png" file="logo.png" layer="board" />
```

Note that the resource directive has a `layer` attribute to specify the layer. The initial CSS file (`board.css`) looks like this:

```
01 body {
02     font-family: Verdana, Arial, Helvetica, sans-serif;
03     background: white;
04     color: black;
05     margin: 0;
06     padding: 0pt;
07 }
08 h1, h2, h3, h4, h5, h6 {
09     font-weight: bold;
10     color: black;
11 }
12 /* Different headers are used for the same purpose,
13    so make them all equal. */
14 h1, h2, h3 {
15     font-size: 20pt;
16     margin-top: 0px;
17     margin-bottom: .8em;
18     border-bottom: solid 1px #1E5ADB;
19 }
20 ...
21 /* Header Stuff */
22 #board_header {
23     background: #EEEEEE;
24     border: solid 1px #AAAAAA;
25     padding: 3pt;
26     clear: both;
27 }
28 ...
29 /* Footer stuff */
30 #footer {
31     background: #EEEEEE;
32     border: solid 1px #AAAAAA;
33     padding: 0.5em;
34     font-size: 85%;
35 }
36 ...
```

For the full style sheet, see the sample code online.

You then register the templates for the board layer, as follows:

```
01 <page
02     for="*"
03     name="skin_macros"
04     permission="zope.View"
05     layer="board"
06     template="template.pt" />
07
08 <page
```

```
09    for="*"
10    name="dialog_macros"
11    permission="zope.View"
12    layer="board"
13    template="dialog_macros.pt" />
```

In the preceding code block, note the following:

- Lines 2 and 9: The * means that this page is available for all objects.
- Lines 5 and 12: The additional layer attribute is enough to specify the layer.

Step 4: Adding a Message Board Intro Screen

The simplest view of the message board is some sort of introduction screen for the message board because it is just a simple page template. The template looks like this:

```
01 <html metal:use-macro="views/standard_macros/page">
02   <body>
03     <div id="content" metal:fill-slot="body"
04         i18n:domain="messageboard">
05
06       <h2 i18n:translate="">Welcome to the Message Board</h2>
07
08       <p class="board_description" tal:content="context/description">
09         Description of the Message Board goes here.
10       </p>
11
12       <div id="login_link">
13         <a href="./posts.html">Click here to enter the board.</a>
14       </div>
15
16     </div>
17   </body>
18 </html>
```

You can place the template in the skin directory and name it board_intro.pt. The view must be registered for the layer by using the following:

```
01 <page
02    for="book.messageboard.interfaces.IMessageBoard"
03    name="intro.html"
04    permission="book.messageboard.View"
05    layer="board"
06    template="board_intro.pt" />
```

When you restart Zope 3 now, you should be able to reach this view (see Figure 24.1) by using `http://localhost:8080/++skin++board/board/@@intro.html`, assuming that the `MessageBoard` instance is called `board` and lives in the root folder.

Figure 24.1   The message board introduction screen of the `board` skin.

Step 5: Viewing a List of All Message Board Posts

When the user enters the message board, he or she should see a list of all the top-level messages (currently it leads nowhere). In the actions section, the user should have an option to add a new message to the board. Administrators should be able to go to a review screen to publish messages that are still pending. You can find the source of the template in `board_posts.pt`, in the `skin` directory of the message board sample code online.

You configure the view by issuing the following instruction:

```
01  <page
02      for="book.messageboard.interfaces.IMessageBoard"
03      name="posts.html"
04      permission="book.messageboard.View"
05      layer="board"
06      class=".views.Posts"
07      template="board_posts.pt" />
```

As you can see, the page uses a view class, which is located in `views.py`. The template `board_posts.pt` uses a method of the view that returns a list containing a dictionary with detailed information for each message. However, this does nothing new. You have functionality like this in the existing views, so it does not need to be explained here.

As shown in Figure 24.2, you should now be able to see a list of posts of the message board (but only those that are in the published workflow state).

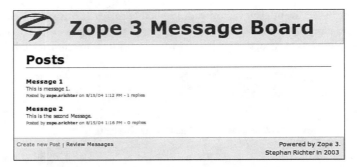

Figure 24.2   Posted message board messages.

Step 6: Adding a Post to the Message Board

When looking at the posts screen, you might have already clicked the Create New Post link and added a new message. You will have noticed that the Add view does not bring you back to the posts overview; instead, it brings you back to a management screen. To change that, you have to create a customized Add view that specifies the return URL. The implementation in the `views.py` module looks like this:

```
01 class AddMessage:
02     """Add-Form supporting class."""
03
04     def nextURL(self):
05         return '../@@posts.html'
```

This is straightforward. Now you just need to configure it.

By default, you can enter a message ID for the message. This is undesirable for your user-friendly skin. You might have noticed that you can leave the ID field empty, in which case the message ID will be something like Message or Message-2. That's because there is a mechanism that creates these generic names. The Add view uses this mechanism if no name is specified. You can tell the Add view to always use this mechanism for the `MessageBoard` and `Message` components by having them implement the `IContainerNamesContainer` interface. You can do this by adding the following directive to the `zope:content` directive of both objects in the main `configure.zcml` file:

```
01 <implements
02     interface="zope.app.container.interfaces.IContainerNamesContainer"
03     />
```

Finally, you have to configure the new Add view by using the following:

```
01 <addform
02     label="Add Message"
03     name="AddMessage.html"
```

```
04        schema="book.messageboard.interfaces.IMessage"
05        content_factory="book.messageboard.message.Message"
06        permission="book.messageboard.Add"
07        class=".views.AddMessage"
08        layer="board"/>
```

This was not very hard, was it? After you restart Zope, you can admire the correct functionality of the Add view.

Step 7: Reviewing Pending Messages

Try to add a message. Where does it go? Remember that only published messages are visible.

Although you have a message review screen for the management interface, it is not very usable. You need to develop simplified functionality in the board skin that can only publish messages. The following template displays all the pending messages and provides a check box for the moderator to select whether this message is about to be published (board_review.pt):

```
01 <html metal:use-macro="views/standard_macros/page">
02   <body>
03     <div metal:fill-slot="body" i18n:domain="messageboard">
04
05       <h2 i18n:translate="">Review Pending Posts</h2>
06
07       <form action="updateStatus.html" method="POST">
08
09         <div id="message_line"
10             tal:repeat="post view/getPendingMessagesInfo">
11           <input type="checkbox" name="messages" value=""
12             tal:attributes="value post/path" />
13           <a href="" tal:attributes="href post/url"
14             tal:content="post/title">Message Title</a>
15           <div style="font-size: 70%">
16             (Posted by <b tal:content="post/creator">Creator</b>
17             on <b tal:replace="post/created">2003/01/01</b>)
18           </div>
19         </div>
20         <br />
21         <input type="submit" value="Publish"
22             i18n:attributes="value" />
23
24       </form>
25
26     </div>
27     <div id="actions" metal:fill-slot="actions">
28       <a href="posts.html" i18n:translate="">View Posts</a>
```

```
29     </div>
30    </body>
31 </html>
```

In the corresponding Python view class, you can simply reuse the code you developed for the management version:

```
01 from zope.app.import zapi
02 from zope.app.dublincore.interfaces import ICMFDublinCore
03 from zope.app.interfaces.workflow import IProcessInstanceContainer
04
05 from book.messageboard.browser.messageboard import ReviewMessages
06
07 class Review(ReviewMessages):
08     """Review messages for publication."""
09
10     def getPendingMessagesInfo(self):
11         """Get all the display info for pending messages"""
12         msg_infos = []
13         for msg in self.getPendingMessages(self.context):
14             dc = ICMFDublinCore(msg)
15             info = {}
16             info['path'] = zapi.getPath(msg)
17             info['title'] = msg.title
18             info['creator'] = dc.creators[0]
19             formatter = self.request.locale.dates.getFormatter(
20                 'dateTime', 'medium')
21             info['created'] = formatter.format(dc.created)
22             info['url'] = zapi.getView(
23                 msg, 'absolute_url', self.request)() + \
24                 '/@@details.html'
25             msg_infos.append(info)
26         return msg_infos
27
28     def updateStatus(self, messages):
29         """Upgrade the stati from 'pending' to 'published'."""
30         if not isinstance(messages, (list, tuple)):
31             messages = [messages]
32
33         for path in messages:
34             msg = zapi.traverse(self.context, path)
35
36             adapter = IProcessInstanceContainer(msg)
37             adapter['publish-message'].fireTransition('pending_published')
38
39         return self.request.response.redirect('@@review.html')
```

In the preceding code block, note the following:

- Lines 5, 7, and 13: You reuse some code from the original implementation.
- Lines 28–39: This interesting method actually fires the transition from pending to published status.

  Lines 33–34: Because you were clever, you passed the path as a check box value, so you can now simply traverse to it.

  Lines 36–37: When you have the message, you get its workflow process instance container and fire the transition.

The new review view can now be registered, using the `pages` directive:

```
01 <pages
02     for="book.messageboard.interfaces.IMessageBoard"
03     class=".views.Review"
04     permission="book.messageboard.PublishContent"
05     layer="board">
06   <page name="review.html" template="board_review.pt"/>
07   <page name="updateStatus.html" attribute="updateStatus"/>
08 </pages>
```

Now you can restart Zope 3. Before you can enjoy publishing messages, you need to automate the transition from private to pending status. To do that, you go to the `default` Site-Management folder, and from there to your `publish-message` workflow definition. There you will find an option called Manage Transitions. You should click it and choose the transition named `private_pending`. In the following edit form, a Trigger Mode option is set to Manual. You should set it to Automatic. This causes the messages to move automatically from initial to pending status. If you now create a message, it is automatically placed on the review list, from which you, as message board moderator, can then publish it. If you do not want any workflow at all, you can also set the `pending_published` Trigger Mode setting to Automatic, and all newly created messages are automatically published (see Figure 24.3).

Figure 24.3   Reviewing all pending messages.

Step 8: Viewing Message Details

Although the ZMI-based Message Details screen is very clear and detailed, it is not suitable for the end user. The new message details view implements a better version of that screen and also adds the replies thread at the end. One of the available actions is to reply to the message. You'll look at this screen next.

As usual, the code can be found online. The result is shown in Figure 24.4. Because there is nothing new or very interesting going on in the code, let's skip over it and move directly to the next view.

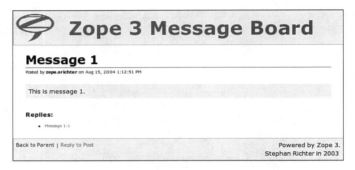

Figure 24.4   Displaying all details of a message.

Step 9: Replying to Messages

Can you really create another Add view? Yes, of course. The Reply to Message Add view is a bit special, though, because it should contain dynamic default values. For example, if the original message had a title called My Title, the suggested title for the new reply message should be Re: My Title. Similarly, every text line of the original message body should be prefixed with >.

The best place to insert the dynamic default values is in the private _setUpWidgets() methods, which creates a data dictionary that is passed to the widget instantiater. The code for the entire Add view class looks like this:

```
01 from zope.app.form.interfaces import IinputWisget
02 from zope.app.form.utility import setUpWidgets
03
04 class ReplyMessage:
05     """Add-Form supporting class."""
06
```

```
07      def nextURL(self):
08          return '../@@details.html'
09
10      def _setUpWidgets(self):
11          """Allow addforms to also have default values."""
12          parent = self.context.context
13          title = parent.title
14          if not title.startswith('Re:'):
15              title = 'Re: ' + parent.title
16
17          dc = ICMFDublinCore(parent)
18          formatter = self.request.locale.dates.getDFormatter(
19              'dateTime', 'medium')
20          body = '%s on %s wrote:\n' %(dc.creators[0],
21                                       formatter.format(dc.created))
22          body += '> ' + parent.body.replace('\n', '\n> ')
23
24          setUpWidgets(self, self.schema, IInputWisget
25                      initial={'title': title, 'body': body},
26                      names=self.fieldNames)
```

In the preceding code block, note the following:

- Lines 24–26: This is pretty much the original content of the `_setUpWidgets()` method, except for the `initial` argument, which carries the default values of the widgets.

You just register the form as follows:

```
01 <addform
02     label="Reply to Message"
03     name="ReplyMessage"
04     schema="book.messageboard.interfaces.IMessage"
05     content_factory="book.messageboard.message.Message"
06     permission="book.messageboard.Add"
07     class=".views.ReplyMessage"
08     layer="board"/>
```

When you restart Zope 3, you should be able to see the Reply to Message screen, as shown in Figure 24.5.

At this point, this is as far as you need to go with creating a nice, end–user–friendly interface. You could do much more to make the package attractive, but the new code would not contain much new content and would be boring to read about. Instead, you should think about what further improvements you would like to make.

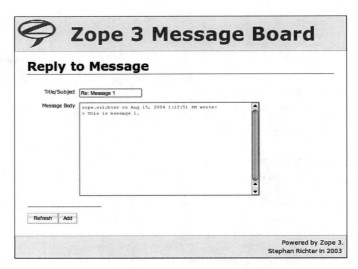

Figure 24.5   Replying to a message.

V

Other Components

From earlier chapters, you know that content objects are not the only type of component you want to write. This part covers several of the various other components, such as utilities and resources.

Chapter 25: Building and Storing Annotations

Because it is desirable to leave an object as untouched as possible, Zope 3 provides a mechanism, known as *annotations*, to associate data with an object. Annotations are commonly stored in a special attribute on the object. This chapter describes how to develop an alternative way to store annotations.

Chapter 26: New Principle-Source Plug-ins

Different people have very different requirements for what mechanism an authentication service should have, and Zope 3 respects this need. There is an authentication service that accepts plug-ins to provide principal data from external data sources.

Chapter 27: Principal Annotations

A common task is to append data to principals. Because principals are often imported from external data sources, they are not attribute annotatable. This chapter makes use of the principal annotation service to store additional data.

Chapter 28: Creating New Browser Resources

This short chapter describes how to implement a new filesystem-based resource (in other words, a context-independent view).

Chapter 29: Registries with Global Utilities

Utilities can be used to implement Zope-wide registries. Because registries are so very useful, this chapter is a must.

Chapter 30: Local Utilities

You have already seen how simple it is to write global utilities, but there is some more work to do for local utilities, as described in this chapter.

Chapter 31: Vocabularies and Related Fields/Widgets

Vocabularies are a powerful extension to the schema framework, and they provide a generic method for creating fields with variable- and context-dependent selection lists.

Chapter 32: Exception Views

In Zope 3, exceptions are simply objects that can have different views. These different views make objects capable of being represented on any output medium (usually the browser). Every exception has a standard view, but for a professional website, you need better screens.

25

Building and Storing Annotations

Difficulty

Sprinter

Skills

- You should be familiar with the concept of annotations and how they are used. See Chapter 36, "Registering New WebDAV Namespaces," for a good example of how to use annotations.
- You should be comfortable with the component architecture and ZCML.

Problem/Task

Currently, every object that comes with Zope 3 and can have some sort of annotation uses attribute annotations. Attribute annotations store the annotation data directly in the objects. This implementation works fine, as long as the object is persistent and is stored in the ZODB. But what if you have SQL-based objects, such as in relational-to-object mapping solutions? Storing annotations on the attribute of the object would certainly not work. In such scenarios it becomes necessary to implement a custom annotations implementation. This chapter demonstrates how to do that.

B EFORE YOU CAN DIVE IN to developing a new annotation adapter, it is important that you understand the inner-workings of annotation adapters. First, there exists an interface named `IAnnotatable`. By providing this interface, an object declares that it is possible to store annotations for itself.

However, `IAnnotatable` is too general because it does not specify how the annotation can be stored. It should therefore never be provided directly by an object. You should never assume that one method works for all possible objects.

By default, Zope 3 comes with an `IAttributeAnnotatable` interface. By providing the `IAttributeAnnotatable` interface, an object declares that annotations can be stored on the object itself, in a special attribute called __annotations__. This works well for any object whose instances are stored in the ZODB.

As a second part to the equation, Zope 3 comes with the `IAnnotations` interface, which provides a simple mapping (that is, dictionary-like) API that allows you to look up annotation data by using a unique key. This interface is commonly implemented as an adapter that requires `IAnnotatable` and provides `IAnnotations`. Thus you need to provide an implementation for `IAnnotations` to have your own annotations storage mechanism.

For `IAttributeAnnotable`, you have an `AttributeAnnotations` adapter. Note that, by definition, `IAnnotations` extends `IAnnotable` because an `IAnnotations` interface can always adapt to itself. It might be helpful to also look at the `zope.app.annotation` package for more information.

Another important aspect about annotations is the key (unique ID) that is used in the mapping. Because annotations may contain a large amount of data, it is important to choose keys such that they will always be unique. The simplest way to ensure this is to include the package name in the key. So for Dublin Core metadata, for example, instead of using `ZopeDublinCore` as the key, you should use `zope.app.dublincore.ZopeDublinCore`. Some people also use a URI-based namespace notation (for example, `http://namespace.zope.org/dublincore/ZopeDublinCore/1.0`). This chapter uses the Dublin Core example to test for the correct behavior of annotations.

Implementing an Alternative Annotations Mechanism

Let's say you cannot store annotations in an attribute on the object because the object is volatile. Where could you store the annotation data in that case? One possibility would be to use relational databases (RDBs), which makes sense if your object's data is also stored in an RDB. A derivative of this solution would be to use files; but that is hard to get working with transactions.

You also have to bear in mind that Zope uses annotations to store metadata such as Dublin Core metadata or workflow data. It would be hard to store that data in an RDB. So the ZODB is still a good place to store the annotation data. One way would be to develop some sort of annotations container that lives in the ZODB. But it would be even better if the annotations could store their data to a nearby object that implements `IAttributeAnnotable`. This would allow almost any persistent object in the ZODB to serve as an annotation keeper.

Step 1: Developing the Interfaces

You don't want to put the burden of holding another object's annotations on just any object you can find. Instead, an object should declare that it is willing to keep annotations of other objects by implementing an interface named `IAnnotationKeeper`.

Objects that want their annotations to be stored in annotation keepers need to implement `IKeeperAnnotatable`.

By the way, for an object to find a keeper, it must also implement `ILocation`. Clearly, the keeper annotation design makes sense only if you expect the object to be stored in a traversable path and is therefore not generally applicable either.

For writing the interfaces, you first need to start a new package in `ZOPE3/src/book` called `keeperannotations`. Then you add the following contents in `interfaces.py`:

```
01 from zope.interface import Interface
02 from zope.app.annotation.interfaces import IAnnotatable
03
04 class IAnnotationKeeper(Interface):
05     """Marker indicating that an object is willing to store other object's
06     annotations in its own annotations.
07
08     This interface makes only sense, if the object that implements this
09     interface also implements 'IAnnotatable' or any sub-class.
10     """
11
12 class IKeeperAnnotatable(IAnnotatable):
13     """Marker indicating that an object will store its annotations in an
14     object implementing IAnnotationKeeper.
15
16     This requires the object that provides this interface to also implement
17     ILocation.
18
19     This interface does not specify how the keeper may be found. This is up
20     to the adapter that uses this interface to provide 'IAnnotations'.
21     """
```

Both interfaces are just markers because there is no direct duty involved in implementing these interfaces.

Step 2: Implementing the `KeeperAnnotations` Adapter

Implementing the keeper annotations adapter is simply a matter of implementing the `IAnnotations` interface's mapping methods. The tricky part of the implementation is to find the object that is the annotation keeper. This should be no problem, as long as the object has a location and a keeper is available in the path of the object.

This first issue is important. When an object has just been created, an `ObjectCreatedEvent` event is sent out, and the Dublin Core mechanism listens to it. The Dublin Core mechanism then tries to set the creation and modification dates on the object, using annotations. This is, of course, a problem because the object has no location at this point. In these cases, you need some sort of temporary storage that can keep the annotation until the object has a location.

You can safely ignore the second issue. The easiest thing to do at this point would be to simply make the root folder an `IAnnotationKeeper` interface. This way, the lookup for a keeper will never fail, provided that the object has a location. In the __init__.py file of your package, you can add the following adapter code:

```
01 from BTrees.OOBTree import OOBTree
02
03 from zope.interface import implements
04 from zope.proxy import removeAllProxies
05
06 from zope.app import zapi
07 from zope.app.annotation.interfaces import IAnnotations
08
09 from interfaces import IKeeperAnnotatable, IAnnotationKeeper
10
11 keeper_key = 'book.keeperannotation.KeeperAnnotations'
12
13 tmp = {}
14
15 class KeeperAnnotations(object):
16     """Store the annotations in a keeper.
17     """
18     implements(IAnnotations)
19     __used_for__ = IKeeperAnnotatable
20
21     def __init__(self, obj):
22         self.obj = obj
23         self.obj_key = removeAllProxies(obj)
24         self.keeper_annotations = None
25
26         # Annotations might be set when object has no context
27         if not hasattr(obj, '__parent__') or obj.__parent__ is None:
28             self.keeper_annotations = tmp
29             return
30
31         for parent in zapi.getParents(obj):
32             if IAnnotationKeeper.providedBy(parent):
33                 # We found the keeper, get the annotation that will store
34                 # the data.
35                 annotations = IAnnotations(parent)
```

```
36                  if not annotations.has_key(keeper_key):
37                      annotations[keeper_key] = OOBTree()
38                  self.keeper_annotations = annotations[keeper_key]
39
40          if self.keeper_annotations == None:
41              raise ValueError, 'No annotation keeper found.'
42
43          # There are some temporary stored annotations; add them to the keeper
44          if tmp.has_key(obj):
45              self.keeper_annotations[self.obj_key] = tmp[obj]
46              del tmp[obj]
47
48      def __getitem__(self, key):
49          """See zope.app.annotation.interfaces.IAnnotations"""
50          annotations = self.keeper_annotations.get(self.obj_key, {})
51          return annotations[key]
52
53      def __setitem__(self, key, value):
54          """See zope.app.annotation.interfaces.IAnnotations"""
55          if not self.keeper_annotations.has_key(self.obj_key):
56              self.keeper_annotations[self.obj_key] = OOBTree()
57          self.keeper_annotations[self.obj_key][key] = value
58
59      def get(self, key, default=None):
60          """See zope.app.annotation.interfaces.IAnnotations"""
61          try:
62              return self[key]
63          except KeyError:
64              return default
65
66      def __delitem__(self, key):
67          """See zope.app.annotation.interfaces.IAnnotations"""
68          del self.keeper_annotations[self.obj_key][key]
```

In the preceding code block, note the following:

- Line 11: This string is used in the keeper's annotations to store the other objects' annotations.

- Line 13: This is the temporary annotations variable, which holds annotations for objects that have not yet been located (that is, have no parent and name).

- Line 23: Here you use the object itself as a key in the annotations. This works well for persistent objects, but volatile content components would still not work. (Note that you could not use the path of the object yet either because the object might not have been located yet.)

- Lines 27–29: In the case that no location has been assigned to the object yet, you can use the temporary storage.

- Lines 31–38: You walk through all the parents and try to find the closest keeper. When a keeper is found, you use it. Next, you add a keeper BTree, if none exists yet.

- Lines 40–41: If no keeper is found, you raise a `ValueError` exception. The condition should never be true because that would cause a lot of application code to fail. So, you need to make sure that a keeper can always be found.

- Lines 44–46: If there are some temporary annotation entries, it is time to move them to the real keeper now and delete them from the temporary storage.

- Lines 48–51: You specify a straightforward implementation that simply looks for the key at the correct place. You pass in a default because the annotation for the given object might not even exist yet.

- Lines 53–57: First, the code checks whether an annotation entry already exists for the object in the keeper. If not, a new entry is added. Finally, the new annotation for the object is set.

- Lines 59–64: This implementation reuses the `__getitem__()` method to avoid code duplication.

- Lines 66–68: You delegate the deletion request to the correct entry.

This `KeeperAnnotations` adapter implementation is not meant to be used in production but to serve as a simple demonstration.

Step 3: Writing and Performing Unit Tests

The problem with writing annotations is that they are used by other content objects. The correct way of writing the tests for the annotations adapter would be to develop dummy content objects. But in order to keep the testing code as small as possible, you can just depend on some of the existing content implementations, namely `Folder` and `File`. The most well-defined annotation is probably `ZopeDublinCore`, and you can use it to declare and test some annotations.

You should use doc strings to write the tests. The doc string tests are not listed in this chapter, but you can find the test code in the class doc string of `KeeperAnnotations` at `http://svn.zope.org/book/trunk/keeperannotations/`.

Now you just have to write a test module to execute the doctests. To do so, you can create a file called `tests.py` and add the following lines:

```
01 import unittest
02
03 from zope.interface import classImplements
04 from zope.testing.doctestunit import DocTestSuite
05
06 from zope.app.annotation.attribute import AttributeAnnotations
07 from zope.app.folder import Folder
08 from zope.app.dublincore.annotatableadapter import ZDCAnnotatableAdapter
```

```
09 from zope.app.annotation.interfaces import \
10     IAnnotations, IAnnotatable, IAttributeAnnotatable
11 from zope.app.dublincore.interfaces import IWriteZopeDublinCore
12 from zope.app.location.interfaces import ILocation
13 from zope.app.traversing.interfaces import IPhysicallyLocatable
14 from zope.app.location.traversing import LocationPhysicallyLocatable
15 from zope.app.tests import ztapi
16 from zope.app.tests.placelesssetup import setUp, tearDown
17
18 from book.keeperannotations.interfaces import IKeeperAnnotatable
19 from book.keeperannotations import KeeperAnnotations
20
21 def customSetUp(test):
22     setUp()
23     classImplements(Folder, IAttributeAnnotatable)
24     ztapi.provideAdapter(IKeeperAnnotatable, IAnnotations,
25                          KeeperAnnotations)
26     ztapi.provideAdapter(ILocation, IPhysicallyLocatable,
27                          LocationPhysicallyLocatable)
28     ztapi.provideAdapter(IAnnotatable, IWriteZopeDublinCore,
29                          ZDCAnnotatableAdapter)
30     ztapi.provideAdapter(IAttributeAnnotatable, IAnnotations,
31                          AttributeAnnotations)
32
33 def test_suite():
34     return unittest.TestSuite((
35         DocTestSuite('book.keeperannotations',
36                      setUp=customSetUp, tearDown=tearDown),
37         ))
38
39 if __name__ == '__main__':
40     unittest.main(defaultTest='test_suite')
```

There are a lot of imports because you have to register a bunch of adapters for the testing code to work.

You can now execute the tests from the Zope 3 root directory by using this:

```
python2.3 bin/test -vpu --dir lib/python/book/keeperannotations
```

Step 4: Configuring the `KeeperAnnotations` Component

To use the `KeeperAnnotations` adapter, you need to register it.

In `configure.zcml`, you add the following lines:

```
01 <configure
02     xmlns="http://namespaces.zope.org/zope"
03     xmlns:browser="http://namespaces.zope.org/browser"
```

```
04      i18n_domain="zope">
05
06   <adapter
07       for=".interfaces.IKeeperAnnotatable"
08       provides="zope.app.annotation.interfaces.IAnnotations"
09       factory=".KeeperAnnotations" />
10
11 </configure>
```

The final step is to hook the code into the Zope 3 framework. All you have to do is create the file *Zope3-Instance*/etc/package-includes/keeperannotations-configure.zcml, which should contain the following line:

```
01 <include package="book.keeperannotations" />
```

And that's it for the package. The annotations keeper adapter is now set up and can be used by other components.

Step 5: Writing Functional Tests and Configuration

Functional tests are very important for this package because you do not know whether you thought of all exceptions until you test the keeper annotations code in a fully running Zope 3 environment. In a running Zope 3 setup, you cannot use File as a test object anymore because it already implements IAttributeAnnotable. Instead, you can use the KeeperFile class, which inherits from File and register it separately. In a new file named ftests.py, you add the new content type:

```
01 from zope.app.file import File
02
03 class KeeperFile(File):
04     pass
```

You now need to register this new content type. You could add the registration directives to configure.zcml and be done, but because this content type is for testing only, it is better to create a separate configuration file and hook it up with the functional testing configuration directly.

You register the KeeperFile class in almost identically the same way as the regular File class. In addition, the KeeperAnnotations adapter must be registered. For simplicity, you can make every Folder class an IAnnotationKeeper adapter.

Next, you need to create a new file called keeper.zcml and add the following lines to it:

```
01 <configure
02       xmlns="http://namespaces.zope.org/zope"
03       xmlns:browser="http://namespaces.zope.org/browser"
04       i18n_domain="zope">
05
```

```
06    <content class="zope.app.folder.Folder">
07      <implements
08        interface=".interfaces.IAnnotationKeeper"
09        />
10    </content>
11
12    <content class=".ftests.KeeperFile">
13      <factory
14          id="book.keeperannotations.KeeperFile"
15          title="Keeper File"
16          description="A Keeper File" />
17
18      <require
19          permission="zope.View"
20          interface="zope.app.filerepresentation.interfaces.IReadFile" />
21
22      <require
23          permission="zope.ManageContent"
24          interface="zope.app.filerepresentation.interfaces.IWriteFile"
25          set_schema="zope.app.filerepresentation.interfaces.IReadFile"
26          />
27
28      <implements
29        interface=".interfaces.IKeeperAnnotatable"
30        />
31    </content>
32
33    <browser:addMenuItem
34        class=".ftests.KeeperFile"
35        title="Keeper File"
36        permission="zope.ManageContent"
37        view="KeeperFile"
38        />
39
40    <browser:addform
41        schema="zope.app.file.interfaces.IFile"
42        label="Add a Keeper File"
43        content_factory=".ftests.KeeperFile"
44        name="AddKeeperFile"
45        permission="zope.ManageContent"
46        />
47
48 </configure>
```

If you do not understand these directives, read Chapters 13, "Writing New Content Objects," and 14 "Adding Views for Content Objects," which explain them in detail.

You now need to tell the functional configuration setup that it should evaluate `keeper.zcml`. You do so by adding the following to *Zope3-Instance*/etc/ `ftesting.zcml`:

```
01 <include package="book.keeperannotations" file="keeper.zcml" />
```

This file is the main configuration file for functional tests. It is used in the same way that `site.zcml` is used for a real startup.

Now the testing environment should be configured, and you can concentrate on writing the test itself. The test should emulate the unit tests. Here is the setup, which you should add to `ftests.py`:

```
01 import time
02 import unittest
03
04 from zope.app.tests.functional import BrowserTestCase
05
06 from book.keeperannotations import keeper_key
07
08
09 class Test(BrowserTestCase):
10     """Funcional tests for Keeper Annotations.
11     """
12
13     def test_DC_Annotations(self):
14         # Create file
15         response = self.publish(
16             "/+/action.html?type_name=book.keeperannotations.KeeperFile",
17             basic='mgr:mgrpw')
18
19         self.assertEqual(response.getStatus(), 302)
20         self.assertEqual(response.getHeader('Location'),
21                          'http://localhost/@@contents.html')
22
23         # Update the file's title
24         self.publish("/@@contents.html",
25                      basic='mgr:mgrpw',
26                      form={'retitle_id' : 'KeeperFile',
27                            'new_value' : u'File Title'})
28
29         root = self.getRootFolder()
30         file = root['KeeperFile']
31         ann = root.__annotations__[keeper_key][file]
32         dc_ann = ann['zope.app.dublincore.ZopeDublinCore']
33         self.assert_(dc_ann[u'Date.Created'][0] > u'2004-01-01T12:00:00')
34         self.assert_(dc_ann[u'Date.Created'][0] == dc_ann[u'Date.Modified'][0])
35         self.assertEqual(dc_ann[u'Title'][0], u'File Title')
36
```

```
37 def test_suite():
38     return unittest.TestSuite((
39         unittest.makeSuite(Test),
40         ))
41
42 if __name__=='__main__':
43     unittest.main(defaultTest='test_suite')
```

In the preceding code block, note the following:

- Lines 15–21: You add a keeper file to the root folder and make sure the correct HTTP response its provided.

- Lines 24–27: You change the title of the file. The title is provided by the Dublin Core, which in turn uses annotations to store its values.

- Lines 29–35: Testing the correct behavior using HTML views would be too tedious, so you just grab the root folder directly and analyze the annotations for correct entries, as you did with the unit tests.

You can now run the tests:

```
python2.3 bin/test -vpf --dir lib/python/book/keeperannotations
```

You can also try the annotation keeper with the message board. You simply make the message board an annotation keeper for messages.

You can find the complete source code for this chapter at
`http://svn.zope.org/book/trunk/keeperannotations`.

26

New Principal-Source Plug-ins

Difficulty

Sprinter

Skills

- You should have a basic understanding of the Zope 3 component architecture.
- You need to understand the purpose and differences between permissions, roles, and principals.
- Basic knowledge about the authentication service is helpful. Optional.

Problem/Task

Many systems provide their own mechanisms for authentication. Examples include /etc/passwd, LDAP, NIS, Radius, and relational databases. For a generic platform such as Zope, it is critical that you provide facilities to connect to these external authentication sources.

Zope 3 has an advanced authentication service that provides an interface you can use to integrate any external authentication source by simply developing a small plug-in, called a *principal source*. In this chapter you'll create such a plug-in and register it with the authentication service.

ALTHOUGH YOU CAN BECOME VERY FANCY in implementing a feature-rich principal-source implementation, this chapter concentrates on a very simple case.

The goal of this chapter is to create a file-based principal source that should be able to read an /etc/passwd-like file. (It will not actually be able to read passwd files because you do not know whether everyone has the crypt module installed on their machines.)

The following is the format of the file that you want to be able to read and parse (note that users are separated by a newline character):

login:password:title:other_stuff

Let's now turn to the principal source. The goal is to provide a source that will work together with the pluggable authentication service in `zope.app.pluggableauth.intefaces`. A component implementing `ILoginPasswordPrincipalSource` (which extends `IPrincipalSource`) promises to provide three simple methods:

- **`getPrincipal(id)`** —This method gets a particular principal by its ID, which is unique for this particular source. If no principal with the supplied ID is found, a `NotFoundError` exception should be raised.

- **`getPrincipals(name)`** —This method returns a list of principals whose logins somehow contain the substring specified in `name`. If `name` is an empty string, all principals of this source are returned.

- **`authenticate(login, password)`** —This method is actually required by the `ILoginPasswordPrincipalSource` interface, and it provides authentication for the provided principal. There are other ways to implement authentication for these principals, but they add unnecessary complexity. `None` is returned if no match is made.

The next step is to provide an implementation of `ILoginPasswordPrincipalSource` for password files. You need to create a new subpackage called `passwdauth` in the `book` package. Then you can define the interfaces, as usual.

Step 1: Defining the Interface

You might wonder what interface you need when dealing with a principal-source plug-in. In order for a file-based principal-source plug-in to provide principals, you need to know what file contains the data; knowing about this file is certainly part of the API for this plug-in. So you want to create a specific interface that contains a filename. If you make this attribute a schema field, you can even use the interface/schema to create auto-generated add and edit forms.

In the `passwdauth` directory, you add an `interfaces.py` file and add the following contents to it:

```
01 from zope.schema import TextLine
02 from zope.app.i18n import ZopeMessageIDFactory as _
03
04 from zope.app.pluggableauth.interfaces import IPrincipalSource
05
06 class IFileBasedPrincipalSource(IPrincipalSource):
07     """Describes file-based principal sources."""
08
09     filename = TextLine(
```

```
10          title = _(u'File Name'),
11          description=_(u'File name of the data file.'),
12          default = u'/etc/passwd')
```

In the preceding code block, note the following:

- Line 1: Here you have the usual imports of the `TextLine` field for the `filename` property.

- Line 2: This is the typical I18n boilerplate code; all text strings wrapped by the underscore function will be internationalized (that is, they will be localizable).

- Line 4: The file-based principal source is still of type `IPrincipalSource`, so you make it the base interface.

- Lines 9–12: You include the typical internationalized text line field declaration, making `/etc/passwd` the default value (even though the package will not work with this file due to the `crypt` module issue). You might want to add a different default, based on the operating system you are using.

Step 2: Writing the Tests

At this point you need to write some unit tests to ensure that the file parser does its job correctly. But first you need to develop a small data file with which you can test the plug-in. You need to create a file called `passwd.sample` and add the following two principal entries to it:

```
01 foo1:bar1:Foo Bar 1
02 foo2:bar2:Foo Bar 2
```

Now you have a user with the login `foo1` and one known as `foo2`, having `bar1` and `bar2` as passwords, respectively.

The following test code tests only the aforementioned three methods of the principal source. The file-reading code is not separately checked because you will test it through other tests later on.

You need to create a `tests.py` file and add the following code to it:

```
01 import os
02 import unittest
03
04 from zope.exceptions import NotFoundError
05
06 from book import passwdauth
07
08
09 class PasswdPrincipalSourceTest(unittest.TestCase):
10
11     def setUp(self):
12         dir = os.path.dirname(passwdauth.__file__)
```

```
13          self.source = passwdauth.PasswdPrincipalSource(
14              os.path.join(dir, 'passwd.sample'))
15
16      def test_getPrincipal(self):
17          self.assertEqual(self.source.getPrincipal('\t\tfoo1').password, 'bar1')
18          self.assertEqual(self.source.getPrincipal('\t\tfoo2').password, 'bar2')
19          self.assertRaises(NotFoundError, self.source.getPrincipal, '\t\tfoo')
20
21      def test_getPrincipals(self):
22          self.assertEqual(len(self.source.getPrincipals('foo')), 2)
23          self.assertEqual(len(self.source.getPrincipals('')), 2)
24          self.assertEqual(len(self.source.getPrincipals('2')), 1)
25
26      def test_authenticate(self):
27          self.assertEqual(self.source.authenticate('foo1', 'bar1')._id, 'foo1')
28          self.assertEqual(self.source.authenticate('foo1', 'bar'), None)
29          self.assertEqual(self.source.authenticate('foo', 'bar1'), None)
30
31  def test_suite():
32      return unittest.makeSuite(PasswdPrincipalSourceTest)
33
34  if __name__=='__main__':
35      unittest.main(defaultTest='test_suite')
```

In the preceding code block, note the following:

- Lines 1 and 12–14: The reason you imported os was to be able to get to the directory of the code, as shown in line 12. When you have the directory, it is easy to build up the data file path and initialize the principal source (lines 13–14).

- Lines 16–19: You test the getPrincipal(id) method. The last test checks that the correct error is thrown in case of a failure. The full principal ID is usually a tab-separated string of a service-identifying earmark, the principal source name, and the principal ID. Because you do not have an earmark or a principal source name specified in the unit tests, these two values are empty, and the full principal ID has two tab characters at the beginning.

- Lines 21–24: The test for getPrincipals(name) mainly tests that the resulting user list is correctly filtered based on the name parameter value.

- Lines 26–29: The authentication test concentrates on checking that only a valid login name and password pair receives positive authentication by returning the principal object.

- Lines 31–35: You provide the usual test boilerplate code.

You can later run the tests either by using Zope's test.py test runner or by executing the script directly; the latter method requires the Python path to be set to *Zope3-Instance*/lib/python.

Step 3: Implementing the Plug-in

The implementation of the plug-in should be straightforward and bear no surprises. The tests already express all the necessary semantics. The only thing we have not discussed yet is the data structure of the principal itself. In this case, you can reuse the `SimplePrincipal` class, which is a basic `IUser` implementation that contains all the data fields (`IUserSchemafied`) relevant to a principal: ID, login (username), password, title, and description.

Note that in Zope 3 the principal knows absolutely nothing about its roles, permissions, or anything else about security. That information is handled by other components of the system and is subject to policy settings.

Now you are ready to implement the principal source. In the `__init__.py` file of the passwdauth package, you add the following implementation:

```
01 import os
02 from persistent import Persistent
03
04 from zope.exceptions import NotFoundError
05 from zope.interface import implements
06
07 from zope.app.container.contained import Contained
08 from zope.app.location import locate
09 from zope.app.pluggableauth import SimplePrincipal
10 from zope.app.pluggableauth.interfaces import IContainedPrincipalSource
11 from zope.app.pluggableauth.interfaces import ILoginPasswordPrincipalSource
12
13 from interfaces import IFileBasedPrincipalSource
14
15 class PasswdPrincipalSource(Contained, Persistent):
16     """A Principal Source for /etc/passwd-like files."""
17
18     implements(ILoginPasswordPrincipalSource, IFileBasedPrincipalSource,
19                IContainedPrincipalSource)
20
21     def __init__(self, filename=''):
22         self.filename = filename
23
24     def readPrincipals(self):
25         if not os.path.exists(self.filename):
26             return []
27         file = open(self.filename, 'r')
28         principals = []
29         for line in file.readlines():
30             if line.strip() != '':
31                 user_info = line.strip().split(':', 3)
32                 p = SimplePrincipal(*user_info)
```

```
33                     locate(p, self, p._id)
34                     p._id = p.login
35                     principals.append(p)
36          return principals
37
38     def getPrincipal(self, id):
39         """See `IPrincipalSource`."""
40         earmark, source_name, id = id.split('\t')
41         for p in self.readPrincipals():
42             if p._id == id:
43                 return p
44         raise NotFoundError, id
45
46     def getPrincipals(self, name):
47         """See `IPrincipalSource`."""
48         return filter(lambda p: p.login.find(name) != -1,
49                       self.readPrincipals())
50
51     def authenticate(self, login, password):
52         """See `ILoginPasswordPrincipalSource`. """
53         for user in self.readPrincipals():
54             if user.login == login and user.password == password:
55                 return user
```

In the preceding code block, note the following:

- Lines 2 and 15: You make sure the principal-source object itself is persistent so that it can be stored in the authentication service.

- Line 4: NotFoundError is a Zope-specific exception, and you need to import it.

- Lines 7 and 15: Because the principal source is stored inside an authentication service, you need to make it an IContained object.

- Line 8: The locate() method helps you assign locations to objects, in this case principals. Because principals are contained by principal sources, you need to assign a parent and a name to each one when it is created.

- Line 9: Here you can see where the SimplePrincipal class is defined. There is really no need to implement your own version, even though it is a persistent class; you never add it to any object in the ZODB anyway.

- Lines 9–11 and 18–19: You import the three principal-source interfaces you promise to implement in the new principal source. The IContainerPrincipalSource interface makes sure that the principal source can only be added to a pluggable authentication service and nowhere else.

- Lines 21–22: You need to make sure the filename attribute always exists. Optionally, it can even be passed to the constructor; you will make use of this fact in the autogenerated add form.

- Lines 24–36: The `readPrincipals()` method does all the heavy lifting because it is responsible for reading and parsing the file. It contains all the logic for interpreting the file format. `readPrincipals()` is just a helper method and is therefore not defined in any interface.

  Lines 25–26: In the first `if` statement, the algorithm checks that the file really exists and returns an empty list if it does not. This prohibits Zope from crashing if the file is not found. This is desirable because otherwise, if you just made a simple typo, you would not be able to access Zope because any authentication check would fail because it passes through this code for every authentication call.

  Line 29: As mentioned earlier, you assume that there is one line per user.

  Line 30: You can ignore empty lines; they just cause headaches.

  Lines 31–32: You make another assumption; the entries in the file correspond directly to the arguments of the `SimplePrincipal` constructor, which is valid as long as the constructor signature of `SimplePrincipal` does not change.

  Line 33: You assign a location to the principal so that you know where it came from.

  Line 34: The principal's `login` field is generally different from its `id` field. Because you do not just want to support `/etc/passwd` files, you do not reuse the Unix user ID; rather, you simply use the login for its ID.

- Lines 38–44: This implementation of the `getPrincipal()` method reads all principals in and checks whether one with a matching ID is found; if not, you raise a `NotFoundError` exception. Of course, this is horribly inefficient, and you should use caching instead.

  The principal ID that is passed into this method argument really exists as three parts, separated by tabs. The first part is the earmark (or unique ID) of the authentication service, the second is the name of the principal source, and the third is the ID of the principal (line 38). However, you are only interested in the last part, which you use for comparison.

- Lines 46–49: Again, you simply use the `readPrincipals()` method's result to build up the list of matching principals.

- Lines 51–55: The `authenticate()` method simply wades through all the users and tries to find a matching `login/password` pair. When a match is found, the principal object is returned. Note that Python returns `None` if no return value is specified, which is the case if no match was determined.

You should now run the unit tests to make sure that the implementation behaves as expected.

Step 4: Registering the Principal Source and Creating Basic Views

You now have to register the `PasswdPrincipalSource` plug-in as content and create a basic add/edit form because you need to allow the user to specify a data file. You need to create a configuration file named `configure.zcml` and add the following directives to it:

```
01 <configure
02     xmlns="http://namespaces.zope.org/zope"
03     xmlns:browser="http://namespaces.zope.org/browser"
04     i18n_domain="demo_passwdauth">
05
06 <content class=".PasswdPrincipalSource">
07   <factory
08       id="zope.app.principalsources.PasswdPrincipalSource"
09       />
10   <allow interface=".interfaces.IFileBasedPrincipalSource"
11       />
12   <require
13       permission="zope.ManageContent"
14       set_schema=".interfaces.IFileBasedPrincipalSource"
15       />
16 </content>
17
18 <browser:addform
19     schema=".interfaces.IFileBasedPrincipalSource"
20     label="Add file-based Principal Source in /etc/passwd style"
21     name="AddPasswdPrincipalSourceForm.html"
22     content_factory=".PasswdPrincipalSource"
23     arguments="filename"
24     permission="zope.ManageContent"
25     />
26
27 <browser:addMenuItem
28     title="/etc/passwd Principal Source"
29     class=".PasswdPrincipalSource"
30     view="AddPasswdPrincipalSourceForm.html"
31     permission="zope.ManageServices"
32     />
33
34 <browser:editform
35     schema=".interfaces.IFileBasedPrincipalSource"
36     label="Edit file-based Principal Source"
37     name="edit.html"
38     menu="zmi_views" title="Edit"
39     permission="zope.ManageContent"
40     />
41 </configure>
```

In the preceding code block, note the following:

- Lines 6–16:You define the principal source as content, create a factory for it, and make the appropriate security declarations for the interfaces. Although the factory ID (line 8) is usually the same as the Python object path, this is not the case here. However, this poses no problem because the only requirement is that the ID be globally unique.

- Lines 18–25:You create a simple autogenerated add form.You also specify that the filename is the first and only argument for the constructor.

- Lines 27–32:You register the add form with the add menu so that it will be available in the pluggable authentication service.

- Lines 34–40: Like the add form, this is a simple edit form for the filename. Plain and simple is enough in this case.

You must take one last step before you can test the package:You need to incorporate the package into the system. Therefore, you should add a file named `passwdauth-configure.zcml` into the `Zope3-Instance`/etc/package-includes directory, and it should have the following content:

```
01 <include package="book.passwdauth" />
```

Now you can (re)start your Zope server and try the new plug-in.

Step 5: Taking the Plug-in for a Test Run

After you have restarted Zope, you should use a web browser to access `http://localhost:8080/`. From the contents screen, you need to go to software space by clicking the Manage Site link.You are then likely to be prompted to log in.You need to make sure you log in as a user who has the `zope.Manager` role.

If you do not have an authentication service yet, you should add one by clicking the Add Service link, selecting Authentication Service, and giving the service the name `auth_service`. The service is then automatically registered and activated for you. After this is done, you are left in the Registration view of the authentication service. In the Add: box on the left side, you should now see two entries, one of which is /etc/passwd `Principal Source`.When you click this entry, you are presented with the source's add form.

In this screen you are asked to enter the path of the file and its name.You might think you do not have a file yet. But don't worry—you still have the file you used for the tests, and you can reuse it here (and as a bonus, you know it works). So, you should enter the following path, replacing *Zope3-Instance* with the path to your Zope 3 instance:

`Zope3-Instance`/lib/python/book/passwdauth/passwd.sample

For the name, you simply use `passwd`. After submitting the form, you end up in the Contents view of the authentication service again. Unfortunately, you have not added a screen that tells whether the file exists and whether it successfully found users.You can try creating such a screen as an exercise.

Before you can use the new principals, however, you have to assign roles to them. Therefore, you need to go to `http://localhost:8080/@@contents.html`. In the top-right corner you will see a Grant menu option, which you should click. In the next screen, you should click Grant Roles to Principals. Now you should be convinced that the new principal source works because the principals with the titles Foo Bar 1 and Foo Bar 2 should appear in the list of principals. You should select Foo Bar 1 and all the listed roles and then submit the form by clicking Filter. In the next screen, you simply select Allow for all available roles, which assigns them to this user. Then you store the changes by clicking Apply.

You are finally ready to test the principal! To do so, you open another browser and enter the following URL: `http://localhost:8080/@@contents.html`. You should be prompted to log in. If you enter `foo1` as username and `bar1` as password, you should see a screen which indicates that the user was authenticated and the `Site Manager` role was appropriately assigned. You should also see `User: Foo Bar 1` somewhere near the top of the screen.

27

Principal Annotations

Difficulty

Sprinter

Skills

- You should understand the concept of annotations.
- You should be familiar with adapters and how to register them.

Problem/Task

A common task is to append metadata to principals. However, principals are often imported from external data sources, and in such cases, they are not attribute annotatable. Therefore, a different solution is desirable. The principal annotation service was developed to always allow annotations for a principal. This chapter shows how to use the principal annotation service to store additional data.

Y OU WANT TO STORE ADDITIONAL METADATA for the principal, but what do you want to store? To make this chapter short, you'll provide an email address and an IRC nickname. Because you do not want to hand-code the HTML forms but autogenerate them, you will describe the two metadata elements by a schema as usual.

But before you can write the interface, you need to create a new package named principalinfo in the book package. You need to remember to add the __init__.py file to the package.

Step 1: Creating the Principal Information Interface

You need to add a file called interfaces.py to the newly created package. Then you should place the following interface in it:

```
01 from zope.i18n import MessageIDFactory
02 from zope.interface import Interface
03 from zope.schema import TextLine
04
05 _ = MessageIDFactory('principalinfo')
06
07
08 class IPrincipalInformation(Interface):
09     """This interface additional information about a principal."""
10
11     email = TextLine(
12         title=_("E-mail"),
13         description=_("E-mail Address"),
14         default=u"",
15         required=False)
16
17     ircNickname = TextLine(
18         title=_("IRC Nickname"),
19         description=_("IRC Nickname"),
20         default=u"",
21         required=False)
```

The interface is straightforward. The two data elements are simply two text lines. If you wanted to, you could write a special Email field that also checks for valid email addresses.

Step 2: Creating the Information Adapter

At this point you need to provide an adapter that is able to adapt from IPrincipal to IPrincipalInformation, using the principal annotation service to store the data. In a new module named info.py, you need to add the following adapter code:

```
01 from persistent.dict import PersistentDict
02 from zope.interface import implements
03 from zope.app import zapi
04
05 from interfaces import IPrincipalInformation
06
07 key = 'book.principalinfo.Information'
08
09 class PrincipalInformation(object):
10     r"""Principal Information Adapter"""
```

```
11      implements(IPrincipalInformation)
12
13      def __init__(self, principal):
14          annotationsvc = zapi.getService('PrincipalAnnotation')
15          annotations = annotationsvc.getAnnotations(principal)
16          if annotations.get(key) is None:
17              annotations[key] = PersistentDict()
18          self.info = annotations[key]
19
20      def __getattr__(self, name):
21          if name in IPrincipalInformation:
22              return self.info.get(name, None)
23          raise AttributeError, "'%s' not in interface." %name
24
25      def __setattr__(self, name, value):
26          if name in IPrincipalInformation:
27              self.info[name] = value
28          else:
29              super(PrincipalInformation, self).__setattr__(name, value)
```

In the preceding code block, note the following:

- Line 7: The key is used to uniquely identify the annotation that is used by this adapter.

- Line 8: You get the principal annotation service. Note that this code assumes that such a service exists. If it does not, a `ComponentLookupError` exception is raised, and the initialization of the adapter fails. Luckily, when the ZODB is first generated, it adds a principal annotation service to the root site manager.

- Line 9: You retrieve the set of annotations for the principal that was passed in. Internally, the annotation service uses the principal's ID to store the annotations. Therefore, it is important that a principal always keep its ID, or, when it is changed, the annotation must be moved.

- Lines 10–11: If the key was not yet registered for the principal, you need to initialize a persistent dictionary, which you will use to store the values of the fields.

- Line 12: You set the persistent data dictionary to be available as `info`.

- Lines 14–17: If the name of the attribute you are trying to get is in the `IPrincipalInformation` interface, you need to retrieve the value from the `info` dictionary. If the name does not correspond to a field in the interface, you need to raise an attribute error. Note that `__getattr__` is called only after the normal attribute lookup fails.

- Lines 19–23: Similarly to the previous method, if the name corresponds to a field in the `IPrincipalInformation` interface, you need to store the value in the data dictionary. If it does not, you use the original `__getattr__()` method to store the value.

This was not that hard, was it?

Step 3: Registering the Components

Now that you have an adapter, you need to register it as such. Also, you need to create an edit form that allows you to edit the values. Here's the code to do these things:

```
01 <configure
02     xmlns="http://namespaces.zope.org/zope"
03     xmlns:browser="http://namespaces.zope.org/browser"
04     i18n_domain="principalinfo">
05
06    <adapter
07        factory=".info.PrincipalInformation"
08        provides=".interfaces.IPrincipalInformation"
09        for="zope.app.security.interfaces.IPrincipal"
10        permission="zope.ManageServices"
11        />
12
13    <browser:editform
14        name="userInfo.html"
15        schema=".interfaces.IPrincipalInformation"
16        for="zope.app.security.interfaces.IPrincipal"
17        label="Change User Information"
18        permission="zope.ManageServices"
19        menu="zmi_views" title="User Info" />
20 </configure>
```

In the preceding code block, note the following:

- Lines 6–11: The adapter is registered for all objects that implement `IPrincipal`. The entire `IPrincipalInformation` schema is available under the `zope.ManageServices` permission. This might not be desirable, but it is sufficient for this example. For a real project, you would probably give the accessor a less strict permission than the attribute mutator. You can do this with a `zope:class` directive that contains `zope:require` directives.

- Lines 13–19: This edit form is registered for `IPrincipal` components so that it will be available as a view for all principals. However, the schema that is being edited is `IPrincipalInformation`. The edit form will automatically look up the adapter from `IPrincipal` to `IPrincipalInformation`.

You need to register the configuration with the Zope 3 framework by adding a file named `principalinfo-configure.zcml` to `Zope3-Instance/etc/package-includes`. That file should contain the following one line directive:

```
01 <include package="book.principalinfo" />
```

You can now restart Zope 3, and the view should be available. The usage of the view is described in the section, "Step 5: Playing with the New Feature," later in this chapter.

Step 4: Testing the Adapter

Before you use the Web interface to test the view, you need to first write a test for the adapter to ensure the correct functioning. The most difficult part about the unit tests in this case is actually setting up the environment, including defining and registering a principal annotation service. You will implement the test as a doc test in the `PrincipalInformation` class' doc string, where all code doc test snippets in this section should be placed.

You need to set up the environment.

```
01 >>> from zope.app.tests import setup
02 >>> from zope.app.principalannotation.interfaces import \
03 ...       IPrincipalAnnotationService
04 >>> from zope.app.principalannotation import PrincipalAnnotationService
05
06 >>> site = setup.placefulSetUp(site=True)
07 >>> sm = zapi.getGlobalServices()
08 >>> sm.defineService('PrincipalAnnotation',
09 ...                   IPrincipalAnnotationService)
10 >>> svc = setup.addService(site.getSiteManager(), 'PrincipalAnnotation',
11 ...                   PrincipalAnnotationService())
```

In the preceding code block, note the following:

- Line 1: The `setup` module contains some extremely helpful convenience functions.

- Lines 2–3: You import the interface that a principal annotation service must provide.

- Line 4: You import the implementation of the service.

- Line 6: You create a placeful setup and make the root folder a site, which is returned.

- Lines 7–9: A new service type can only be defined via the global service manager, so you get it first. Then you define the service type by name and interface.

- Lines 10–11: You add a principal annotation service to the site of the root folder.

Now that the service is set up, you need a principal to use the adapter on. You could use an existing principal implementation, but all that the principal annotation service needs from the principal is the ID, which you can easily provide via a stub implementation:

```
01 >>> class Principal(object):
02 ...      id = 'user1'
03 >>> principal = Principal()
04
05 Now create the principal information adapter:
06
07 >>> info = PrincipalInformation(principal)
```

Before you give the fields any values, they should default to None. Any field not listed in the information interface should cause an AttributeError exception. Let's check that behavior:

```
01 >>> info.email is None
02 True
03 >>> info.ircNickname is None
04 True
05 >>> info.phone
06 Traceback (most recent call last):
07 ...
08 AttributeError: 'phone' not in interface.
```

Next, you try to set a value for the email and make sure that it is even available if you reinstantiate the adapter:

```
01 >>> info.email = 'foo@bar.com'
02 >>> info.email
03 'foo@bar.com'
04
05 >>> info = PrincipalInformation(principal)
06 >>> info.email
07 'foo@bar.com'
```

Finally, you need to make sure that the data is really stored in the service:

```
01 >>> svc.annotations['user1']['book.principalinfo.Information']['email']
02 'foo@bar.com'
```

You need to be careful to clean up after yourself:

```
01 >>> setup.placefulTearDown()
```

To make the tests runnable via the test runner, you add the following test setup code to tests.py:

```
01 import unittest
02 from zope.testing.doctestunit import DocTestSuite
03
04 def test_suite():
05     return DocTestSuite('book.principalinfo.info')
06
07 if __name__ == '__main__':
08     unittest.main(defaultTest='test_suite')
```

Now you need to make sure that the test passes before you proceed by running the tests.

Step 5: Playing with the New Feature

When the tests pass and the components are configured, you can worry about the edit form. You need to restart Zope 3. Then you need to go to `http://localhost:8080/++etc++site/default/manage` and select Authentication Service in the Add box. After the authentication service is added, you need to go to its Contents tab. You should select Add Principal Source in the Add box and call it `btree` because it is a BTree-based, persistent source. You then need to enter the source's management screen and add a principal, choosing any values you want. After you enter the principal by clicking it from the source's Content view, you will see that a tab named User Info is available; this tab provides you with the edit form created in this chapter, as shown in Figure 27.1. You can now go there and add the email and IRC nickname of the principal.

Figure 27.1   The principal's User Info tab.

Creating New Browser Resources

Difficulty

Newcomer

Skills

- You need some basic ZCML knowledge.
- You should be familiar with the component architecture, especially presentation components and views.

Problem/Task

Certain elements of a presentation, such as images and style sheets, are not associated with any other components, so you cannot create a view. To solve this problem, the Zope 3 developers came up with the concept of resources, which are presentation components that do not require any context. This chapter demonstrates how resources are created and registered with Zope 3.

Creating a Resource File

The first goal of this chapter is to register a simple plain-text file called `resource.txt` as a browser resource. You start this process by creating the file anywhere you want on the filesystem and adding the following content:

```
01 Hello, I am a Zope 3 Resource Component!
```

Now you just register the resource in a ZCML configuration file by using the `browser:resource` directive:

```
01 <browser:resource
02    name="resource.txt"
03    file="resource.txt"
04    layer="default" />
```

In the preceding code block, note the following:

- Line 2: This is the name under which the resource will be known in Zope.
- Line 3: The `file` attribute specifies the path to the resource on the filesystem. The current working directory (.) is always the directory in which the configuration file is located. So, in the preceding example, the file `resource.txt` file is located in the same folder as the configuration file.
- Line 4: The optional `layer` attribute specifies the layer the resource is added to. By default, the `default` layer is selected.

After you hook up the configuration file to the main configuration path and restart Zope 3, you should be able to access the resource via a browser by using `http://localhost:8080/@@/resource.txt`. The `@@/` in the URL tells the traversal mechanism that the following object is a resource. This shortcut to the more explicit `http://localhost:8080/++resource++resource.txt` syntax is only available from sites, so `http://localhost:8080/somefile/resource.txt` would not work.

Image Resources

If you have an image resource, you might want to use a different configuration. You can create a simple image called `img.png` and register it as follows:

```
01 <browser:resource
02    name="img.png"
03    image="img.png"
04    permission="zope.ManageContent" />
```

In the preceding code block, note the following:

- Line 3: As you can see, instead of the `file` attribute, you use the `image` attribute. Internally, this will create an `Image` object, which is able to detect the content type and return it correctly. There is a third possible attribute, named `template`. If it is specified, a page template is executed when the resource is called.

Note

Only one of the attributes `file`, `image`, and `template` can be specified inside a resource directive.

- Line 4: A final optional attribute is the permission a user needs in order to view the resource. To demonstrate the security, you can set the permission required for viewing the image to `zope.ManageContent`, so that the user must log in as an administrator/manager to be able to view it. The default of the attribute is `zope.Public` so that everyone can see the resource.

If you have many resource files to register, it can be very tedious to write a single directive for every resource. For this purpose, the `resourceDirectory` directive is provided, and you can use it to simply declare an entire directory, including its content, as resources. In this way, the filenames of the files are reused as the names for the resource that is available. Assuming that you put your two previous resources in a directory called `resource`, you can use the following:

```
01 <browser:resourceDirectory
02     name="resources"
03     directory="../resource" />
```

The image will then be publicly available under the URL `http://local-host:8080/@@/resources/img.png`

The DirectoryResource Object

The `DirectoryResource` object uses a simple resource type recognition. It looks at the filename extensions to discover the type. For page templates, currently the extensions `.pt`, `.zpt` and `.html` are registered, and for an image, `.gif`, `.png`, and `.jpg` are registered. All other extensions are converted to file resources. Note that it is not necessary to have a list of all image types because only browser-displayable images must be recognized.

29

Registries with Global Utilities

Difficulty

Contributor

Skills

- You need to be familiar with the component architecture.
- You need to be comfortable with ZCML.
- You should be familiar with the message board example.

Problem/Task

You need registries all the time. In fact, the component architecture itself depends heavily on registered component lookups to provide functionality. These registries, especially the utility service, can be used to provide application-level registries as well.

THE GOAL OF THIS CHAPTER IS TO develop a mechanism that provides image-representations of text-based smileys. For example, the text :-) should be converted to ☺. To further complicate the problem, it is undesirable to just store smileys without any order. Many applications support multiple themes of smileys, and you want to make that possible in this case as well. For example, the message board administrator should be able to choose the desired smiley theme for a message board.

Based on these requirements, you want a registry of smiley themes that the user can choose from. Therefore, you need to develop the theme as a utility and register it with a specific interface, ISmileyTheme. Thus, the entire utility service acts as a huge registry, but you can easily simulate subregistries by specifying a particular interface for a utility. You can then ask the Zope component API to return a list of all utilities providing ISmileyTheme or simply return a single ISmileyTheme interface that has a specific name.

Let's now take a look on how to handle the smileys themselves. Inside the theme, you simply need a mapping (that is, a dictionary) from the text representation to the image. However, should you really store the image data? In fact, it would be better to declare the image itself as a resource and only store the URL, so that you can support external links (which is not done in this chapter) and so that you do not have to worry about publishing the images.

After creating the code to do this, you will implement a couple new ZCML directives to make the registration of new smiley themes as easy as possible. A message board editor will then be able to easily upload his or her favorite theme and use it. You'll actually add a final step to the message board example, incorporating smiley themes at the end of this chapter.

To allow the smiley theme utility to be distributed independently of the message board application, you need to develop its code in a new package, called smileyutility, which you should place in *Zope3-Instance*/lib/python/book. You need to be sure to add an __init__.py file to that directory.

Step 1: Defining the Interfaces

Before you start coding away, you need to spend some time thinking about the API that you want to expose. In Chapter 30, "Local Utilities," you'll develop a local/placeful equivalent of the utility, so the base interface, ISmileyTheme, should be general enough to support both implementations and not include any implementation-specific methods. You will then derive another interface, IGlobalSmileyTheme, from the general one that will specify methods to manage smileys for the global implementation. Note that the utility will still be registered as a ISmileyTheme.

You need to place the following interface implementation in the interfaces.py module:

```
01 from zope.interface import Interface
02
03 class ISmileyTheme(Interface):
04     """A theme is a collection of smileys having a stylistic theme.
05
06     Themes are intended to be implemented as named utilities, which will be
07     available via a local smiley service.
08     """
09
10     def getSmiley(text, request):
11         """Returns a smiley for the given text and theme.
12
13         If no smiley was found, a ComponentLookupError should be raised.
14         """
15
16     def querySmiley(text, request, default=None):
```

```
17          """Returns a smiley for the given text and theme.
18
19          If no smiley was found, the default value is returned.
20          """
21
22      def getSmileysMapping(request):
23          """Return a mapping of text to URL.
24
25          This is incredibly useful when actually attempting to substitute the
26          smiley texts with a URL.
27          """
28
29
30 class IGlobalSmileyTheme(ISmileyTheme):
31      """A global smiley theme that also allows management of smileys."""
32
33      def provideSmiley(text, smiley_path):
34          """Provide a smiley for the utility."""
```

Note

You might think that this interface seems a bit wordy, but in widely available components such as this, it is extremely important to document the specific semantics of each method, and the documentation should leave no question or corner case uncovered. Many people will depend on the correctness of the API.

In the preceding code block, note the following:

- Lines 1 and 3: Notice that a utility does not have to inherit any special interfaces. Until you declare a utility to be a utility, it is just a general component.

- Lines 10–14: You retrieve a smiley, given its text representation. Note that you need the request because the URL could be built on-the-fly, and you need all the request information to generate an appropriate URL.

- Lines 16–20: You specify a method similar to the `getSmiley()` method, except that it returns the default instead of raising an error if the smiley is not found.

- Lines 22–25: By returning a complete list of text-to-URL mappings, the application using this utility can simply do a search and replace of all smiley occurrences.

Note

In the beginning I envisioned a method that would take a string as argument and return a string, with all the smiley occurrences being replaced by image tags. But this would have been rather limiting because the utility would need to guess the usage of the URL; not everyone wants to generate HTML. This implementation does not carry that restriction because it makes no assumption on how the URLs will be used.

- Lines 33–34: As an extension to the `ISmileyTheme` interface, you include a method that adds a new smiley to the theme. `smiley_path` will be expected to be a relative path to a resource—something like `++resource++plainsmile.png`. Because the path must be unique across all themes, it is a good idea to encode the theme name into it by convention—but let's not introduce that restriction in the theme.

Now that you have all the interfaces defined, you can look at the implementation, which should be straightforward.

Step 2: Implementing the Utility

The global theme for this utility should use a simple dictionary that maps a text representation to the path of a smiley. When smileys are requested, this path should be converted to a URL and returned. The only tricky part of the utility will be to obtain the root URL because the utility does not know anything about locations.

However, there is a fast solution: You create a containment root component stub that implements the `IContainmentRoot` interface, and the traversal mechanism looks for that while generating a path or URL. Here is what you can do to obtain the root URL:

```
01 from zope.app import zapi
02 from zope.app.traversing.interfaces import IContainmentRoot
03 from zope.interface import implements
04
05 class Root:
06     implements(IContainmentRoot)
07
08 def getRootURL(request):
09     return str(zapi.getView(Root(), 'absolute_url', request))
```

In the preceding code block, note the following:

- Lines 8–9: You return the root URL for a given request. The reason you need this request object is that it might contain information about the server name and port, as well as additional namespaces, such as skin declarations or virtual hosting information.

The `absolute_url` view is defined for all objects and returns the URL at which the object is reachable, as long as it has enough context information.

Now you have all the pieces to implement the utility. You can just use `pyskel` to create the skeleton and then fill it. You need to place the following code and the `getRootURL()` code in a file called `globaltheme.py`:

```
01 from zope.component.exceptions import ComponentLookupError
02 from interfaces import IGlobalSmileyTheme
03
04 class GlobalSmileyTheme(object):
```

```
05   """A filesystem based smiley theme."""
06   implements(IGlobalSmileyTheme)
07
08   def __init__(self):
09       self.__smileys = {}
10
11   def getSmiley(self, text, request):
12       "See book.smileyutility.interfaces.ISmileyTheme"
13       smiley = self.querySmiley(text, request)
14       if smiley is None:
15           raise ComponentLookupError, 'Smiley not found.'
16       return smiley
17
18   def querySmiley(self, text, request, default=None):
19       "See book.smileyutility.interfaces.ISmileyTheme"
20       if self.__smileys.get(text) is None:
21           return default
22       return getRootURL(request) + '/' + self.__smileys[text]
23
24   def getSmileysMapping(self, request):
25       "See book.smileyutility.interfaces.ISmileyTheme"
26       smileys = self.__smileys.copy()
27       root_url = getRootURL(request)
28       for name, smiley in smileys.items():
29           smileys[name] = root_url + '/' + smiley
30       return smileys
31
32   def provideSmiley(self, text, smiley_path):
33       "See book.smileyutility.interfaces.IGlobalSmileyTheme"
34       self.__smileys[text] = smiley_path
```

In the preceding code block, note the following:

- Lines 8–9: You initialize the registry, which is a simple dictionary. You want this registry to be totally private to this class; no one else should be able to reach it.

- Lines 11–16: This method does not do much because you turn over all the responsibility to the next method. All you do is complain with a `ComponentLookupError` exception if there is no result (that is, if `None` is returned).

- Lines 18–22: First, if the theme does not contain the requested smiley, you simply return the default value. When you know that there is a smiley available, you construct the URL by appending the smiley path to the URL root.

- Lines 24–30: You make a copy of the whole smiley map. If the theme does not exist, an empty dictionary is created. In lines 43–44, you update every smiley path with a smiley URL.

- Lines 32–34: You add the smiley path, with the text being the key of the mapping.

The utility is now complete. However, you have not created a way to declare a default theme. To make life simple, the default theme is simply available under the name `default` (place the code in `globaltheme.py`):

```
01 from interfaces import ISmileyTheme
02
03 def declareDefaultSmileyTheme(name):
04     """Declare the default smiley theme."""
05     utilities = zapi.getService(zapi.servicenames.Utilities)
06     theme = zapi.getUtility(ISmileyTheme, name)
07     # register the utility simply without a name
08     utilities.provideUtility(ISmileyTheme, theme, 'default')
```

In this code, you simply look up the utility by its original name and then register it again, using the name `default`. (This is totally legal and often practiced. One utility instance can be registered multiple times, using different interfaces and/or names.)

Now, you need to test your new utility.

Step 3: Writing Tests

Writing tests for global utilities is usually fairly simple because you usually do not have to start up the component architecture. In this case, however, you have to do so because you are looking up a view when asking for the root URL. You also have to register this view (`absolute_url`) in the first place, so it can be found later.

You need to create a package called `tests`, which should include the `__init__.py` file. In the `tests` package you should create a file called `test_doc.py`, where you insert the following setup and tear-down:

```
01 import unittest
02
03 from zope.interface import Interface
04 from zope.testing.doctestunit import DocTestSuite
05
06 from zope.app.tests import ztapi, placelesssetup
07
08 class AbsoluteURL:
09     def __init__(self, context, request):
10         pass
11     def __str__(self):
12         return ''
13
14 def setUp(test):
15     placelesssetup.setUp()
16     ztapi.browserView(Interface, 'absolute_url', AbsoluteURL)
17
18
```

```
19 def test_suite():
20     return unittest.TestSuite((
21         DocTestSuite('book.smileyutility.globaltheme',
22                      setUp=setUp, tearDown=placelesssetup.tearDown),
23         ))
24
25 if __name__ == '__main__':
26     unittest.main(defaultTest='test_suite')
```

In the preceding code block, note the following:

- Lines 8–12: This is a stub implementation of the absolute URL. You simply return nothing as the root of the URL.

- Lines 14–16: You have seen a placeless unit test setup before; in this case, `placelesssetup.setUp()` brings up the basic component architecture and clears all the registries from possible entries. In line 16 you then register your stub implementation of `AbsoluteURL` as a view.

- Lines 21–22: Here you create a doc test suite, using the custom setup function.

Now you just have to write the tests. In the doc string of the `GlobalSmileyTheme` class, you add the following doc test code:

```
01 Let's make sure that the global theme implementation actually fulfills the
02 `ISmileyTheme` API.
03
04 >>> from zope.interface.verify import verifyClass
05 >>> verifyClass(IGlobalSmileyTheme, GlobalSmileyTheme)
06 True
07
08 Initialize the theme and add a couple of smileys.
09
10 >>> theme = GlobalSmileyTheme()
11 >>> theme.provideSmiley(':-)', '++resource++plain__smile.png')
12 >>> theme.provideSmiley(';-)', '++resource++plain__wink.png')
13
14 Let's try to get a smiley out of the registry.
15
16 >>> from zope.publisher.browser import TestRequest
17
18 >>> theme.getSmiley(':-)', TestRequest())
19 '/++resource++plain__smile.png'
20 >>> theme.getSmiley(':-(', TestRequest())
21 Traceback (most recent call last):
22 ...
23 ComponentLookupError: 'Smiley not found.'
24 >>> theme.querySmiley(';-)', TestRequest())
25 '/++resource++plain__wink.png'
```

```
26 >>> theme.querySmiley(';-(', TestRequest()) is None
27 True
28
29 And finally we'd like to get a dictionary of all smileys.
30
31 >>> map = theme.getSmileysMapping(TestRequest())
32 >>> len(map)
33 2
34 >>> map[':-)']
35 '/++resource++plain__smile.png'
36 >>> map[';-)']
37 '/++resource++plain__wink.png'
```

In the preceding code block, note the following:

- Lines 4–6: You ensure that the interface was correctly implemented.
- Lines 8–12: You test the `provideSmiley()` method.
- Lines 14–27: You test the simple smiley accessor methods of the utility. Note that doc tests also handle exceptions nicely.
- Lines 29–37: You make sure that the `getSmileyMapping()` method gives the right output. Note that dictionaries cannot be directly tested in doc tests because their representation depends on the computer architecture, due to the fact that their item order is arbitrary.

Now you need to run the tests and make sure they all pass.

Step 4: Providing a User-Friendly UI

Although the current API is functional, it is not very practical to the developer because he or she first needs to look up the theme by using the component architecture's utility API, and only then can the developer make use of the smiley theme features. It would be much nicer if you had only a smiley-theme-related API to work with. Thus, you can create some convenience functions in the package's `__init__.py` file:

```
01 from zope.app import zapi
02
03 from interfaces import ISmileyTheme
04
05 def getSmiley(text, request, theme='default'):
06     theme = zapi.getUtility(ISmileyTheme, theme)
07     return theme.getSmiley(text, request)
08
09 def querySmiley(text, request, theme='default', default=None):
10     theme = zapi.queryUtility(ISmileyTheme, theme)
11     if theme is None:
12         return default
```

```
13        return theme.querySmiley(text, request, default)
14
15  def getSmileyThemes():
16        return [name for name, util in zapi.getUtilitiesFor(ISmileyTheme)
17                if name != 'default']
18
19  def getSmileysMapping(request, theme='default'):
20        theme = zapi.getUtility(ISmileyTheme, theme)
21        return theme.getSmileysMapping(request)
```

The functions integrate the theme utility more tightly into the API.
In the preceding code block, note the following:

- Lines 15–17: You return a list of the names of all available themes, excluding the
  default one.

The tests for these functions are very similar to the tests of the theme utility, so they are
not described here. You can find the complete code, including methods, in the code
repository at http://svn.zope.org/book/trunk/smileyutility.

Step 5: Implementing ZCML Directives

You might have already wondered how this utility can be useful, if it does not even deal
with the smiley images. This functionality is reserved for the configuration. When a smiley registration is made, the directive receives a path to an image, but it does not just register the path with the smiley theme. Instead, it first creates a resource for the image and
then passes the resource's relative path to the smiley theme.

There are three steps to writing a ZCML directive: create the directive schema,
implement the directive handlers, and write the meta-ZCML configuration. They are
described in the following sections.

But first, you need to decide what directives you want to create. The first one,
smiley:theme, defines a new theme and allows a subdirective, smiley:smiley, that
registers new smileys for this theme. A second directive, smiley:smiley, allows you to
register a single smiley for an existing theme, so that other packages can add additional
smileys to a theme. The third and final directive, smiley:defaultTheme, lets you specify
the theme that will be known as the default one. The specified theme must exist already.

Declaring the Directive Schemas

Each ZCML directive is represented by a schema that defines the type of content for
each element/directive attribute. Each field is also responsible for knowing how to convert the attribute value into something that is useful. All the usual schema fields are available. In addition, some specific configuration fields can also be used. They are listed in
Chapter 9, "Introduction to the Zope Configuration Markup Language (ZCML)." Now
that you know what you can use, you need to define the schemas, which, by convention,
are placed in a file called metadirectives.py:

```
01 from zope.interface import Interface
02 from zope.configuration.fields import Path
03 from zope.schema import TextLine
04
05 class IThemeDirective(Interface):
06     """Define a new theme."""
07
08     name = TextLine(
09         title=u"Theme Name",
10         description=u"The name of the theme.",
11         default=None,
12         required=False)
13
14 class ISmileySubdirective(Interface):
15     """This directive adds a new smiley using the theme information of the
16     complex smileys directive."""
17
18     text = TextLine(
19         title=u"Smiley Text",
20         description=u"The text that represents the smiley, i.e. ':-)'",
21         required=True)
22
23     file = Path(
24         title=u"Image file",
25         description=u"Path to the image that represents the smiley.",
26         required=True)
27
28 class ISmileyDirective(ISmileySubdirective):
29     """This is a standalone directive registering a smiley for a certain
30     theme."""
31
32     theme = TextLine(
33         title=u"Theme",
34         description=u"The theme the smiley belongs to.",
35         default=None,
36         required=False)
37
38 class IDefaultThemeDirective(IThemeDirective):
39     """Specify the default theme."""
```

In the preceding code block, note the following:

- Lines 5–12: The theme directive requires a name attribute that gives the theme its name.
- Lines 14–26: Every smiley is identified by its text representation and the image file. (The theme is already specified in the subdirective.)

- Lines 28–36: A single directive specifies all information at once. You simply reuse the previously defined `smiley` subdirective interface and specify the theme.

- Lines 38–39: The default theme directive is simple because it takes just a theme name.

Implementing ZCML Directive Handlers

Next, you need to implement the directive handlers themselves. This is the really fun part because it actually represents some important parts of the package's logic. By convention, you should place the following code in the `metaconfigure.py` file:

```
01 import os
02
03 from zope.app import zapi
04 from zope.app.component.metaconfigure import utility
05 from zope.app.publisher.browser.resourcemeta import resource
06
07 from interfaces import ISmileyTheme
08 from globaltheme import GlobalSmileyTheme, declareDefaultSmileyTheme
09
10 __registered_resources = []
11
12 def registerSmiley(text, path, theme):
13     theme = zapi.queryUtility(ISmileyTheme, theme)
14     theme.provideSmiley(text, path)
15
16 class theme(object):
17
18     def __init__(self, _context, name):
19         self.name = name
20         utility(_context, ISmileyTheme,
21                 factory=GlobalSmileyTheme, name=name)
22
23     def smiley(self, _context, text, file):
24         return smiley(_context, text, file, self.name)
25
26     def __call__(self):
27         return
28
29 def smiley(_context, text, file, theme):
30     name = theme + '__' + os.path.split(file)[1]
31     path = '/++resource++' + name
32
33     if name not in __registered_resources:
34         resource(_context, name, image=file)
```

```
35            __registered_resources.append(name)
36
37      _context.action(
38          discriminator = ('smiley', theme, text),
39          callable = registerSmiley,
40          args = (text, path, theme),
41          )
42
43 def defaultTheme(_context, name=None):
44      _context.action(
45          discriminator = ('smiley', 'defaultTheme',),
46          callable = declareDefaultSmileyTheme,
47          args = (name,),
48          )
```

In the preceding code block, note the following:

- Line 10: You want to keep track of all resources that you have already added so that you do not register any resource twice, which would raise a component error.

- Lines 12–14: Actually sticking the smileys into the theme must be delayed until the configuration actions are executed. This method is used as the smiley registration callable object that is called when the smiley registration action is executed.

- Lines 16–27: Because `theme` is a complex directive (it can contain other directives), it is implemented as a class. The parameters of the constructor resemble the arguments of the XML element, except for _context, which is always passed in as the first argument and represents the configuration context.

  Each subdirective (in this case, `smiley`) is a method of the class and takes the element attributes as parameters. In this implementation, you forward the configuration request to the main `smiley` directive; there is no need to implement the same code twice.

  Every complex directive class must be callable (that is, it must implement __call__()). This method is called when the closing element is parsed. Usually, all the configuration action happens here, but not in this case.

- Lines 29–41: The first task is to separate the filename from the file path and construct a unique name and path for the smiley. On lines 33–35 you register the resource. You do that only if you have not registered it before, which can happen if there are two text representations for a single smiley image—for example, :) and :-). On lines 37–41 you then tell the configuration system it should add the smiley to the theme. Note that these actions are not executed at this time because the configuration mechanism must first resolve possible overrides and conflict errors.

- Lines 43–48: You provide a simple handler for the `defaultTheme` directive. It calls the previously developed `declareDefaultSmileyTheme()` function.

Writing the Meta-ZCML Directives

Now that you have completed the Python side of things, you need to register the new ZCML directives by using the `meta` namespace in ZCML. By convention, you place the ZCML directives in a file named `meta.zcml`:

```
01 <configure xmlns:meta="http://namespaces.zope.org/meta">
02
03   <meta:directives namespace="http://namespaces.zope.org/smiley">
04
05     <meta:complexDirective
06         name="theme"
07         schema=".metadirectives.IThemeDirective"
08         handler=".metaconfigure.theme">
09
10       <meta:subdirective
11           name="smiley"
12           schema=".metadirectives.ISmileySubdirective" />
13
14     </meta:complexDirective>
15
16     <meta:directive
17         name="smiley"
18         schema=".metadirectives.ISmileyDirective"
19         handler=".metaconfigure.smiley" />
20
21     <meta:directive
22         name="defaultTheme"
23         schema=".metadirectives.IDefaultThemeDirective"
24         handler=".metaconfigure.defaultTheme" />
25
26   </meta:directives>
27
28 </configure>
```

Each metadirective, whether it is `directive`, `complexDirective`, or `subdirective`, specifies the name of the directive and the schema it represents. The first two metadirectives also take a `handler` attribute, which describes the callable object that will execute the directive.

You register this meta ZCML file with the system by placing in the *Zope3-Instance*/etc/package-includes directory a file called `smileyutility-meta.zcml` that has the following content:

```
01 <include package="book.smileyutility" file="meta.zcml" />
```

Testing the Directives

Now you are ready to test the directives. First, you create a test ZCML file in `tests`, called `smiley.zcml`. You write the directives such that you assume you are in the `tests` directory during its execution:

```
01 <configure
02     xmlns:zope="http://namespaces.zope.org/zope"
03     xmlns="http://namespaces.zope.org/smiley">
04
05   <zope:include package="book.smileyutility" file="meta.zcml" />
06
07   <theme name="yazoo">
08     <smiley text=":(" file="../smileys/yazoo/sad.png"/>
09     <smiley text=":)" file="../smileys/yazoo/smile.png"/>
10   </theme>
11
12   <theme name="plain" />
13
14   <smiley
15       theme="plain"
16       text=":("
17       file="../smileys/yazoo/sad.png"/>
18
19   <defaultTheme name="plain" />
20
21 </configure>
```

In the preceding code block, note the following:

- Line 5: First, you read the meta configuration.
- Lines 7–19: Here you use the three directives.

Now you need to create a module called `test_directives.py` (directive test modules are usually called this way) and add the following test code to it:

```
01 import unittest
02
03 from zope.app import zapi
04 from zope.app.tests.placelesssetup import PlacelessSetup
05 from zope.configuration import xmlconfig
06
07 from book.smileyutility import tests
08 from book.smileyutility.interfaces import ISmileyTheme
09
10 class DirectivesTest(PlacelessSetup, unittest.TestCase):
11
12     def setUp(self):
```

```
13          super(DirectivesTest, self).setUp()
14          self.context = xmlconfig.file("smiley.zcml", tests)
15
16      def test_SmileyDirectives(self):
17          self.assertEqual(
18              zapi.getUtility(ISmileyTheme,
19                              'default')._GlobalSmileyTheme__smileys,
20              {u':(': u'/++resource++plain__sad.png'})
21          self.assertEqual(
22              zapi.getUtility(ISmileyTheme,
23                              'plain')._GlobalSmileyTheme__smileys,
24              {u':(': u'/++resource++plain__sad.png'})
25          self.assertEqual(
26              zapi.getUtility(ISmileyTheme,
27                              'yazoo')._GlobalSmileyTheme__smileys,
28              {u':)': u'/++resource++yazoo__smile.png',
29               u':(': u'/++resource++yazoo__sad.png'})
30
31      def test_defaultTheme(self):
32          self.assertEqual(zapi.getUtility(ISmileyTheme, 'default'),
33                           zapi.getUtility(ISmileyTheme, 'plain'))
34
35  def test_suite():
36      return unittest.TestSuite((
37          unittest.makeSuite(DirectivesTest),
38          ))
39
40  if __name__ == '__main__':
41      unittest.main()
```

As you can see, directive unit tests can be very compact, thanks to the `xmlconfig.file()` call.

In the preceding code block, note the following:

- Lines 4 and 10: Because you are registering resources during the configuration, you need to create a placeless setup.

- Line 14: You execute the configuration.

- Lines 16–29: You make sure that all entries in the smiley themes have been created.

- Lines 31–33: You quickly check to determine whether the default theme was set correctly.

- Lines 35–41: You provide the necessary unit test boilerplate code.

Now you need to make sure the tests pass. You will notice that they will actually fail miserably because you have not provided any smileys yet. The easiest way to get some smileys is to copy the `smileys` directory from `http://svn.zope.org/book/trunk/smileyutility/` into your `smileyutility` package. When you are done with that, you can try to run the tests again, and all tests should pass.

Step 6: Setting Up Some Smiley Themes

The service functionality is complete, and you are now ready to hook it up to the system. You need to define the service and provide an implementation to the component architecture before you add two smiley themes. Therefore, in the `configure.zcml` file, you add this:

```
01 <configure
02     xmlns="http://namespaces.zope.org/smiley"
03     i18n_domain="smileyutility">
04
05   <theme name="plain">
06     <smiley text=":("   file="./smileys/plain/sad.png"/>
07     <smiley text=":-("  file="./smileys/plain/sad.png"/>
08     <smiley text=":)"   file="./smileys/plain/smile.png"/>
09     <smiley text=":-)"  file="./smileys/plain/smile.png"/>
10     ...
11   </theme>
12
13   <theme name="yazoo">
14     <smiley text=":("   file="./smileys/yazoo/sad.png"/>
15     <smiley text=":-("  file="./smileys/yazoo/sad.png"/>
16     <smiley text=":)"   file="./smileys/yazoo/smile.png"/>
17     <smiley text=":-)"  file="./smileys/yazoo/smile.png"/>
18     ...
19   </theme>
20
21   <defaultTheme name="plain" />
22
23 </configure>
```

In the preceding code block, note the following:

- Lines 5–19: You provide two smiley themes. The list here has been abbreviated somewhat from the actual size to keep things simple.
- Line 21: You set the default theme to `plain`.

You can now activate the configuration by placing a file named `smileyutility-configure.zcml` in `Zope3-Instance`/etc/package-includes. It should have the following content:

```
01 <include package="book.smileyutility" />
```

Step 7: Integrating Smiley Themes into the Message Board

Now you have these smiley themes, but you do not use them anywhere. So that it will be easier for you to see the smiley themes in action, you can extend the `messageboard` package example by yet another step. The new code consists of two parts: First, you allow the message board to select one of the available themes and then you use smileys on the Preview tab of the message board.

The Smiley Theme Selection Adapter

You can best implement the additional functionality by using an adapter and annotations. The interface you need is as follows:

```
01 from zope.schema import Choice
02
03 class ISmileyThemeSpecification(Interface):
04
05     theme = Choice(
06         title=u"Smiley Theme",
07         description=u"The Smiley Theme used in message bodies.",
08         vocabulary=u"Smiley Themes",
09         default=u"default",
10         required=True)
```

You should add this interface to the `interfaces.py` file of the message board. This interface refers to a vocabulary called Smiley Themes, but you have not yet specified that vocabulary. You expect this vocabulary to provide a list of names of all available smiley themes. Luckily, you can easily create vocabularies for utilities or utility names by using a single ZCML directive:

```
01 <vocabulary
02     name="Smiley Themes"
03     factory="zope.app.utility.vocabulary.UtilityVocabulary"
04     interface="book.smileyutility.interfaces.ISmileyTheme"
05     nameOnly="true" />
```

In the preceding code block, note the following:

- Line 3: This is a special utility vocabulary class that is used to quickly create utility-based vocabularies.
- Line 4: This is the interface by which the utilities will be looked up.
- Line 5: If `nameOnly` is specified, the vocabulary will provide utility names instead of the utility component itself.

Next, you create the adapter. You need to place the following class in `messageboard.py`:

```
01 from zope.app.annotation.interfaces import IAnnotations
02 from book.messageboard.interfaces import ISmileyThemeSpecification
03
04 ThemeKey = 'http://www.zope.org/messageboard#1.0/SmileyTheme'
05
```

```
06 class SmileyThemeSpecification(object):
07
08     implements(ISmileyThemeSpecification)
09     __used_for__ = IMessageBoard
10
11     def __init__(self, context):
12         self.context = self.__parent__ = context
13         self._annotations = IAnnotations(context)
14         if self._annotations.get(ThemeKey, None) is None:
15             self._annotations[ThemeKey] = 'default'
16
17     def getTheme(self):
18         return self._annotations[ThemeKey]
19
20     def setTheme(self, value):
21         self._annotations[ThemeKey] = value
22
23     # See .interfaces.ISmileyThemeSpecification
24     theme = property(getTheme, setTheme)
```

As you can see, this is a very straightforward implementation of the interface, using annotations and the adapter concept, both of which are introduced in Part III, "Content Components—The Basics," and Part IV, "Content Components—Advanced Techniques."

The adapter registration and security is a bit tricky because you must use a trusted adapter. It is not enough to just specify the `permission` attribute in the adapter directive because it will only affect attribute access, and not mutation. Instead of specifying the `permission` attribute, you need to do a full security declaration by using the `zope:class` and `zope:require` directives:

```
01 <class class=".messageboard.SmileyThemeSpecification">
02   <require
03       permission="book.messageboard.View"
04       interface=".interfaces.ISmileyThemeSpecification"
05       />
06   <require
07       permission="book.messageboard.Edit"
08       set_schema=".interfaces.ISmileyThemeSpecification"
09       />
10 </class>
11
12 <adapter
13     factory=".messageboard.SmileyThemeSpecification"
14     provides=".interfaces.ISmileyThemeSpecification"
15     for=".interfaces.IMessageBoard"
16     trusted="true" />
```

Finally, you need to create a view to set the value. You can simply use `browser:editform`. You configure the view with the following directive in `browser/configure.zcml`:

```
01  <editform
02      name="smileyTheme.html"
03      schema="book.messageboard.interfaces.ISmileyThemeSpecification"
04      for="book.messageboard.interfaces.IMessageBoard"
05      label="Change Smiley Theme"
06      permission="book.messageboard.Edit"
07      menu="zmi_views" title="Smiley Theme" />
```

The edit form will automatically know how to look up the adapter and use it instead of the `MessageBoard` instance. If you now restart Zope 3, you should be able to change the theme to whatever you like.

Using the Smiley Theme

At this point you need to use all the machinery you've created. To do so, you need to add a method called `body()` to the `MessageDetails` (located in `browser/message.py`) class:

```
01  def body(self):
02      """Return the body, but mark up smileys."""
03      body = self.context.body
04
05      # Find the messageboard and get the theme preference
06      obj = self.context
07      while not IMessageBoard.providedBy(obj) and \
08              obj is not None:
09          obj = zapi.getParent(obj)
10
11      if obj is None:
12          theme = None
13      else:
14          theme = ISmileyThemeSpecification(obj).theme
15
16      for text, url in getSmileysMapping(self.request, theme).items():
17          body = body.replace(
18              text,
19              '<img src="%s" label="%s"/>' %(url, text))
20
21      return body
```

Note

In order for this code to function correctly, you also have to import several other objects. You need to place the following lines to the import statements of the module:

```
01 from book.messageboard.interfaces import IMessageBoard
02 from book.messageboard.interfaces import ISmileyThemeSpecification
03 from book.smileyutility import getSmileysMapping
```

In the preceding code block, note the following:

- Lines 5–14: This code finds the `MessageBoard` instance and, when it is found, gets the desired theme.
- Lines 16–19: Using the theme, you get the smiley mapping and convert one smiley after another from the text representation to an image tag that references the smiley.

In the `details.pt` template, line 33, you now just have to change the call from `context/body` to `view/body` so that the preceding method is used. After you do that, you are ready to restart Zope 3 and enjoy the smileys, as shown in Figure 29.1.

Figure 29.1   The message Preview screen, featuring the smileys.

Local Utilities

Difficulty

Contributor

Skills

- You need to be comfortable with the component architecture, specifically utilities.
- You need to be familiar with the site management Web GUI.
- You should be familiar with this book's message board example.
- You should be familiar with Chapter 29, "Registries with Global Utilities," because this chapter is its local companion.

Problem/Task

It is great to have the global smiley theme utilities you created in Chapter 29. They work just fine. But what if you want to provide different icon themes for different message boards on the same Zope installation? Or what if you want to allow your online users to upload new themes? In such a case, the global smiley theme is not sufficient anymore, and you need a local and persistent version. In this chapter you will create a local smiley theme utility.

T HE SEMANTICS OF LOCAL UTILITIES ARE OFTEN very different from the ones for global utilities; thus, they have a very different implementation. For one thing, local utilities can be fully managed, which means they can be added, edited, and deleted. Only the first one of these actions—full management—is possible for their global counterparts. Furthermore, and most importantly, local utilities must know how to delegate requests to other utilities higher up, including the global version of the utility. All these facts create a very different problem domain, which is addressed in this chapter.

You know that the purpose of the global smiley utility is to manage smileys (in a very limited way). Because the local smiley theme must be able to manage smileys fully, it is best to make the utility also a container that can contain only smileys. A smiley component will simply be a glorified image that can only be contained by local smiley themes. Thus, you need to develop an `ILocalSmileyTheme` interface that extends `IContainer`. This interface must also limit its containable items to be only smileys. The second interface will be `ISmiley`, which simply extends `IImage` and allows only itself to be added to smiley themes.

Like all other local components, local utilities must be registered. One way to do this would be to write a custom registration component; however, a simpler method is to have the local smiley theme provide the `ILocalUtility` marker interface. A registration component (including all necessary views) exists for any object that provides this interface, making the implementation of a local utility much simpler than the implementation of a global utility.

The code developed in this chapter should be placed in the existing *Zope3-Instance*`/lib/python/book/smileyutility` package.

Step 1: Defining the Interfaces

As mentioned earlier in this chapter, you need two new interfaces. The first one is the `ISmiley` interface:

```
01 from zope.schema import Field
02
03 from zope.app.container.constraints import ContainerTypesConstraint
04 from zope.app.file.interfaces import IImage
05
06 class ISmiley(IImage):
07     """A smiley is just a glorified image"""
08     __parent__ = Field(
09         constraint = ContainerTypesConstraint(ISmileyTheme))
```

As mentioned previously, the smiley component is simply an image that can be added only to smiley themes. The second interface is `ILocalSmileyTheme`, which will manage all the smileys in a typical container-like fashion:

```
01 from zope.app.container.constraints import ItemTypePrecondition
02 from zope.app.container.interfaces import IContainer
03
04 class ILocalSmileyTheme(ISmileyTheme, IContainer):
05     """A local smiley themes that manages its smileys via the container API"""
06
07     def __setitem__(name, object):
08         """Add a IMessage object."""
09
10     __setitem__.precondition = ItemTypePrecondition(ISmiley)
```

After you make the local smiley theme a container, you declare that it can contain only smileys. If you do not know about preconditions and constraints in interfaces, you need to read Chapter 13, "Writing New Content Objects."

Step 2: Implementing a Smiley

Implementing a smiley is trivial. In a new Python file called `localtheme.py`, you need to add the following code:

```
01 from zope.interfaces import implements
02 from zope.app.file.image import Image
03 from interfaces import ISmiley
04
05 class Smiley(Image):
06     implements(ISmiley)
```

Now you just need to provide an implementation for the theme. As before, you can use `BTreeContainer` as a base class that provides you with a full implementation of the `IContainer` interface. Then all that you have to worry about are the three `ISmileyTheme` API methods. You need to add the following implementation to `localtheme.py`:

```
01 from zope.component.exceptions import ComponentLookupError
02
03 from zope.app import zapi
04 from zope.app.container.btree import BTreeContainer
05 from zope.app.component.localservice import queryNextService
06
07 from interfaces import ISmileyTheme, ILocalSmileyTheme
08
09 class SmileyTheme(BTreeContainer):
10     """A local smiley theme implementation."""
11     implements(ILocalSmileyTheme)
12
13     def getSmiley(self, text, request):
14         "See book.smileyutility.interfaces.ISmileyTheme"
15         smiley = self.querySmiley(text, request)
16         if smiley is None:
17             raise ComponentLookupError, 'Smiley not found.'
18         return smiley
19
20     def querySmiley(self, text, request, default=None):
21         "See book.smileyutility.interfaces.ISmileyTheme"
22         if text not in self:
23             theme = queryNextTheme(self, zapi.name(self))
24             if theme is None:
25                 return default
```

```
26                else:
27                    return theme.querySmiley(text, request, default)
28            return getURL(self[text], request)
29
30      def getSmileysMapping(self, request):
31          "See book.smileyutility.interfaces.ISmileyTheme"
32          theme = queryNextTheme(self, zapi.name(self))
33          if theme is None:
34              smileys = {}
35          else:
36              smileys = theme.getSmileysMapping(request)
37
38          for name, smiley in self.items():
39              smileys[name] = getURL(smiley, request)
40
41          return smileys
42
43
44  def queryNextTheme(context, name, default=None):
45      """Get the next theme higher up."""
46      theme = default
47      while theme is default:
48          utilities = queryNextService(context, zapi.servicenames.Utilities)
49          if utilities is None:
50              return default
51          theme = utilities.queryUtility(ISmileyTheme, name, default)
52          context = utilities
53      return theme
54
55  def getURL(smiley, request):
56      """Get the URL of the smiley."""
57      url = zapi.getView(smiley, 'absolute_url', request=request)
58      return url()
```

In the preceding code block, note the following:

- Lines 13–18: This implementation is identical to the global one. The
  querySmiley() method does the work.

- Lines 20–28: If the requested smiley is available in the theme, you simply return its
  URL. However, if the smiley is not found, you should not give up too quickly. It
  might be defined in a theme (with the same name) in a level higher up. The high-
  est level holds the global components. If a theme of the same name exists higher
  up, you can try to get the smiley from there. If no such theme exists, you need to
  give up and return the default value.

This generalizes very nicely to all local components. Local components should
only be concerned with querying and searching their local place and not stretch
out into other places. For utilities, the request should then always be forwarded to

the next occurrence at a higher place. This method will automatically be able to recursively search the entire path, all the way up. The termination condition is usually the global utility, which always has to return and will never refer to another place. If you do not have a global version of the utility available, you need to put a condition in your local code and terminate when no other utility is found.

- Lines 30–41: This method has to be very careful about the procedure it uses to generate the result. The same exact smiley—defined by its text and theme—might be declared in several locations along the path, but only the last declaration (that is, the one closest to the current location) should make it into the smiley mapping. Therefore, you first get the acquired results and then merge the local smiley mapping into it, so that the local smileys are always added last. Note that this implementation makes this method also recursive, ensuring that all themes with the matching name are considered.

- Lines 44–53: You specify a method that returns the next matching theme up. Starting at `context`, the `queryNextService()` method walks up the tree, looking for the next site in the path. If a site is found, the `queryNextService()` method sees whether it finds the specified service (in this case, the utility service) in the site. If it does not, it keeps walking. It terminates its search when it reaches the global site (that is, when `None` is returned) or when it finds a service.

  If the utilities service is found, you need to then ensure that it also has a matching theme. If it does not, you have to keep looking by finding the next utilities service. If a matching theme is found, the `while` loop's condition is fulfilled, and the theme is returned.

- Lines 55–58: Because smiley entries are not URLs in the local theme, you look up their URLs by using the `absolute_url` view.

As you can see, the implementation of the local theme is a bit more involved than the implementation of the global theme because you have to worry about the delegation of the requests. But it is downhill from here on. What you get for free is a full management and registration user and programming interface for the local themes and smileys, which is the equivalent of the ZCML directives you had to develop for the global theme.

Until now, you have always written tests right after doing the implementation. However, tests for local components very much reflect their behavior in the system, and the tests in this chapter will be easier to understand if you get everything working first. Therefore, you will next develop the necessary registrations, followed by providing some views.

Step 3: Registering the Themes

You need to register the local theme as a new content type and local utility. Making it a local utility will also ensure that it can be added only to site management folders. You need to add the following directives to your configuration file:

```
01 <zope:content class=".localtheme.SmileyTheme">
02   <zope:factory
03       id="book.smileyutility.SmileyTheme"
04       title="Smiley Theme"
05       description="A Smiley Theme"
06       />
07   <zope:implements
08       interface="zope.app.utility.interfaces.ILocalUtility"
09       />
10   <zope:implements
11       interface="zope.app.container.interfaces.IContentContainer"
12       />
13   <zope:implements
14       interface="zope.app.annotation.interfaces.IAttributeAnnotatable"
15       />
16   <zope:allow
17       interface="zope.app.container.interfaces.IReadContainer"
18       />
19   <zope:require
20       permission="zope.ManageServices"
21       interface="zope.app.container.interfaces.IWriteContainer"
22       />
23   <zope:allow
24       interface=".interfaces.ISmileyTheme"
25       />
26 </zope:content>
```

Note

The reason you use the zope: prefix in the directives here is that you use the smiley namespace as the default. You also have to add the zope namespace to the configure element.

In the preceding code block, note the following:

- Lines 7–9: You declare the local theme component to be a local utility. Because this is just a marker interface, you don't need to implement any special methods or attributes.

- Lines 10–12: In order for the precondition of __setitem__() to work, you need to make the smiley theme an IContentContainer interface, which is just another marker interface.

- Lines 13–15: All local components should be annotatable, so that you can append Dublin Core and other metadata.

- Lines 16–18: You allow everyone to just access the smileys as they wish.

- Lines 19–22: For changing the theme, you require the service management permission.

- Line 23–25: You make the theme's API methods publicly available.

Now you just have to declare the `Smiley` class as a content type:

```
01 <zope:content class=".localtheme.Smiley">
02    <zope:require
03        like_class="zope.app.file.image.Image"
04        />
05 </zope:content>
```

In the preceding code block, note the following:

- Lines 2–4: You just give the `Smiley` class the same security declarations as the image. Because the smiley does not declare any new methods and attributes, you don't have to make any further security declarations.

The components are registered now, but you will still not be able to do much because you have not added any menu items to the Add menu or any other management view.

Step 4: Providing Views

As you will see, the browser code for the theme is minimal. Therefore, you do not need to create a separate `browser` package; instead, you can place the browser code in the main configuration file. As always, you need to add the `browser` namespace first:

```
01 xmlns:browser="http://namespaces.zope.org/browser"
```

Now you create Add menu entries for each content type:

```
01 <browser:addMenuItem
02     class=".localtheme.Smiley"
03     title="Smiley"
04     description="A Smiley"
05     permission="zope.ManageServices"
06     />
07
08 <browser:addMenuItem
09     class=".localtheme.SmileyTheme"
10     title="Smiley Theme"
11     description="A Smiley Theme"
12     permission="zope.ManageServices"
13     />
```

You also want the standard container management screens to be available in the theme, so you just add the following directive:

```
01 <browser:containerViews
02     for=".localtheme.SmileyTheme"
03     index="zope.View"
04     contents="zope.ManageServices"
05     add="zope.ManageServices"
06     />
```

At this point, you can restart Zope 3 and test the utility, and everything should work as expected. However, you should now create a couple more convenience views to make the utility a little bit nicer.

First, you might have noticed the Tools tab in the site manager. Tools are mainly meant to make the management of utilities simpler, and a tools entry requires only one simple directive:

```
01 <browser:tool
02     interface=".interfaces.ISmileyTheme"
03     title="Smiley Themes"
04     description="Smiley Themes allow you to convert text-based to icon-based
05                  smileys."
06     />
```

In the preceding code block, note the following:

- Line 1: Because tools are not components, but just views on the site manager, the directive is part of the `browser` namespace.
- Line 2: You specify the interface under which the utility is registered.
- Lines 3–5: Here you provide a human-readable title and description for the tool, which is used in the tools Overview tab.

The second step is to create a nice Overview tab that tells what local and acquired smileys are available for a particular theme. The first step is to create a view class, which provides one method for retrieving all locally defined smileys and one method that retrieves all acquired smileys from higher themes. In a new file called `browser.py`, you add the following code:

```
01 from zope.app import zapi
02
03 from localtheme import queryNextTheme, getURL
04
05 class Overview(object):
06
07     def getLocalSmileys(self):
08         return [{'text': name, 'url': getURL(smiley, self.request)}
09                 for name, smiley in self.context.items()]
10
11     def getAcquiredSmileys(self):
12         theme = queryNextTheme(self.context, zapi.name(self.context))
13         map = theme.getSmileysMapping(self.request)
14         return [{'text': name, 'url': path} for name, path in map.items()
15                 if name not in self.context]
```

In the preceding code block, note the following:

- Lines 7–9: Getting all the locally defined smileys is easy; you simply get all the items from the container and convert the smiley object to a URL. The return object will be a list of dictionaries with the following form:
  - text—This is the text representation of the smiley; in this case, it is the name of the smiley object.
  - url—This is the URL of the smiley, as located in the theme. You already developed a function for getting the URL (getURL()), so you can reuse it here.

- Lines 11–15: You know that getSmileysMapping() will get you all local and acquired smileys. But if you get the next theme first and then call the method, you will only get the acquired smileys with respect to this theme. You only need to make sure that you exclude smileys that are also defined locally. From the mapping, you then create the same output dictionary as in the previous function.

The template that will make use of these two view methods, which you should place in a new file called overview.pt, could look something like this:

```
01 <html metal:use-macro="views/standard_macros/view">
02 <head>
03   <title metal:fill-slot="title"
04          i18n:translate="">Smiley Theme</title>
05 </head>
06 <body>
07 <div metal:fill-slot="body">
08
09   <h2 i18n:translate="">Local Smileys</h2>
10   <ul>
11     <li tal:repeat="smiley view/getLocalSmileys">
12     <b tal:content="smiley/text"/> &#8594;
13     <img src="" tal:attributes="src smiley/url"/>
14     </li>
15   </ul>
16
17   <h2 i18n:translate="">Acquired Smileys</h2>
18   <ul>
19     <li tal:repeat="smiley view/getAcquiredSmileys">
20       <b tal:content="smiley/text"/> &#8594;
21       <img src="" tal:attributes="src smiley/url"/>
22     </li>
23   </ul>
24
25 </div>
26 </body>
27 </html>
```

All that's left now is to register the view, using a simple `browser:page` directive:

```
01 <browser:page
02     name="overview.html"
03     menu="zmi_views" title="Overview"
04     for=".localtheme.SmileyTheme"
05     permission="zope.ManageServices"
06     class=".browser.Overview"
07     template="overview.pt" />
```

Step 5: Working with the Local Smiley Theme

You need to test the new local theme by walking through the steps of creating a utility via the Web interface. This will help you understand the tests you will have to write at the end. First, you need to restart Zope 3 and log in as a user who is also a manager. Then you need to go to the contents view of the root folder and click the Manage Site link, just below the tabs. When the screen is loaded, you click the Tools tab and choose the Smiley Themes tool. You can then add a new theme by clicking the Add button. When the new page appears, you enter the name of the theme in the text field and click the Add button. You should choose a name for the theme that is already used as a global theme as well, such as `plain`. This way, you can test the acquisition of themes better. When the browser is done loading the following page, you should be back in the Smiley Themes tool Overview tab, which lists the `plain` theme, which is already registered as being active, as shown in Figure 30.1.

Figure 30.1   An overview of all smiley themes.

To add a new smiley, you click `plain`, which brings you to the theme's Contents view. Right beside the Add button is a text field where you should enter the name `:-)` before you click Add. You have now created a new smiley. You can click `:-)` to upload a new image. Then you can choose an image in the Data row and click Change, which uploads the image. You should repeat the procedure for the `:)` smiley. To see the contrast, you might want to upload smileys from the `yazoo` theme.

When you are done, you can click the Overview tab, and you should see (see Figure 30.2) the two local smileys and a bunch of acquired smileys, which are provided by the global `plain` smiley theme.

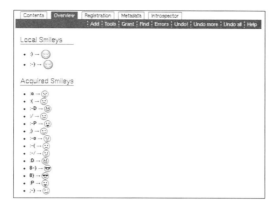

Figure 30.2   An overview of all available smileys in this theme.

If you like, you can now go to the message board and ensure that the local smiley definitions are preferred over the global ones for the `plain` theme.

Step 6: Writing Tests

Although you now have a working system, you should still write tests so that you can figure out whether all aspects of the local smiley theme are working correctly. The truly interesting part about testing any local component is the setup; when you get that right, you can quickly write the tests.

When testing local components, you must basically bring up an entire bootstrap ZODB with folders and site managers. Luckily, there are some very nice utility functions that help with this tedious setup. You can find them in `zope.app.tests.setup`. The following functions are commonly useful to developers:

- `setUpAnnotations()`—This function registers the attribute annotations adapter. This function is also useful for placeless setups.

- `setUpTraversal()`—This function sets up a wide range of traversal-related adapters and views, including everything that is needed to traverse a path, get an object's parent path, and traverse the `etc` namespace. The `absolute_url` view is also registered.

- `placefulSetUp(site=False)`—Like the placeless setup, this function registers all the interfaces and adapters required for doing anything useful. Included are annotations, a dependency framework, traversal hooks, and the registration machinery. If `site` is set to `True`, a root folder with a `ServiceManager` instance (also known as site manager) inside will be created, and the site manager is returned.

- `placefulTearDown()`—Like the placeless equivalent, this function correctly shuts down the registries.

- **buildSampleFolderTree()**—A sample folder tree is built to support multiple-place settings, which is important for testing acquisition of local components. The structure shown in Figure 30.3 is created.

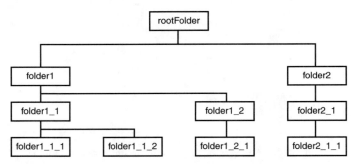

Figure 30.3   The folder structure, after buildSampleFolderTree() is called.

- **createServiceManager(folder, setsite=False)**—This function creates a local service/site manager for the specified folder. Note that the function can be used for any object that implements ISite. If setsite is True, the thread global site variable will be set to the new site as well.

- **addService(servicemanager, name, service, suffix="")**—This function adds a service instance to the specified service manager and registers it. The service will be available as name, and the instance will be stored as name+suffix.

- **addUtility(servicemanager, name, iface, utility, suffix="")**—With this function, you register to the specified service manager a utility that provides the interface iface and has the name name. The utility will be stored in the site management folder under the name name+suffix.

Now you are ready to look into writing tests. As for the global theme, you can write doc tests for the theme. Thus, you should add the following lines in tests/test_doc.py, after line 41:

```
01 DocTestSuite('book.smileyutility.localtheme')
```

You should add the following tests to the doc string or the SmileyTheme class. You begin by calling the placefulSetUp() function and setting up the folder tree:

```
01 >>> from zope.app.tests import setup
02 >>> from zope.app.utility.utility import LocalUtilityService
03 >>> site = setup.placefulSetUp()
04 >>> rootFolder = setup.buildSampleFolderTree()
```

Next, you write a convenience function that lets you quickly add a new smiley to a
local theme:

```
01 Setup a simple function to add local smileys to a theme.
02
03 >>> import os
04 >>> import book.smileyutility
05 >>> def addSmiley(theme, text, filename):
06 ...     base_dir = os.path.dirname(book.smileyutility.__file__)
07 ...     filename = os.path.join(base_dir, filename)
08 ...     theme[text] = Smiley(open(filename, 'r'))
```

Now that the framework is all set up, you can add some smiley themes in various
folders:

```
01 Create components in root folder
02
03 >>> site = setup.createServiceManager(rootFolder)
04 >>> utils = setup.addService(site, zapi.servicenames.Utilities,
05 ...                         LocalUtilityService())
06 >>> theme = setup.addUtility(site, 'plain', ISmileyTheme, SmileyTheme())
07 >>> addSmiley(theme, ':)', 'smileys/plain/smile.png')
08 >>> addSmiley(theme, ':(', 'smileys/plain/sad.png')
09
10 Create components in `folder1`
11
12 >>> site = setup.createServiceManager(rootFolder['folder1'])
13 >>> utils = setup.addService(site, zapi.servicenames.Utilities,
14 ...                         LocalUtilityService())
15 >>> theme = setup.addUtility(site, 'plain', ISmileyTheme, SmileyTheme())
16 >>> addSmiley(theme, ':)', 'smileys/plain/biggrin.png')
17 >>> addSmiley(theme, '8)', 'smileys/plain/cool.png')
```

In the preceding code block, note the following:

- Line 3: First, you make the root folder a site.
- Lines 4–5: By default, there are no local services in a new site. Before you can add utilities, you first need to add a local utility service to the site.
- Lines 6–8: First, you create the theme and add it as a utility to the site. Then you just add two smileys to it.
- Lines 10–17: You use a setup similar to the root folder for `folder1`.

Now you have completely set up the system and can test the API methods. First, you
need to test the `getSmiley()` and `querySmiley()` methods via the package's API convenience functions:

```
01 Now test the single smiley accessor methods
02
03 >>> from zope.publisher.browser import TestRequest
04 >>> from zope.app.component.localservice import setSite
05 >>> from book.smileyutility import getSmiley, querySmiley
06
07 >>> setSite(rootFolder)
08 >>> getSmiley(':)', TestRequest(), 'plain')
09 'http://127.0.0.1/++etc++site/default/plain/%3A%29'
10 >>> getSmiley(':(', TestRequest(), 'plain')
11 'http://127.0.0.1/++etc++site/default/plain/%3A%28'
12 >>> getSmiley('8)', TestRequest(), 'plain')
13 Traceback (most recent call last):
14 ...
15 ComponentLookupError: 'Smiley not found.'
16 >>> querySmiley('8)', TestRequest(), 'plain', 'nothing')
17 'nothing'
18
19 >>> setSite(rootFolder['folder1'])
20 >>> getSmiley(':)', TestRequest(), 'plain')
21 'http://127.0.0.1/folder1/++etc++site/default/plain/%3A%29'
22 >>> getSmiley(':(', TestRequest(), 'plain')
23 'http://127.0.0.1/++etc++site/default/plain/%3A%28'
24 >>> getSmiley('8)', TestRequest(), 'plain')
25 'http://127.0.0.1/folder1/++etc++site/default/plain/8%29'
26 >>> getSmiley(':|', TestRequest(), 'plain')
27 Traceback (most recent call last):
28 ...
29 ComponentLookupError: 'Smiley not found.'
30 >>> querySmiley(':|', TestRequest(), 'plain', 'nothing')
31 'nothing'
```

In the preceding code block, note the following:

- Line 7: You set the current site to the root folder. All requests are now executed with respect to that site.

- Lines 8–11: You make sure that the basic local access works. Note that the TestRequest class defines the computer's IP address to be 127.0.0.1 and is not computer specific.

- Lines 12–17: You make sure that a ComponentLookupError exception is raised if a smiley is not found or the default is returned and if querySmiley() was used.

- Lines 19–31: You repeat the tests, using folder1 as location. Specifically interesting are lines 22–23 because the smiley is not found locally but is retrieved from the root folder's theme.

You can now test the getSmileysMapping() method. To do so, you create a small helper method that helps you compare dictionaries:

```
01 >>> from pprint import pprint
02 >>> from book.smileyutility import getSmileysMapping
03 >>> def output(dict):
04 ...      items = dict.items()
05 ...      items.sort()
06 ...      pprint(items)
07
08 >>> setSite(rootFolder)
09 >>> output(getSmileysMapping(TestRequest(), 'plain'))
10 [(u':(', 'http://127.0.0.1/++etc++site/default/plain/%3A%28'),
11  (u':)', 'http://127.0.0.1/++etc++site/default/plain/%3A%29')]
12
13 >>> setSite(rootFolder['folder1'])
14 >>> output(getSmileysMapping(TestRequest(), 'plain'))
15 [(u'8)', 'http://127.0.0.1/folder1/++etc++site/default/plain/8%29'),
16  (u':(', 'http://127.0.0.1/++etc++site/default/plain/%3A%28'),
17  (u':)', 'http://127.0.0.1/folder1/++etc++site/default/plain/%3A%29')]
18 >>> getSmileysMapping(TestRequest(), 'foobar')
19 Traceback (most recent call last):
20 ...
21 ComponentLookupError:
➡ (<InterfaceClass book.smileyutility.interfaces.ISmileyTheme>, 'foobar')
```

In the preceding code block, note the following:

- Lines 8–17: You test the method for two locations so that acquisition can be tested.
- Lines 18–21: You make sure you do not accidentally find any non-existent themes.

After all the tests are complete, you need to cleanly shut down the test case:

```
01 >>> setup.placefulTearDown()
```

You should now run the tests and see that they all pass. Another interesting function that deserves careful testing is queryNextTheme(). That test is not explained here because it is very similar to the previous one; you should look in the code, located at http://svn.zope.org/book/trunk/smileyutility/localtheme.py, for the test or even try to develop it yourself.

Vocabularies and Related Fields/Widgets

Difficulty

Sprinter

Skills

- You need to be familiar with the `zope.schema` package.
- You should be familiar with the `zope.app.widget` package.

Problem/Task

Schemas in combination with widgets and forms are pretty cool. The days of writing boring HTML forms and data verification are over. However, the standard Zope 3 fields make it hard (if not impossible) to create a dynamic list of possible values to choose from. To solve this problem, the Zope 3 development team created the vocabularies and their corresponding fields and widgets. This chapter demonstrates one of the common usages of vocabularies in Zope 3.

A COMMON USER INTERFACE PATTERN is to provide the user with a list of available or possible values from which to select one or more items. This pattern is used to reduce the number of errors the user could possibly make. Often, the list of choices is static, meaning that the list does not change over time and is not dependent on a particular situation. On the other hand, user interfaces also commonly have choices for a field that depend strongly on the situation you are presented with.

In this chapter, you'll use the `Choice` field to allow users to select a value from a provided list. If you pass the keyword argument `values` to the list, the field lets you always choose from this static list of values. However, if you specify a vocabulary via the vocabulary argument, then it will be used to provide the list of available choices. By the way, the argument accepts either a vocabulary object or a vocabulary name (string). If you want to select multiple items from a list of choices, you can either use the Tuple, List, or Set fields; these fields accept a value_type argument, which specifies the type of values that can reside in these collection types. If you pass a Choice field as value_type, then a widget is chosen that lets you select only from the choices in the Choice field.

Vocabularies in themselves are not difficult to understand, but their application ranges from the generation of a static list of elements to providing a list of all available RDB connections, for example. But at the end of the day, vocabularies just provide a list of items or terms, which is the correct jargon.

Generally, there are two scenarios of vocabulary usage in Zope 3: the ones that do and others that do not need a place to generate the list of terms. Vocabularies that do not need a place can be created as singletons and would be useful when data is retrieved from a file, an RDB, or any other Zope-external data source. In this chapter, however, you are going to implement a vocabulary that provides a list of all items in a container (or any other IReadMapping object). Thus, the location clearly matters.

Vocabularies that need a location to provide their terms cannot exist as singletons, but the location must be passed into the constructor. Zope 3 provides a vocabulary registry with which you can register vocabulary factories (which are usually just the classes) by name. The ZCML directive zope:vocabulary can be used as follows:

```
01 <vocabulary
02    name="VocabularyName"
03    factory=".vocab.Vocabulary" />
```

You can then use the vocabulary in a schema by declaring a Choice field:

```
01 from zope.schema import Choice
02
03 field = Choice(
04    title=u"...",
05    description=u"...",
06    vocabulary="VocabularyName")
```

If the vocabulary argument value is a string, then it is used as a vocabulary name, and the vocabulary is created with a context whenever needed. But the argument also accepts IVocabulary instances, which are directly used.

In the following sections you'll experiment with using vocabularies.

Step 1: The Vocabulary and Its Terms

A vocabulary has a very simple interface. It is much like a simple collection object with some additional functionality. The main idea is that a vocabulary provides ITerm objects. A term simply has a value attribute that can be any Python object. However, for Web forms (and other user interfaces), this minimalistic interface does not suffice because you have no way of reliably specifying a unique ID (an ASCII string) for a term, which you need to do to create any HTML input element with the terms. To solve this problem, the Zope 3 development team came up with the `ITokenizedTerm` interface, which provides a `token` attribute that must be a string that uniquely identifies the term. Another extension to the `ITokenizedTerm` interface is the `ITitledTokenizedTerm` interface, which additionally provides a title for the term that is used for representing the term in a user interface.

Because your vocabulary deals with folder item names, your `ITerm` interface's `value` attribute can be used to generate the `token` value. Because the token must be ASCII, you simply encode the value to UTF-8 (because it can be Unicode) and then use base 64 to ensure that it is ASCII. The title is just the same as the `value` attribute. Therefore, you only need a minimal implementation of `ITitledTokenizedTerm`, as shown here:

```
01 from zope.interface import implements
02 from zope.schema.interfaces import ITitledTokenizedTerm
03
04 class ItemTerm(object):
05     """A simple term implementation for items."""
06     implements(ITitledTokenizedTerm)
07     def __init__(self, value):
08         self.value = self.title = value
09         self.token = value.encode('utf8').encode('base64')[:-1]
```

Next, you need to create a new package called `itemvocabulary` in *Zope3-Instance*/lib/python/book and place the preceding code in the __init__.py file. Next, you need to implement the vocabulary. Because the context of the vocabulary is an `IReadMapping` object, the implementation is straightforward (put it in the __init__.py file):

```
01 from zope.schema.interfaces import IVocabulary, IVocabularyTokenized
02 from zope.interface.common.mapping import IEnumerableMapping
03
04 class ItemVocabulary(object):
05     """A vocabulary that provides the keys of any IEnumerableMapping object.
06
07     Every dictionary will qualify for this vocabulary."""
08     implements(IVocabulary, IVocabularyTokenized)
09     __used_for__ = IEnumerableMapping
10
11     def __init__(self, context):
12         self.context = context
13
14     def __iter__(self):
15         """See zope.schema.interfaces.IIterableVocabulary"""
16         return iter([ItemTerm(key) for key in self.context.keys()])
17
```

```
18    def __len__(self):
19        """See zope.schema.interfaces.IIterableVocabulary"""
20        return len(self.context)
21
22    def __contains__(self, value):
23        """See zope.schema.interfaces.IBaseVocabulary"""
24        return value in self.context
25
26    def getTerm(self, value):
27        """See zope.schema.interfaces.IBaseVocabulary"""
28        if value not in self.context:
29            raise LookupError, value
30        return ItemTerm(value)
31
32    def getTermByToken(self, token):
33        """See zope.schema.interfaces.IVocabularyTokenized"""
34        token = str(token)
35        return self.getTerm(token.decode('base64').decode('utf8'))
```

In the preceding code block, note the following:

- Line 8: You need to make sure you implement both IVocabulary and IVocabularyTokenized so that the widget mechanism will work correctly later.

- Lines 14–16: You need to make sure the values of the iterator are ITitledTokenizedTerm objects and not simple strings. If you only implement IVocabulary, the objects just have to implement ITerm, but then you cannot use Zope 3's form framework because widgets only work for ITokenizedTerm objects.

- Lines 26–30: You must be careful here and not just create an ItemTerm instance from the value because the interface specifies that if the value is not available in the vocabulary, a LookupError exception should be raised.

- Lines 32–35: The token should always be a string, not Unicode. However, because the token is often coming from a Web form, it is Unicode, so that you have to convert it to a string first, which is no problem because you know the string only consists of ASCII characters. Because the token value is derived from the value attribute of the term, you can just forward the request to getTerm() when the value is decoded.

Because the vocabulary requires a context for initiation, you need to register it with the vocabulary registry. The vocabulary is also used in untrusted environments, so you have to make security assertions for it and for the term. You need to place the following ZCML directives in the configure.zcml file of the itemvocabulary package:

```
01 <configure
02     xmlns="http://namespaces.zope.org/zope"
03     i18n_domain="itemvocabulary">
04
```

```
05 <vocabulary
06    name="Items"
07    factory=".ItemVocabulary" />
08
09 <class class=".ItemVocabulary">
10   <allow interface="zope.schema.interfaces.IVocabularyTokenized" />
11 </class>
12
13 <class class=".ItemTerm">
14   <allow interface="zope.schema.interfaces.ITitledTokenizedTerm"/>
15 </class>
16
17 </configure>
```

In the preceding code block, note the following:

- Lines 5–7: You register the vocabulary under the name Items. The vocabulary directive is available in the default zope namespace.
- Lines 9–15: You simply open all the interfaces to the public because the objects that provide the data are themselves protected.

That was easy, right? Next, you can write some quick tests for this code.

Step 2: Testing the Vocabulary

The tests are as straightforward as the vocabulary code itself. You are going to test only the vocabulary because the implementation of the term is trivial and will be tested through the vocabulary anyway. In the docstring of the ItemVocabulary class, you need to add the following example and test code:

```
01 Example:
02
03 >>> data = {'a': 'Anton', 'b': 'Berta', 'c': 'Charlie'}
04 >>> vocab = ItemVocabulary(data)
05 >>> iterator = iter(vocab)
06 >>> iterator.next().token
07 'a'
08 >>> len(vocab)
09 3
10 >>> 'c' in vocab
11 True
12 >>> vocab.getQuery() is None
13 True
14 >>> vocab.getTerm('b').value
15 'b'
16 >>> vocab.getTerm('d')
17 Traceback (most recent call last):
18 ...
```

```
19 LookupError: d
20 >>> vocab.getTermByToken('b').token
21 'b'
22 >>> vocab.getTermByToken('d')
23 Traceback (most recent call last):
24 ...
25 LookupError: d
```

Note that you can simply use a dictionary as your test context because it fully provides `IEnumerableMapping`. The tests are activated via a doc test that is initialized in `tests.py` with the following code:

```
01 import unittest
02 from zope.testing.doctestunit import DocTestSuite
03
04 def test_suite():
05     return unittest.TestSuite((
06         DocTestSuite('book.itemvocabulary'),
07         ))
08
09 if __name__ == '__main__':
10     unittest.main(defaultTest='test_suite')
```

You can execute the tests as usual via the Zope 3 test runner or call the test file directly after you have set the correct Python path.

Step 3: The Default Item Folder

To see the vocabulary working, you can develop a special folder that simply keeps track of a default item (whatever *default* may mean in the context). Because the folder is part of a browser demonstration, you place the following folder interface and implementation of the folder in the file `browser.py`:

```
01 from zope.interface import implements, Interface
02 from zope.schema import Choice
03 from zope.app.folder import Folder
04
05 class IDefaultItem(Interface):
06
07     default = Choice(
08         title=u"Default Item Key",
09         description=u"Key of the default item in the folder.",
10         vocabulary="Items")
11
12 class DefaultItemFolder(Folder):
13     implements(IDefaultItem)
14
15     default = None
```

In the preceding code block, note the following:

- Lines 7–10: Here you can see the `Choice` field in a very common setup and usage. The `vocabulary` argument can either be the vocabulary name or a vocabulary instance, as pointed out earlier in this chapter.
- Lines 12–15: You implement a trivial content component that combines `IFolder` and `IDefaultItem`.

Now you only have to register the new content component, make some security assertions, and create an Edit view for the `default` value. You can do all this with the following three ZCML directives in `configure.zcml`:

```
01 <content class=".browser.DefaultItemFolder">
02   <require like_class="zope.app.folder.Folder"/>
03
04   <require
05       permission="zope.View"
06       interface=".browser.IDefaultItem" />
07
08   <require
09       permission="zope.ManageContent"
10       set_schema=".browser.IDefaultItem" />
11 </content>
12
13 <browser:addMenuItem
14     class=".browser.DefaultItemFolder"
15     title="Default Item Folder"
16     permission="zope.ManageContent" />
17
18 <browser:editform
19     schema=".browser.IDefaultItem"
20     for=".browser.IDefaultItem"
21     label="Change Default Item"
22     name="defaultItem.html"
23     permission="zope.ManageContent"
24     menu="zmi_views" title="Default Item" />
```

You also need to register the `browser` namespace in the `configure` tag:

```
01 xmlns:browser="http://namespaces.zope.org/browser"
```

Finally, you have to tell the system about the new package so that it will read its configuration. You need to place a file called `itemvocabulary-configure.zcml` in the `package-includes` directory, and the file needs to contain the following one-line directive:

```
01 <include package="book.itemvocabulary" />
```

You are now ready to go. You can restart Zope 3. When you refresh the ZMI, you will see that you can now select the option Default Item Folder. You should create such a folder and add to it a couple other components, such as images and files. If you then click the Default Item tab, you see a selection box with the names of all contained objects. If you select one and submit the form, you store the name of the object that will be considered the default. As you can see, there are widgets that know how to display a vocabulary field.

32

Exception Views

Difficulty

Newcomer

Skills

- You should be knowledgeable about writing page templates.
- You should have some basic ZCML knowledge.

Problem/Task

Zope 3 has the capability to provide views for exceptions and errors. It provides views for some of the most common user errors, such as `NotFound` (a page was not found), and even a generic view for all exceptions. However, when you have a specific application error, you usually want to provide a customized error message.

EXCEPTIONS ARE POWERFUL TOOLS in programming. However, sometimes it is hard to deal with them, especially at the point where they reach the user. Zope 3 allows exceptions to have views, so that the user can always see a friendly message when an error occurs. This is a way to clearly differentiate between errors that are raised due to programming errors (bugs) and errors that are raised on purpose to signal user errors.

Programming errors should never occur in a production-quality application, and as Jim Fulton has said, "I want to discourage people from trying to make all errors look good." Thus Zope 3's default is to provide only a very minimalistic view, saying only "System Error." An exception to that is the view for `NotFoundError`, which displays a very nice message that explains what happened. But even the best applications have bugs, and before publishing a Zope 3 application, you should probably provide a more polite message for programming errors. For development, the debug skin contains a nice view for IException that shows the exception class and value, as well as the traceback.

User and application errors, on the other hand, often have very fancy and elaborate views. User errors commonly implement IUserError, which is defined in zope.app.exceptions.interfaces. A simple example of a user error is the message shown when you forgot to enter a name when adding a new content type, such as an image. A good example of an application error is Unauthorized, which is raised if a user is not allowed to access a particular resource. Its view actually raises an HTTP challenge, which means your browser asks you for a username and password.

Overall, you should be very careful about classifying exceptions according to those that should reach the users and those that shouldn't. In this chapter, you will create an exception that is raised when a payment is required to access a certain page. You will then test the Payment Required exception view by writing a small page that raises the exception.

Step 1: Creating an Exception

To begin creating an exception, you need to create a new package called exceptionview in *Zope3-Instance*/lib/python/book. Then you should create a file called interfaces.py and add the following exception interface and class to it:

```
01 from zope.interface import implements
02 from zope.interface.common.interfaces import IException
03
04 class IPaymentException(IException):
05     """This is an exception that can be raised by my application."""
06
07 class PaymentException(Exception):
08     implements(IPaymentException)
09
10     # We really do nothing here.
```

In the preceding code block, note the following:

- Line 2: The interfaces for all common exceptions are defined in zope.interface.common.interfaces.
- Line 4: You should always inherit IException in any exception interface.
- Line 7: You should always inherit Exception for any self-written exception. Note that exceptions are considered to be part of a package's API and are therefore always implemented in the interfaces module.

Step 2: Providing an Exception View

Now that you have a payment exception, you just have to provide a view for it. However, when the exception occurs, you do not want to return the HTTP status code

200. Instead, you want the status to be 402, which is the Payment Required status. In a new module named `browser.py`, you need to add the following view class:

```
01  class PaymentExceptionView(object):
02      """This is a view for `IPaymentException` exceptions."""
03
04      def __call__(self, *args, **kw):
05          self.request.response.setStatus(402)
06          return self.index(*args, **kw)
```

In the preceding code block, note the following:

- Line 4: Because this view will be template based, the __call__() method is usually used to render the template.
- Line 5: Before executing the template, you set the HTTP return status to 402.
- Line 6: You render the template, which is always available under the attribute index.

Now you just need a template to render the view. You should add the following ZPT code in a file named `error.pt`:

```
01  <html metal:use-macro="context/@@standard_macros/dialog">
02    <body>
03      <div metal:fill-slot="body">
04
05        <h1>402 - Payment Required</h1>
06
07        <p>Before you can use this feature of the site, you have to make a
08           payment to Stephan Richter.</p>
09
10      </div>
11    </body>
12  </html>
```

There is nothing interesting going on in the template because it has no dynamic components. In `configure.zcml` you can register the page now by using the following:

```
01  <configure
02      xmlns="http://namespaces.zope.org/browser"
03      i18n_domain="exceptionview">
04
05    <page
06        name="index.html"
07        template="error.pt"
08        for=".interfaces.IPaymentException"
09        class=".browser.PaymentExceptionView"
10        permission="zope.Public"
11        />
12
13  </configure>
```

To register the new package, you add a file named `exceptionview-configure.zcml` to `package-includes`, and that file should contain the following line:

```
01 <include package="book.exceptionview" />
```

You can now restart Zope 3. But how can you test whether the view works if there is currently no code that raises the exception? Read on.

Step 3: Testing the Exception View

The easiest way to raise an exception is to write a simple view that does it. It could look something like this (in `browser.py`):

```
01 from book.exceptionview.interfaces import PaymentException
02
03 class RaiseExceptionView(object):
04     """The view that raises the exception"""
05
06     def raisePaymentException(self):
07         raise PaymentException, 'You are required to pay.'
```

Now you can register the class method as a view on a folder:

```
01 <page
02     name="raiseError.html"
03     for="zope.app.folder.interfaces.IFolder"
04     class=".browser.RaiseExceptionView"
05     attribute="raisePaymentException"
06     permission="zope.View"
07     />
```

At this point, you need to restart Zope now and enter the URL `http://localhost:8080/raiseError.html` in your browser. You should now see the Payment Required exception view, as shown in Figure 32.1.

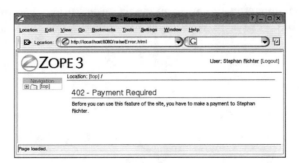

Figure 32.1   The view for the `PaymentException` error.

In your console you should see the following output:

```
01 ------
02 2004-08-23T12:38:01 ERROR SiteError http://localhost:8080/raiseError.html
03 Traceback (most recent call last):
04 ...
05 PaymentException: You are required to pay.
```

You can easily cast this little experiment into a functional test. In a new file called ftests.py, you add the following test code:

```
01 import unittest
02
03 from zope.app.tests.functional import BrowserTestCase
04
05 class Test(BrowserTestCase):
06
07     def test_PaymentErrorView(self):
08         response = self.publish("/raiseError.html", handle_errors=True)
09
10         self.assertEqual(response.getStatus(), 402)
11         body = response.getBody()
12         self.assert_('402 - Payment Required' in body)
13         self.assert_('payment to Stephan Richter' in body)
14
15 def test_suite():
16     return unittest.TestSuite((
17         unittest.makeSuite(Test),
18         ))
19
20 if __name__=='__main__':
21     unittest.main(defaultTest='test_suite')
```

In the preceding code block, note the following:

- Line 8: You make sure that handle_errors is set to True; otherwise, the publication of this URL will raise a PaymentException error and cause the test to fail.
- Line 10: Using the response's getStatus() method, you can even get to the HTTP return status, which should be 402. Note that this is not as easily testable using the browser as in this test.
- Lines 11–13: You need to make sure the page contains the right contents.

If you are not familiar with functional tests, you should read Chapter 42, "Writing Functional Tests."

You can verify the test by executing this from your *Zope3-Instance* directory:

```
python bin/test -vpf --dir lib/python/book/exceptionview
```

VI

Advanced Topics

Not everything you ever want to develop is a component that you want to allow the user to add and manipulate. This part contains a collection of chapters that deal mainly with packages outside zope.app that are often useful both inside and outside Zope 3.

Chapter 33: Writing New ZCML Directives

This chapter discusses how new directives can be added to a ZCML namespace, using metadirectives as well as how to create a new namespace from scratch.

Chapter 34: Implementing TALES Namespaces

In Zope 3, Zope page templates (that is, TALES expressions) can contain namespaces to provide easier access to an object's data and metadata. Although Zope 3 provides a zope namespace, it is sometimes extremely helpful to develop your own namespace to expose your product-specific API.

Chapter 35: Changing Traversal Behavior

As in Zope 2, in Zope 3 you can change the traversal (lookup) behavior for an object, except that this functionality is much more flexible in Zope 3.

Chapter 36: Registering New WebDAV Namespaces

WebDAV is allowed to store and request any namespace on any resource. However, you want to have some control over the namespaces and their values. This chapter explains how to bind Zope 3 attributes and annotations to WebDAV namespaces.

Chapter 37: Using TALES Outside Page Templates

TALES is a powerful expression mechanism that certainly does not find use only in page templates. This chapter describes how to incorporate TALES into your own Python applications and scripts.

Chapter 38: Developing New TALES Expressions

TALES is powerful in itself, but you can make it even more powerful by implementing custom expressions. This chapter explains step-by-step how to create a SQL expression.

Chapter 39: The Life of a Request

This chapter shows a request's exciting journey through the server, publisher, and publication frameworks.

33

Writing New ZCML Directives

Difficulty

Sprinter

Skills

- You should be familiar with using ZCML. If necessary, you should read Chapter 9, "Introduction to the Zope Configuration Markup Language (ZCML)."
- You should have in mind a purpose for creating or extending a namespace.

Problem/Task

As you know by now, you use ZCML to configure the Zope 3 framework, especially for globally available components. When developing complex applications, it is sometimes very useful to develop new and custom ZCML directives to reduce the work involved with repetitive tasks or simply make something configurable that would otherwise require Python code manipulation. In this chapter you will implement a small `browser:redirect` directive that defines a view which simply redirects to another URL.

O NE OF THE MAJOR DESIGN GOALS of ZCML is to make it very easy for a developer to create new ZCML directives. There is a distinction between simple and complex directives. A simple directive consists of one XML element that causes a set of actions. A complex directive is a wrapper-like directive that can contain subdirectives. Complex directives usually do not cause actions themselves, but they provide data that is applicable to most of the subdirectives. In this chapter, you will just create a simple directive; the complex ones are not much more difficult.

There are three simple steps to implementing a directive:

1. You need to develop the directive's schema, which describes the attributes the XML element can and must have. As with any schema, you can specify whether an attribute is required. When the XML is parsed, the Unicode values that are returned from the parser are automatically converted to Python values, as described by the field. Besides the common fields, such as `TextLine` and `Int`, you also have special configuration fields, such as `GlobalObject`, which automatically converts a Python reference to a Python object. A full list of additional fields is provided in Chapter 9. Directive schemas are commonly placed in a file called `metadirectives.py`.

2. You need to develop a handler for the directive, which for simple directives is a function that takes the attributes as arguments. The first argument of the handler is the context of the configuration. If you have a complex directive, the handler is usually a class, where the constructor takes the attributes of the directive as arguments. Each subdirective is then a method of the class. The class must also be callable, so that it can be called when the complex directive is closed. It is very important to note that the directives should *not perform any actions*; they should only declare the actions, as you will see later in this chapter. This way, the configuration mechanism can detect configuration conflicts. By convention, the handlers are stored in `metaconfigure.zcml`.

3. When the directive schema and handler are written, you can register the ZCML directive, using the ZCML `meta` namespace, which is usually done in a configuration file named `meta.zcml`. The meta configuration file is then registered in `packages-includes`, using a filename such as *package*-`meta.zcml`.

Now that you have an overview of the necessary tasks, you can get your hands dirty. As mentioned previously, the goal is to provide a directive that creates a view which makes a simple redirect. A view must always be defined for a particular object and needs a name under which it can be accessible. You should also optionally allow a layer to be specified. Usually, you also want to specify a permission, but because this view just redirects to another, you simply make the view public. The final attribute you need for the directive is the `url` attribute, which specifies the URL you want to direct to. To start the implementation, you need to first create a package named `redirect` in *Zope3-Instance*/`lib/python/book/` (and don't forget to add `__init__.py`).

Step 1: Developing the Directive Schema

In a new file named `metadirectives.py`, you need to add the following schema:

```
01 from zope.interface import Interface
02 from zope.configuration.fields import GlobalObject
03 from zope.schema import TextLine
04
```

```
05 class IRedirectDirective(Interface):
06     """Redirects clients to a specified URL."""
07
08     name = TextLine(
09         title=u"Name",
10         description=u"The name of the requested view.")
11
12     for_ = GlobalObject(
13         title=u"For Interface",
14         description=u"The interface the directive is used for.",
15         required=False)
16
17     url = TextLine(
18         title=u"URL",
19         description=u"The URL the client should be redirected to.")
20
21     layer = TextLine(
22         title=u"Layer",
23         description=u"The layer the redirect is defined in.",
24         required=False)
```

In the preceding code block, note the following:

- Line 2: As you can see, all configuration-specific fields, such as `GlobalObject`, are defined in `zope.configuration.fields`.

- Line 3: You can also use any of the conventional fields.

- Line 5: The directive schemas are just schemas like any other schemas. No special base class is required.

- Line 12: Whenever you have an attribute whose name is a Python keyword, you simply add an underscore behind it; the underscore will be safely ignored during runtime.

Step 2: Implementing the Directive Handler

You need to add the following handler to `metaconfigure.py`:

```
01 from zope.app.publisher.browser.viewmeta import page
02
03 class Redirect(object):
04     """Redirects to a specified URL."""
05     url = None
06
07     def __call__(self):
08         self.request.response.redirect(self.url)
09
```

```
10 def redirect(_context, name, url, for_=None, layer='default'):
11     # define the class that performs the redirect
12     redirectClass = type(str("Redirect %s for %s to '%s'" %(name, for_, url)),
13         (Redirect,), {'url' : url})
14
15     page(_context, name, 'zope.Public', for_, layer, class_=redirectClass)
```

In the preceding code block, note the following:

- Line 1: Because you are just defining a new page, why not reuse the page-directive handler? This makes the implementation of the handler much simpler.

- Lines 3–8: This is the base view class. You simply allow a URL to be set on it. When the view is called, you simply redirect the HTTP request. There is no need to implement `IBrowserPublisher` or `IBrowserView` here because the `page()` function will mix in all these APIs, plus implementation.

- Lines 10–15: This is the actual handler of the directive. The first step is to create a customized version of the view class by merging in the URL (lines 12–13). Then you simply call the page-directive handler, where you use the public permission. The page-directive handler hides a lot of the gory details of defining a full-blown view, including creating configuration actions.

You create an action by calling `_context.action()`. This function supports the following arguments:

- **discriminator**—You use this unique identifier to recognize a particular action. It is very important that no two actions have the same discriminator when you start Zope 3. `discriminator` is used for conflict resolution and to spot duplicate actions. It is usually a tuple.

- **callable**—Here you specify the method or function that is called when the action is executed.

- **args and kw**—These are arguments and keywords that are passed to `callable` as arguments at execution time.

Step 3: Writing the `meta` Configuration

Now that you have all the pieces of the directive, you can register it in `meta.zcml`:

```
01 <configure
02     xmlns="http://namespaces.zope.org/meta">
03
04   <directives namespace="http://namespaces.zope.org/browser">
05     <directive
06       name="redirect"
07       schema=".metadirectives.IRedirectDirective"
08       handler=".metaconfigure.redirect"
```

```
09        />
10    </directives>
11
12  </configure>
```

In the preceding code block, note the following:

- Line 2: You use the `meta` namespace to define new ZCML directives.
- Lines 4 and 10: You use the `meta:directives` directive to specify the namespace under which the directives will be available. In this case, it is the `browser` namespace.
- Lines 5–9: You use the `meta:directive` directive to register a simple directive. `name` is the name by which the directive will be known/accessible. The `schema` specifies the directive schema and the `handler` the directive handler, both of which you developed earlier in this chapter.

  If you develop a complex directive, you use the `meta:complexDirective` directive, which supports the same attributes as the `meta:simpleDirective` directive. Inside a complex directive you can then place `meta:subdirective` directives, which define the subdirectives of the complex directive. (See Chapter 29, "Registries with Global Utilities," for an example of a relatively simple complex directive.)

You now have to register the new directive with the Zope 3 system by placing a file named `redirect-meta.zcml` in *Zope3-Instance*/etc/package-includes. It should have the following content:

```
01 <include package="book.redirect" file="meta.zcml" />
```

The next time you restart Zope, the directive should be available.

Step 4: Testing the Directive

The best way to test the directive is to use it. For example, you could have the view `manage.html` be redirected to `manage` for all folders. In a new configuration file, `configure.zcml`, you add the following directives:

```
01 <configure
02     xmlns="http://namespaces.zope.org/browser">
03
04   <redirect
05       name="manage.html"
06       for="zope.app.folder.interfaces.IFolder"
07       url="manage" />
08
09 </configure>
```

In the preceding code block, note the following:

- Line 2: As specified, the `redirect` directive is available via the `browser` namespace.
- Line 5: The name is the view that must be called to initiate the redirection.
- Line 6: The redirection will be available only for folders.
- Line 7: The target URL is the relative name `manage`.

Add to `Zope3-Instance/etc/package-includes` the `redirect-configure.zcml` file, which contains the following:

```
01 <include package="book.redirect" />
```

Now you need to restart Zope 3. Then you should be able to call the URL `http://localhost:8080/@@manage.html`, which should bring you to `http://localhost:8080/@@contents.html` because `manage` just redirects to `contents.html`.

You can easily duplicate this functionality in a functional test. You simply put the following test case into a file named `ftests.py`:

```
01 import unittest
02
03 from zope.app.tests.functional import BrowserTestCase
04
05
06 class Test(BrowserTestCase):
07
08     def test_RedirectManageHtml(self):
09         response = self.publish("/manage.html")
10
11         self.assertEqual(response.getStatus(), 302)
12         self.assertEqual(response.getHeader('Location'), 'manage')
13
14
15 def test_suite():
16     return unittest.makeSuite(Test)
17
18 if __name__=='__main__':
19     unittest.main(defaultTest='test_suite')
```

If you are not familiar with the `BrowserTestCase` API, I suggest you read Chapter 42, "Writing Functional Tests." Otherwise, the test is straightforward, and you can execute in the usual manner.

34

Implementing TALES Namespaces

Difficulty

Newcomer

Skills

- You should be familiar with TAL and TALES (in the context of page templates).
- You should feel comfortable with ZCML.

Problem/Task

Zope 3 exposes a fair amount of its API in TAL and TALES, through expression types (path, python, string, and sql [add-on]) as well as the TALES namespaces, such as zope. However, sometimes all these APIs are not powerful enough or still requires a lot of Python view class coding. For this reason, Zope 3 allows you to add new TALES namespaces. This chapter demonstrates how to write and register a new TALES namespace.

TALES NAMESPACES USE PATH ADAPTERS to implement the adaptation. You use path adapters to adapt an object to another interface while traversing a path. The name of the adapter is used in the path to select the correct adapter. An example is the zope TALES namespace:

```
01 <p tal:content="context/zope:modified" />
```

In this example, the object is adapted to IZopeTalesAPI, which provides many convenience methods, including one that exposes the Dublin Core. Then the modified() method is called on the adapter, and it returns the modification date of the context object.

Although the standard zope TALES namespace deals with retrieving additional data about the component, it does not handle the output format of the data. So it would be a good idea to specify a new namespace that deals exclusively with the formatting of objects. This chapter concentrates on the full display of dates, times, and date/times. The user's locale functions are used to do the actual formatting, so your development effort will be minimal, and the output will be correctly localized.

The code for this chapter's example is located in *Zope3-Instance/lib/python/book/formatns*. Therefore, you need to create this package now and place a `__init__.py` file in the directory.

Step 1: Defining the Namespace Interface

You need to start out by defining the interface of the namespace you'll be creating. Here's how it should look:

```
01 from zope.interface import Interface
02
03 class IFormatTalesAPI(Interface):
04
05     def fullDate(self):
06         """Returns the full date using the user's locale.
07
08         The context of this namespace must be a datetime object,
09         otherwise an exception is raised.
10         """
11
12     def fullTime(self):
13         """Returns the full time using the user's locale.
14
15         The context of this namespace must be a datetime object,
16         otherwise an exception is raised.
17         """
18
19     def fullDateTime(self):
20         """Returns the full datetime using the user's locale.
21
22         The context of this namespace must be a datetime object,
23         otherwise an exception is raised.
24         """
```

The interface specifies all the functions that will be available in the namespace. Note that the code available in the repository at `http://svn.zope.org/book/trunk/formatns/` has a lot more functions than are shown here, but because the code is fairly repetitive, it is not all included here.

Although every TALES namespace also has to implement `ITALESFunctionNamespace`, you do not inherit from this interface here; you simply merge it into he implementation. The advantage of this method is that the IFormatTalesAPI interface can be reused elsewhere.

Step 2: Implementing the Namespace

The actual code of the namespace is not much harder than that of the interface, if you have played with the user locales before. You just add the following implementation in the package's __init__.py file:

```
01 from zope.interface import implements
02 from zope.tales.interfaces import ITALESFunctionNamespace
03 from zope.security.proxy import removeSecurityProxy
04 from interfaces import IFormatTalesAPI
05
06
07 class FormatTalesAPI(object):
08
09     implements(IFormatTalesAPI, ITALESFunctionNamespace)
10
11     def __init__(self, context):
12         self.context = context
13
14     def setEngine(self, engine):
15         """See zope.tales.interfaces.ITALESFunctionNamespace"""
16         self.locale = removeSecurityProxy(engine.vars['request']).locale
17
18     def fullDate(self):
19         """See book.formatns.interfaces.IFormatTalesAPI"""
20         return self.locale.dates.getFormatter(
21             'date', 'full').format(self.context)
22
23     def fullTime(self):
24         """See book.formatns.interfaces.IFormatTalesAPI"""
25         return self.locale.dates.getFormatter(
26             'time', 'full').format(self.context)
27
28     def fullDateTime(self):
29         """See book.formatns.interfaces.IFormatTalesAPI"""
30         return self.locale.dates.getFormatter(
31             'dateTime', 'full').format(self.context)
```

In the preceding code block, note the following:

- Line 2: Here you see from where you import the ITALESFunctionNamespace interface. Note that this interface is not totally necessary, but without it, the engine will not be set on the namespace, which makes it impossible to reach the request.

- Lines 11–12: All TALES function namespaces must be implemented as adapters. The object they adapt is the object that was evaluated from the previous part of the path expression.

- Lines 14–16: This method implements the only requirement the `ITALESFunctionNamespace` interface poses. The `setEngine()` method provides some additional context about the user and the entire request. For this namespace, however, you are only interested in the locale, so you get it. Interestingly, the engine is security-wrapped, so the request is automatically security-wrapped, which is unusual. This means that no security declaration exists for accessing the `locale` attribute. Therefore, you have to remove all the security proxies from the `request` object before accessing the `locale` object. Note that this is safe because all the namespace functions read data from the locale but do not perform any write operations.

- Lines 18–31: These are the trivial implementations of the namespace functions. The `locale` object provides all the functionality you need. From the locale itself, you can retrieve the date, time, or date/time formatting objects by using `locale.dates.getFormat()`. The method expects the name of the format to be specified. The four names supported by ICU (on which the locale support is based) are `short`, `medium`, `long`, and `full`. The formatting objects have a method called `format()` that converts the `datetime` object into a localized string representation.

That was easy, wasn't it? Next you are going to test the functionality of the namespace.

Step 3: Testing the Namespace

At this point you are only going to test whether the namespace works by itself; you are not checking whether the namespace will work correctly in TALES because that should be tested in the TALES implementation. The tricky part of this test is to create a sufficient `Engine` object so that the code can access the `request` instance. Here is the complete test code that you should place in `tests.py`:

```
01 import unittest
02 from datetime import datetime
03 from zope.publisher.browser import TestRequest
04 from zope.testing.doctestunit import DocTestSuite
05 from book.formatns import FormatTalesAPI
06
07 class Engine:
08     vars = {'request': TestRequest(environ={'HTTP_ACCEPT_LANGUAGE': 'en'})}
09
10 def getFormatNamespace(context):
11     ns = FormatTalesAPI(context)
12     ns.setEngine(Engine())
```

```
13      return ns
14
15 def fullDate():
16      """
17      >>> ns = getFormatNamespace(datetime(2003, 9, 16, 16, 51, 01))
18      >>> ns.fullDate()
19      u'Tuesday, September 16, 2003'
20      """
21
22 def fullTime():
23      """
24      >>> ns = getFormatNamespace(datetime(2003, 9, 16, 16, 51, 01))
25      >>> ns.fullTime()
26      u'4:51:01 PM +000'
27      """
28
29 def fullDateTime():
30      """
31      >>> ns = getFormatNamespace(datetime(2003, 9, 16, 16, 51, 01))
32      >>> ns.fullDateTime()
33      u'Tuesday, September 16, 2003 4:51:01 PM +000'
34      """
35
36 def test_suite():
37      return DocTestSuite()
38
39 if __name__ == '__main__':
40      unittest.main(defaultTest='test_suite')
```

In the preceding code block, note the following:

- Lines 7–8: This is the most minimal stub implementation of the engine. It sufficiently provides the request, as it is required by the namespace.

- Lines 10–13: This helper function creates the namespace instance for you and also
  sets the engine, so that you are ready to use the returned namespace object.

- Lines 15–34: These are the tests, in the Zope doc test format, which are easy to
  read. You can see what's going on: The code inside the doc string is executed, and
  it checks whether the returned value equals the expected value.

- Lines 36–40: This is the usual unit doc test boilerplate code. The only difference is
  that you create a DocTestSuite constructor without passing in the module name.
  If no name is specified to the DocTestSuite constructor, the current module is
  searched for tests.

You can run the tests as usual by using this:

```
python2.3 bin/test -vpu --dir lib/python/book/formatns
```

Step 4: Wiring the `format` Namespace into Zope 3

Now you are ready to hook up the `format` namespace to the rest of the framework. You do this by simply registering a normal adapter that provides the `IPathAdapter` interface. You place the following code into the `configure.zcml` file:

```
01 <configure
02     xmlns="http://namespaces.zope.org/zope">
03
04   <adapter
05     for="*"
06     provides="zope.app.traversing.interfaces.IPathAdapter"
07     factory=".FormatTalesAPI"
08     name="format" />
09
10 </configure>
```

In the preceding code block, note the following:

- Line 5: You register this namespace as an adapter for all possible objects, even though in this case you could restrict it to `IDateTime` instances. However, the idea is that the `format` namespace will support many different object types.

- Line 8: The name of the adapter is extremely important because it is the name by which the adapter will be available in the path expressions.

Now you can hook the configuration into Zope 3 by adding to *Zope3-Instance*/etc/package-includes a file called `formatns-configure.zcml` that has the following line as content:

```
01 <include package="book.formatns" />
```

Step 5: Trying the `format` Namespace

To try the `format` namespace, you need to restart Zope. Then you need to create a ZPT page in the Web user interface and add the following content to it:

```
01 <html>
02   <body>
03     <h1 tal:content="context/zope:modified/format:fullDateTime">
04       Tuesday, September 16, 2003 04:51:01 PM +000
05     </h1>
06   </body>
07 </html>
```

In the preceding code block, note the following:

- Lines 3–5: This line displays the modification `datetime` of the root folder as a full `datetime`. The output is even localized to the user's preferred language and format.

A great aspect of the function namespace concept is that several namespace calls can be piped together. In the preceding example, you can see how the `zope` namespace extracts the modification datetime of the root folder and this datetime object is then passed to the `format` namespace to create the localized, human-readable representation.

35

Changing Traversal Behavior

Difficulty

Sprinter

Skills

- You should be familiar with the Zope 3 component architecture and testing framework.
- Some knowledge about the container interfaces is helpful. Optional.

Problem/Task

Zope 3 uses a mechanism called *traversal* to resolve an object path, such as the path given by a URL, to the actual object. Obviously, there is some policy involved in the traversal process, as objects must be found, namespaces must be resolved, and even components, such as views, must be looked up in the component architecture. This also means that these policies can be changed and replaced. This chapter shows how to change the traversal policy so that the container items are not case-sensitive anymore.

I N ZOPE 3 *traversers*, objects that are responsible for using a path segment to get from one object to another, are implemented as views of the respective presentation type. In principle, the traverser only has to implement `IPublishTraverse` (located in `zope.publisher.interfaces`), which specifies a method named `publishTraverse(request, name)`, which returns the traversed object. The browser implementation, for example, is simply a view that tries to resolve `name` by using its context. Whether the method tries to access sub-objects or look up views called `name` is up to the specific implementation, such as `zope.app.container.traversal.ContainerTraverser` for the browser.

Step 1: Creating a Non–Case–Sensitive Folder

In this chapter you'll implement a case-insensitive traverser and a sample folder, called `CaseInsensitiveFolder`, that uses this traverser. You'll develop the latter component first. All you need for the case-insensitive folder is an interface and a factory that provides this interface for a normal `Folder` instance.

First, you need to create a package called `insensitivefolder` in the `book` package. In the `__init__.py` file, you add the following interface and factory:

```
01 from zope.component.interfaces import IFactory
02 from zope.app.folder import Folder
03 from zope.app.folder.interfaces import IFolder
04 from zope.interface import implements, implementedBy
05 from zope.interface import directlyProvides, directlyProvidedBy
06
07 class ICaseInsensitiveFolder(IFolder):
08     """Marker for folders whose contained items keys are case insensitive.
09
10     When traversing in this folder, all names will be converted to lower
11     case. For example, if the traverser requests an item called `Foo`, in
12     reality the first item matching `foo` or any upper-and-lowercase
13     variants are looked up in the container."""
14
15 class CaseInsensitiveFolderFactory(object):
16     """A Factory that creates case-insensitive Folders."""
17     implements(IFactory)
18
19     def __call__(self):
20         """See zope.component.interfaces.IFactory
21
22         Create a folder and mark it as case insensitive.
23         """
24         folder = Folder()
25         directlyProvides(folder, directlyProvidedBy(folder),
26                         ICaseInsensitiveFolder)
27         return folder
28
29     def getInterfaces(self):
30         """See zope.component.interfaces.IFactory"""
31         return implementedBy(Folder) + ICaseInsensitiveFolder
32
33 caseInsensitiveFolderFactory = CaseInsensitiveFolderFactory()
```

Instead of developing a new content type, you create a factory that tags on the `ICaseInsensitiveFolder` interface, making the `Folder` instance a case-insensitive folder. This is a classic example of declaring and using a factory directly. Factories are used in many places, but usually they are autogenerated in ZCML handlers.

You simply register the factory in ZCML by using the following:

```
01 <configure
02     xmlns="http://namespaces.zope.org/zope"
03     xmlns:browser="http://namespaces.zope.org/browser"
04     i18n_domain="zope">
05
06 <factory
07     id="zope.CaseInsensitiveFolder"
08     component=".caseInsensitiveFolderFactory"
09     />
10
11 <browser:addMenuItem
12     factory="zope.CaseInsensitiveFolder"
13     title="Case insensitive Folder"
14     description="A simple case insensitive Folder."
15     permission="zope.ManageContent"
16     />
17
18 <browser:icon
19     name="zmi_icon"
20     for=".ICaseInsensitiveFolder"
21     file="cifolder_icon.png"
22     />
23
24 </configure>
```

In the preceding code block, note the following:

- Lines 6–9: You declare the factory. The `id` attribute must be a valid `id` field value.

- Lines 11–16: You declare an add menu item entry, using the factory ID, as specified in the `id` attribute on line 7.

- Lines 18–22: You register a custom icon for the non-case-sensitive folder so that you can differentiate it from the other folders. You can find this custom icon in the repository at `http://svn.zope.org/book/trunk/insensitivefolder/`.

Step 2: Creating the Traverser

Now you have a new content type, but it does not do anything special. You have to implement the special traverser for the non-case-sensitive folder. Luckily, you do not have to implement a new container traverser from scratch; you can just use the standard `ContainerTraverser` class and replace the `publishTraverse()` method to be a bit more flexible and ignore the case of the item names. In the `__init__.py` file, you add the following traverser implementation:

```
01 from zope.publisher.interfaces import NotFound
02
03 from zope.app import zapi
04 from zope.app.container.traversal import ContainerTraverser
05
06 class CaseInsensitiveFolderTraverser(ContainerTraverser):
07
08     __used_for__ = ICaseInsensitiveFolder
09
10     def publishTraverse(self, request, name):
11         """See zope.publisher.interfaces.browser.IBrowserPublisher"""
12         subob = self._guessTraverse(name)
13         if subob is None:
14             view = zapi.queryView(self.context, name, request)
15             if view is not None:
16                 return view
17
18             raise NotFound(self.context, name, request)
19
20         return subob
21
22     def _guessTraverse(self, name):
23         for key in self.context.keys():
24             if key.lower() == name.lower():
25                 return self.context[key]
26         return None
```

In the preceding code block, note the following:

- Line 8: This traverser is only meant to be used with `ICaseInsensitiveFolder` components. However, the implementation of the traverser is generic enough that it would work with any object implementing `IReadContainer`. Note that the most generic container traverser is registered for `ISimpleReadContainer`, which is not sufficient here because you make use of the `keys()` method, which is not available in `ISimpleReadContainer`.

- Lines 10–20: First, you try to find the name by using the private `_guessTraverse()` method. If no object is found in the items of the container, you check whether `name` could be a view and return it. If `name` does not point to an item or a view, you need to raise a `NotFound` error.

  Note that the implementation of this method could be more efficient. You could first try to get the object by using `_guessTraverse()` and upon failure forward the request to the original `publishTraverse()` method of the base class. Then the code would look like this:

```
01 def publishTraverse(self, request, name):
02     subob = self._guessTraverse(name)
03     if subob is not None:
```

```
04          return subob
05      return super(CaseInsensitiveFolderTraverser,
06                  self).publishTraverse(request, name)
```

However, this would hide some of the insights on how `publishTraverse()` should behave.

- Lines 22–26: Here you try to look up the name without caring about the case. This works both ways. The keys of the container *and* the provided `name` value are converted to all lowercase. You then compare the two. If a match is found, the value for the key is returned. Note that you need to keep the original key (which has uppercase and lowercase letters) because the container still manages the keys in a case-sensitive manner.

The traverser is registered via ZCML by using the `zope:view` directive:

```
01 <view
02     for=".ICaseInsensitiveFolder"
03     type="zope.publisher.interfaces.browser.IBrowserRequest"
04     factory=".CaseInsensitiveFolderTraverser"
05     provides="zope.publisher.interfaces.browser.IBrowserPublisher"
06     permission="zope.Public"
07     />
```

In the preceding code block, note the following:

- Line 2: You register the view only for non–case-sensitive folders.

- Line 3: You make sure that this traverser is only used for browser requests.

- Line 5: It is very important to specify the provided interface here, so that you know that the object is a browser publisher and implements the sufficient interfaces for traversal.

- Line 6: You want to allow everyone to be able to traverse through the folder because it does not provide the user with any special access. All methods of the returned object are protected separately anyway.

To register the product with Zope 3, you add a file named `insensitivefolder-configure.zcml` to *Zope3-Instance*`/etc/package-includes`. It should contain the following line:

```
01 <include package="book.insensitivefolder" />
```

When you restart Zope 3, the new folder should be available to you.

Step 3: Creating and Running Unit Tests

You can quickly write unit tests in for the traverser because you can make use of the original container traverser's unit tests and setup. You simply need to open a `tests.py` file and insert the following test code:

```
01 import unittest
02 from zope.app.container.tests import test_containertraverser
03 from book.insensitivefolder import CaseInsensitiveFolderTraverser
04
05 class Container(test_containertraverser.TestContainer):
06
07     def keys(self):
08         return self.__dict__.keys()
09
10     def __getitem__(self, name):
11         return self.__dict__[name]
12
13 class InsensitiveCaseTraverserTest(test_containertraverser.TraverserTest):
14
15     def _getTraverser(self, context, request):
16         return CaseInsensitiveFolderTraverser(context, request)
17
18     def _getContainer(self, **kw):
19         return Container(**kw)
20
21     def test_allLowerCaseItemTraversal(self):
22         self.assertEquals(
23             self.traverser.publishTraverse(self.request, 'foo'),
24             self.foo)
25         self.assertEquals(
26             self.traverser.publishTraverse(self.request, 'foO'),
27             self.foo)
28
29 def test_suite():
30     return unittest.TestSuite((
31         unittest.makeSuite(InsensitiveCaseTraverserTest),
32         ))
33
34 if __name__ == '__main__':
35     unittest.main(defaultTest='test_suite')
```

In the preceding code block, note the following:

- Lines 7–11: The original test container has to be extended to support keys() and __getitem__() because both of these methods are needed for the non-case-sensitive traverser.

- Lines 15–16: You specify a setup helper method that returns the traverser. This method is used in the setUp() method to construct the environment.

- Lines 18–19: You specify another helper method that allows you to specify a custom container. This method is used in the setUp() method to construct the environment.

- Lines 21–27: Most of the functionality is already tested in the base test case. Here you just test that the case of the letters is truly ignored.

- Lines 29–35: You use the usual unit test boilerplate code.

As always, the tests are directly executable when Zope 3 is in your path or uses the test runner.

Step 4: Creating and Running Functional Tests

Before you let the traverser code be run in the wild, you should test it some more in a fairly contained environment. The following functional test is pretty straightforward and mimics the unit tests.

You need to open a file called `ftests.py` and add the following to it:

```
01 import unittest
02 from zope.app.tests.functional import BrowserTestCase
03 from zope.publisher.interfaces import NotFound
04
05 class TestCaseInsensitiveFolder(BrowserTestCase):
06
07     def testAddCaseInsensitiveFolder(self):
08         # Step 1: add the case insensitive folder
09         response = self.publish(
10             '/+/action.html',
11             basic='mgr:mgrpw',
12             form={'type_name': u'book.CaseInsensitiveFolder',
13                   'id': u'cisf'})
14         self.assertEqual(response.getStatus(), 302)
15         self.assertEqual(response.getHeader('Location'),
16                          'http://localhost/@@contents.html')
17         # Step 2: add the file
18         response = self.publish('/cisf/+/action.html',
19                                 basic='mgr:mgrpw',
20                                 form={'type_name': u'zope.app.content.File',
21                                       'id': u'foo'})
22         self.assertEqual(response.getStatus(), 302)
23         self.assertEqual(response.getHeader('Location'),
24                          'http://localhost/cisf/@@contents.html')
25         # Step 3: check that the file is traversed
26         response = self.publish('/cisf/foo')
27         self.assertEqual(response.getStatus(), 200)
28         response = self.publish('/cisf/foO')
29         self.assertEqual(response.getStatus(), 200)
30         self.assertRaises(NotFound, self.publish, '/cisf/bar')
31
32
```

```
33 def test_suite():
34     return unittest.TestSuite((
35         unittest.makeSuite(TestCaseInsensitiveFolder),
36         ))
37
38 if __name__ == '__main__':
39     unittest.main(defaultTest='test_suite')
```

There is really nothing interesting about this test. If you are not familiar with functional tests, you should read Chapter 42, "Writing Functional Tests."

In Zope 2 it is common to change the traversal behavior of objects and container-like objects. In Zope 3, however, you do not need to implement your own traversers because most of the time it is better (and easier) to write a custom `IReadContainer` content component.

You can find the complete code of the traverser product discussed in this chapter at `http://svn.zope.org/book/trunk/insensitivefolder/`. It was originally written by Vincenzo Di Somma and has been maintained by many developers throughout the development of Zope 3.

Registering New WebDAV Namespaces

Difficulty

Sprinter

Skills

- You should be familiar with Zope 3's component architecture.
- You should be familiar with the WebDAV standard, as proposed in RFC 2518.

Problem/Task

WebDAV, as an advanced application of HTTP and XML, supports an unlimited amount metadata to be associated with any resource. Although this guarantees an ultimate flexibility in WebDAV, it is often not that useful to Zope because it does not know how to deal with the data in a structured manner. In order for Zope 3 to make use of some of the data sent via WebDAV, the Zope 3 development team created a namespace registry that manages the list of all available namespaces per content type (interface). This chapter shows how to enable a new namespace called `photo` for an `IImage` object.

W<small>EBDAV'S UNLIMITED SUPPORT FOR</small> XML namespaces makes WebDAV very powerful but also makes it very difficult to deal with the data. Therefore, you need to control an object's WebDAV namespaces as well as the permissions required to access and modify the namespace's attributes, if you want to use the data for other parts of the framework.

First of all, namespaces with attributes are really just schemas, so you are able to describe a namespace by using the Zope 3 zope.schema package. Now you are even able to write WebDAV widgets for the schema field types. You use adapters to connect a WebDAV namespace to a content type or any other object. By using schemas, widgets, and adapters, you are able to completely describe the namespace and the storage of the data.

The last step of the process is to register the schema as a WebDAV namespace. You do this by registering the schema as an IDAVNamespace utility, where the name of the utility is the WebDAV namespace URI. However, the dav ZCML namespace provides a nice directive, provideInterface, that registers the utility for you.

If you want to provide a new namespace for a given object, your main task consists of creating a schema for the namespace and providing an adapter from the object to the schema. The goal of this chapter is to provide some additional metadata information about images that have been taken by digital cameras—images that are photos.

Before you begin the following steps, you need to create a new package called photodavns in *Zope3-Instance*/lib/python/book.

Step 1: Creating the Namespace Schema

The schema of the photo should contain some information that is usually provided by the camera. To implement the schema, you open a new file called interfaces.py and add the following code to it:

```
01 from zope.interface import Interface
02 from zope.schema import Text, TextLine, Int, Float
03
04 photodavns = "http://namespaces.zope.org/dav/photo/1.0"
05
06 class IPhoto(Interface):
07     """A WebDAV namespace to store photo-related meta data.
08
09     The 'IPhoto' schema/namespace can be used in WebDAV clients to determine
10     information about a particular picture. Obviously, this namespace makes
11     only sense on Image objects.
12     """
13
14     height = Int(
15         title=u"Height",
16         description=u"Specifies the height in pixels.",
17         min=1)
18
19     width = Int(
20         title=u"Width",
21         description=u"Specifies the width in pixels.",
22         min=1)
23
```

```
24    equivalent35mm = TextLine(
25        title=u"35mm equivalent",
26        description=u"The photo's size in 35mm is equivalent to this amount")
27
28    aperture = TextLine(
29        title=u"Aperture",
30        description=u"Size of the aperture.")
31
32    exposureTime = Float(
33        title=u"Exposure Time",
34        description=u"Specifies the exposure time in seconds.")
```

In the preceding code block, note the following:

- Line 4: The name of the namespace is also part of the interface, so you declare it here. The name must be a valid URI; otherwise, the configuration directive that registers the namespace will fail.

There is nothing more of interest in this code; at this time, you should be very comfortable with interfaces and schemas. If you're not, please read Chapters 6, "An Introduction to Interfaces," and 8, "Zope Schemas and Forms."

Step 2: Implementing the `IPhoto` to `IImage` Adapter

Next, you need to implement the adapter, which will use annotations to store the attribute data. This means the `IImage` object must also implement `IAttributeAnnotable`. With the knowledge you gained in previous chapters, the following implementation should seem simple. You need to place it in the `__init__.py` file of the `photodavns` package:

```
01 from persistent.dict import PersistentDict
02 from zope.interface import implements
03 from zope.schema import getFieldNames
04 from zope.app.annotation.interfaces import IAnnotations
05 from zope.app.file.interfaces import IImage
06 from interfaces import IPhoto, photodavns
07
08 class ImagePhotoNamespace(object):
09     """Implement IPhoto namespace for IImage."""
10
11     implements(IPhoto)
12     __used_for__ = IImage
13
14     def __init__(self, context):
15         self.context = context
16         self._annotations = IAnnotations(context)
```

```
17              if not self._annotations.get(photodavns):
18                  self._annotations[photodavns] = PersistentDict()
19
20      def __getattr__(self, name):
21          if not name in getFieldNames(IPhoto):
22              raise AttributeError, "'%s' object has no attribute '%s'" %(
23                  self.__class__.__name__, name)
24          return self._annotations[photodavns].get(name, None)
25
26      def __setattr__(self, name, value):
27          if not name in getFieldNames(IPhoto):
28              return super(ImagePhotoNamespace, self).__setattr__(name, value)
29          field = IPhoto[name]
30          field.validate(value)
31          self._annotations[photodavns][name] = value
```

In the preceding code block, note the following:

- Lines 14–18: During initialization, you get the annotations for the IImage object and create a dictionary where all the attribute values will be stored. You need to make sure that the dictionary is a PersistentDict instance; otherwise, the data will not be stored permanently in the ZODB.

- Lines 20–24: If the name of the requested attribute corresponds to a field in IPhoto, you get the value from the annotations; otherwise, the lookup fails with an attribute error.

- Lines 26–31: You want to set attributes differently if they are fields in the IPhoto schema. If the name is a field, then the first task is to get the field that is then used to validate the value. This way, you can enforce all specifications provided for the fields in the schema. If the validation passes, you store the value in the annotations.

Step 3: Unit-Testing and Configuring the Adapter

For the unit tests of the adapter, you use doc tests. To do so, you extend the adapter's class doc string so that it looks like this:

```
01 """Implement IPhoto namespace for IImage.
02
03 Examples:
04
05 >>> from zope.app.file.image import Image
06 >>> image = Image()
07 >>> photo = IPhoto(image)
08
09 >>> photo.height is None
```

```
10 True
11 >>> photo.height = 768
12 >>> photo.height
13 768
14 >>> photo.height = u'100'
15 Traceback (most recent call last):
16 ...
17 WrongType: (u'100', (<type 'int'>, <type 'long'>))
18
19 >>> photo.width is None
20 True
21 >>> photo.width = 1024
22 >>> photo.width
23 1024
24
25 >>> photo.equivalent35mm is None
26 True
27 >>> photo.equivalent35mm = u'41 mm'
28 >>> photo.equivalent35mm
29 u'41 mm'
30
31 >>> photo.aperture is None
32 True
33 >>> photo.aperture = u'f/2.8'
34 >>> photo.aperture
35 u'f/2.8'
36
37 >>> photo.exposureTime is None
38 True
39 >>> photo.exposureTime = 0.031
40 >>> photo.exposureTime
41 0.031
42
43 >>> photo.occasion
44 Traceback (most recent call last):
45 ...
46 AttributeError: 'ImagePhotoNamespace' object has no attribute 'occasion'
47 """
```

You can see that this code covers pretty much every possible situation.

In the preceding code block, note the following:

- Lines 5–7: You use the standard `Image` content component as a context for the adapter. Then you use the component architecture to get the adapter. This tests whether the constructor—which is not trivial in this case—does not cause an exception.

- Lines 14–17: You test that the validation of the field's values works correctly.

- Lines 43–46: You also need to make sure that no non-existing attributes can be assigned values.

To make the tests runnable, you add a file named `tests.py` and add the following test code to it:

```
01 import unittest
02 from zope.interface import classImplements
03 from zope.testing.doctestunit import DocTestSuite
04 from zope.app.annotation.interfaces import IAttributeAnnotatable
05 from zope.app.file.image import Image
06 from zope.app.file.interfaces import IImage
07 from zope.app.tests import ztapi, placelesssetup, setup
08 from book.photodavns.interfaces import IPhoto
09 from book.photodavns import ImagePhotoNamespace
10
11 def setUp(test):
12     placelesssetup.setUp()
13     ztapi.provideAdapter(IImage, IPhoto, ImagePhotoNamespace)
14     setup.setUpAnnotations()
15     classImplements(Image, IAttributeAnnotatable)
16
17 def test_suite():
18     return unittest.TestSuite((
19         DocTestSuite('book.photodavns',
20                     setUp=setUp, tearDown=placelesssetup.tearDown),
21         ))
22
23 if __name__ == '__main__':
24     unittest.main(defaultTest='test_suite')
```

In the preceding code block, note the following:

- Lines 13–15: You need to set up some additional adapters to make the tests work. First, of course, you need to register your adapter. Then you need to provide the attribute adapter so that the `ImagePhotoNamespace` adapter will find the annotations for the image. Luckily, the `zope.app.tests.setup` module has a convenience function to do that. Finally, because the `Image` class does not implement `IAttributeAnnotable` directly (that is usually done in a ZCML directive), you need to declare it manually for the unit tests.

- Lines 19–20: You pass the `setUp()` and `tearDown()` functions for a doc test as keyword arguments to the `DocTestSuite` constructor.

From the Zope 3 instance directory, you can now execute the tests by using the following:

```
python2.3 bin/test -vpu --dir lib/python/book/photodavns
```

Step 4: Registering the WebDAV Schema

As mentioned previously in this chapter, registering a new WebDAV namespace is a simple two-step process. First, you declare the IPhoto schema to be a WebDAV namespace, and then you register an adapter for it, making it available for images. In the configure.zcml file, you add the following two directives:

```
01 <configure
02    xmlns="http://namespaces.zope.org/zope"
03    xmlns:dav="http://namespaces.zope.org/dav">
04
05 <dav:provideInterface
06    for="http://namespaces.zope.org/dav/photo/1.0"
07    interface=".interfaces.IPhoto" />
08
09 <adapter
10    provides=".interfaces.IPhoto"
11    for="zope.app.file.interfaces.IImage"
12    permission="zope.Public"
13    factory=".ImagePhotoNamespace"
14    trusted="True"/>
15
16 </configure>
```

In the preceding code block, note the following:

- Lines 5–7: The `for` attribute specifies the name of the schema as it will be available via WebDAV, and `interface` specifies the Zope schema for this namespace.

- Lines 9–14: You register the adapter from `IImage` to `IPhoto`. Note that the adapter must be trusted because you are manipulating annotations and need a bare object to be passed as the context of the adapter.

To register the new namespace with the Zope 3 framework, you add a file called photons-configure.zcml to *Zope3-Instance*/etc/package-includes. This file should include the following line:

```
01 <include package="book.photodavns" />
```

You can now restart Zope 3 to make the namespace available.

Step 5: Creating and Running Functional Tests

Now it's time to see your new namespace in action. Unfortunately, there are no WebDAV tools that can handle any namespace in a generic fashion. Therefore, you need to use functional tests to confirm the correct behavior.

First, you need to test whether PROPFIND will understand the namespace and return the right values from the annotation of the image. Here is the complete code for the functional test; you should place it in a file called ftests.py:

```
01 import unittest
02 from transaction import get_transaction
03 from xml.dom.minidom import parseString as parseXML
04 from zope.app.file.image import Image
05 from zope.app.dav.ftests.dav import DAVTestCase
06 from book.photodavns.interfaces import IPhoto
07 from book.photodavns import ImagePhotoNamespace
08
09 property_request = '''\
10 <?xml version="1.0" encoding="utf-8" ?>
11 <propfind xmlns="DAV:">
12   <prop xmlns:photo="http://namespaces.zope.org/dav/photo/1.0">
13     <photo:height />
14     <photo:width />
15     <photo:equivalent35mm />
16     <photo:aperture />
17     <photo:exposureTime />
18   </prop>
19 </propfind>
20 '''
21
22 data = {'height': 768, 'width': 1024, 'equivalent35mm': u'41 mm',
23         'aperture': u'f/2.8', 'exposureTime': 0.031}
24
25 class IPhotoNamespaceTests(DAVTestCase):
26
27     def createImage(self):
28         img = Image()
29         photo = ImagePhotoNamespace(img)
30         for name, value in data.items():
31             setattr(photo, name, value)
32         root = self.getRootFolder()
33         root['img.jpg'] = img
34         get_transaction().commit()
35
36     def test_propfind_fields(self):
37         self.createImage()
38         response = self.publish(
39             '/img.jpg/',
40             env={'REQUEST_METHOD':'PROPFIND',
41                  'HTTP_Content_Type': 'text/xml'},
42             request_body=property_request)
43         self.assertEqual(response.getStatus(), 207)
44         xml = parseXML(response.getBody())
45         node = xml.documentElement.getElementsByTagName('prop')[0]
46
```

```
47          for name, value in data.items():
48              attr_node = node.getElementsByTagName(name)[0]
49              self.assertEqual(attr_node.firstChild.data, unicode(value))
50
51 def test_suite():
52      return unittest.TestSuite((
53          unittest.makeSuite(IPhotoNamespaceTests),
54          ))
55
56 if __name__ == '__main__':
57      unittest.main(defaultTest='test_suite')
```

In the preceding code block, note the following:

- Lines 9–20: This is the XML request that will be sent to the Zope 3 WebDAV server. Note that you need to make sure that the first line starts at the beginning of the string; otherwise, the XML parser causes a failure. In the string, you explicitly request all attributes of the photo namespace.

- Lines 22–23: Here you specify the data that is being set up in the annotation and that you expect to receive it from the PROPFIND request.

- Lines 27–34: This helper method creates an image and sets the photo data on the image so that you can access it. Note that you have to commit a transaction at this point; otherwise, the image will not be found in the ZODB.

- Lines 36–49: First, you create the image so that it will be available. Then you just publish your request with a carefully constructed environment. To make the request a PROPFIND call, you need to create an environment variable named REQUEST_METHOD. Because you send XML as the body of the request, you need to set the content type to text/xml, which you do with an HTTP_Content_Type environment entry.

  The answer you receive from the server should be 207, which signals that the PROPFIND call was successful and the data is enclosed in the body. You then parse the XML body by using Python's built-in xml.dom.minidom package. The rest of the test code simply uses DOM to ensure that all the requested attributes were returned and the data is correct.

When you are done with the functional test, you can run it as follows:

```
python2.3 bin/test -vpf --dir lib/python/book/photodavns
```

The -f option executes only functional tests. Functional tests are recognized by their module name, which is ftests. (tests is the module name for regular unit tests.)

Using TALES Outside Page Templates

Difficulty

Newcomer

Skills

- You should be familiar with TALES and know how TALES expressions are used in Zope page templates.
- Advanced Python knowledge is required in this chapter. Being familiar with the os and os.path standard module is advantageous because this chapter uses the directory hierarchy as the data source.

Problem/Task

As you have noticed by now, Zope 3 comes with a lot of technologies, and many of them can be used outside their common environment. TALES expressions are no exception. You can use TALES in any application without adding much overhead, as this chapter demonstrates.

THIS BOOK USES PAGE TEMPLATES and therefore TALES (Template Attribute Language Expression Syntax) expressions extensively. You might have already thought that using TALES outside templates might be quite useful, either to provide simple access to objects via path expressions, to enable users to enter Python code in a controlled environment, or simply to specify logical expressions. The latter use case has frequently been applied in Zope 2 applications.

What is there to know about running TALES in an application? TALES mainly consists of three concepts: the expression engine, expression objects, and contexts.

The *expression engine* is an object that can compile the expression code and returns an expression object that can be executed or called. It is also responsible for the setup environment. In the expression engine, you can register the expressions that should be available in TALES and register objects via names that are always available as base objects. A good example of building a simple engine is given in the `tales.engine` module.

An *expression object* is able to handle certain input. The most common one is the path expression (that is, `zope.tales.expressions.PathExpr`), which takes a filesystem- or URL-like path and tries to resolve it to a Python object by traversing through the path segments. Another one is the string expression (that is, `zope.tales.expressions.StringExpr`), which simply returns a string but can contain path expressions (for example, `string:  The object id is ${context/id}.`). A final common expression is the Python expression (that is, `zope.tales.expressions.PythonExpr`), which is simply able to execute the given expression code as Python and returns the output of the operation. Chapter 38, "Developing New TALES Expressions," shows how to create a new TALES expression.

A *context* (for example, `zope.tales.tales.Context`) is responsible for providing runtime variables and information for the execution of an expression. When you execute an expression, you always have to provide a context. A context object has many other methods, but they are mainly available for TAL and are not required for understanding TALES.

The TALES Filesystem Runner

In this chapter you'll learn about the TALES-based filesystem accessor, which provides a great tree with lots of nodes. Your first task is to provide some objects that represent directories and regular files and that ignore other file types. Directories should be simple, read-only mapping objects (that is, they should behave like dictionaries). That should not be too hard to do.

To begin creating the filesystem simulation, you need to open a new file called `talesrunner.py` and add the following two classes to it:

```
01 import os
02
03 class Directory(object):
04
05     def __init__(self, path):
06         self.path = path
07         self.filename = os.path.split(path)[1]
08
09     def __getitem__(self, key):
10         path = os.path.join(self.path, key)
11         if not os.path.exists(path):
```

```
12                raise KeyError, "No file '%s' in '%s'" %(key, self.filename)
13            elif os.path.isdir(path):
14                value = Directory(path)
15            else:
16                value = File(path)
17            return value
18
19    def get(self, key, default=None):
20        try:
21            return self.__getitem__(key)
22        except KeyError:
23            return default
24
25    def keys(self):
26        return os.listdir(self.path)
27
28    def items(self):
29        return [(key, self[key]) for key in self.keys()]
30
31    def values(self):
32        return [value for key, value in self.items()]
33
34 class File(object):
35
36    def __init__(self, path):
37        self.path = path
38        self.filename = os.path.split(path)[1]
39
40    def read(self):
41        return open(self.path, 'r').read()
```

As you can see, you do not need to worry about writing interfaces for this demo. Also, these are really simple implementations that do not include anything advanced, such as creation and modification date, size, or permissions.

In the preceding code block, note the following:

- Line 7: You want to always provide the name of the directory.

- Lines 9–17: If the requested file does not exist in the directory, you raise a KeyError exception, saying that the file does not exist. By using the os.path module, you can easily determine whether a given key represents a file or directory and create a corresponding object for it accordingly.

- Lines 25–26: The keys of a directory are simply the names of all the files it contains.

- Lines 34–41: There is not much you can say about a file, so you want to at least provide a method that shows its data.

Now that you have a way of providing a nice data tree, you can implement the TALES runner. You simply add the following few lines to the `talesrunner.py` file:

```
01 import sys
02 from zope.tales.engine import Engine
03 from zope.tales.tales import Context
04
05 if __name__ == '__main__':
06     path = sys.argv[1]
07     context = Context(Engine, {'root': Directory(path)})
08     while 1 == 1:
09         expr = raw_input("TALES Expr: ")
10         if expr == 'exit':
11             break
12         try:
13             bytecode = Engine.compile(expr)
14             print bytecode(context)
15         except Exception, error:
16             print error
```

In the preceding code block, note the following:

- Lines 2–3: For this example, the standard engine and context objects are fine. If you want to create your own engine because you want to reduce the number of available expression types, you can just look at `zope.tales.engine` to see how the engine was created. The engine constructor is a simple method that is easily understandable.

- Line 6: When the program is executed, the runner expects a single command-line argument, which is the path to the directory that is being used as root.

- Line 7: You create a context for the TALES expressions. You need to make the root directory available under the name `root`.

- Lines 13–14: You can easily compile any expression by calling `Engine.compile()`. The `bytecode` object is simply an instance of one of the registered expressions. As mentioned previously, you execute expressions simply by calling them. The `__call__()` method expects a context, so you pass one in. This ensures that `root` is available during the execution.

That was easy, wasn't it? Note that you often do not need to mess with the `Context` object. On the other hand, it is pretty reasonable to expect that people will change the engine—for example, to exclude the Python expression—because it is simply too powerful for some applications. Conversely, sometimes you might want to add additional expression types to an engine.

Trying Out the New TALES Runner

After you set *Zope3-Installation*/lib/python as part of your Python path, you can execute the runner by using the following:

python2.3 talesrunner.py /

  This uses the Unix root directory as the root for the TALES expressions. Here is an example of a session:

```
01 $ python talesrunner.py /
02 TALES Expr: root/keys
03 ['boot', 'dev', 'etc', 'usr', 'lib', 'bin', 'opt', ...]
04 TALES Expr: exists: root/us
05 0
06 TALES Expr: exists: root/usr
07 1
08 TALES Expr: root/usr
09 <__main__.Directory object at 0x4036e12c>
10 TALES Expr: root/usr/filename
11 usr
12 TALES Expr: string: This is the ${root/usr/path} directory.
13  This is the /usr directory.
14 TALES Expr: root/etc/motd/read
15 Welcome!
16
17 TALES Expr: python: root['usr'].keys()
18 ['share', 'bin', 'lib', 'libexec', 'include', ...]
19 TALES Expr: exit
```

Developing New TALES Expressions

Difficulty

Contributor

Skills

- You need to have solid knowledge about TAL and TALES, as well as page templates.
- You should have detailed insight into Zope 3's relational database (RDB) integration.
- You should have access to a PostGreSQL database (or any other database with which you can connect to Zope 3) and be able to install the corresponding Python and Zope 3 database adapter.
- Basic API knowledge of the `ExpressionEngine` and `Context` components is desirable. Optional.

Problem/Task

TAL, in combination with TALES, provides an incredibly powerful templating system for many types of applications (not only Zope). However, a templating system must be able to adjust to the needs of its various uses. Zope makes extensive use of this flexibility and implements custom versions of the `ExpressionEngine`, `Context`, and expression components.

A way of extending TAL/TALES is to provide additional expressions, including `python`, `string`, and `path` (which is the implicit default). In this chapter you will create an expression that evaluates SQL expressions and returns the result.

THE GOAL OF THIS CHAPTER is to be able to have TAL code such as this:

```
01 <html tal:define="rdb string:zope.da.PsycopgDA; dsn string:dbi://test">
02   <body>
03     <ul>
04       <li tal:repeat="contact sql: SELECT * FROM contact">
05         <b tal:content="contact/name" />
06       </li>
07     </ul>
08   </body>
09 </html>
```

be evaluated to this:

```
01 <html>
02   <body>
03     <ul>
04       <li>[Contact Name 1]</li>
05       <li>[Contact Name 2]</li>
06       ...
07     </ul>
08   </body>
09 </html>
```

In the preceding code block, note the following:

- Line 1: You tell the system that you want a connection to a PostGreSQL database via the psycopg database adapter, which you can download online, at http://svn.zope.org/psycopgda/. You also tell the system that you would like to connect anonymously to a database called test. Alternatively, to always specify the database and the database source name (DSN), it is helpful to specify a Zope database adapter object directly:

```
01 <html tal:define="sql_conn string:psycopg_test">
02   ...
03 </html>
```

- Line 4: Here you can see that generally a SQL expression should return a result set that contains the various rows bundled as result objects. This is really fortunate because it is exactly the way Zope database connections return the data anyway.

It should of course also be possible to insert path expressions into the SQL expression so that the SQL can be dynamic:

```
01 <ul tal:define="name string:Stephan; table string:contact">
02   <li tal:repeat="
03     contact sql: SELECT * FROM ${table} WHERE name = '${name}'">
04     <b tal:content="contact/name" />
05   </li>
06 </ul>
```

Note that expression code should also be responsible for quoting string input correctly.

An Overview of TALES Expressions

Next, let's take a closer look at the expression component itself. A TALES expression is actually a very simple object, which only has a constructor and a call method:

- The constructor takes three arguments: name, expr, and engine. The name argument is actually not used and can simply be ignored. The expr argument contains the string that is being evaluated; it contains basically the user's source code. The engine argument is an instance of the ExpressionEngine component, which manages all the different expressions.

- The __call__() method takes only one argument: econtext. The expression context provides expression-external runtime information, such as declared variables. This allows the expression to behave differently in different contexts and to accept custom user input. It is the responsibility of the using code, such as TAL, to provide and manage the context-sensitive variables.

  This method should return any value that would be expected. For the path expression, it is an object that was located, and for the string expression it would be a string. It is up to the user's code to deal with the output correctly.

You should probably also implement the str and repr methods, but they are for cosmetic and debugging purposes only, so they are not that interesting.

Step 1: Implementing the SQL Expression

The SQL expression is almost identical to the string expression, except that instead of returning a string from the __call__() method, you evaluate the computed string as a SQL statement and return the result. This means that you can safely use the StringExpr class as a base for your expression.

All the other code samples for this book are located in the book package, whereas the SQL expression became so popular that it was added to the Zope trunk (although it is not distributed with Zope X3.0). Therefore, you need to create a package called sqlexpr in zope.app. Inside it, you need to create a module called sqlexpr.py and add the following code to it:

```
01 from zope.component.exceptions import ComponentLookupError
02 from zope.interface import implements
03 from zope.tales.interfaces import ITALESExpression
04 from zope.tales.expressions import StringExpr
05 from zope.app import zapi
06 from zope.app.exception.interfaces import UserError
07 from zope.app.rdb import queryForResults
08 from zope.app.rdb.interfaces import IZopeDatabaseAdapter, IZopeConnection
09
```

```
10 class ConnectionError(UserError):
11     """This exception is raised when the user did not specify an RDB
12     connection."""
13
14 class SQLExpr(StringExpr):
15     """SQL Expression Handler class"""
16
17     def __call__(self, econtext):
18         if econtext.vars.has_key('sql_conn'):
19             conn_name = econtext.vars['sql_conn']
20             adapter = zapi.queryUtility(IZopeDatabaseAdapter, conn_name)
21             if adapter is None:
22                 raise ConnectionError, \
23                     ("The RDB DA name, '%s' you specified is not "
24                      "valid." %conn_name)
25         elif econtext.vars.has_key('rdb') and econtext.vars.has_key('dsn'):
26             rdb = econtext.vars['rdb']
27             dsn = econtext.vars['dsn']
28             try:
29                 adapter = zapi.createObject(None, rdb, dsn)
30             except ComponentLookupError:
31                 raise ConnectionError, \
32                     ("The factory id, '%s', you specified in the `rdb` "
33                      "attribute did not match any registered factory." %rdb)
34
35             if not IZopeDatabaseAdapter.providedBy(adapter):
36                 raise ConnectionError, \
37                     ("The factory id, '%s', you specifed did not create a "
38                      "Zope Database Adapter component." %rdb)
39          else:
40             raise ConnectionError, \
41                 'You did not specify a RDB connection.'
42
43         connection = adapter()
44         vvals = []
45         for var in self._vars:
46             v = var(econtext)
47             if isinstance(v, (str, unicode)):
48                 v = sql_quote(v)
49             vvals.append(v)
50         query = self._expr % tuple(vvals)
51         return queryForResults(connection, query)
52
53     def __str__(self):
54         return 'sql expression (%s)' % `self._s`
55
```

```
56     def __repr__(self):
57         return '<SQLExpr %s>' % `self._s`
58
59
60 def sql_quote(value):
61     if value.find("\'") >= 0:
62         value = "''".join(value.split("\'"))
63     return "%s" %value
```

In the preceding code block, note the following:

- Lines 5–8: Most TALES expressions do not depend on zope.app, which makes them usable outside Zope. However, for this expression, you use much of the Zope relational infrastructure, so this particular expression depends on zope.app.

- Lines 10–12: Of course it is not guaranteed that the user correctly specified the required variables rdb/dsn or sql_conn. If an error occurs while retrieving a Zope RDB connection from this data, this exception is raised. It is a UserError exception because these exceptions are not due to a system failure but to wrong user input.

- Lines 18–43: It is necessary to figure out whether you actually have the right variables defined to create and use a database connection.

  Lines 18–24: A Zope database adapter has been specified, so you try to look it up. If no adapter is found, you raise a ConnectionError exception.

  Lines 25–38: If the rdb/dsn pair is specified, you assume that rdb is the factory ID, and you try to initialize the database adapter by using the dsn value. If the rdb value is not a valid factory ID, you raise a ConnectionError exception (lines 32–34). If the created object is not a IZopeDatabaseAdapter object, you also raise a ConnectionError exception (lines 36–38).

  Lines 39–41: Neither of the two options was specified, so you raise an error.

  Line 43: You get a connection from the database adapter by calling it.

- Lines 44–49: First, you evaluate all the path expressions. Then you quote all string/Unicode values.

- Lines 50–51: You make final preparations by inserting the path expression results in the query, and then you execute the query and return the result.

- Lines 60–63: The SQL quoting function simply replaces each single quotes with two single quotes, which is the correct escaping for this character.

The main code for the expression has now been written. Now you only need to add the expression to the Zope TAL engine. To do that, you create a configuration file and add the following directive to it:

```
01 <configure
02     xmlns="http://namespaces.zope.org/zope"
03     xmlns:tales="http://namespaces.zope.org/tales"
```

```
04      i18n_domain="zope"
05      >
06
07   <tales:expressiontype
08      name="sql"
09      handler=".sqlexpr.SQLExpr"
10      />
11
12 </configure>
```

To insert the new expression into the Zope 3 framework, you add to package-includes a file called sqlexpr-configure.zcml that has the following line:

```
01 <include package="zope.app.sqlexpr" />
```

Step 2: Preparing and Implementing the Tests

Writing tests for the code in this chapter is actually quite painful because you have to simulate an entire database connection and result objects. Furthermore, you have to bring up the component architecture because the RDB connection is created by using the createObject() function, which uses factories. In tests.py, you need to add the following:

```
01 import unittest
02
03 from zope.interface import implements
04 from zope.component.factory import Factory
05 from zope.component.interfaces import IFactory
06 from zope.component.tests.placelesssetup import PlacelessSetup
07 from zope.tales.tests.test_expressions import Data
08 from zope.tales.engine import Engine
09
10 from zope.app.tests import ztapi
11 from zope.app.rdb.interfaces import IZopeDatabaseAdapter, IZopeConnection
12 from zope.app.rdb.tests.stubs import ConnectionStub
13 from zope.app.sqlexpr.sqlexpr import SQLExpr, ConnectionError
14
15
16 class AdapterStub(object):
17     implements(IZopeDatabaseAdapter)
18
19     def __init__(self, dsn):
20         return
21
22     def __call__(self):
23         return ConnectionStub()
24
```

```
25 class ConnectionStub(object):
26     implements(IZopeConnection)
27
28     def __init__(self):
29         self._called = {}
30
31     def cursor(self):
32         return CursorStub()
33
34 class CursorStub(object):
35
36     description = (('id', 0, 0, 0, 0, 0, 0),
37                    ('name', 0, 0, 0, 0, 0, 0),
38                    ('email', 0, 0, 0, 0, 0, 0))
39
40
41     def fetchall(self, *args, **kw):
42         return ((1, 'Stephan', 'srichter'),
43                 (2, 'Foo Bar', 'foobar'))
44
45     def execute(self, operation, *args, **kw):
46         if operation != 'SELECT num FROM hitchhike':
47             raise AssertionError(operation, 'SELECT num FROM hitchhike')
48
49
50 class SQLExprTest(PlacelessSetup, unittest.TestCase):
51
52     def setUp(self):
53         super(SQLExprTest, self).setUp()
54         ztapi.provideUtility(IFactory, Factory(AdapterStub),
55                              'zope.da.Stub')
56         ztapi.provideUtility(IFactory, Factory(lambda x: None),
57                              'zope.Fake')
58         ztapi.provideUtility(IZopeDatabaseAdapter, AdapterStub(''),
59                              'test')
60
61     def test_exprUsingRDBAndDSN(self):
62         context = Data(vars = {'rdb': 'zope.da.Stub', 'dsn': 'dbi://test'})
63         expr = SQLExpr('name', 'SELECT num FROM hitchhike', Engine)
64         result = expr(context)
65         self.assertEqual(1, result[0].id)
66         self.assertEqual('Stephan', result[0].name)
67         self.assertEqual('srichter', result[0].email)
68         self.assertEqual('Foo Bar', result[1].name)
69
70     def test_exprUsingSQLConn(self):
71         context = Data(vars = {'sql_conn': 'test'})
```

```
72            expr = SQLExpr('name', 'SELECT num FROM hitchhike', Engine)
73            result = expr(context)
74            self.assertEqual(1, result[0].id)
75            self.assertEqual('Stephan', result[0].name)
76            self.assertEqual('srichter', result[0].email)
77            self.assertEqual('Foo Bar', result[1].name)
78
79    def test_exprUsingRDBAndDSN_InvalidFactoryId(self):
80            context = Data(vars = {'rdb': 'zope.da.Stub1', 'dsn': 'dbi://test'})
81            expr = SQLExpr('name', 'SELECT num FROM hitchhike', Engine)
82            self.assertRaises(ConnectionError, expr, context)
83
84    def test_exprUsingRDBAndDSN_WrongFactory(self):
85            context = Data(vars = {'rdb': 'zope.Fake', 'dsn': 'dbi://test'})
86            expr = SQLExpr('name', 'SELECT num FROM hitchhike', Engine)
87            self.assertRaises(ConnectionError, expr, context)
88
89    def test_exprUsingSQLConn_WrongId(self):
90            context = Data(vars = {'sql_conn': 'test1'})
91            expr = SQLExpr('name', 'SELECT num FROM hitchhike', Engine)
92            self.assertRaises(ConnectionError, expr, context)
93
94    def test_noRDBSpecs(self):
95            expr = SQLExpr('name', 'SELECT num FROM hitchhike', Engine)
96            self.assertRaises(ConnectionError, expr, Data(vars={}))
97
98
99 def test_suite():
00    return unittest.TestSuite((
01            unittest.makeSuite(SQLExprTest),
02            ))
03
04 if __name__ == '__main__':
05    unittest.main(defaultTest='test_suite')
```

In the preceding code block, note the following:

- Lines 16–23: You implement a database adapter stub that can only create connection stubs. You even ignore the DSN.

- Lines 25–32: This connection object does not implement the entire interface, of course; you only need the cursor() method here.

- Lines 34–47: Whatever SQL query will be made, only a simple result is returned, and it should have two rows with three entries: id, name, and email. If a query is successful, you should expect this result. Note that only the query SELECT num FROM hitchhike is considered a valid SQL statement.

- Lines 54–57: You create two factories. The first one is a factory for a valid Zope database adapter component, and other one is a dummy factory. Having the dummy factory will allow you to cause one of the anticipated failures.

- Lines 58–59: You register an existing database adapter instance so that the use of `sql_conn` can be tested.

- Lines 61–68: You run a simple test that uses the `rdb` and `dsn` values to see whether a simple query executes correctly.

- Lines 70–77: You run another simple test, this time using the `sql_conn` variable.

- Lines 79–96: These tests all attempt to cause `ConnectionError` exceptions. All possible cases are covered.

Now you should run the tests and make sure they work; you should also fix errors if necessary.

Step 3: Trying Your New Expression in Zope

Before you do the following walk-through, you need to have installed and started PostGreSQL. Then you should make sure that the `psycopg` module is installed for your Python. Furthermore, you should have installed the `psycopgda` database adapter in your Python path somewhere (for example, `Zope3-Instance/lib/python`). You can get the database adapter at `http://svn.zope.org/psycopgda/trunk/`. Before you can come back to Zope, you will need to create a database user that should have the same login name as the user running Zope 3. With that new database user, you need to create a database called `test`. You can use the following commands from the shell:

```
createuser zope3
createdb test
```

Now you need to enter the database by using `psql test` and add a table called `contact` that has at least one column called `name`. Then you should add a couple entries to the table:

```
CREATE TABLE contact (name varchar);
INSERT INTO contact VALUES ('Stephan');
INSERT INTO contact VALUES ('Claudia');
INSERT INTO contact VALUES ('Jim');
```

Next, you restart Zope and go to the management interface, where you add a `ZPT Page` content component that has the following content:

```
01 <html tal:define="rdb string:zope.da.PsycopgDA; dsn string:dbi://test">
02   <body>
03     <ul>
04       <li tal:repeat="contact sql: SELECT * FROM contact">
05         <b tal:content="contact/name" />
06       </li>
```

```
07        </ul>
08      </body>
09  </html>
```

After you save the code, you can click the Preview tab, and you should see a bulleted list of all your `contact` entries names. You should feel free to test the path expression functionality and directly test the usage of a database connection.

The Life of a Request

Difficulty

Contributor

Skills

- You should be familiar with the Zope 3 framework.
- Having a general idea of Internet server design is helpful. Optional.

Problem/Task

When developing Zope 3 applications, you commonly deal with the request object to create views, but you don't often think much about the details of how the request gets into the view and what happens with the response that is constructed in it. This is fine because it is often not necessary to know. But in certain cases, it is good to know the general design of the Zope servers and publishers.

THIS CHAPTER TAKES YOU ON A JOURNEY through the life of a request, using a browser (special HTTP) request as an example.

What Is a Request?

The term *request* appears often in discussions of Zope 3. But what is a request? In technically concrete situations, a request is usually an object that implements IRequest. These objects are responsible for embedding protocol-specific details and represent the protocol semantics to provide them for usage by presentation components.

It is not enough to only think of request objects, though. Anything that the client sends to the server after connection negotiations is considered a request. So on the very lowest level, when the user agent (in this case, the classic Web browser) sends this HTTP string:

```
GET /index.html HTTP/1.1
```

it could be considered a request (raw).

Finding the Origin of a Request

Now that you have an idea of what a request is, let's discuss how connections are handled technically and how a request is born in the midst of much indirection and many abstraction layers.

When a server starts up, it binds a socket to an address on the local machine (`bind(address)`) and then starts to listen for connections by calling `listen(backlog)`. When an incoming connection is detected, the `accept()` method is called, and this method returns a connection object and the address of the computer to which the connection was made. All this is part of the standard Python `socket` library and is documented in the `zope.server.interfaces.ISocket` interface.

The server, which is mainly an `IDispatcher` implementation, has a simple interface to handle the specific events, by calling its corresponding `handle_event()` methods. A complete list of all events that are managed this way is given in the `IDisplatcherEventHandler` interface. So when a connection comes in, `handle_accept()` is called, and it is overridden in the `zope.server.serverbase.ServerBase` class, around line 130. This method tries to get the connection by calling `accept()`. If the connection is successfully created, the connection is used to create a `ServerChannel` instance, which is the next level of abstraction. Most of the other dispatcher functionality is provided by the standard `async.dispatcher` module, which fully implements `IDispatcher`. Figure 39.1 shows a diagram of the process.

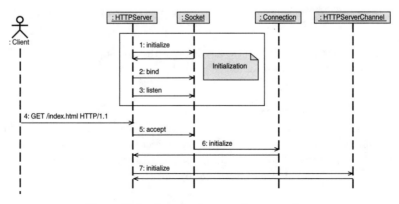

Figure 39.1   Low-level setup of a connection.

At this stage, the channel, which is just another dispatcher, is taking over. So the channel starts to collect the incoming data (see `received(data)`) and sends it right away to the request parser, which is an instance of a class specified as `parser_class`. (Obviously, this class will be different for every server implementation.) The way the parser functions is not that important. All you have to know is that it implements `IStreamConsumer`, which has a way of saying when it has completed parsing a request. When all the data is received, the `IServerChannel` method `receivedCompleteRequest(req)` is called; its goal is to schedule the request to be executed. But only one request of the channel can be running at a time. So if the channel is busy, you need to queue the request until the running task is completed.

Whenever the channel becomes available (see `end_task(close)`), the next request from the queue is converted to an `ITask` object. The task is then immediately sent to the server for execution, using `IServer.addTask(task)`. There, it is added to a task dispatcher (see `ITaskDispatcher`), which schedules the task for execution. Why all this redirection through a task and a task dispatcher? Until now, all the code in this chapter has run on a single thread. But in order to scale the servers better and to support long-running requests without blocking the entire server, it is necessary to be able to start several threads to handle the requests. It is now up to the `ITaskDispatcher` implementation to decide how to spread the requests. Theoretically, the `ITaskDispatcher` implementation could even consult other computers to execute a task. By default, you use the `zope.server.taskthreads.ThreadedTaskDispatcher` class. Using this class' `setThreadCount(count)` method, the Zope startup code is able to specify the maximum number of threads running at a time.

When it is the task's turn to be serviced, the task dispatcher calls `ITask.service()`, which should finally execute the request. Specifically, when the `HTTPTask` instance is serviced, the method `executeRequest(task)` of the `HTTPServer` class is called. The `zope.server.http.publisherhttpserver.PublisherHTTPServer` class, which is the one used for Zope 3, creates an `IHTTPRequest` object from the task and publishes the request with `zope.publisher.publish(request)`. The server has an attribute `request_factory` in which the request class that is used to create the request is stored.

What have you accomplished so far? You have taken an incoming connection, read all the incoming data and parsed it, scheduled it for execution, and created a request that was published with the Zope 3 publisher. Except for the last step, there is nothing Zope-specific about this code, so all this could be replaced by any other Web server, such as Twisted's. (See Figure 39.2.)

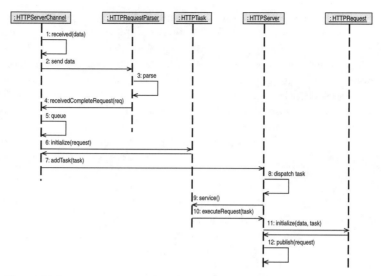

Figure 39.2   Data reception through the initialization of the request object.

The Request and the Publisher

As the request begins on its path, entering the publisher by using `zope.publisher.`
`publish.publish()`, it also enters a Zope-pure domain. In fact, Zope does not really
care how a request was created, as long as it implements `IRequest`. For example, when
functional tests are executed, they create the request purely from fictional data and pass it
through the publisher to analyze the response afterward.

From a high-level point of view, the publisher's `publish()` method is responsible for
interpreting the request's information and causing the correct actions to occur. It starts
out by traversing the given object path to an actual object, it calls the object, and, finally,
it writes the result in the response. Everything else in this method has to do with handling errors and exceptions as well as providing enough hooks for other components to
step in.

The `publish()` method is so central to the Zope 3 framework that the rest of this
chapter goes through it very carefully, so you can understand each step's purpose.
Wherever necessary, you can take a rest and examine side paths more closely. If you open
the `zope.publisher.publish` module at this point, you can more easily follow the text.

The work of the `publish()` method starts with a infinite `while` loop. The loop exists
because the publication process might fail the first time, and you want to be able to try
to publish the request again. It will be up to some policy to decide in which way and
how many times a request can be retried.

The first step inside the loop is to get the publication. The publication provides the
publisher with hooks to accomplish application-specific tasks that are related to data

storages, transactions, and security. The default implementation is `DefaultPublication`, which is located in `zope.publisher.base` and can be used by software that does not make use of the entire Zope framework. For Zope 3, however, there is a specific Zope implementation in `zope.app.publication.zopepublication`.

Wrapped inside three `try/except` statements, you tell the request to look at its data and process whatever needs to be processed. In the case of a browser request, such as the one used as an example in this chapter, the `processInputs()` method tries to parse all HTML form data, cookies, and HTTP headers that might have been sent by the browser and convert that data to Python objects. Note that the publisher is based on the CGI standard. Much of the responsibility of the server code was to put the HTTP data in a CGI-friendly format and, in fact, the `processInputs()` method uses the standard Python CGI module to do most of its work.

The next step is to convert the request's object path to an object—the process of *traversal*. Besides calling all the event–hooks, the first step of the traversal process is to determine the application—in other words, the object root. For a common Zope 3 installation, the application is an object called `Application` inside the root dictionary of the ZODB. Then you use the request's `traverse(object)` method to get to the desired object. Let's have a closer look at this method for the `BrowserRequest` class.

First, you should notice that the `BrowserRequest` class' traverse method does not do any of the heavy lifting; it only covers a few browser-specific corner cases, such as choosing a default view and using the HTML form data (by inspecting form variable names for the suffix `:method`) for possible additional traversal steps. It turns out that the `BaseRequest` class' traverse method does all the work; see `zope/publisher/base.py`, starting at line 247. At the beginning of the method are several private attributes that are pulled into the local namespace and set up. Here is a list of the attributes, including a small description of each:

- **`publication`**—This is simply the `publication` object you encountered before, which gives you access to the application-specific functionality.

- **`_traversal_stack`**—This is a simple stack (that is, list) of names that must be traversed. These names come from the parsed path of the URL. For example `/path/to/foo/bar/index.html` would be parsed to `['path', 'to', 'foo', 'bar', 'index.html']`. The traversal stack stores the names in reverse order because a stack starts popping objects from the end.

- **`_traversed_names`**—This is a list of names that have already been successfully traversed. The names are simply the entries coming from `_traversal_stack`. However, the names in that list have the reverse order from that of the traversal stack.

- **`_last_obj_traversed`**—This variable keeps track of the last object that was found in the traversal process.

Now you just work through the traversal stack until it has been completely emptied. The interesting call here is `publication.traverseName(request, object, name)`, which tries to determine the next object using the name from the traversal stack and the request. The `traverseName()` method can be very complex. The Zope 3 application version, found in `zope.app.publication.publicationtraverse.` `PublicationTraverse`, must be able to handle namespaces (`++namespace++`), views (`@@`), and pluggable traverser lookups, so that objects can implement their own traversers. Discussing the details of this method would be beyond the scope of this chapter. How to develop a custom traverser is discussed in Chapter 35, "Changing Traversal Behavior."

If everything goes well and no exception is raised, meaning that the object specified in the path was found, the `traverse()` method returns the found object, and you are back in the publisher's `publish()` function. The next step is to execute the object.

Calling the object assumes that the object is callable in the first place. Therefore, the traversal process should always end in a view or a method on a view. But because all common content objects have browser-specific default views, you are guaranteed that the object is callable. For other presentation types, similar default options exist. Even though the object is formally executed by calling `publication.callObject(request,` `object)`, eventually `mapply()`, which is defined in the `zope.publisher.publish` module, is called. `mapply()` does not just call the object; it also takes great care in determining the arguments and finding values for them. `mapply()` is the heart of the object request broker (ORB) for Python objects. What you have done here is to marshal a CGI request into a Python object call.

When an object is called, it can either write the result directly to the request's response object or return a result object. In the latter case, the `publish()` method adds the result to the body of the response. No assumptions are made about the type of the result object. It is totally up to the response object to handle the result correctly.

For the Zope application, the `afterCall(request)` execution is of importance because it commits the transaction to the ZODB. This process can cause a failure, so it is very important that you not return any data to the server until the transaction is committed.

When all this has successfully finished, you call `outputBody()` on the response, which sends the data out to the world; the data then goes through the task, channel, and eventually the socket to the connected machine. Note that the `output(data)` method, which is called from `outputBody()`, is responsible for converting the internally kept Unicode strings to valid ASCII, using an encoding. If no encoding is specified, UTF-8 is used by default.

After the response has sent out its data, the request is closed by the `publish()` method calling `close()` on the request, which releases all locks on resources. This also finishes the running task, closes the channel, and eventually disconnects the socket. This marks the end of the request. Figure 39.3 provides an overview of the path of the request inside the publisher.

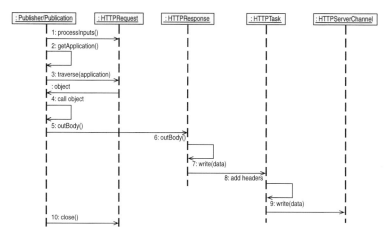

Figure 39.3   The request in the publisher.

Let's now look at some of the possible failure scenarios. The most common failure is a ZODB write conflict, in which case you simply want to rollback the transaction and retry the request. But where does the `Retry` error come from, when the ZODB raises a `ConflictError` exception? A quick look in the publication's `handleException()` method reveals that if a write conflict error is detected, it is logged, and then a `Retry` exception is raised, so the next exception handler is used. Here you simply reset the request and the response and allow the publishing process to start all over again. (Remember that you have an everlasting `while` loop over all this code.)

In general, though, exceptions are handled by the `handleException()` method, which logs each error and even allows errors to be formatted in the appropriate output format, using a view. See Chapter 32, "Exception Views," for details on how to define your own views on exceptions.

This concludes our journey through the life of a request. Sometimes this chapter intentionally ignores details to stay focused and not overwhelm you. The interfaces of the various involved components serve well as further documentation, especially for the publisher.

VII

Writing Tests

Writing tests for every bit of functionality is of utmost importance in Zope 3. Testing can be done in many ways, from Java-like unit tests to Pythonic doc testing.

Chapter 40: Writing Basic Unit Tests

This chapter shows how to develop basic unit tests for your code and explains in detail how various pieces of functionality can be tested.

Chapter 41: Doc Tests: Example-Driven Unit Tests

Sometimes regular unit tests are not instructive enough to someone reviewing the code. This chapter shows how example-driven doc tests can become useful in these cases.

Chapter 42: Writing Functional Tests

Unit tests are great for testing isolated components, but they are impractical for testing entire sections of a system. For these type of tests, you use a functional testing framework, which is introduced in this chapter in some detail.

Chapter 43: Creating Functional Doc Tests

For the same reason doc tests were developed to supersede unit tests, functional doc tests are intended to be a more descriptive solution to developing functional tests.

Chapter 44: Writing Tests Against Interfaces

If an interface is commonly implemented multiple times, it is a good idea to write tests directly against the interface as a base for the implementation tests. This chapter shows how to do that and expands on the motivation for it.

40

Writing Basic Unit Tests

Difficulty

Newcomer

Skills

- You need to know some Python.

Problem/Task

As you know by now, Zope 3 is incredibly stable because all its code is tested in great detail. Currently, the most common testing method in the Python world is to write unit tests, as described in this chapter.

T HIS CHAPTER INTRODUCES UNIT TESTS—which are Zope 3 independent—and explains some of their subtleties.

Implementing the Sample Class

Before you can write tests, you have to write some code that you can test. In this case, you will implement a simple class called `Sample` with public attributes `title` and `description` that are accessed via `getDescription()` and mutated using `setDescription()`. Further, the description must be either a regular or Unicode string.

Because this code does not depend on Zope, you should open a file named `test_sample.py` anywhere and add the following class to it:

```
01 Sample(object):
02     """A trivial Sample object."""
03
04     title = None
```

```
05
06     def __init__(self):
07         """Initialize object."""
08         self._description = ''
09
10     def setDescription(self, value):
11         """Change the value of the description."""
12         assert isinstance(value, (str, unicode))
13         self._description = value
14
15     def getDescription(self):
16         """Change the value of the description."""
17         return self._description
```

In the preceding code block, note the following:

- Line 4: `title` is publicly declared, and the value `None` is given. Therefore, this is just a regular attribute.

- Line 8: The actual description string will be stored in `_description`.

- Line 12: You make sure that the description is only a regular or Unicode string, as is stated in the requirements.

If you want, you can now manually test the class with the interactive Python shell. You just start Python by entering `python` in your shell prompt. Note that you should be in the directory in which `test_sample.py` is located when you start Python (an alternative is, of course, to specify the directory in `PYTHONPATH`.) The following is a sample session using the Python interactive prompt:

```
01 >>> from test_sample import Sample
02 >>> sample = Sample()
03 >>> print sample.title
04 None
05 >>> sample.title = 'Title'
06 >>> print sample.title
07 Title
08 >>> print sample.getDescription()
09
10 >>> sample.setDescription('Hello World')
11 >>> print sample.getDescription()
12 Hello World
13 >>> sample.setDescription(None)
14 Traceback (most recent call last):
15   File "<stdin>", line 1, in ?
16   File "test_sample.py", line 31, in setDescription
17     assert isinstance(value, (str, unicode))
18 AssertionError
```

As you can see in the test, nonstring object types are not allowed as descriptions, and an `AssertionError` exception is raised.

Writing Unit Tests

The goal of writing unit tests is to convert your informal, manual, and interactive testing session into a formal test class. Python provides a module called `unittest` for this purpose; it is a port of the Java-based unit-testing product JUnit, by Kent Beck and Erich Gamma. There are three levels to the testing framework. (The following descriptions of the levels deviate a bit from the original definitions, as found in the Python library documentation at `www.python.org/doc/current/lib/module-unittest.html`.)

The smallest element of the unit test is a *test*, which is a single method in a `TestCase` class that tests the behavior of a small piece of code or a particular aspect of an implementation. A *test case* is a collection of tests that share the same setup/inputs. On top of all this sits the *test suite*, which is a collection of test cases and/or other test suites. Test suites combine tests that should be executed together. With the correct setup (as shown shortly in an example below), you can then execute test suites. For large projects such as Zope 3, it is useful to know that there is also the concept of a *test runner*, which manages the test run of all or a set of tests. Besides providing many testing options, the test runner also provides good feedback about the testing session.

But enough about the theory. The following example, which you can simply put into the same file as the preceding code, shows a test in common Zope 3 style:

```
01 import unittest
02
03 class SampleTest(unittest.TestCase):
04     """Test the Sample class"""
05
06     def test_title(self):
07         sample = Sample()
08         self.assertEqual(sample.title, None)
09         sample.title = 'Sample Title'
10         self.assertEqual(sample.title, 'Sample Title')
11
12     def test_getDescription(self):
13         sample = Sample()
14         self.assertEqual(sample.getDescription(), '')
15         sample._description = "Description"
16         self.assertEqual(sample.getDescription(), 'Description')
17
18     def test_setDescription(self):
19         sample = Sample()
20         self.assertEqual(sample._description, '')
21         sample.setDescription('Description')
22         self.assertEqual(sample._description, 'Description')
23         sample.setDescription(u'Description2')
24         self.assertEqual(sample._description, u'Description2')
25         self.assertRaises(AssertionError, sample.setDescription, None)
26
27
```

```
28 def test_suite():
29     return unittest.TestSuite((
30         unittest.makeSuite(SampleTest),
31         ))
32
33 if __name__ == '__main__':
34     unittest.main(defaultTest='test_suite')
```

In the preceding code block, note the following:

- Lines 3–4: You usually develop test classes, which must inherit from `TestCase`. Although it is often not done, it is a good idea to give the class a meaningful doc string that describes the purpose of the tests it includes.

- Lines 6, 12, and 18: When a test case is run, a method called `runTests()` is executed. Although it is possible to override this method to run tests in a different way, the default option looks for any method whose name starts with `test` and executes it as a single test. This way, you can create a test method for each aspect, method, function, or property of the code to be tested. This default is very sensible and is used everywhere in Zope 3.

- Lines 8, 10, 14,…: The `TestCase` class implements a handful of methods that aid you with the testing. The following test-validation methods are some of the most frequently used ones:

  - `assertEqual(first, second[, msg])`—This method checks whether the `first` and `second` values are equal. If the test fails, `msg` or `None` is returned.

  - `assertNotEqual(first, second[, msg])`—This is simply the opposite of `assertEqual()`; it checks for non-equality.

  - `assertRaises(exception, callable, ...)`—You expect the `callable` argument to raise the `exception` argument when executed. After the `callable` argument, you can specify any number of positional and keyword arguments for the callable. If you expect a group of exceptions from the execution, you can make `exception` a tuple of possible exceptions.

  - `assert_(expr[, msg])`—This method checks whether the specified expression executes correctly. If it does not, the test fails, and `msg` or `None` is returned.

  - `failUnlessEqual(first, second[, msg])`—This testing method is equivalent to `assertEqual()` but is rarely used.

  - `failUnless(expr[, msg])`—This method is equivalent to `assert_(expr[, msg])` but is rarely used.

  - `failIf(expr[, msg])`—This method is the opposite of `assert_()`.

  - `fail([msg])`—This method fails the running test without any evaluation. This is commonly used for testing various possible execution paths at once, when you want to signify a failure if an improper path was taken.

Note

For a complete list of methods, see the standard Python documentation, at `www.python.org/doc/current/lib/module-unittest.html`.

- Lines 6–10: This method tests the `title` attribute of the `Sample` class. The first test should be that the attribute exists and has the expected initial value (line 8). Then the title attribute is changed, and you check whether the value was really stored. This might seem like overkill, but later you might change the title such that it uses properties instead. In that case, it is very important to check whether this test still passes.

- Lines 12–16: First, you simply check that `getDescription()` returns the correct default value. Because you do not want to use other API calls, such as `setDescription()`, you set a new value of the description via the implementation-internal `_description` attribute (line 15). This is okay. Unit tests can make use of implementation-specific attributes and methods. Finally, you just check that the correct value is returned.

- Lines 18–25: On lines 21–24, you check whether both regular and Unicode strings are set correctly. In the last line of the test, you make sure that no other type of objects can be set as a description and that an error is raised.

- Lines 28–31: This method returns a test suite that includes all test cases created in this module. The Zope 3 test runner uses this method when it picks up all available tests. You basically add the line `unittest.makeSuite(TestCaseClass)` for each additional test case.

- Lines 33–34: In order to make the test module capable of running by itself, you execute `unittest.main()` when the module is run.

Running the Tests

You can run the test you created in the preceding section by simply calling `python test_sample.py` from the directory you saved the file in. Here is the result you should see:

```
...
----------------------------------------------------------------------
Ran 3 tests in 0.001s

OK
```

The three dots (...) represent the three tests that were run. If a test failed, the failure would be reported, and you would know which test failed and receive a small traceback.

When you use the default Zope 3 test runner, tests are picked up as long as they follow some conventions:

- The tests must be in either a package or a module called `tests`.
- If `tests` is a package, then all test modules inside must also have a name that starts with `test`, as is the case with the filename `test_sample.py`.
- The test module must be somewhere in the Zope 3 source tree because the test runner looks for files there only.

In this case, you could simply create a `tests` package in *Zope3-Instance*/lib/python (do not forget the `__init__.py` file). Then you would place the `test_sample.py` file in that directory.

You can use the test runner as follows to run only the sample tests from the Zope 3 instance directory:

```
python2.3 bin/test -vp -dir lib/python/tests/
```

The `-v` option stands for verbose mode, which means detailed information about a test failure is provided. The `-p` option enables a progress bar that tells you how many of the tests have been completed. You can specify many more options; you can get a full list of them by using the option `-h`:

```
python2.3 bin/test -h
```

The preceding call has the following output:

```
Configuration file found.
Running UNIT tests at level 1
Running UNIT tests from /opt/zope/Zope3
  3/3 (100.0%): test_title (tests.test_sample.SampleTest)
------------------------------------------------------------------
Ran 3 tests in 0.002s

OK
Running FUNCTIONAL tests at level 1
Running FUNCTIONAL tests from /opt/zope/Zope3


------------------------------------------------------------------
Ran 0 tests in 0.000s

OK
```

In the preceding code block, note the following:

- Line 1: The test runner uses a configuration file for some setup. This allows developers to use the test runner for other projects as well. This message simply tells you that the configuration file was found.
- Lines 2–8: The unit tests are run. On line 4 you can see the progress bar.
- Lines 9–15: The functional tests are run because the default test runner runs both types of tests. Because you do not have any functional tests in the specified module, there are no tests to run. To just run the unit tests, you use the options `-u` and `-f`. See Chapter 42, "Writing Functional Tests," for more details on functional tests.

Doc Tests: Example-Driven Unit Tests

Difficulty

Newcomer

Skills

- You should have read Chapter 40, "Writing Basic Unit Tests," because this chapter depends heavily on the work done there.

Problem/Task

Unit tests are nice, but they are not the best implementation of what eXtreme Programming expects of testing. Testing should also serve as documentation—a requirement that the conventional unit test module pattern does not provide. This chapter shows you an alternative way of writing unit tests that can also serve well as documentation. It is now the preferred method for writing tests in Zope 3.

Python provides doc strings for classes and methods, and they serve—as the name suggests—as documentation for the object. If you could write tests in the doc strings of classes and methods and execute them during test runs, the documentation requirement of a testing framework would be fulfilled. Even better, the tests would automatically become part of the documentation. This way, the documentation reader would always see a working example of the code. Because most people learn by example, this would also speed up the learning process of the technology.

Thus doc tests were developed, with exactly the described behavior. If you embed Python-prompt-like sample code in the doc strings of objects and register the contained module as one that has doc tests, the Python code in the doc strings is executed for testing. Each doc string is then counted as a single test.

Integrating a Doc Test

How will the example from the previous chapter change in light of doc tests? First of all, you can completely get rid of the TestSample class. Next, you can add the following lines to the doc string of the Sample class:

```
01 Examples::
02
03   >>> sample = Sample()
04
05   Here you can see how the 'title' attribute works.
06
07   >>> print sample.title
08   None
09   >>> sample.title = 'Title'
10   >>> print sample.title
11   Title
12
13   The description is implemented using a accessor and mutator method
14
15   >>> sample.getDescription()
16   ''
17   >>> sample.setDescription('Hello World')
18   >>> sample.getDescription()
19   'Hello World'
20   >>> sample.setDescription(u'Hello World')
21   >>> sample.getDescription()
22   u'Hello World'
23
24   'setDescription()' only accepts regular and unicode strings
25
26   >>> sample.setDescription(None)
27   Traceback (most recent call last):
28     File "<stdin>", line 1, in ?
29     File "test_sample.py", line 31, in setDescription
30       assert isinstance(value, (str, unicode))
31   AssertionError
```

In the preceding code block, note the following:

- Line 1: The double colon on this line is not a mistake. Zope 3's documentation tools assume that all doc strings are written in structured text by default, a plain-text format that allows you to insert some markup without diminishing the readability of the text. The double colon signifies the beginning of a code segment.

- Lines 5, 13, and 24: It is possible to insert additional comments for better documentation. This way, you can explain examples step-by-step.
- Lines 26–31: These lines demonstrate that you can also test for raised exceptions. However, often it is very tedious to provide the entire traceback when you just want to check for the raised exception type and value. To solve the problem, you can simply use three dots (. . .) to replace the traceback between the first and last lines. The test would then look like this:

```
01    >>> sample.setDescription(None)
02    Traceback (most recent call last):
03    ...
04    AssertionError
```

Next, you need to change the test suite construction to look for the doc tests in the `Sample` class's doc string. To do so, you import the `DocTestSuite` class and change the `test_suite()` function as follows:

```
01 from zope.testing.doctestunit import DocTestSuite
02
03 def test_suite():
04     return unittest.TestSuite((
05         DocTestSuite(),
06         ))
```

The first argument to the `DocTestSuite` constructor is a string that is the dotted Python path to the module that is to be searched for doc tests. If no module is specified, the current one is chosen. The constructor also takes two keyword arguments, `setUp` and `tearDown`, which specify functions that are called before and after each tests. These are the equivalent methods to the `TestCase` class's `setUp()` and `tearDown()` methods.

You can now execute the test as before, using `Python test_sample.py`, except that `Zope3-Installation`/`lib/python` must be in the `PYTHONPATH` Path list. The output is similar to that of the regular unit tests:

```
.
----------------------------------------------------------------------
Ran 1 test in 0.003s

OK
```

As you can see, the three different unit tests collapse to one doc test.

Doc Tests in a File

As you might suspect, not all tests are well suited to be embedded in the doc strings of objects. Sometimes tests check an overall functionality of many components, and other times tests are just too lengthy to be included in the code. For these situations, the Zope 3 developers decided to also make regular text files doc tests. In these cases, you would simply store the test code in a simple text file. The test file can then be registered by using this:

```
01 doctest.DocFileSuite('filename.txt')
```

The `DocFileSuite` class constructor supports the same arguments as the `DocTestSuite` class's constructor. These documentation test files have become very popular among the Zope 3 developers and are used to write narrative documentation of newly developed features.

As you can see, using doc tests is a much more natural way to test your code than using regular unit tests. However, you need to be aware of a couple issues using doc tests.

Shortcomings of Doc Tests

The most obvious problem with doc tests is that if you like to test attributes and properties, there is no doc string in which to place the tests. You can usually solve this problem by testing attributes implicitly in the context of other tests and/or place these tests in the class's doc string. This solution is good because attributes by themselves usually do not have much functionality, but they are used in combination with methods to provide functionality.

Next, it is not easy to test for certain outputs. The prime example here is `None` because it has no representation. The easy way around this issue is to make the testing statement a condition. So the statement `methodReturningNone()`, which should return `None`, is tested using `methodReturningNone() is None`, and the test should return `True`. There are also some issues when you're testing statements that return output whose representation is longer than a line because the doc string checker is not smart enough to remove the indentation whitespace. Good examples of such objects are lists and tuples. The best solution to this problem is to use the pretty printer module, `pprint`, which always represents objects in lines no longer than 80 characters and uses nice indentation rules for clarity.

Another problematic object to test is the dictionary because its representation might change from one time to another, based on the way the entries are hashed. The simplest solution to this problem is to always convert the dictionary to a list, using the `items()` method, and sort the entries. This should give you a uniquely identifiable representation of the dictionary.

Using doc tests tends to make developers write sloppy tests. Many times developers think of the tests as examples to show how the class is supposed to work, so they often neglect to test for all aspects and possible situations a piece of code could come into. You can solve this problem by either writing some additional classic unit tests or by creating a special testing module that contains further doc tests.

Although doc tests cover 98% of all test situations well, some tests require heavy programming. A good example of this is a test in the internationalization support that makes sure all XML locale files can be parsed and some of the most important data is correctly evaluated. It is completely fine to use regular unit tests for these scenarios.

Still, overall doc tests are the way to go, due to their great integration into documentation.

Writing Functional Tests

Difficulty

Newcomer

Skills

- Knowing how Zope 3–generated forms works is helpful. Optional.

Problem/Task

Unit tests cover a large part of the testing requirements listed in the eXtreme Programming literature, but they are not everything. There are also integration and functional tests. Whereas integration tests can be handled with unit tests and doc tests, functional tests cannot. For this reason, the Zope 3 community developed an extension to `unittest` that handles functional tests. That package is introduced in this chapter.

U NIT TESTS ARE VERY GOOD FOR testing the functionality of a particular object in the absence of the environment the object will eventually live in. Integration tests build on unit tests by testing the behavior of an object in a limited environment. Finally, functional tests test the behavior of an object in a fully running system. Therefore, functional tests often check the user interface behavior, and it is not surprising that they are found in the `browser` packages of Zope 3. In fact, in Zope 3's implementation of functional tests, there exists a base test case class for each view type, such as `zope.tests.functional.BrowserTestCase` and `zope.app.dav.ftests.dav.DAVTestCase`.

The Browser Test Case

Each custom functional test case class provides some valuable methods that help you write the tests in a fast and efficient manner. The `BrowserTestCase` class provides the following methods:

- `getRootFolder()`—This method returns the root folder of the database. This method is available in every functional test case class.

- `commit()`—This method commits a transaction to the database. This is particularly useful when you add objects to the database before publishing a request. If the transaction is not committed after the setup of the object, the object will not be available when calling the publishing process. This method is available in every functional test case class.

- `abort()`—This method aborts a transaction of the database. It is available in every functional test case class.

- `makeRequest(path=", basic=None, form=None, env=, outstream=None)`— This method creates a new `BrowserRequest` instance that can be used for publishing a request with the Zope publisher. Here are its arguments:

  - `path`—This is the absolute path of the URL (that is, the URL minus the protocol, server, and port) of the object that is being accessed.

  - `basic`—This provides the authentication information, in the format *login:password*. When Zope 3 is brought up for functional testing, a user with the login `mgr` and the password `mgrpw` is automatically created, and it is assigned the role `zope.Manager`. Therefore, usually you use `mgr:mgrpw` as the basic argument.

  - `form`—This argument is a dictionary that contains all fields that would be provided by an HTML form. Note that you should have already converted the data to the native Python format; you need to be sure to only use Unicode for strings.

  - `env`—This variable is also a dictionary, and in it, you can specify further environment variables, such as HTTP headers. For example, the header *X-Header: value* would be an entry in the `env` dictionary of the form `'HTTP_X_HEADER': value`.

  - `outstream`—Optionally, you can define the stream to which the outputted HTML is sent. If you do not specify one, one is created for you.

  You would often not use this method directly because it does not actually publish the request. Instead, you use the `publish()` method, described next.

- `publish(self, path, basic=None, form=None, env=, handle_errors=False)`—This method creates a request as described for the `makeRequest()` method that is then published with a fully running Zope 3 instance and then returns a regular browser response object that is enhanced by a couple methods:

- **getOutput()**—This method returns all the text that was pushed to the out-
  stream.

- **getBody()**—This method only returns all the HTML of the response. It
  therefore excludes HTTP headers.

- **getPath()**—This method returns the path that was passed to the request.

path, basic, form, and env have the same semantics as the arguments to
makeRequest() that have the same names. If handle_errors is False, any exceptions that occur are not caught. If handle_errors is True, the default view of an
exception is used, and a formatted HTML page is returned. As you can imagine,
having handle_errors set to False is often more useful for testing.

- **checkForBrokenLinks(body, path, basic=None)**—Given an output body and a
  published path, this method checks whether the contained HTML contains any
  links and checks that those links are not broken. Because the availability of pages
  and therefore links depends on the permissions of the user, you might want to
  specify a login/password pair in the basic argument. For example, if you have
  published a request as a manager, it will be very likely that the returned HTML
  contains links that require the manager role.

Testing ZPT Page Views

Now that you know how the BrowserTestCase class extends the FunctionalTestCase
class (which in turn extends the normal unittest.TestCase class), you can use it to
write some functional tests for the Add, Edit, and Index views of the ZPT Page content
type.

You need to create a file called test_zptpage.py and add the following functional
testing code to it:

```
01 import time
02 import unittest
03
04
05 from zope.app.tests.functional import BrowserTestCase
06 from zope.app.zptpage.zptpage import ZPTPage
07
08 class ZPTPageTests(BrowserTestCase):
09     """Funcional tests for Templated Page."""
10
11     template = u'''\
12     <html>
13       <body>
14         <h1 tal:content="modules/time/asctime" />
15       </body>
16     </html>'''
17
```

```
18    template2 = u'''\
19    <html>
20      <body>
21        <h1 tal:content="modules/time/asctime">time</h1>
22      </body>
23    </html>'''
24
25    def createPage(self):
26        root = self.getRootFolder()
27        root['zptpage'] = ZPTPage()
28        root['zptpage'].setSource(self.template, 'text/html')
29        self.commit()
30
31    def test_add(self):
32        response = self.publish(
33            "/+/zope.app.zptpage.ZPTPage=",
34            basic='mgr:mgrpw',
35            form={'add_input_name' : u'newzptpage',
36                  'field.expand.used' : u'',
37                  'field.source' : self.template,
38                  'field.evaluateInlineCode.used' : u'',
39                  'field.evaluateInlineCode' : u'on',
40                  'UPDATE_SUBMIT' : 'Add'})
41
42        self.assertEqual(response.getStatus(), 302)
43        self.assertEqual(response.getHeader('Location'),
44                         'http://localhost/@@contents.html')
45
46        zpt = self.getRootFolder()['newzptpage']
47        self.assertEqual(zpt.getSource(), self.template)
48        self.assertEqual(zpt.evaluateInlineCode, True)
49
50    def test_editCode(self):
51        self.createPage()
52        response = self.publish(
53            "/zptpage/@@edit.html",
54            basic='mgr:mgrpw',
55            form={'field.expand.used' : u'',
56                  'field.source' : self.template2,
57                  'UPDATE_SUBMIT' : 'Change'})
58        self.assertEqual(response.getStatus(), 200)
59        self.assert_('&gt;time&lt;' in response.getBody())
60        zpt = self.getRootFolder()['zptpage']
61        self.assertEqual(zpt.getSource(), self.template2)
62        self.checkForBrokenLinks(response.getBody(), response.getPath(),
63                                 'mgr:mgrpw')
64
```

```
65     def test_index(self):
66         self.createPage()
67         t = time.asctime()
68         response = self.publish("/zptpage", basic='mgr:mgrpw')
69         self.assertEqual(response.getStatus(), 200)
70         self.assert_(response.getBody().find('<h1>'+t+'</h1>') != -1)
71
72 def test_suite():
73     return unittest.TestSuite((
74         unittest.makeSuite(ZPTPageTests),
75         ))
76
77 if __name__=='__main__':
78     unittest.main(defaultTest='test_suite')
```

In the preceding code block, note the following:

- Lines 25–29: This is a perfect example of the helper methods that are often used in Zope's functional tests. It creates a ZPT Page content object called zptpage. To write the new object to the ZODB, you have to commit the transaction by using self.commit().

- Lines 31–48: To understand this test completely, it is helpful to be familiar with the way Zope 3 adds new objects and how the widgets create an HTML form. The + in the URL is the Add view for a folder. The path that follows is simply the factory ID of the content type (line 32). Instead of the factory ID, you sometimes also find the name of the object's Add view there.

  The form dictionary is another piece of information that must be carefully constructed. First, the field.expand.used and field.evaluateInlineCode.used keys are required, whether you want to activate expand and evaluateInlineCode or not. This is required by the corresponding widgets. The add_input_name key contains the name the content object will receive, and UPDATE_SUBMIT just tells the form generator that the form was actually submitted and action should be taken. Also note that each form entry representing a field has a field. prefix, which is added by the widgets mechanism. (You can find all these variable names by creating a ZPT page in the browser and looking at the HTML source for the names and values.)

  On line 42, you check whether the request was successful. Code 302 signals a redirect, and on lines 43–44 you check that you are redirected to the correct page.

  Now it is time to check in the ZODB to see whether the object has really been created and to ensure that all data has been set correctly. On line 46 you retrieve the object itself and consequently you check that the source is set correctly and the evaluateInlineCode flag was turned on (line 48), as the request demanded in the form (line 39).

- Lines 50–63: Before you can test whether the data of a ZPT page can be edited correctly, you have to create one. Here the `createPage()` method comes in handy; it quickly creates a page that you can use. Because you have done previous tests already, the contents of the `form` dictionary should be obvious.

  Because the edit page returns itself, the status of the response should be 200. You also inspect the body of the response to make sure the template was stored correctly.

  One extremely useful feature of the `BrowserTestCase` class is the check for broken links in the returned page. You should do this test whenever an HTML page is returned by the response.

- Lines 65–70: Here you simply test the default view of the ZPT page. No complicated forms or environments are necessary. You just need to make sure that the template is executed correctly.

Running Functional Tests

The testing code directly depends on the Zope 3 source tree. It is not wise to run the tests directly because doing so requires a lot of unnecessary setup. Instead, you should use the test runner to execute the tests. From the *Zope3-Instance* directory you can run the tests as follows:

```
python2.3 bin/test -vpf --dir path/to/ftests/
```

These tests take 3 to 10 seconds to run. This is okay because the functional tests have to bring up the entire Zope 3 system, which by itself takes about 2 to 8 seconds. The output of the test run should be something like this:

```
Configuration file found.
Running FUNCTIONAL tests at level 1
Running FUNCTIONAL tests from /opt/zope/Zope3/Zope3-Fresh
Parsing ftesting.zcml
  3/3 (100.0%): test_index (ftests.test_zptpage.ZPTPageTests)
------------------------------------------------------------------
Ran 3 tests in 0.292s

OK
```

Creating Functional Doc Tests

Difficulty

Sprinter

Skills

- You should be familiar with how to start Zope 3 and use the Web user interface, the ZMI.

Problem/Task

Chapter 42, "Writing Functional Tests," suggests that when writing functional tests, you first use the Web user interface to see what and how you want to test. You also often need to look at the HTML code to determine all the important form data elements. Then you start to write some Python code to mimic this behavior, which is often very frustrating and tedious, to say the least. Wouldn't it be nice if some mechanism would record your actions and then simply convert the recorded session to a test that you can simply comment on? This chapter tells you exactly how to do this by using functional doc tests.

I N CHAPTER 42 YOU DEVELOPED SOME functional tests for the common tasks of a ZPT page: creating the component, editing the content, and calling the default view to render the page. In this chapter, you will re-create only the rendering of the template, for the sake of simplicity.

Creating functional doc tests requires some specific setup of Zope 3 and a nice Python script called tcpwatch.py (written by Shane Hathaway). TCPWatch will record the HTTP requests and responses for you, and you will then use the responses to create the functional tests. Next, you'll use a script called `dochttp.py` to convert the TCPWatch output to a functional doc test, which you can then document and adjust as you desire.

Setting Up the Zope 3 Environment

The best way to run a recording session is to have a clean ZODB. Therefore, you need to save your old `Data.fs` as `Data.fs.orig` and remove `Data.fs`. This way, you'll start at the same position as the functional testing framework. Also, the functional tests know about only one user, with login `mgr` and the password `mgrpw`. The user has the `zope.Manager` role. You need to set up this user if you want to be able to access all screens. You can easily add the user by placing the following two directives in `principals.zcml`:

```
01 <principal
02     id="zope.mgr"
03     title="Manager"
04     login="mgr"
05     password="mgrpw" />
06
07 <grant role="zope.Manager" principal="zope.mgr" />
```

In fact, you can simply copy the first directive from the *Zope3-Instance*/etc/ `ftesting.zcml` file, which is actually used when running the functional tests. During the functional test run, the `zope.Manager` role is granted to the user using Python.

Now you simply start Zope 3. The rest of this chapter assumes that Zope runs on port 8080. Because you only want to test the rendering of the ZPT, you can add a new ZPT page called `newzptpage` via the Web GUI; it should have the following template code:

```
01 <html>
02   <body>
03     <h1 tal:content="modules/time/asctime" />
04   </body>
05 </html>
```

Setting Up TCPWatch

As mentioned previously, you use TCPWatch to record a Web GUI session. You can find the TCPWatch script on Shane Hathaway's website, `http://hathawaymix.org/Software/TCPWatch`. You should download the latest version.

When the download is complete, you need to untar the archive:

```
tar xvzf tcpwatch-1.x.tar.gz
```

Next, you enter the newly created directory `tcpwatch`. You can then install the script by calling the following:

```
python setup.py install
```

You might have to be root to call this command because Python might be installed in a directory you do not have write access to.

Now you need to create a temporary directory that TCPWatch can use to store the collected requests and responses:

```
mkdir tmp
```

Next, you start the script by using the following:

```
/path/to/python/bin/tcpwatch.py -L 8081:8080 -s -r tmp
```

The `-L` option tells TCPWatch to listen on port 8081 for incoming connections, `-s` outputs the result to `stdout` instead of to a graphical window, and `-r <dir>` specifies the directory to record the session.

After you start TCPWatch, you can access Zope also via port 8081, except that all communication between the client and the server is also reported by TCPWatch.

Recording a Session

When everything is set up according to the directions in the preceding section, you can do whatever you want via port 8081. Don't forget to log in as `mgr` on port 8081 so that the authentication will also work via the functional test. In this case, you just call the URL `http://localhost:8081/newzptpage`, which renders the result, all of which is recorded, to the page output.

When you are done recording, you need to shut down TCPWatch by pressing Ctrl+C. You might also want to shut down Zope 3.

Creating and Running the Test

After the session is recorded, you can convert it to a functional test by using the following:

```
python2.3 Zope3-Installation/lib/python/zope/app/tests/dochttp.py \
path/to/tmp > zptpage_raw.txt
```

You might want to store the output of this script in a temporary file (`zptpage_raw.txt`) and copy it, request-for-request, into the final text file. The raw functional test should look like this:

```
01 >>> print http(r"""
02 ... GET /newzptpage HTTP/1.1
03 ... Cache-Control: no-cache
04 ... Pragma: no-cache
05 ... """)
```

```
06 HTTP/1.1 200 Ok
07 Content-Length: 72
08 Content-Type: text/html;charset=utf-8
09 <BLANKLINE>
10 <html>
11   <body>
12     <h1>Thu Aug 26 12:24:26 2004</h1>
13   </body>
14 </html>
15 <BLANKLINE>
```

The final functional test will be stored in `zptpage.txt`, though. Because you added the `newzptpage` object before the recording session, your final test file must add this object via Python code. Here is the final version of `zptpage.txt`:

```
01 ========
02 ZPT Page
03 ========
04
05 This file demonstrates how a page template is rendered in content
06 space. Before we can render the page though, we have to create one. The
07 template content will be:
08
09   >>> template = u'''\
10   ... <html>
11   ...   <body>
12   ...     <h1 tal:content="modules/time/asctime" />
13   ...   </body>
14   ... </html>'''
15
16 Next we have to create the ZPT Page in the root folder. The root folder of the
17 test setup can be simply retrieved by calling getRootFolder(). At the end we
18 have to commit the transaction, so that the page will be stored in the ZODB
19 and available for requests to be accessed.
20
21   >>> from transaction import get_transaction
22   >>> from zope.app.zptpage.zptpage import ZPTPage
23   >>> root = getRootFolder()
24   >>> root['newzptpage'] = ZPTPage()
25   >>> root['newzptpage'].setSource(template, 'text/html')
26   >>> get_transaction().commit()
27
28 Now that we have the page setup, we can just send the HTTP request by calling
29 the function http(), which will return the complete HTTP response. When
30 comparing the result, we make use of '...' to signalize variable content.
31
32   >>> print http(r"""
```

```
33    ... GET /newzptpage HTTP/1.1
34    ... Cache-Control: no-cache
35    ... Pragma: no-cache
36    ... """)
37    HTTP/1.1 200 Ok
38    Content-Length: 72
39    Content-Type: text/html;charset=utf-8
40    <BLANKLINE>
41    <html>
42      <body>
43        <h1>...</h1>
44      </body>
45    </html>
46    <BLANKLINE>
```

In the preceding code block, note the following:

- Lines 21–26: Here you add a ZPT page named `newzptpage` to the root folder. This is identical to the method you created in Chapter 42.

- Line 43: Here you replace the datetime string with the three dots (...) wildcard characters, which means that the content is variable. This is necessary because the session and the functional test are run at different times.

Now that the test is written, you can make it runnable with a test setup. In a file named `ftests.py`, you add the following code:

```
01 import unittest
02 from zope.app.tests.functional import FunctionalDocFileSuite
03
04 def test_suite():
05     return FunctionalDocFileSuite('zptpage.txt')
06
07 if __name__ == '__main__':
08     unittest.main(defaultTest='test_suite')
```

When running a functional doc test, you just use the `FunctionalDocFileSuite` class to create a doc test suite. You can then run the tests with the test runner, as usual.

Writing Tests Against Interfaces

Difficulty

Newcomer

Skills

- You should be familiar with Python interfaces. If necessary, you should read Chapter 6, "An Introduction to Interfaces."
- You should know about the `unittest` package, especially the material covered in Chapter 40, "Writing Basic Unit Tests."

Problem/Task

When you expect an interface to be implemented multiple times, it is good to provide a set of generic tests that verify the correct semantics of that interface. In Zope 3, these abstract tests are referred to as *interface tests*. This chapter describes how to implement and use such tests, using two different implementations of a simple interface.

ZOPE 3 HAS MANY INTERFACES that you expect to be implemented multiple times. The prime example is the `IContainer` interface, which is primarily implemented by the `Folder` class but also by many other objects that contain some other content. It would be useful to implement a set of tests which could verify that `Folder` and other classes correctly implement `IContainer`.

Interface tests are abstract tests—that is, they do not run by themselves because they do not know about any implementation—that provide a set of common tests. The advantage of these tests is that the implementer of the interface immediately has some feedback about his or her implementation of the interface. However, you should not mistake the interface tests for replacements of a complete set of unit tests; rather, they are a supplement. Interface tests, by definition, cannot test implementation details, as is required of unit tests. Additional tests also ensure a higher quality of code.

You will be able to recognize a couple characteristics in any interface test. First, an interface should always have a test that verifies that the interface implementation fulfills the contract. This type of test can be created by using the `verifyObject(`*interface*`,` *instance*`)` method, which is found at `zope.interface.verify`. Second, although the interface test is abstract, it needs to get an instance of the implementation from somewhere. For this reason, an interface test should always provide an abstract method that returns an instance of the object. By convention, this method is called `makeTestObject`, and it should look like this:

```
01 def makeTestObject(self):
02     raise NotImplemented()
```

Each test case that inherits from the interface test should then realize this method by returning an instance of the object to be tested.

But how can you determine what should be part of an interface test? The best way to approach this problem is by thinking about the functionality that the attributes and methods of the interface provide. You might also ask about the interface's behavior inside the system. Interface tests often model actual usages of an object, whereas implementation tests also cover a lot of corner cases and exceptions. That is often hard to do with interface tests because they are bound to the interface-declared methods and attributes. From another point of view, because tests should document an object, you can think of interface tests as documentation of how the interface should be used and normally behave.

The `ISample` Interface

Reusing the examples from Chapters 40 and 41, "Doc Tests: Example-Driven Unit Tests", you can now develop an `ISample` interface that provides a `title` attribute and uses the methods `getDescription()` and `setDescription()` for dealing with the description of the object.

Again, you want to keep the code contained in one file for simplicity, so you need to open a file called `test_isample.py` anywhere and add the following interface to it:

```
01 from zope.interface import implements, Interface, Attribute
02
03 class ISample(Interface):
04     """This is a Sample."""
05
06     title = Attribute('The title of the sample')
07
08     def setDescription(value):
09         """Set the description of the Sample.
10
11         Only regular and unicode values should be accepted.
```

```
12          """
13
14      def getDescription():
15          """Return the value of the description."""
```

By this point you should know about interfaces, so there is nothing interesting here.

The `ISample` **Interface Tests**

The next step is to write the interface tests. You should add the following `TestCase` class:

> **Note**
>
> You will notice how similar these tests are to the ones developed in Chapters 40 and 41.

```
01 import unittest
02 from zope.interface.verify import verifyObject
03
04 class TestISample(unittest.TestCase):
05      """Test the ISample interface"""
06
07      def makeTestObject(self):
08          """Returns an ISample instance"""
09          raise NotImplemented()
10
11      def test_verifyInterfaceImplementation(self):
12          self.assert_(verifyObject(ISample, self.makeTestObject()))
13
14      def test_title(self):
15          sample = self.makeTestObject()
16          self.assertEqual(sample.title, None)
17          sample.title = 'Sample Title'
18          self.assertEqual(sample.title, 'Sample Title')
19
20      def test_setgetDescription(self):
21          sample = self.makeTestObject()
22          self.assertEqual(sample.getDescription(), '')
23          sample.setDescription('Description')
24          self.assertEqual(sample.getDescription(), 'Description')
25          self.assertRaises(AssertionError, sample.setDescription, None)
```

In the preceding code block, note the following:

- Lines 7–9: Here is the promised method to create object instances.
- Lines 11–12: As mentioned earlier, every interface test case should check whether the object implements the tested interface. This is the easiest test you will ever write, and it is one of the most important ones.

- Lines 14–18: This test is equivalent to the test you wrote in Chapter 40, except that you do not create the sample instance by using the class; rather, you use some indirection by asking the `makeTestObject()` method to create one for you.
- Lines 20–25: In interface tests, it does not make much sense to test the accessor and mutator methods of a particular attribute separately because you do not know how the data is stored. So, similarly to the test in Chapter 40, you test some combinations of calling the description getter and description setter.

Now that you have an interface and some tests for it, you are ready to create an implementation. In fact, you should create two so that you can see the specificity of the interface tests to different implementations.

Implementations of the `ISample` Interface

The first implementation is equivalent to the one you used in Chapter 40, except that now you should call it `Sample1` and tell it that it implements the `ISample` interface:

```
01 class Sample1(object):
02     """A trivial ISample implementation."""
03
04     implements(ISample)
05
06     # See ISample
07     title = None
08
09     def __init__(self):
10         """Create objects."""
11         self._description = ''
12
13     def setDescription(self, value):
14         """See ISample"""
15         assert isinstance(value, (str, unicode))
16         self._description = value
17
18     def getDescription(self):
19         """See ISample"""
20         return self._description
```

The second implementation uses Python's `property` feature to implement its `title` attribute, and it uses a different attribute name, `desc`, to store the data of the description:

```
01 class Sample2(object):
02     """A trivial ISample implementation."""
03
04     implements(ISample)
05
06     def __init__(self):
```

```
07          """Create objects."""
08          self.__desc = ''
09          self.__title = None
10
11      def getTitle(self):
12          return self.__title
13
14      def setTitle(self, value):
15          self.__title = value
16
17      def setDescription(self, value):
18          """See ISample"""
19          assert isinstance(value, (str, unicode))
20          self.__desc = value
21
22      def getDescription(self):
23          """See ISample"""
24          return self.__desc
25
26      description = property(getDescription, setDescription)
27
28      # See ISample
29      title = property(getTitle, setTitle)
```

In the preceding code block, note the following:

- Line 26: Although this implementation chooses to provide a convenience property to setDescription() and getDescription(), it is not part of the interface and should not be tested in the interface tests. However, the specific implementation tests should cover this feature.

Writing Tests for the Implementations

These two implementations are different enough that the interface tests would fail if you had included implementation-specific testing code. You can now implement the tests quickly:

```
01 class TestSample1(TestISample):
02
03      def makeTestObject(self):
04          return Sample1()
05
06      # Sample1-specific tests are here
07
08
09 class TestSample2(TestISample):
10
```

```
11      def makeTestObject(self):
12          return Sample2()
13
14      # Sample2-specific tests are here
15
16
17 def test_suite():
18     return unittest.TestSuite((
19         unittest.makeSuite(TestSample1),
20         unittest.makeSuite(TestSample2)
21         ))
22
23 if __name__ == '__main__':
24     unittest.main(defaultTest='test_suite')
```

In the preceding code block, note the following:

- Lines 1–6 and 9–14: You can easily realize the `TestISample` tests by implementing the `makeTestObject()` method. (This code does not include any implementation-specific test, in order to keep the code snippets small and concise.)
- Lines 17–24: You specify the usual test environment boilerplate code.

Running the Tests

To run the tests directly, you need to make sure you have *Zope3-Installation*/lib/python in your PYTHONPATH variable because this code depends on `zope.interface`. Then you can simply execute the tests by using the following:

```
python2.3 test_sampleiface.py
```

from the directory containing the `test_sampleiface.py` file.

```
Configuration file found.
Running UNIT tests at level 1
Running UNIT tests from /opt/zope/Zope3/Zope3-Cookbook
  6/6 (100.0%): test_verifyInterfaceImplementation (...leiface.TestSample2)
----------------------------------------------------------------
Ran 6 tests in 0.004s

OK
```

Of course you could also just use the test runner, which would have saved you from setting the Python path.

You have just written three tests, but for the two implementations, you have done six test runs. Using interface tests is a great way to add additional tests (that multiply quickly), and it is a great motivation to keep on writing tests—a task that can be annoying at times.

Attribution-NonCommercial-NoDerivs License 2.0

THE WORK (AS DEFINED BELOW) IS PROVIDED UNDER THE TERMS OF THIS CREATIVE COMMONS PUBLIC LICENSE ("CCPL" OR "LICENSE"). THE WORK IS PROTECTED BY COPYRIGHT AND/OR OTHER APPLICABLE LAW. ANY USE OF THE WORK OTHER THAN AS AUTHORIZED UNDER THIS LICENSE OR COPYRIGHT LAW IS PROHIBITED. BY EXERCISING ANY RIGHTS TO THE WORK PROVIDED HERE, YOU ACCEPT AND AGREE TO BE BOUND BY THE TERMS OF THIS LICENSE. THE LICENSOR GRANTS YOU THE RIGHTS CONTAINED HERE IN CONSIDERATION OF YOUR ACCEPTANCE OF SUCH TERMS AND CONDITIONS.

1. **Definitions**

   (a) **"Collective Work"** means a work, such as a periodical issue, anthology or encyclopedia, in which the Work in its entirety in unmodified form, along with a number of other contributions, constituting separate and independent works in themselves, are assembled into a collective whole. A work that constitutes a Collective Work will not be considered a Derivative Work (as defined below) for the purposes of this License.

   (b) **"Derivative Work"** means a work based upon the Work or upon the Work and other pre-existing works, such as a translation, musical arrangement, dramatization, fictionalization, motion picture version, sound recording, art reproduction, abridgment, condensation, or any other form in which the Work may be recast, transformed, or adapted, except that a work that constitutes a Collective Work will not be considered a Derivative Work for the purpose of this License. For the avoidance of doubt, where the Work is a musical composition or sound recording, the synchronization of the Work in timed-relation with a moving image ("synching") will be considered a Derivative Work for the purpose of this License.

(c) **"Licensor"** means the individual or entity that offers the Work under the terms of this License.

(d) **"Original Author"** means the individual or entity who created the Work.

(e) **"Work"** means the copyrightable work of authorship offered under the terms of this License.

(f) **"You"** means an individual or entity exercising rights under this License who has not previously violated the terms of this License with respect to the Work, or who has received express permission from the Licensor to exercise rights under this License despite a previous violation.

2. **Fair Use Rights**. Nothing in this license is intended to reduce, limit, or restrict any rights arising from fair use, first sale or other limitations on the exclusive rights of the copyright owner under copyright law or other applicable laws.

3. **License Grant.** Subject to the terms and conditions of this License, Licensor hereby grants You a worldwide, royalty-free, non-exclusive, perpetual (for the duration of the applicable copyright) license to exercise the rights in the Work as stated below:

(a) to reproduce the Work, to incorporate the Work into one or more Collective Works, and to reproduce the Work as incorporated in the Collective Works;

(b) to distribute copies or phonorecords of, display publicly, perform publicly, and perform publicly by means of a digital audio transmission the Work including as incorporated in Collective Works;

The above rights may be exercised in all media and formats whether now known or hereafter devised. The above rights include the right to make such modifications as are technically necessary to exercise the rights in other media and formats, but otherwise you have no rights to make Derivative Works. All rights not expressly granted by Licensor are hereby reserved, including but not limited to the rights set forth in Sections 4(d) and 4(e).

4. **Restrictions.** The license granted in Section 3 above is expressly made subject to and limited by the following restrictions:

(a) You may distribute, publicly display, publicly perform, or publicly digitally perform the Work only under the terms of this License, and You must include a copy of, or the Uniform Resource Identifier for, this License with every copy or phonorecord of the Work You distribute, publicly display, publicly perform, or publicly digitally perform. You may not offer or impose any terms on the Work that alter or restrict the terms of this License or the recipients' exercise of the rights granted hereunder. You may not sublicense the Work. You must keep intact all notices that refer to this License and to the disclaimer of warranties. You may not distribute, publicly display, publicly perform, or publicly digitally perform the Work with any technological measures that control access or use of the Work in a manner inconsistent with the terms of this License Agreement. The above applies to the Work as incorporated in a Collective Work, but this does not require the Collective Work apart from the Work itself to be made subject to the terms of this License. If You create a Collective Work, upon notice from any Licensor You must, to the extent practicable, remove from the Collective Work any reference to such Licensor or the Original Author, as requested.

(b) You may not exercise any of the rights granted to You in Section 3 above in any manner that is primarily intended for or directed toward commercial advantage or private monetary compensation. The exchange of the Work for other copyrighted works by means of digital file-sharing or otherwise shall not be considered to be intended for or directed toward commercial advantage or private monetary compensation, provided there is no payment of any monetary compensation in connection with the exchange of copyrighted works.

(c) If you distribute, publicly display, publicly perform, or publicly digitally perform the Work, You must keep intact all copyright notices for the Work and give the Original Author credit reasonable to the medium or means You are utilizing by conveying the name (or pseudonym if applicable) of the Original Author if supplied; the title of the Work if supplied; and to the extent reasonably practicable, the Uniform Resource Identifier, if any, that Licensor specifies to be associated with the Work, unless such URI does not refer to the copyright notice or licensing information for the Work. Such credit may be implemented in any reasonable manner; provided, however, that in the case of a Collective Work, at a minimum such credit will appear where any other comparable authorship credit appears and in a manner at least as prominent as such other comparable authorship credit.

(d) For the avoidance of doubt, where the Work is a musical composition:

　　i. **Performance Royalties Under Blanket Licenses.** Licensor reserves the exclusive right to collect, whether individually or via a performance rights society (e.g. ASCAP, BMI, SESAC), royalties for the public performance or public digital performance (e.g. webcast) of the Work if that performance is primarily intended for or directed toward commercial advantage or private monetary compensation.

　　ii. **Mechanical Rights and Statutory Royalties.** Licensor reserves the exclusive right to collect, whether individually or via a music rights agency or designated agent (e.g. Harry Fox Agency), royalties for any phonorecord You create from the Work ("cover version") and distribute, subject to the compulsory license created by 17 USC Section 115 of the US Copyright Act (or the equivalent in other jurisdictions), if Your distribution of such cover version is primarily intended for or directed toward commercial advantage or private monetary compensation.

(e) **Webcasting Rights and Statutory Royalties.** For the avoidance of doubt, where the Work is a sound recording, Licensor reserves the exclusive right to collect, whether individually or via a performance-rights society (e.g. SoundExchange), royalties for the public digital performance (e.g. webcast) of the Work, subject to the compulsory license created by 17 USC Section 114 of the US Copyright Act (or the equivalent in other jurisdictions), if Your public digital performance is primarily intended for or directed toward commercial advantage or private monetary compensation.

5. **Representations, Warranties, and Disclaimer**

UNLESS OTHERWISE MUTUALLY AGREED BY THE PARTIES IN WRITING, LICENSOR OFFERS THE WORK AS-IS AND MAKES NO REPRESENTATIONS OR WARRANTIES OF ANY KIND CONCERNING THE WORK, EXPRESS, IMPLIED, STATUTORY OR OTHERWISE, INCLUDING, WITHOUT LIMITATION, WARRANTIES OF TITLE, MERCHANTIBILITY, FITNESS FOR A PARTICULAR PURPOSE, NON-INFRINGEMENT, OR THE ABSENCE OF LATENT OR OTHER DEFECTS, ACCURACY, OR THE PRESENCE OF ABSENCE OF ERRORS, WHETHER OR NOT DISCOVERABLE. SOME JURISDICTIONS DO NOT ALLOW THE EXCLUSION OF IMPLIED WARRANTIES, SO SUCH EXCLUSION MAY NOT APPLY TO YOU.

6. **Limitation on Liability.** EXCEPT TO THE EXTENT REQUIRED BY APPLICABLE LAW, IN NO EVENT WILL LICENSOR BE LIABLE TO YOU ON ANY LEGAL THEORY FOR ANY SPECIAL, INCIDENTAL, CONSEQUENTIAL, PUNITIVE OR EXEMPLARY DAMAGES ARISING OUT OF THIS LICENSE OR THE USE OF THE WORK, EVEN IF LICENSOR HAS BEEN ADVISED OF THE POSSIBILITY OF SUCH DAMAGES.

7. **Termination**

(a) This License and the rights granted hereunder will terminate automatically upon any breach by You of the terms of this License. Individuals or entities who have received Collective Works from You under this License, however, will not have their licenses terminated provided such individuals or entities remain in full compliance with those licenses. Sections 1, 2, 5, 6, 7, and 8 will survive any termination of this License.

(b) Subject to the above terms and conditions, the license granted here is perpetual (for the duration of the applicable copyright in the Work). Notwithstanding the above, Licensor reserves the right to release the Work under different license terms or to stop distributing the Work at any time; provided, however that any such election will not serve to withdraw this License (or any other license that has been, or is required to be, granted under the terms of this License), and this License will continue in full force and effect unless terminated as stated above.

8. Miscellaneous

(a) Each time You distribute or publicly digitally perform the Work or a Collective Work, the Licensor offers to the recipient a license to the Work on the same terms and conditions as the license granted to You under this License.

(b) If any provision of this License is invalid or unenforceable under applicable law, it shall not affect the validity or enforceability of the remainder of the terms of this License, and without further action by the parties to this agreement, such provision shall be reformed to the minimum extent necessary to make such provision valid and enforceable.

(c) No term or provision of this License shall be deemed waived and no breach consented to unless such waiver or consent shall be in writing and signed by the party to be charged with such waiver or consent.

(d) This License constitutes the entire agreement between the parties with respect to the Work licensed here. There are no understandings, agreements or representations with respect to the Work not specified here. Licensor shall not be bound by any additional provisions that may appear in any communication from You. This License may not be modified without the mutual written agreement of the Licensor and You.

B

Zope Public License (ZPL) Version 2.1

A COPYRIGHT NOTICE ACCOMPANIES this license document that identifies the copyright holders.

This license has been certified as open source. It has also been designated as GPL compatible by the Free Software Foundation (FSF).

Redistribution and use in source and binary forms, with or without modification, are permitted provided that the following conditions are met:

1. Redistributions in source code must retain the accompanying copyright notice, this list of conditions, and the following disclaimer.

2. Redistributions in binary form must reproduce the accompanying copyright notice, this list of conditions, and the following disclaimer in the documentation and/or other materials provided with the distribution.

3. Names of the copyright holders must not be used to endorse or promote products derived from this software without prior written permission from the copyright holders.

4. The right to distribute this software or to use it for any purpose does not give you the right to use Servicemarks (SM) or Trademarks (TM) of the copyright holders. Use of them is covered by separate agreement with the copyright holders.

5. If any files are modified, you must cause the modified files to carry prominent notices stating that you changed the files and the date of any change.

Disclaimer

THIS SOFTWARE IS PROVIDED BY THE COPYRIGHT HOLDERS "AS IS" AND ANY EXPRESSED OR IMPLIED WARRANTIES, INCLUDING, BUT NOT LIMITED TO, THE IMPLIED WARRANTIES OF MERCHANTABILITY AND FITNESS FOR A PARTICULAR PURPOSE ARE DISCLAIMED. IN NO EVENT SHALL THE COPYRIGHT HOLDERS BE LIABLE FOR ANY DIRECT, INDIRECT, INCIDENTAL, SPECIAL, EXEMPLARY, OR CONSEQUENTIAL DAMAGES (INCLUDING, BUT NOT LIMITED TO, PROCUREMENT OF SUBSTITUTE GOODS OR SERVICES; LOSS OF USE, DATA, OR PROFITS; OR BUSINESS INTERRUPTION) HOWEVER CAUSED AND ON ANY THEORY OF LIABILITY, WHETHER IN CONTRACT, STRICT LIABILITY, OR TORT (INCLUDING NEGLIGENCE OR OTHERWISE) ARISING IN ANY WAY OUT OF THE USE OF THIS SOFTWARE, EVEN IF ADVISED OF THE POSSIBILITY OF SUCH DAMAGE.

Index

N - O

P

U – V

W

Your Guide to Computer Technology

www.informit.com